Teaching
Modern
Science

Arthur A. Carin
Queens College
Robert B. Sund

Teaching Modern Science

Fourth Edition

Charles E. Merrill Publishing Company
A Bell & Howell Company
Columbus Toronto London Sydney

Photo credits:
Strix Pix, pp. iii, 3, 16; SCIS, p. 19; Charles
Quinlan, pp. 1, 41, 67, 68, 78, 79, 81, 101, 115,
124, 125 top, middle, bottom, 133, 138, 145,
149, 160, 164, 165, 201, 209, 223, 231, 241,
267, Don Birdd, pp. 75, 99, 208, 216,
219, 227; Courtesy of Columbus Public Schools,
p. 102; Ben Chandler, pp. 163 left, 226; Harvey
R. Phillips, Phillips Photo Illustrators, p. 218.

Published by
Charles E. Merrill Publishing Co.
A Bell & Howell Company
Columbus, Ohio 43216

This book was set in Souvenir.
Production Editor: Jeffrey Putnam
Cover Design Coordination: Cathy Watterson
Text Designer: Cynthia Brunk
Cover Photograph by Strix Pix

Library of Congress Catalog Card Number:
84-42911
International Standard Book Number:
0-675-20221-3
Printed in the United States of America
3 4 5 6 7 8 9 10—89 88 87

Preface

Science should be an integral part of the school curriculum, and this book presents an approach to teaching scientific topics that will interest students by allowing them to actively participate in the learning process. While the "guided discovery teaching/learning approach" is not the only approach to teaching science that has merit, finding answers through experimentation will be exciting and fun, as well as educational, for both teachers and students.

Before implementing this approach in the classroom, you must decide what topics to teach and why you are going to teach them. Chapters 1–5 of this text will help you reach conclusions after focusing on how people develop, grow, and view the world around them; this general process is referred to as "science" and is a natural way to enrich children's development. Their curiosity for learning is called "discovery" in this book.

Chapters 6–9 give practical methods for planning and organizing the classroom to implement the guided discovery approach. You learn how to improve your questioning and listening skills, learn to create guided laboratory lessons, and take ideas from innovative science programs. In addition, a new chapter on arranging and managing an activity-based guided discovery science classroom has been included in this edition.

You can use the guided discovery approach presented with children of all grade levels and abilities, as chapter 10, "How Can You Individualize Science for *All* Children?", illustrates. With this chapter as background material, you can proceed to chapters 11 and 12, which show you how to correlate science with communication, social studies, art, music, physical activities, and mathematics. Chapter 13 gives examples of how to use microcomputers in your science teaching. Use this book regularly to help make science enjoyable, exciting, and instructive for both you and your students.

Contents

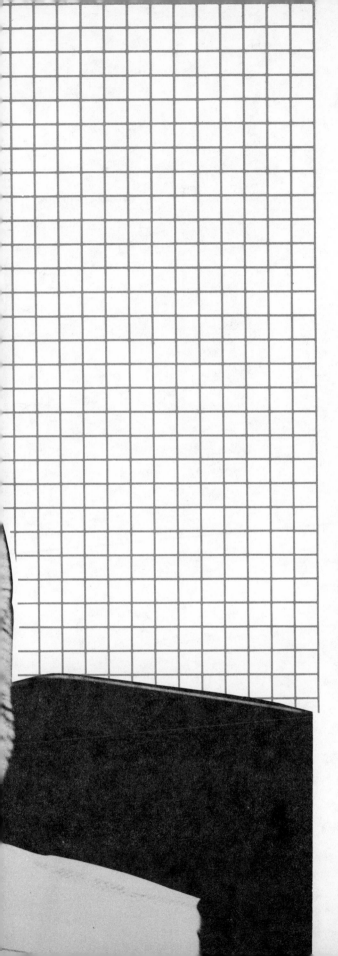

Teaching
Science
Through
Discovery

1

What Is Modern Science?

"The new insights coming out of particle physics tend to disprove the myth that the cosmos is an inexorable machine. To see the universe as evolving like life, like thought, as subject to chance just as our lives are subject to chance, is to deepen our sense that we have a rightful place in nature. This result is all the more intriguing for having arisen from a science that is out not to make nature seem more accommodating, but simply to comprehend it." (Timothy Ferris, "Physics' Newest Frontier," *New York Times Magazine* [September 26, 1982], p. 70.)

What you think about science influences what you choose to teach in your science program, as well as how you teach it. This chapter examines the spirit, orderliness, structure, beauty, and function of science in our modern society, and how it can be taught in our elementary schools.

But first, what do *you* think science is? Write down your ideas and share them with your professor, your teaching colleagues, and your fellow students. Do you agree or disagree with their definitions? Be thinking during your reading of this chapter whether or not you agree with the definition given in this text.

Obviously, a human endeavor as complex, encompassing, and divergent as science can hardly be "covered" in one chapter. What will be discussed, however, is how science is relevant in guiding children to become sensitive, curious, compassionate, and scientifically literate citizens. After reading this chapter, you will be better prepared to select, plan, and carry out activities with the children you teach.

SCIENCE—WHAT IS IT?

There are many ways to define *science*, but consider this working definition:

Science is the system of knowing about the universe through data collected by observation and controlled experimentation. As data are collected, theories are advanced to explain and account for what has been observed. The true test of a theory in science is threefold:

(1) its ability to explain what has been observed;

(2) its ability to predict what has not yet been observed; and

(3) its ability to be tested by further experimentation and to be modified as required by the acquisition of new data.[1]

As you analyze this definition, you will see two major elements: processes (or methods) and products. In addition, it implies that science is a human endeavor, a personal way of exploring and knowing.

Elements of Science

☐ *Human attitudes*—Certain beliefs, values, opinions, for example, suspending judgment until enough data have been collected relative to the problem. Constantly endeavoring to be objective.

☐ *Processes or methods*—Certain ways of investigating problems, observing, for example, making hypotheses, designing and

carrying out experiments, evaluating data, measuring, and so on.

☐ *Products*—Facts, principles, laws, theories, for example, the scientific principle: metals when heated expand.

AN ORDERLY AND REGULAR WORLD

Scientists look at the world's objects and phenomena believing that no matter how mysterious they may seem, there is a natural explanation. These investigators are persistent, creative, and cautious. They assume the world is regular, orderly, and predictable. Finding explanations for mysteries motivates and challenges the senses of both scientists and children. It's a task Jean Piaget described like this:

$$S \longleftarrow O$$
$$S \longrightarrow O$$

The human subjects (S) take in data from the objects (O) of the world (S ← O) and organize that data in terms of their own developing knowledge (S → O). Organizing the data allows people to go beyond the empirical observations of events and circumstances. If people's investigations stopped at the empirical level we would not have progressed to the point that science and scientific thinking have brought us, namely, finding the hidden patterns and relationships that occur in nature. Science looks for different kinds of patterns and relationships, such as relationships between different things, relationships between the parts of things, relationships between properties possessed by several things, etc.

After discovering relationships, the scientist formulates statements that describe them. These statements become the laws and principles of science. What kind of people enjoy this work?

SCIENTISTS AND THEIR WORK

Scientists are persons trained in some field of science who study phenomena through observation, experimentation, and other rational, analytical activities. They use attitudes, such as the desire for objectivity, while collecting, evaluating, and interpreting their data. They also follow a variety of experimental and statistical procedures in their efforts to clarify the marvelous mysteries of our universe; these activities are called the *processes* of science. They make discoveries, and these findings become the *products* of science. Figure 1–1 shows the relationships among the investigation of phenomena, scientific processes, and scientific products. As you read the next sections on science processes and products, see if you can think how these processes and products apply to our examination of real or imagined phenomena such as UFO sightings, astrology, and pyramidology.

SCIENTISTS' ATTITUDES

Fascination with the World Around Us

Human urges and needs are the forces that drive people to seek rational answers to questions about their world. These forces were the catalyst for the development of science. Young children enjoy discovering the texture, size, weight, color—even the taste—of sand at the seashore or in the sandbox because sand intrigues them. Similarly, scientists study the marvels of nature because they delight in them. This dynamic—almost compulsive—involvement of child or adult searching for answers provides the fuel for the vehicle of investigation. Without this attitude of discovery for discovery's sake, there would be no scientific inquiry. Charles P. Snow has captured this motivation well:

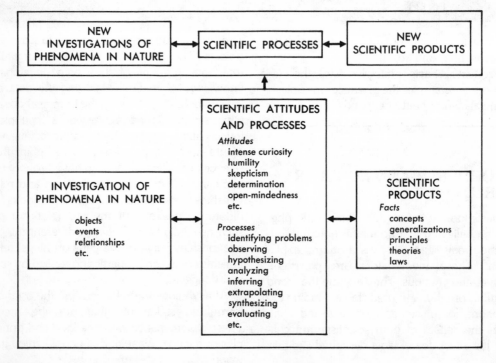

FIGURE 1–1
Relationships among the investigation of phenomena, scientific processes, and scientific products

Anyone who has ever worked in a science knows how much esthetic joy he has obtained. That is, in the actual activity of science, in the process of making a discovery, however humble it is, one can't help feeling an awareness of beauty.[2]

Scientists, because of their thirst for knowing, become perpetual learners: constantly curious, continually seeking knowledge, and always inquiring. But the more they know, the more they discover how little they know. This in turn fosters other scientific attitudes—*humility* and *skepticism*.

Humility and Skepticism

Being *humble,* that is, being free from arrogance and false pride, grows out of two aspects of scientists' working habits. First, there is the constant observation of human beings and their natures, strengths, and frailties. Second, scientists must constantly guard against *their own* tendencies as humans to be dogmatic; they must avoid accepting things blindly, without questioning. Healthy *skepticism* is a vital ingredient. Scientists must avoid having their minds so imprinted with static thoughts that alternative ideas do not occur to them. Also, when alternatives are pointed out, they must attempt to evaluate them objectively. *Authoritarianism*—favoring obedience to authority rather than freedom to question—is the enemy of healthy skepticism. Therefore, it is antiscientific.

Opinionated, pedantic, and categorical bigots are antiscientific because their minds are sealed to new ideas. On the other hand, scientists cannot be gullible and succumb to the latest fads. Scientists are wary of these human frailties and build checks and balances into their methods of research, safeguards that have gradually evolved from the work of thousands of scientists over hundreds of years. This heritage has been continually modified and formed into the processes of science collectively known as the *scientific method*. Recognizing that the methods of science are human activities, this caution is given to us: "One of the great achievements of science is to have developed scientific methods that work almost independently of the people on whom they operate."

Thinking Positively about "Failure"

We all have a tendency to become discouraged, especially if months of study end in little progress or failure to resolve a problem. Scientists try to overcome this human trait by adopting a very realistic, practical, and healthy approach to their work. All effort in science is viewed as a continuum, and all discovered knowledge has value to both present and future scientists. At any given point, scientists see the results of their efforts as incomplete, be-

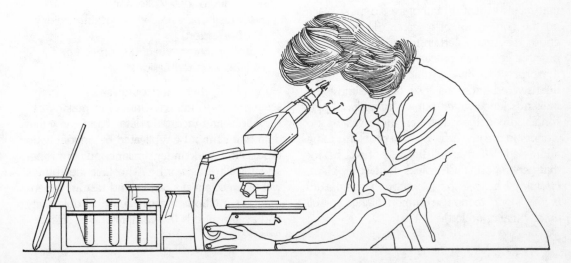

cause future work will reveal more about the subject. Failure to the nonscientist then, is a kind of success to the scientist. This failure—or success—says to the scientist: "This is not the answer you are seeking, so now you know you must try another route to resolve your problem."

The historical records are full of successes stemming from "failures." Dr. Paul Ehrlich, 1908 Nobel Prize winner in medicine and physiology, developed Salvarsan for the treatment of syphilis after 605 "unsuccessful" experiments. In Polaroid's search for instant color pictures, Howard Rogers, a chemist, spent 15 years experimenting with over 5,000 different chemical compounds before inventing a new chemical molecule. (For this absorbing story, read "Instant Color Pictures," *Life,* January 25, 1963, pp. 74–88.) Scientists thus succeed in the long run because of their daily, intelligent failures, and we can follow this example in our own everyday attempts to solve problems of living, teaching, human relations, and so forth.

Change and Uncertainty: Nature's One Constant

Most people who make science their career discover there is a light shining through the dark haze of daily frustration and failure in their work: the knowledge that the only certainty in scientific work is uncertainty and change. This discovery usually comes when scientists realize that failure is just a temporary stopping place on the continuum of research. Their current efforts may make certain tentative conclusions possible from their collected data. However, in the process of investigating a problem, other unanswered questions arise. Isaac Asimov, the brilliant science writer, put it very aptly: "I personally dread the day when there will be no wonder in the universe, no new problems to be addressed. What a dull universe it will be for that generation which solves the last problem. *Happily, I believe there is enough complexity in the world to amuse human beings for all time*"[3] (italics added).

Why Scientists Must Guard Against Themselves

Scientists must guard against their own biases and strive for objectivity. Unscientific, nonobjective individuals select or twist information to conform to their own biases. They seem to be saying: "My mind is made up. Don't confuse me with the facts." We all have a tendency to think this way because we bring certain perceptions, biases, and attitudes to each new situation. Psychologists call this process of trying to understand the world as it is perceived and experienced through the eyes of another individual *phenomenology.* Existentialists also assume that each of us has a world design or reference point from which we interpret everything that exists. How *I* see something, they say, is colored by my uniqueness, what previous experiences I have had, and so on, and not only by the realities of the object itself. Scientists, however, must try to maintain an open mind and base their decisions upon evidence; they must not extrapolate beyond the facts and should *always suspend judgments until they have sufficient data.*

Struggling for Objectivity

Scientists must continually remind themselves to strive for objectivity:

> *How do I know what I know?* (checking validity of data collection)
> *How well do I know it?* (checking validity of assertion)
> *Can I or others repeat this procedure?* (checking replication)

By applying these and other such questions, scientists try to minimize errors in making observations and recording data. They know that data that cannot be replicated by anyone who repeats the work under similar conditions is not scientifically trustworthy. The fact that others will use a scientist's results and test an experimenter's methods is a safeguard of objectivity and accuracy; it is the cornerstone of science.

Precision and objectivity in the observing and recording of data have improved as scientific instruments have become more sophisticated. Today, in most scientific experiments, scientists rely less on their feelings, observations, and senses and more on objective devices such as photographic instruments, data processors, and electronic computers.

Scientists have adopted these attitudes as their rules for conducting scientific investigations:

1. Curiosity
2. Humility
3. Skepticism
4. Open-mindedness
5. Avoidance of dogmatism or gullibility
6. Positive approach to failure
7. Objectivity

How well scientists follow these rules determines how well they will be able to use the processes of science to make significant discoveries. Average citizens can also use these rules to solve everyday problems in a better way.

SCIENTIFIC INQUIRY AND PROCESSES

Broadly defined, *scientific inquiry* is a search for truth and knowledge. If you are scientific, you are able to identify problems, make educated guesses or hypotheses, and investigate them. These attitudes influence scientists' discovery behaviors. The discovery behaviors of scientists in turn result in scientific methods, which are referred to in science for elementary school children as the *processes of science*.

Elementary School Processes of Science

☐ Observing
☐ Classifying
☐ Measuring

□ Hypothesizing or predicting
□ Describing
□ Inferring or making conclusions from data
□ Asking insightful questions about nature
□ Formulating problems
□ Designing investigations including experiments
□ Carrying out experiments
□ Constructing principles, laws, and theories from data

Acting like a scientist means using these attitudes and processes. As you will discover in chapter 9, innovative elementary school science projects and textbook series stress the seven scientific attitudes and the eleven processes of science.

Searching Means Asking Good Questions

Both young children exploring their sensory world and scientists working on deep intellectual problems ask many questions. These three types of questions are the essence of science inquiry.

What?

What-questions generally ask for descriptions and are the simplest type. Examples: "What bird is on that fence?" "What kind of rock is that?"

How?

How-questions require greater inquiry because they usually use some *process*. Example: "How is heat or thermal energy conducted through a piece of iron?" Answers to these questions are frequently suggested by the question and involve a process. To answer this question, you must know about molecular structure of matter, action of heat on molecules, interaction of "stimulated" molecules, transfer of energy from molecule to molecule, and so on.

Why?

Why-questions are the most difficult to answer. They rarely have a final answer, and each successive answer leads to another, more fundamental question. Example: A young child asks, "Daddy, why is grass green?" Father answers, "Because grass has chlorophyll," to which child immediately asks, "Well, why is chlorophyll *green*?" This could go on indefinitely because each question leads back to more basic conceptional information.

Because questioning is the heart of scientific inquiry and the foundation of teaching by discovery, chapter 6 is entirely devoted to the specifics of questioning and listening techniques.

Avoid Unscientific Answers

Sometimes in our frustration or ignorance, we respond to *why*-questions with answers that are not very scientific. We may give an *anthropomorphic* response. That is, we give human form or qualities to nonhuman things (*anthropomorphic* comes from the Greek *anthropos,* "man," and *morphos,* "form"). An example of this is Lassie's actions and ascribed qualities on television, which make it appear she can think, reason, and act as a human.

Occasionally we may respond to questions that attribute end purpose, design, or will to nonhuman things. This is called *teleological* from the Greek word *teleos* meaning "end." Stating that "water seeks its own level" is an example of teleological explanation. It is the same as saying that water has the end purpose of being at some given level. It is more scientific to say that water actually moves because of the actions of forces upon it.

Scientists do not answer questions in anthropomorphic or teleological terms because these descriptions do not contribute to a better understanding of the phenomena. These answers are vague, untrue, and lead to dead ends. For example, if you are told a plant bends toward a light source because "it likes light" (anthropomorphic), you have no need to find out how light stimulates plant hormones so cells grow more rapidly on one side of the plant, bending it toward the light source. Anthropomorphic and teleological answers discourage efforts to look deeper at cause and effect.

Search for Cause and Effect

Scientists try to find cause and effect relationships between seemingly unrelated data. Whenever possible, scientists use the *controlled experiment* to test cause and effect. Each separate condition is isolated and controlled as accurately as possible. These isolated and controlled conditions are called the *variables* of an experiment: temperature, light, moisture, or any other aspect to be tested. Scientists observe, record, and analyze differences by setting up two identical experiments and precisely altering one variable in one of the experiments. An example of a simple controlled experiment for young children is seeds germinated on a wet sponge.

This experiment establishes a cause-effect relationship between water and seed germination. It is very probable that seeds will germinate on the wet sponge in a few days but not on the dry sponge. Children are helped to see some cause-effect relationship between water and seed germination, if other conditions of temperature and light are constant and suitable. Thus, water is the *variable,* the condition that is changed to test whether it affects germination. The unchanged variables, in this case temperature and light, are the *control.*

WITH WATER

WITHOUT WATER

CONTROLLED EXPERIMENT; variable is water

Controlled experiments are one of the most important contributions of science to people's search for reliable, repeated data. However, it is extremely difficult to precisely control *all* variables at *all* times. Even slight changes in conditions may yield significant differences in findings. Scientists try to account for these slight changes and build degrees of accuracy, tolerance, and measurement into the standards of their work.

Using Scientific Procedures

Some people think that once scientists are aware of a problem, all they have to do is apply "the" scientific method. Then, by some mysterious process, their answers come pouring forth. This common misconception stems from our memorization, usually in high school or college science, of "the" scientific method

1. State problem.
2. Suggest hypotheses.
3. Experiment.
4. Observe.
5. Collect and analyze data.
6. Reexperiment to verify data.
7. Draw conclusions from data.

When scientists investigate problems, they *may* follow all these procedures, but not necessarily in the sequence given, and the actual methods may vary from scientist to scientist. They may need to spend much time defining the problem and making *several* hypotheses. Often, many experimental approaches are planned and numerous conclusions inferred. In addition to sharing common procedures, scientists also share the tested cumulative data of centuries, knowledge that influences their hypotheses or educated guesses.

The Products of Science

Scientists have been collecting data for centuries. From these data, scientists have formulated concepts, principles, and theories. The factual data, concepts, principles, and theories are the *products* of science.

A *concept* is an idea generalized from particular and relevant experiences. Examples are magnetic poles, electrical current, plant, cell, and sound. Try to name some other science concepts.

Scientific principles are generalizations involving several related concepts. For example: "Metals expand when heated." This statement has three concepts: metals, heat, and expand. Can you think of other scientific principles?

A *theory* is a broader set of related scientific principles explaining a variety of scientific phenomena. Theories explain, relate, and predict different experimental and observational findings in the simplest and most efficient ways. For instance, if we had not had a theory of gravitation, we would not have been able to go to the moon because it would have been impossible to determine how much fuel was needed to compensate for gravitational changes between the earth and the moon. Evolution, cell structure, and molecular structure are some examples of science theories. Try to identify other theories.

Science: By Humans, For Humans

We should not forget that scientific investigations are done by people, making science a human enterprise. Countless men and women inquire into the unknown through creative activities, combining their talents and labors. Nationalities often become unimportant in the free interchange of research efforts, which we called the products of science. Chapters 3 and 4 explore the humanistic values and ecological aspects of science and their implications for teaching science to elementary school children.

A Real Scientist

There are many accounts of the work of real scientists, who use the attitudes, processes, and skills we have discussed. The book *Search for Solutions,* which accompanies the film series of the same name, is an especially good source. Here is a conversation with Jocelyn Bell Burnell, the astronomer who discovered pulsars in 1967. In discussing her discovery and ensuing efforts to verify and explain pulsars, she refers to various processes and products of science, as well as the attitudes she and her team used.

As you read this excerpt, look for the examples of science processes, products, and attitudes discussed in this chapter. Notice also the scientist's human side and how she reacts in many situations like any other person.

A Conversation with Jocelyn Bell Burnell [4]

Jocelyn Bell (she is now Jocelyn Bell Burnell) came to Cambridge as a graduate student in 1965. For as far back as she can remember she had wanted to be an astronomer. She was born in Northern Ireland, where her father was an architect. Her father, in fact, designed an observatory and planetarium in the town of Armagh, and as a child Jocelyn sometimes went with him when he had work to do at the observatory. "The astronomers there were very good to me, when they knew I was interested," she said not long ago. "They gave me a lot of advice. One bit of advice was that if you want to be good at astronomy you've got to be able to stay up late at night. And even as a teenager I knew that I wasn't able to stay up at night, so I went home that day very depressed.

"I found out fairly soon after that that there was a new branch of astronomy, called radio astronomy, and you didn't normally have to be able to stay up late at night to do that. . . . So I had—I thought—a daytime type of astronomy," she said. "So we built ourselves this enormous antenna system. It covered about four and a half acres of ground. And we sledgehammered wooden posts into the ground, about a thousand posts, and strung the actual antennas, copper wires, between the posts, and laid cables connecting them all together. I think it was 120 miles of wire and cable. It took a couple of years to build.

"And when it was built, then it was my job to start operating it, and to analyze the data that came pouring out. They came out on a strip of paper, a long sheet of blue-squared paper that the tracing pen moved over. We got a hundred feet of chart paper every day. I operated the telescope for six months, which meant that there was three and a half miles of chart recording by the end. Anybody else would have got the computer to analyze it, but Muggins"—she gestured to herself—"sat down to analyze it by hand. Well, perhaps you wouldn't give it to the computer straight away, because with new equipment you want to get the feel of how it's performing and check that all's going okay.

"Fairly quickly you got used to picking out the twinkling sources. But unfortunately, the other thing that the radio astronomer gets is man-made interference. Radio telescopes are very sensitive. They have to be to pick up cosmic signals, which are very weak, coming from far across space. The energy you use to turn a single page of a book is more than all the radio telescopes have collected since the beginning of radio astronomy. The signals need amplification by factors of ten to the power of thirty before they can be recorded and studied. So almost anything in the vicinity that produces electrical interference will be picked up by the radio telescope. You get problems with badly suppressed motor-car ignitions. Thermostats kicking on and off. Arc welders. If the rules reserving frequencies to radio astronomers haven't been strictly observed, you pick up taxi radios, airplane altimeters, police-car radios. But fairly quickly you get used to recognizing the characteristics of the twinkling sources and the man-made interference.

"After a bit of chart analysis, I noticed there was something slightly peculiar on the record, late at night, from one particular patch of sky. It didn't look exactly like a twinkling source, and anyway twinkling sources shouldn't twinkle in the middle of the night. They only twinkle when they're in the daytime sky. And it didn't look exactly like man-made interference, either. It occurred a number of times when we were looking at that patch of sky. I discussed it with Tony Hewish, and we agreed that perhaps it deserved a closer look. It might have been some kind of flare on a star, where it temporarily becomes much brighter and then fades again. Or it might be a point source. One thing we were trying to do, as well as detecting the twinkling sources, was measure their angular diameter. How broad across were they? And you do that by studying the amount of scintilla-

tion—of twinkling. But it was difficult to calibrate that. And you remember, of course, that a point has zero radius. So we wondered if we had stumbled across some kind of source that was virtually a point source—because that would have helped with calibration a lot.

"The way you get a closer look is much the same way you get a photographic enlargement. You run your chart paper under the pen much faster than it normally runs, and everything becomes more spread out and enlarged and you can see it. As the student, it was my job to go out to the observatory each day at the time that source was passing through the telescope beam, and to switch the chart recorder onto a high speed. I did this very conscientiously for several weeks. No sign of anything, just the usual receiver noise. And garbage. One day, in disgust, I deliberately skipped it and went to a rather interesting lecture. Next day, on my recording there was this funny little bit of scruff again. So it hadn't gone and died on me. The next day I went out again to the observatory, all diligent and enthusiastic, and ran the fast recording, and it came through!

"It was this series of blips on the recording. And they were equally spaced, about one and a third seconds. Which is a suspicious frequency. If somebody had been playing around with a signal generator in one of the labs nearby, that's just the sort of frequency they might have set their signal generator to. I telephoned Tony Hewish. 'Oh, well, that settles it,' he said. 'It must be man-made.'

"Even so he came out to the observatory the next day, at the right time, and bless its little heart, once again the thing produced a series of pulses. Flashes. In retrospect, I appreciate how lucky I was, because we all know these things rarely perform to order. Just when you want them to put on a good display, they never do. But it was there.

"And that's where the problem started, to be honest. We weren't leaping up and down shouting 'Eureka!' We were really rather worried. We had never seen anything like this before from the sky; we didn't expect to see anything like this from the sky. We couldn't believe it could be a star, because it was flash-ing at the rather rapid rate of one and a third seconds. Stars are big cumbersome things, when you get to them. We knew of stars that flash at periods of some *hours.*

"The precision and rapidity—one and a third seconds—is suspiciously man-made. If it's going to flash at that kind of rate, you expect the object to be something much, much smaller. More nippy, more agile, to flash at that kind of rate. We tried to explain it as being something man-made, and this didn't fit very well because it was going around with the stars. It kept the same place in the sky all the time. Whereas if it had been somebody on earth, he would have been operating to earth time, where the day is twenty-four hours—while in star time the day is twenty-three hours and fifty-six minutes." The four-minute difference comes from the fact that the earth, turning on its axis once a day, is also going around the sun—but not around the stars. "So if it was Joe Bloggs going home from work in a badly sup-pressed car, he was getting home about four minutes earlier, each night.

"So it couldn't be a star. And it wasn't man-made interference. But it went round the sky with the stars. So it *had* to be a star—or some-thing out there. We had a couple of months of agony. We had to think of ways the *equipment* could be causing this. One of the nicest things was when another telescope at the observatory picked it up. That showed it was not something wrong with the antenna and receiver. But was it somebody's radar signals bouncing off the moon? Was it a satellite in a funny sort of orbit, going *bleep-bleep-bleep?* That didn't make sense either.

"One of the ideas we facetiously entertained was that it might be little green men—a civiliza-tion outside in space somewhere trying to com-municate with us. Now, radio astronomers don't really want to believe that little green men will contact us. There may well be other civiliza-tions out there in space, but I think the chances of making contact are pretty small. So it did seem to be a little bit going off the deep end to say we had detected signals from another civi-lizaton. But the name stuck. We referred to this radio source as LGM-1. . . . The evening be-fore I went off for Christmas, just before the lab shut for the night and I would be locked in, I was analyzing a bit of chart from yet another part of sky. When there seemed to be on it something that looked just a little bit familiar—this same sort of scruff! Not exactly a twinkling source, not exactly man-made interference. I searched back through other records of the same patch of sky and, sure enough, it did seem to occur on a number of occasions. We estimated the distance of the source, and reck-oned rather crudely that although it was well outside the solar system it was well within our galaxy.

"One of the tests that Tony Hewish initiated stemmed straight from this idea of it being little green men signaling to us. He argued that they would be on a planet going around their sun, just like us on earth going around our sun. And that as their planet moved around their sun, some of the time it would be coming towards us, and some of the time moving away from us. And when it's coming towards us, the flashes would tend to get piled up on top of each other and the gap between them would be shorter, and when it's moving away, the flashes would get stretched out and the timing would be slightly longer. So he started some very accu-rate timing checks to try to detect this change as their planet went around their sun. In fact, he only succeeded in showing that the earth goes around our sun, no sign of any motion of the source. But that was useful, and it also estab-lished that whatever it was was fiendishly accu-rate—comparable with some of the best clocks man can make. Which implied it had to have great reserves of energy. So that it could keep on flashing dead accurately without any serious depletion of energy. Without any serious slow-ing up.

"Well, the discovery of the second one was quite a relief in one way because it scotched the little green men idea. You don't really expect to have two lots of little green men, both choosing to signal inconspicuous planet Earth, both choosing the same unspecial radio frequency.

"Then one afternoon after Christmas, on a chart from yet another part of the sky, there were *two* lots of this scruff! Slightly different times—an hour or so apart. I did begin to wonder if I was seeing things—had too good a Christmas or something. But later in January we confirmed those two as well. So we then had four of these things from totally different parts of the sky. It definitely couldn't be little green men. It really began to look much more as if it was some kind of star. Then somebody in the group remembered reading a paper about the vibrations of a hypothetical type of star called a neutron star. Way back in the 1930s, there were some theoreticians—with a great elasticity of mind, we felt—who had been studying different states of matter. They reckoned that there could be another stable state of matter so dense that a cubic centimeter, the volume of the tip of your thumb, would weigh a hundred million tons. They reasoned that if you took a star, and somehow forced it to shrink down to this density, it might come to be made up largely of neutrons. And a neutron star would weigh as much as an ordinary star like the sun, but would be only about ten miles across. . . .

"The discovery was almost totally unexpected. We learned later of a radio astronomer at another observatory—I won't say who or where—who several years earlier was observing a portion of the sky to the right of Orion, northward, where we now know there to be a pulsar. And he saw his pen begin to jiggle. And he was about to go home for the day, and thought his equipment was misbehaving. And he kicked the table, and the pen stopped jiggling."

Social Implications of Science

Many scientists and other citizens are becoming increasingly concerned about the social implications of science. Scientific investigation endeavors to reveal truth. What it discovers, however, can be used for our benefit or detriment. Madame Curie, for example, did not know beforehand the value or the danger of radioactive material. Nuclear research has led to cataclysmic harm to the people of Hiroshima and Nagasaki. Radiation has also been used beneficially, for example, to treat cancer, the disease Marie Curie died of.

An increasing number of scientists are trying to educate the lay public about the problems of the population explosion, pollution, insecticide poisoning of the environment, and other ecological concerns. Teachers have the responsibility to show students that scientific discoveries can also help to *prevent* the destruction of the environment. No scientist can know how valuable or dangerous his or her discovery will be in advance. But all citizens should insist that scientific discoveries be used to improve the earth's environment and produce a better life-style.

Implications of Science for Your Teaching

As you find out more about science, you will discover it is not merely a body of information, but also a way of investigating. This way of investigating is called *inquiry* or *discovery;* to become a good inquirer takes years of experience and development.

Scientists are curious about their world and continually improve their investigative skills. If *children* are to understand science and become capable, active problem solvers, they must also have years of active experience in investigating *their* worlds. Children must learn, by doing and then reflecting, how to investigate and discover scientific concepts, theories, and processes. *Inquiry* science teaching sets up a classroom environment to stimulate this active interaction. *Discovery,* the culmination of inquiry processes, should not be left to chance. Rather, you must plan your discovery science lessons carefully so that children reach the goals you have set. Other important ways to approach learning are teacher telling or showing, reading, listening, drawing, and dancing.

You will find a more in-depth look at the guided discovery approach to teaching science in the elementary schools and other implications of science for teaching in chapter 5, with practical suggestions in all the succeeding chapters. Discovery science teaching enhances and reinforces other subjects in the elementary school; chapter 12 discusses this integration.

Here is a poem written by Sharon Elliott, a fourth-grade teacher:

/si əns/is . . .
This word "science," just try to
  define.
What a heck of a task,
What a hell of a time.
How do you capture a mood with a
  pen?
What words can describe the
  excitement within?

(I'm sure what it isn't.
It isn't just passively taking YOUR
  word
but challenging, searching, and
  seeking THE(?) word.

It isn't just looking—but seeing
  beyond

It isn't just hearing—but listening
  for sounds.
No—these things it isn't.

What then?
It's a method, a madness, a race to
  begin.
The compiling of facts that seem
  never to end.
It's the courage to question, the
  freedom to try,
It's the dynamic force of rejecting a
  lie.
It's the dejection of failure without
  giving in.
But it's more than all these,
It's a child's wonder, when the first
  time he sees
The miracle of the mundane.[5]

SUMMARY

Scientific inquiry involves scientific attitudes, processes, and products. Scientists use these attitudes in their work: humility, objectivity, curiosity, skepticism, avoidance of dogmatism, willingness to consider new data, and a positive approach to failure. These attitudes influence the methods used in science. Three kinds of questions form the basis of scientific investigation: "What?" (eliciting descriptions), "Why?" (rarely eliciting final answers), and "How" (eliciting process answers). Scientists avoid giving anthropomorphic or teleological explanations to questions.

Processes of science include observing, identifying problems, formulating hypotheses, designing and carrying out experiments, interpreting data, and using other forms of scientific reasoning.

Products of science are the accumulated and systematized tested body of knowledge including concepts, principles, and theories.

SELF-EVALUATION AND FURTHER STUDY

1. Explain why you agree or disagree with Timothy Ferris's statement at the beginning of this chapter.
2. Identify several scientific discoveries or inventions that have been used to improve the earth's environment and/or benefit people. List also some possible negative effects of using these scientific discoveries.
3. Select several resource science discovery lessons in Part Five and identify the control and variable(s) in each of them.
4. Tape-record or listen to your students' answers and scientific explanations. Reword several *anthropomorphic* and *teleological* responses so they are more scientifically accurate.
5. A scientist once said, "If a scientific experiment can't be done by other scientists following the exact methods reported, the experiment isn't scientific." Why is replicating the exact procedures so important in science?
6. List the kinds of *feelings* that might motivate a person to become a professional scientist.
7. When someone says, "The only constant in the universe is change," what do you think he means? What significance does this have for science and teaching?
8. Are opinionated, pedantic, and categorical people antiscientific? Why?
9. Is the statement, "The earth rotates on its axis," a scientific concept, a principle, or a theory? Explain.
10. A scientist discussing scientific inquiry said this about her cancer research: "What does *not* cure cancer is as much a scientific finding as what may eventually cure cancer." What did she mean?
11. Why do scientists make a thorough survey of scientific literature on a problem *before* starting research or experimentation on it?
12. Draw a picture of a scientist. Write a short description of the scientist. If possible, have school-age children do the same thing. Compare the pictures and descriptions. Why do you feel as you do about scientists?
13. Select a scientist and read about his or her life. What motivated this person to pursue science?
14. Interview a scientist, engineer, physician, science student, or other person engaged in scientific work. Find out what they think science is and how they use each of the processes and attitudes described in this chapter.

ENDNOTES

1. NSTA Position Statements, *Science and Children,* Vol. 18, no. 6 (March 1981), p. 2.
2. Charles P. Snow, "Appreciations in Science," *Science,* no. 133 (January 27, 1961): 256–59.
3. Isaac Asimov, "Convention '78 Revisited" (Address given at NSTA's 26th Annual National Convention in Washington, D.C.), *The Science Teacher* 45, no. 5 (May 1978): 27.
4. Excerpts from Horace Freeland Judson, *The Search for Solutions* (New York: Holt, Rinehart and Winston, 1980), pp. 80–85.
5. Sharon K. Elliott, "/siəns/ is. . . ." Reproduced with permission by *Science and Children,* April 1977. Copyright 1977 by the National Science Teachers Association, 1742 Connecticut Avenue, N.W., Washington, D.C. 20009.

2

How Do Children Develop Mentally? The Relevance of Piagetian Theory to Science Teaching

"Proper academic instruction, especially in science and mathematics, provides the ideal stimulation for brain growth during the concrete operational and formal operational periods. Unfortunately, many schools use written material, textbooks, and worksheets to teach abstract concepts. This practice is directly contrary to the active, *sensory* stimulation which neuroscience research indicates." (Virginia R. Johnson, "Myelin and Maturation: A Fresh Look at Piaget," *The Science Teacher*, Vol. 49, no. 3 [March 1982], p. 43.)

Chapter 1 discussed how *mature* people think about science. However, it takes many years of development before a person is capable of thinking about science in this way. Some people never reach this developmental level. This chapter focuses on the child's mental development. Rewarding experiences are likely to create a rich mind; physical, psychological, nutritional, and social deprivation will hamper the child's mental growth. The quality of the experiences—how the child interacts with them—is vital.

Although most children have the potential for developing good minds, many, unfortunately, never do. The responsibility for helping children develop their mental potential falls upon the schools, and, specifically, on teachers. This chapter tells you how recent research shows that discovery-oriented science teaching facilitates the development of human potential.

REVIEWING WHAT YOU KNOW ABOUT CHILDREN

You have probably learned a lot about children at this stage of your professional life, either by taking courses on child development or intelligently observing children. Look at figure 2–1. What are some of the *differences* you see in the

children in different stages of development? Why would you *not* expect children in the first group to do what those in the last group do?

Why is this question inappropriate for kindergarten children: "Mary is taller than Bruce. Bruce is not as tall as George. How does George's height compare with Mary's?" What evidence do you have for your answer?

Since you have chosen to be an elementary school teacher, you know how children develop and think. You know this question is inappropriate because kindergarten children cannot reason on a level high enough to solve that problem. For the same reason, you know that it would be nonsense to try to teach algebra to primary school children. You know that *a child does not think the way an adult does.*

Questions About Children's Development and Science Teaching

How does a child's mind differ from an adult's? What kinds of thinking are children capable of in preschool compared to primary or upper elementary grades? How does the mind evolve toward adult patterns of thought? How does teaching science through the discovery method enrich mental development? How does teaching and learning science depend on the

FIGURE 2-1
Piaget's four stages of mental development

learner's developmental stage? These are important, but complicated, questions. We still do not have all the answers.

THE FOUR STAGES OF MENTAL DEVELOPMENT

Jean Piaget, assisted by Barbel Inhelder and many others at the University of Geneva in Switzerland, studied children's mental development for almost 60 years. Piaget and his colleagues, supported by other researchers, found that children pass through four qualitatively different stages of mental or cognitive development.

1. Sensorimotor stage (0–2 years)
2. Preoperational stage (2–7 years)
3. Concrete-operational stage (7–11 years)
4. Formal-operational stage (11–14+ years)

As an elementary school teacher, it is important for you to note that

1. The ages are only *averages*. Many children in the same age group may not have devel-

oped the characteristics indicated for that stage.
2. The *sequence* for passing through the four stages is always the same. No person skips a stage.
3. *When* people reach each stage may vary considerably with individual capacities and different cultures, as well as with the kinds of experiences the individual has. It is *not* unusual, for example, for many people to be a year or more behind the sequence indicated. Although they may be slower in neurological and cognitive development, this does not necessarily mean they will not be cognitively superior in later years to those who develop earlier.
4. Many adults who should be capable of performing on a formal-operational stage do not reach this level.
5. In her doctoral study, Barbel Inhelder found that mentally retarded children also do not reach the formal-operational stage. In fact, Piagetian assessments are now being used to determine whether children are retarded.

Piagetian Stages of Development	Epstein Brain Growth Spurts
Sensorimotor (birth to 2 years)	Sensory areas of neocortex developed
Preoperational (2–7 years)	Semiotic functions signal beginning of language
	Brain mechanism for speech in place
	Can process stimuli
Concrete-operational (7–11 years)	Can process and store sensory information
	Has developed language to reconstruct the environment symbolically
Formal-operational (11 and up)	Increased development in nonspecific association area
	Myelination of fibers in rear associative areas
	Development of frontal lobe

Herman Epstein[1] found evidence of brain growth spurts at similar predictable ages. Research in neuron development and performance shows evidence that correlates with Piaget's cognitive process and may account for the Epstein growth spurts.

This chart compares brain growth spurts with the Piagetian stages of development:[2]

Because of wide variations in cognitive development, you will usually have children in your class who are at several different cognitive stages. To teach them as though they were at the same cognitive level, or as if they were adults, would be detrimental to their cognitive development. Therefore, you need to understand Piaget's four stages of mental development so you can recognize cognitive differences in your children and interact with them more appropriately. This is especially important in science since it plays such a significant role in developing cognitive abilities. Following is a review of each Piagetian stage, along with a Piagetian assessment activity. In addition, section 5 of this book gives practical Piagetian types of discovery activities should you wish to further assess your children's mental development.

SENSORIMOTOR STAGE (0–2 YEARS)

The name of the *sensorimotor stage* describes what children do at this level. What is the child in figure 2–1 (sensorimotor stage) doing? How does this drawing symbolize the name for the stage?

Aspects of the Sensorimotor Stage

The sensorimotor child is stimulus-bound and unable to initiate internal thought. Piaget is a *structuralist.* This means he believes that each person has to build his or her own structures of thought. He believes a child at birth has a relatively blank mind, except for the presence of a few instinctional behaviors. It is in the sensorimotor stage that infants begin the long process of devising mental schemes or structures for handling information. But children in this stage are stimulus-bound. The mind during this period mainly interacts to stimuli from without rather than within. Children do not, as yet, have enough schemes to initiate their own thought through interaction with their surroundings. They develop their ability to perceive, touch, move, and so on. Most of their body motions are, in a sense, an experiment with their environment.

The child in figure 2–1 is fascinated by the rattle. When children in this stage see rattles, they try to grasp them, jangle them, and, if given the chance, put them in their mouths. But they cannot think about objects like adults can.

Order and organization begin. Through physical action, children slowly construct physical knowledge and begin the life process of developing action schemes. These schemes help them adapt their behavior so they can interact more appropriately with their environment.

For example, depth perception is in the brain, not in the eye. Babies mainly see things as flat. As they develop, however, they slowly evolve schemes that enable them to perceive depth. The eye only picks up light sensations; the mind must construct schemes to interpret and integrate visual sensations to perceive depth.

This process of forming and modifying schemes is central to Piagetian theory. Children cannot be *told* how to build schemes. They must work them out themselves, although parents and teachers play a significant role in providing the experiences that facilitate this development.

The Importance of Physical Action in Development

Piaget believes the origin of cognitive mental structures is physical action. Children progressively build through cognitive action more elaborate mental schemes as they develop. They begin by adapting their innate reflexes to the objects around them; like the baby with the rattle, they grasp, push, and place things in their mouths. They proceed to coordinate the various actions that are possible on each object, thus learning the object's properties. By grasping, they learn whether the object is hard or soft, cold or warm, heavy or light, and so on.

Later they may use what they have learned about properties to solve practical problems. As they develop and use their minds, children are finally able to recall mentally the properties of objects without having to test them each time they confront them.

The child cannot perform operations mentally without doing them physically. Children at the sensorimotor stage have no imagination for objects or acts. They cannot add, subtract, or even classify objects unless they are acting on them. These thought processes only become meaningful in later stages of mental development. Even the most rudimentary sense of direction and purpose does not develop until later in this stage. For example, children are unable to detour or remove an obstacle without forgetting where they are going.

Later in this period the child is able to label. At the end of this period, children are able to imagine. They can call to mind certain people, animals, objects, and activities. By age two, they have "names" for many things and activities, enabling them to elaborate their concepts in the next stage. Space is limited to the area in which they act, and time is limited to the duration of their actions. Progress occurs as they become more involved with activities concerning space and time.

The reason it is important for you to know about the sensorimotor stage, even though you do not have children at this stage in your classes, is that you should understand that thought development is a continuous process

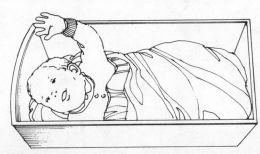

Picture 1

Picture 2

from birth through adolescence. It begins with action schemes or patterns in responses to sensori-stimuli and progresses toward internalization and representation of these actions. This process continues toward fully operational thought.

PREOPERATIONAL STAGE (2–7 YEARS)

The second stage is called *preoperational* and refers to the stage before the time when children perform operations. Piaget defines operations as internalized or mental versions of actions. The internalized actions must be reversible and be grouped with other actions into a structured whole.[3]

Operations include logical processes, such as combining ideas or objects (addition or subtraction), placing things in order (height or weight), or doing "if-then" thinking. Preoperational children are *not* yet capable of rational or

logical processes. Their thinking is often inconsistent and they say things adults think are funny.

The child is stimulus-limited but intuitive. Preoperational children differ from sensorimotor infants because they can internalize actions. They can think of moving an object before they move it. When children internalize actions, they no longer operate only on stimuli from the environment, although their mental images or representations are limited to what they have experienced. Because they can operate on a plane of representation, they can use language. However, during this period they may use the images they have formed in their minds incorrectly. For example, in the early part of this stage, a child may call all men "Daddy." The preoperational stage is said to be *intuitive* because as children develop they begin to sense the difference between things such as an individual item and its class ("Daddy" and other

men) and the difference between singular and plural (this glass and these glasses, man and men).

The child centers but does not decenter attention. Preoperational children usually center their attention on the surface of a problem. The superficial features may stimulate them the most. For example, if you were to try the experiment illustrated in figure 2–2 on a child aged five or six, you would probably receive the response indicated. The reason is that the child notices only one aspect of the change,

length, and will not notice that the putty is also thinner. The child has not decentered his or her attention to include width.

The child focuses on states, not transformations. A preoperational child cannot combine a series of events in the proper order. For example, when six year olds are shown a series of pictures of a pencil falling, they are unable to order the pictures sequentially. They focus on the state of the pencil before and after it has fallen and will probably place the first and last picture in order but be confused about the

---

Conservations of Substance, Interview Activity

1. Take two pieces of clay and make them into two balls, so they are approximately equal.

2. Ask, "Are these two balls equal?" If the child responds no, ask: "Why are they not equal?" The child may say that one is bigger than the other. If this is true, pinch some clay off one, and say: "Are they equal now?" The child will probably say yes.
3. Tell the child you are going to change one of the balls of clay into a hot dog. Roll out the clay.

Ask, "Are the two pieces of clay equal now, or does one have more or less clay than the other?" The child will probably say the rolled-out clay has more.

FIGURE 2–2
Child centers on length; thinks there is more.

others. These children will not be able to tell you when an apple will no longer be an apple as you chop it up to make applesauce.

Thought processes are not reversible. Preoperational children do not reverse their thought processes. For example, if asked, "What is a chicken?" a child will say, "It is a bird." Then if asked, "What would happen if all the birds disappeared or were destroyed? Would there be any chickens left?" the child will probably reply, "Yes." If forced into giving some other answer, the child will usually state an irrational one, such as, "There are chickens left because they run away." The child does not realize that the subclass *chicken* belongs to the class *bird,* and if the class is destroyed, the subclass is also destroyed. To grasp this point, a child would have to conceive of class and subclass and be able to reverse the mental process to go from class to subclass.

TRY THIS WITH YOUR PREOPERATIONAL CHILDREN

1. A chicken is a bird.   A is included in B.

2. If all birds are killed are there any
   chickens? Answer: yes.
   Child does not realize B includes A.

3. If no B'S then there will be no A's.
4. A child does not reverse its thinking.

Reversibility is the ability to simultaneously focus on a part and the whole. Remember that reversibility is *not* an operation itself, but an essential characteristic of *all* operations. An internalized version of an action is not an operation until it is reversible.

Animistic, artificial explanations are common. Children of this preoperational period have animistic and artificial world views. They may believe that anything that moves is alive, an *animistic* view. If you ask how a crater was formed, they are likely to say it was formed by a giant. They are *artificial* because they believe mountains and lakes are made by humans or humanlike creatures, such as giants. They also have names for all kinds of objects and believe the name is inherently a part of the object. They believe they would be different people if they had another name. They further believe all things have a purpose: the moon and sun move because they want to, and so on. The *why* questions these children constantly ask are efforts to find simple purposes for the things they perceive.

Play and reality are confused. Preoperational children cannot discriminate play from reality. In show and tell activities, for example, they may demonstrate such confusion between play and reality.

The child has an egocentric nature. It is difficult for children of this period to understand views other than their own. They talk, for example, with little attention given to whether they are being understood or even listened to. They think the way they see things is the way all people view them. It is futile to expect children to follow the rules of a game until at least age four, because they follow their own rules. This egocentricity subsides in time when they are confronted in social interaction with other individuals' various opinions.

Time and space concepts are expanded. During the preoperational stage, children's impressions of time change from thinking of the immediate present, as in the sensorimotor stage, to thinking of the future and the past. Their understanding of time, however, does not extend very far beyond the present, and the time on a clock has little meaning for them. Because of their increased freedom of movement and mobility, their conceptualization of space has enlarged to include an understanding of their home and neighborhood.

CONCRETE-OPERATIONAL STAGE (7–11 YEARS)

The child is able to perform operations. In the *concrete-operational stage,* children think

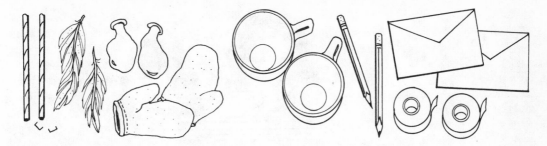

about, and learn mainly through, *concrete experiences*. They are not yet able to perform abstract reasoning processes, and are unable to learn well any abstract science processes such as osmosis and photosynthesis. They also have difficulty conceptualizing abstractions such as love and peace, or molecular theory and gravitation. Among the operations developed during this stage are addition, subtraction, multiplication, division, classification correspondence, and placement in order.

A primary task of the elementary school is to foster the development of the concrete-operational processes. Although these operations appear related to mathematics, their significance is much broader than this. Children mentally develop these operations first through interacting with objects. For example, apples and oranges are fruit; this is an operation of addition. Only after having physical experiences with objects such as fruit are they later able to progress in using the operations in more abstract ways, such as one plus one equals two in mathematics.

Below are some logical operations with examples from a child's school and home life.

Operations in Science

As a teacher of science, you will find examples of these operations useful. Consider giving a child or small group of children a variety of objects, such as pieces of wood, a nail, bottle top, corks, and a candle, and a basin of water.[4] Ask the children:

1. to classify the objects according to whether they will sink or float
2. to explain why they classified it
3. to try them in the basin of water
4. to provide a general explanation of the observation

A child just beginning the concrete operations might classify the objects in two categories:

1. those that float because they are light (wood, paper, etc.)
2. those that sink because they are heavy (pebbles, nail, key, etc.)

Logical Operations	
ADDITION	Combining
SUBTRACTION	Taking away
MULTIPLICATION	Repeating
DIVISION	Repeating subtraction
CORRESPONDENCE (ONE-TO-ONE)	Aligning one row with another row
PLACEMENT IN ORDER	This is greater than or this is less than
SUBSTITUTION	Replacing something similar with another entity
CLASSIFICATION	Grouping according to similarities

The students investigating sinking and floating objects are engaged in concrete operations like those at the bottom of this page.[5]

The child moves through several substages of operational abilities. Piaget's work has shown that there may be several substages of development in a specific operation such as ordering. For example, the majority of eight year olds can order objects by length from one to ten. However, it usually takes two or more years before they can order by weight. Ordering by weight, then, is higher in development than ordering by length.

The child develops classification abilities. Classification develops significantly during the concrete-operational stage. The sequence for the classification hierarchy is shown in table 2–1.

Classifying objects or ideas is basic to intellectual thought. Developing classification skills is paramount to ordering and easily locating information in the mind. *Silverware, furniture, clothing,* and *animals* are classification categories we slowly establish and develop. Once they are mentally coded, we can call upon them to interact better with the environment. For example, young children soon learn the class *silverware.* They can be taken to a new home and asked to get some silverware from the kitchen and will do it relatively easily.

As an outcome of the concrete-operational stage, children conceptually organize their environment into cognitive structures—ideas. Because they can do this, each new encounter with nature does not require extensive examination. They can now call on their classificational abilities and quickly determine an object's properties, structure, and function. This allows for much more efficient response, since

Operation	Activity or Observation
Classifying	Floating versus sinking Heavy versus light Large versus small
Identifying variables and serially ordering them	Weight Volume Density
Placing two sets of variables in correspondence	Large and heavy Small and heavy Large and light Small and light

TABLE 2-1
Classification hierarchy

Classification Task	Age Approximations
1. Grouping by a single characteristic perceptually apparent; for example, groups by color.	3–4 years
2. Grouping by abstracting common property; for example, child sees sticks and notes some are long, then collects only long ones.	3–4 years
3. Multiple classification—can classify by more than one property; for example, color, size, shape.	4–5 years
4. Grouping by realizing all objects are the same in some respects but different in others; for example, fingers all grasp, but vary in shape.	4–5 years
5. Class inclusion—forms subclasses and includes major classes; for example, a bird has feathers (class); some are white and some black (subclass). If asked if there are more black feathers than feathers, will say more feathers.	6–10 years
6. Ascending hierarchy; for example, cat is a mammal.	7–10 years
7. Descending hierarchy; for example, mammals include cats.	9–10 years
8. Establishing multiple criteria for a relatively complex classification system. Defines characteristics for supraordinate and subordinate classes; for example, supraordinate group (mammals) have hair, nurse their young, and so on; subordinate class (humans) stand erect, have opposite thumbs, and so on.	11–14 years

Note: Remember that the ages are only approximations. A third or more of any class may not achieve the levels until a year or more later.

they can go beyond individual things and think of groups. Because concrete-operational children can do reversible thinking, they are able, late in the stage, to classify objects and organisms not only in an ascending but a descending manner as well. For example, they usually realize by age ten that ducks are birds (ascending) and if birds are destroyed there will be no

ducks (descending). Because they ascend from ducks to birds and descend from birds to ducks in their thought processes, concrete-operational children demonstrate they are capable of reversing their thinking. The ability to form classes and groups and relate their characteristics to individual members enables the children to greatly expand their mental activity.

Most elementary science curriculum projects include varied classificational activities to provide the experience necessary for developing this type of operational thinking.

Ascending and Descending Hierarchy

Ascending
7–10

Ducks are birds

Descending
9–10

Birds include ducks

Reversible and descending thought

Limited hypotheses are possible. Concrete-operational children are capable of noting what happens if something is added to the volume of a container, both to the object receiving the liquid and the one being depleted of it. However, in trying to resolve problems, they are usually limited to making only one hypothesis, and this involves only one variable. Furthermore, they are better able to solve problems if they are concretely acting on them. For example, in volume problems, they need to see actual containers before them. It is difficult for children to hold a problem in their minds while trying to resolve it.

Understanding of space and time are greatly expanded. Concrete-operational children's understanding increases significantly over the previous period. They now have some notion of geographical space—town, city, county, state, nation, hemisphere—and of historical time—Egyptians, Romans, Washington, Napoleon, and so on.

The child develops conservation abilities. Here is a task that demonstrates a child's conservation abilities:

1. Present the child with two glasses as illustrated in figure 2-3.
2. The tall glass has liquid in it.
3. Pour the liquid into the shorter, wider glass. Ask, "Is there more or less liquid in the shorter glass than was in the tall one?" Preoperational-level children usually state that the shorter glass has less liquid. Ask, "Why do you think so?" and they will usually give you an illogical response.

Preoperational children give this type of answer because they are overly impressed by perceptions. Piaget says they are "perception-bound." Concrete-operational children, on the other hand, note the differences in the height, but reason that nothing has been added or

taken away. In other words, they have developed the ability to conserve because they can mentally represent actions such as what would happen if the liquid were poured back into the tall glass. They realize that there would be the same amount of liquid as before.

Conservation, like ordering and classification, is hierarchical. It is the realization that changing an object physically (shape, length, direction, or position) does not alter the amount present. Although it is reasonable to expect a child conserving substance to generalize this to conservation of length, weight, volume, area, number, and so on, such is not the case. Refer to table 2-2 for different types of conservation and the approximate age level of attainment.

Look back over the hierarchies for classification and conservation (tables 2-1 and 2-2). Which of these would the children *you* teach have trouble with? Remember to include some operations just above and below your age group. What would you do to help children develop these operations? How would science activities help? Why would you want to involve children in hands-on science experiences for these operations? Why would you have to have some children do many similar activities before they would develop the operations?

Classification and conservation are extremely important operational abilities. It has been found that children who cannot perform them have learning problems in school. When children cannot multiply, classify, conserve substance, and number, they have problems in mathematics and reading. Many words are classifications (fingers, shoes, etc.); they can be rearranged. Fingers can be spread apart or

FIGURE 2-3
Piagetian task on conservation

Tall slender glass

Wide glass

1. Preoperational child thinks there is less in wide glass.
2. Concrete child conserves.

TABLE 2-2
Conservation hierarchy

Types of Conservation	Approximate Age	Cognition
Conservation of substance	6–7	Realizes amount of substance does not change by dividing it
Conservation of length	6–7	Realizes, for example, bending a wire does not change its length
Conservation of number	6½–7	Realizes rearranging objects does not change their number
Conservation of a continuous quantity	6–7	Realizes pouring liquid from one container to another does not change the quantity
Conservation of area	7	Realizes the area of a paper split in half covers just as much area as if it were whole
Conservation of weight	9–12	Realizes a mashed piece of clay weighs the same as when it was a sphere
Conservation of volume	11–12 & beyond	Realizes that a mashed piece of clay immersed in a liquid will occupy as much volume as when it was a sphere

brought close together, and shoes can be separated in different parts of a room. They are, however, still conserved. When children cannot conserve words, they also have difficulty conserving different letters and references to ideas in reading.

The child shows operational thinking by conservation of number. Most elementary teachers, unaware of Piaget's research, assume that if children can count, they know number and should be able to add. Counting is a long way cognitively from knowing the meaning of "number." Most preoperational children can count, "one, two, three," but very few understand number. All they are doing is repeating a memorized sequence.

A simple test to determine whether children who may still be preoperational (ages five to nine) comprehend number is to ask them to count their fingers on both hands. They usually count fairly well. Then ask, "If the tenth finger were number one, what would be the numbers of the longest fingers in each hand?" Those not conserving will give you all kinds of odd answers: 9, 14, 15.

For children to know number, they must

1. Conserve. They must understand that spreading out the fingers does not mean there are more or less.
2. Classify all fingers as being in some respects the same.
3. Cardinate, or arrive at a cardinal number. They must be able to classify objects in a set order to arrive at their number while still realizing that objects are separate entities.
4. Realize that the number of something may depend on its position in a series, such as in a line of children.

5. Order. They should be able to count in sequence without jumping around.

Piaget believes that one of the first indications that operational thinking is starting to take place occurs when children show they really understand and use number. To attempt to involve children in experiences requiring an understanding of number before they have learned the significance of number through working with objects is futile.

Hands-on science activities, where children count and do things with objects, provide experiences that contribute to their development of an understanding of number. This is why many elementary science curriculums have units dealing with material objects.

Science is basic to the three Rs since it helps students develop the operations necessary to read and do mathematics. It is one of the most effective ways to help children grow operationally so they can perform well in other areas.

FORMAL-OPERATIONAL STAGE (11–14+ YEARS)

The child develops abstract, reflexive thinking. Piaget initially believed that most adolescents reached formal-operational thinking by age 15. More recently, however, he questioned this because other investigators have found that many students, even on the university level, do not do well on formal tasks.[6] Research at the University of Northern Colorado has further substantiated that many students in high school and university do not function well formally. If you are an upper-level elementary teacher (grades six and above), you can expect to have students in your classes who are concrete-operational, a few in transition to the formal-operational level, and some who are already formal-operational thinkers.

Roger Webb found no formal-operational children among an academically gifted group of students before age 11. After age 11, the academically gifted (I.Q. 150 and above) seem to develop formal reasoning much faster provided they have stimulating environments.[7]

The age category with this stage, perhaps more than the others, should be thought of as a rough indication of cognitive level. If you teach upper elementary students, you will soon recognize that the ones having little difficulty in grasping abstract ideas are formal in their thinking.

Probability becomes understandable. Formal-operational students think in terms of many possibilities and are not limited to the facts before them. They can think of ideals as opposed to realities, and are capable of understanding probability theory.

Thinking processes are more hypothetical-deductive. Formal adolescents are capable of doing hypothetical-deductive, "if-then" thinking. They formulate hypotheses as testable ideas in their minds and do not regard them necessarily as realities. They are more likely to demonstrate deductive patterns of thought than at previous stages of mental development. For example, they might perform the following operations:

> John really is well liked.
> He has long hair and nice clothes.
> How can I become well liked? (formulates a problem)
> If I had long hair, then . . . (makes a hypothesis)

Reflexive thinking processes begin. One of the main characteristics demarking this stage is the students' ability to do reflexive thinking. They are now capable of thinking back over a series of mental operations and reflecting on them. In other words, they can think about their thinking. In the process of doing this, they represent their own mental operations by symbols. For example, students, asked after finishing an experiment how they could improve their results, will reflect and evaluate everything they have done to come up with better data.

The child can control variables. In science, students in the formal-operational stage are capable of controlling one variable at a time in order to isolate the one affecting a situation.

For example, in determining whether it is the weight, length of string, or height from which a weight is released that affects the frequency of a pendulum's swing, they control all but one variable at a time to determine the answer. They may keep the weight and the height from which it is released the same but change the length of a string. Concrete-operational children, on the other hand, in doing this experiment may change the weight and length of the string at the same time. They seem to become confused in identifying and controlling variables.

The child does ratios and proportions. Formal-operational thinkers can solve ratio and proportional types of problems. For example, they know that if a balance has a 10 gram weight that is 3 centimeters from the pivot point, a 5 gram weight will have to be placed 6 centimeters from this point for it to be in balance. (See illustration below.)

Abstraction Processes More Developed

The student of this period generally is more capable of thinking abstractly, for example, in performing complex mathematical tasks. This is a good summary of a formal-operational person:

". . . the child begins to function intellectually like an adult. This stage marks the child's emancipation from dependence on direct perception of objects as a mediator of thought. In contrast to the concrete operational child, the adolescent thinker can represent his own thoughts by symbols, consider ideals as opposed to realities, form inferences based on stated sets of assumptions (propositional thought), formulate complex and abstract theories, and reflect upon his thought processes. He can carry out "mental" experiments as well as actual ones. Probability is well understood."[8]

To insure that you fully understand the theory, review the characteristics of Piaget's stages of mental development. Now, turn away and try to summarize the characteristics of each stage, so you can better predict what children are capable of doing at various age levels. Then compare your summary with the one in the following section.

SUMMARY OF THE CHARACTERISTICS OF PIAGET'S STAGES OF MENTAL DEVELOPMENT

Sensorimotor (0–2 years). The child

1. is mainly directed by stimuli outside the mind.

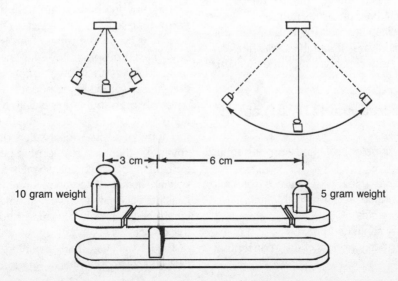

2. is preverbal—no language.
3. has thought proceeding from actions.
4. learns to perceive and identify objects.
5. by end of period distinguishes parents, animals, and knows names.
6. has a rudimentary sense of direction and purpose (appears late in stage).
7. is bound to the present.
8. is bound to the immediate space.

Preoperational (2–7 years). The child

1. cannot perform operations but language develops.
2. does not decenter.
3. is egocentric.
4. shows nonreversible thinking.
5. mainly acts on perceptive impulses.
6. is a static thinker—doesn't think of series of operations—transfers motions.
7. thinks of present, future, and past, but this is limited to short duration.
8. thinks of house, yard, and neighborhood.
9. late in the period, in transition to concrete, may conserve substance, length, number, and continuous quantity.

Concrete-Operational (7–11 Years). The child

1. performs operations: combining, separating, ordering, seriating, multiplying or repeating, dividing, and substituting.
2. can do correspondence (by end of period).
3. analyzes, is aware of variables, classifies.
4. measures and conserves volume, weight, and area.

Formal-Operational (11–15 Years). The child

1. performs hypothetical and propositional thought.
2. is a reflexive thinker—evaluates thinking processes, thinks about own thinking.
3. controls variables.
4. is externally stimulus-free.
5. does *abstract*, nonconcrete conceptual thinking.

6. understands probability.
7. questions ethics (not discussed in text).
8. does ratios, proportions, and combinatorial logic.

PIAGET AND LEARNING

Perhaps the most significant contribution of Piaget to learning theory is his refutation of Rousseau's suggestion that humans are born with faculties. Rather, each person must, through interaction with the environment, *construct his or her own intellect.* Knowledge, then, is not something that is sponged up but, instead, is constructed in the mind through actions of the individual. Children are not *passive receptors* but *active agents* in developing their own minds. Power to form the intellect, therefore, largely lies within the child; knowledge is not somehow stored in the content and techniques of a subject.

Types of Knowledge

Piaget believes there are three types of knowledge: physical, logical mathematical, and social.

Physical knowledge is the first type a child develops. It is basic because it forms the primary mental structures that are the foundation for other forms of knowledge. Physical knowledge develops through the child's observation and interaction with objects. Piaget believes that all young children are naturally drawn to performing actions on objects. Their observation may be of two types. One is where they only *observe* something that happens. The other involves their own *action* on an object that causes something to happen. For example, when children make noises with a spoon, they learn some of its properties. Eventually through this type of active observation, they will discover that there is a relationship between cause and effect. Educationally speaking, activities involving active observation are more likely to facilitate cognitive development than those where children only observe without acting on the object.

Piaget believes that reasoning, or what he calls *logical mathematical knowledge,* evolves out of physical experience. It occurs when children reflect on their actions and relate and organize reality in some way in their minds. For example, when children are confronted with a ball of clay that is then flattened, they may only observe it. They may also reflect and conclude that nothing has been added or taken away from the clay. It therefore has the same amount of material as before. By only observing it, children cannot conclude that the material is conserved. Only if their minds carry on logically consistent processes are they able to derive that the clay is conserved. Conservation occurs in the mind; all nature does is rearrange itself. Logical mathematical experience is what a mind uses to establish operational processes such as conservation, classification, ordering, and logical consistency. It depends on physical knowledge but is separate and different from it.

Social knowledge differs from physical and logical mathematical knowledge in that it evolves from the interaction of *individuals* with each other. Consensus plays an important role in the derivation of social knowledge. A chair is called a chair because people agree that an object having chairlike attributes should be called a chair. Similarly more complex abstract words such as *democracy* derive their meaning from agreed-upon definitions. Social rules of behavior are also determined through social interaction.

Some interpreters of Piaget's work use a broader definition of social knowledge to include all of the *preformed* knowledge that is transmitted to the individual from the culture, either by informal or formal means. They take knowledge to be the refined, highly organized knowledge of the human race developed across the centuries and expressed in some symbolic form, primarily language or mathematics. In your science teaching, social knowledge would be the body of subject matter (products of science): facts, concepts, principles, etc. You can tell your children about these products of science after they have hands-on experiences with the science areas, or you can present them in books, films, etc.

Egocentricity and Decentering

Piaget believes that, as individuals develop, there is a continual lessening of egocentricity.

Physical knowledge   Social knowledge   Logical-mathematical reasoning

All humans are egocentric to some extent, but there are wide differences between an infant, a conceited person, and a mature human with great wisdom. Sensorimotor babies, at birth, do not even separate themselves from their physical world. Through physical encounters over many months they slowly realize they are separate and different from other objects. However, for several years into the preoperational state, they still are very egocentric. For example, when they are with other children of age three to four, they will carry on monologues oblivious to whether or not they are communicating. It is in the upper preoperational stage, when they are confronted by other children's perceptions, that they begin to realize the way they see things in an egocentric manner may differ from the way other children perceive things. Piaget believes it is social conflict that causes children to begin to *decenter*. Social experience, then, is fundamental to the child's learning that there may be alternative perceptions, views, and, eventually, hypotheses related to a problem. Social knowledge is critical if the child is to eventually develop hypothetical-deductive thinking in the formal-operational stage. Many early childhood and preschool programs, although they are not necessarily based on Piagetian theory, use social intervention as a means of helping the child develop both mentally and morally.

Discovery-oriented science instruction plays a significant role in the attainment and development of each of the three types of knowledge and in the decentering process. It focuses on the children having hands-on physical experiences where they make discoveries commensurate with their cognitive level in a social-interactive setting.

Using Piaget's Theory in Science Curriculums

Many curriculum projects are designed to give greater attention to child development, particularly on the elementary level and in science projects. Some of these projects are Science Curriculum Improvement Study (SCIS); Elementary Science Study (ESS); American Association for the Advancement of Science: Science—A Process Approach (SAPA); Outdoor Biology Instructional Strategies (OBIS); Health Activities Project (HAP); Early Childhood Curriculum (ECC); and many others in science, social studies, and mathematics. See Chapter 9 for a description of some of these innovative science programs.

Curriculum developers question whether the child's cognitive development can or should be accelerated. Whether or not it can be does not seem as important as providing experiences for developing good rational thinking in the higher cognitive stages. Piaget believes that involving students in rich experiences at their level of development provides a firm foundation for later stages of cognitive growth. The quality of experiences at each level is more important than quantity.

The paramount concern of teachers, therefore, should be designing activities for students to insure that they have opportunities to perform desirable mental operations at their stage of development. For example, if children are to become good problem-solving adults, they must have opportunities to solve various types of problems throughout their school life. An awareness of the cognitive development of the child, and a translation of this awareness into teaching practice, provide a great challenge. Achieving it makes the difference between teaching as a professional and as a technician.

Practical Suggestions for Facilitating Thinking in Your Science Classroom

Here are some suggestions, based on Piaget's work, for developing rational thought:

1. Stress hands-on, concrete science activities in all grades. Piaget believes only the individual builds his or her own mind. Teachers can, however, facilitate and enhance mental growth through providing activities where the student mentally acts on what is being learned. This requires a shift from the traditional approach of the teacher as the teller and the student as the receiver to the teacher as the facilitator and the student as the actor and doer. To Piaget, there is no learning without action, and action to him means being physically, mentally, and socially involved, rather than simply listening. In the upper elementary level you may have the children read or create something and then share in small groups their views on what each individual thinks is important, how it is creative, what other things they could do, and so on. The groups should decide what they want to report to the whole class for further discussion and evaluation and then present their conclusions.[9]

2. Provide a wide variety of teaching/learning activities. Piaget stresses that children learn best through a variety of activities. Hands-on discovery-type activities are stressed in this textbook, not because children learn *only* by that approach, but as a counterweight to telling, reading to children, using a textbook and the other more familiar activities most teachers feel more comfortable with. *All* ac-

tivities should be used where appropriate to your children's developmental level.

Remember that a wide variety of teaching and learning activities is vital since not all students are at the stages of development suggested by Piaget's age groups, especially at the formal-operational stage (upper elementary grades). Figure 2–4 reveals an enormous variation in proportion of students at each stage. Although it is a British population, similar findings are made with American populations.

Explain things using objects, diagrams, pictures, films and filmstrips and other aids. Avoid using complex verbalizations or abstractions, since many children are not mentally prepared to understand them.

3. Determine the cognitive levels of your children by giving individual Piagetian interviews. You know that paper and pencil tests can be misleading in trying to identify cognitive levels of your students. See pages 60–61 in

Teachers should do less telling.

Children should do more and act on what they learn.

FIGURE 2-4
Proportion of children at different Piagetian stages in a representative British child population[10]

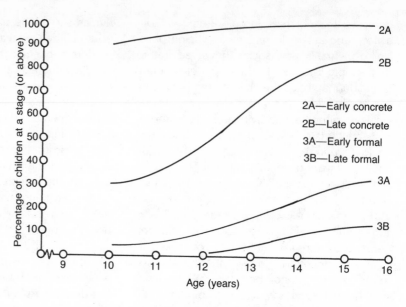

2A—Early concrete
2B—Late concrete
3A—Early formal
3B—Late formal

this text for suggestions on how to do this. Although it takes some time, it will make your teaching, and your children's learning, more effective.

4. Select appropriate cognitive experiences for the children you teach after finding their cognitive levels. For example, ordering, class inclusion, conservation and reflexive thinking.

5. Avoid using terms and introducing concepts unless there is some concrete referent (e.g., objects or photographs).

6. Involve children frequently in operational thinking. This is especially important for helping children attain ordering, conserving, and classifying.

7. In interacting with individual children, ask questions to determine how they think. For example, you may want to determine whether the children have achieved formal thought by asking them to perform reflexive thinking processes. In science and mathematics, you might ask your children to describe the steps they went through in resolving the problem. If students do not perform well with problems of this nature, it indicates they have not yet achieved the formal level of cognitive development.

8. Children in the upper elementary level (grade six and higher), who may be entering the formal level, should be encouraged to perform the following types of operations:

a) hypothetical-deductive thinking, b) propositional thinking, c) evaluation of information, d) origination of problems, e) reflexive thinking. Since the formal-thinking students are capable of determining and synthesizing general properties, theories, values, and ethics, they should be given many opportunities to discuss ethical questions, to devise and discover general laws, principles, and rules, and laws in science. They should also be encouraged to think formally in those areas they are interested in and know something about, since this will increase their level of thinking and involvement in the area.

9. Above all, allow all students many opportunities to use their minds. They may do this by organizing a task, motivating other students to work with them on a project, interacting with other students about a problem, collecting and interpreting data, deciding on a class presentation they will give, or creating something for the class.

SUMMARY

Dr. Jean Piaget conducted research for almost 60 years on how the minds of children develop. He says individuals pass through four stages of cognitive development as they mature. These are the sensorimotor, 0–2 years;

the preoperational, 2–7 years; the concrete-operational, 7–11 years; and the formal-operational, 11–14+ years.

Piaget's work focuses on how an individual is able to perform operations. Operations include mental processes such as adding, subtracting, multiplying, dividing, performing correspondence, ordering, substituting, and reversing. Sensorimotor and preoperational students are unable to perform these operations, but during the concrete-operational period, individuals slowly develop these rational skills. Formal-operational students, in addition to being able to perform hypothetical-deductive thinking, perform propositional reasoning and do reflexive thinking.

Although the ages given for Piaget's periods indicate that by the time of high school individuals should be formal-operational, in fact, many are not. Frequently, instructors have within the same class individuals at varying mental stages, many in transition from one period to another. Teachers should adjust their teaching accordingly. For example, concrete-operational students usually do not perform well verbally. Teachers should, therefore, involve them in concrete activities where there is not a dependence on verbal learning alone.

SELF-EVALUATION AND FURTHER STUDY

1. Obtain the media kit of filmstrips and audio tapes from Charles E. Merrill Publishing Co. entitled *Piaget for Educators Multimedia Program.* Observe several filmstrips and listen to the accompanying audio tapes.
2. Give Piagetian types of interviews to children on several levels. The following sources will be of value to you in preparing to give the interviews.

   □ Robert B. Sund, *Piaget for Educators* (Columbus, Ohio: Charles E. Merrill Publishing Co., 1976).
   □ Robert L. Selman, "Concrete Operational Thought and the Emergence of the Concept of Unseen Force in Children's Theories of Electromagnetism and Gravity," *Science Education,* vol. 66, no. 2 (April 1982), pp. 181–94.
   □ Robert P. Craig, "The Child's Construction of Space and Time," *Science and Children,* vol. 19, no. 3 (Nov.–Dec. 1981), pp. 36–37.

3. To learn more about brain development research and its relevance to Piagetian levels of thinking, read and summarize

   □ Marcel Kinsbourne, "Hemispheric Specialization and the Growth of Human Understanding," *American Psychologist,* vol. 37, no. 4 (April 1982), pp. 411–20.
   □ Virginia R. Johnson, "Myelin and Maturation: A Fresh Look at Piaget," *The Science Teacher,* vol. 49, no. 3 (March 1982), p. 43.
   □ William K. Esler, "What Research Says: Brain Physiology: Research and Theory," *Science and Children,* vol. 19, no. 6 (March 1982), pp. 44–45.

4. Researchers have found that hands-on activities (especially the kind in discovery-type science programs) raise the reading scores of children. To see this connection, read Mary Budd Rowe, "Help Is Denied to Those in Need," *Science and Children,* vol. 12, no. 6 (March 1975), p. 23. How does this article use Piagetian theory to relate concrete experiences to learning?

5. Read chapter 4 to find out about left-brain, right-brain research. See if you can discover relationships in Piagetian theory and right-brain, left-brain development.

ENDNOTES

1. Herman T. Epstein, "Growth Spurts During Brain Development: Implications for Educational Policies and Practices," *Education and the Brain* (Chicago: University of Chicago Press, 1979), pp. 343–70.

2. Information found in D. J. Coulter, *New Paradigms for Understanding the Properties and Functions of the Brain:* Implications for Education. A research project. (Greeley, Colorado: University of Colorado, 1981.)

3. Jean Piaget and Barbel Inhelder, *The Psychology of the Child,* (New York: Basic Books, 1969).

4. For a fuller description of this activity and an analysis of the Piagetian interview tasks, read Michael Shayer and Philip Adey, *Towards a Science of Science Teaching* (Edison, New Jersey: Heineman Educational Books, Inc., 1981), 159 pages.

5. Other examples of the use of these three primary operations with your elementary school children can be found in Barbel Inhelder and Jean Piaget, *The Growth of Logical Thought From Childhood to Adolescence* (New York: Basic Books, Inc., 1957).

6. Jean Piaget, "Intellectual Evolution from Adolescence to Adulthood" (3rd International Convention and Awarding of Foneme Prizes, Foneme Institution for Studies and Research in Human Formation, Milan, Italy, May 9–10, 1970), pp. 160–65.

7. Roger Webb, "Concrete and Formal Operations in Very Bright 6–11 Year Olds," *Human Development* 17 (1974): pp. 292–300.

8. Robert B. Sund and Roger W. Bybee, *Becoming a Better Elementary Science Teacher* (Columbus, Ohio: Charles E. Merrill Publishing Co., 1973), p. 61.

9. Piaget calls this the *constructivist* theory of knowledge, which implies an *active* interaction between the student and the source of knowledge. For additional information, see Constance Kamii and Rhita DeVries, *Physical Knowledge in Preschool Education—Implications of Piaget's Theory* (Englewood Cliffs, N.J.: Prentice-Hall, 1978).

10. Michael Shayer and Philip Adey, *Towards a Science of Science Teaching* (Edison, N.J.: Heineman Educational Books, Inc., 1981), p. 9.

3

**What Are Your
Goals and Objectives
in Teaching Science
and How Do You
Evaluate Progress?**

You can see how the ideas in chapters 1 and 2 form a logical program of science for the elementary schools. You learned that science is a dynamic human activity made up of products, processes, and attitudes that are closely interrelated. Also, you discovered that children are environmental investigators from birth, using all their senses to observe and sample everything around them.

This chapter has two purposes. First, you will see how science in the elementary school has evolved from what is known about both science and children (goals and objectives). Second, you will discover ways to assess to what extent your children are achieving the goals and objectives in your science program (evaluation).

THE INFLUENCE OF SCIENCE EDUCATION ON ALL LEARNING

Elementary school children are inquisitive. They are fascinated by their surroundings, animals, rocks, plants, their bodies, the sky and beyond, and by a variety of phenomena that may appear as magic to them. Many scientists have this same almost childlike fascination with scientific phenomena. This innate "science" interest of your students will help make teaching them science relatively easy and enjoyable for you.

You can readily see that science education not only helps children learn about science, but it contributes to the overall goals and objectives of the elementary school. Reading, 'riting, and 'rithmetic skills are stressed along with the specific science education goals of observing, comparing, classifying, hypothesizing, inferring, interpreting data, etc.

How Science Contributes to the General Objectives of a School

A goal is something a teacher tries to help children attain. One primary goal is the development of good citizens. But what does it mean to be a good citizen? Most people would agree that a good citizen must be a rational, critical, thinking, creative human. He or she should have a wealth of knowledge, problem-solving skills, desirable attitudes, appreciation for the contributions of others, and broad interests. Science teaching, as with all areas of instruction, contributes to these general goals, but, in addition, it has specific objectives that scientists, science educators, and teachers believe contribute to the development of the individual.

The Goals and Objectives of Science Teaching

Our goals and objectives are constantly changing as we acquire new information about how children develop and learn, as science and technology advance, and as the aspirations of individuals and society change. Although many school systems create their own science programs, these have many common objectives. One objective is to promote scientific literacy. The Rockefeller Foundation's Commission on the Humanities emphasized this when it stated that scientific literacy is no less vital a characteristic of an educated person than his or her ability to read and write.[1] The Commission also stressed the *social* implications of science by cautioning us that if science and technology are to make invention both creative and humane, then a knowledge of the humanities must be coupled with science.

In its monograph, *What Research Says to the Science Teacher, Vol. 3,* the National Science Teachers Association lists priorities for science teaching for the remainder of the twentieth century. Robert Yager, one of the editors of the monograph, summarizes these priorities in their order of importance.[2]

1. *A redefinition of goals for science education.* We need both a new rationale and a new statement of purpose, taking into account the fact that our students are soon to be adults in a society even more technological than today's. They will be participating as citizens in science-related decisions affecting the whole of society. Thus, restricting science to the goal of academic preparation is too limiting.

2. *A new concept of the science curriculum to meet new goals.* This includes redesigned courses, new course sequences, and combining science with other disciplines. These new curricula should include components of science not yet defined or used. Direct student experiences, technology, and personal and social concerns should all be stressed.

3. *New programs and procedures for the preparation, certification, placement, and con-* *tinuing education of teachers.* In order for new directions and views of the curriculum to succeed, we must attend to inservice education and also allow for professional development and peer "support systems."

4. *New instructional materials expressing the new philosophy, curriculum structure, and teacher strategies.* These materials should provide concrete examples for moving teachers and students in new directions.

5. *Means for translating new research findings into practical programs.* The separation of researcher from practitioner is a problem in science education. Science educators from all facets of the profession must work cooperatively so that genuine progress can occur.

6. *Renewed attention to the meaning of evaluation in science education.* To realize well-ordered, purposeful change, we should use such methods as self-assessment techniques, a questioning attitude, and gathering of evidence to enable thoughtful decisions about instructional goals.

7. *Greater attention, on the local level, to developing systems for implementation, as well as support for exemplary teaching and programs.* At the moment, a serious problem in science education is the erosion of support systems for effecting change and improvement.

Project Synthesis Study of Science Education

Science education in the United States is considered to be in transition by many observers currently assessing this field of teaching, and significant research has been done in the past few years to determine its status. The National Science Foundation (NSF) funded three studies of science teaching in grades K through 12. The National Assessment of Educational Progress (NAEP) added substantially to its third assessment of science teaching. Many professional organizations started large scale studies to determine prior accomplishments, as well as what is happening in science teaching currently. Project Synthesis was funded by NSF in 1977 to define the *desired* state of science education, compare that ideal with the *actual* status of science education, and make recommendations for the future.

FOUR MAJOR GOAL AREAS FOR SCIENCE TEACHING

Growing out of the priorities identified by Project Synthesis are four major goal areas for science curricula: personal needs, societal needs, academic needs, and career awareness. Note that the focus is on both the students' and the society's needs.[3]

Goal Cluster I: Personal Needs

Students will:

☐ Be able to exhibit effective consumer behavior. This requires the skills to evaluate the quality of products, the accuracy of advertising, and the personal needs for the product.
☐ Use effective personal health practices.
☐ Have knowledge of one's self, both personal and physical.
☐ Possess a variety of skills and procedures to gather knowledge for personal use.
☐ Be able to learn when presented with new ideas and data.
☐ Use information and values to make rational decisions and evaluate the personal consequences.
☐ Recognize that their lives influence their environment and are influenced by it.
☐ Recognize and accept the ways in which each individual is unique.
☐ Be aware of the constant changes in themselves.

Goal Cluster II: Societal Issues

Students will:

☐ Recognize that the solution to one problem can create new problems.
☐ Use information and values to make decisions and evaluate the consequences for others in the community.

☐ Recognize that some data can be interpreted differently by different people depending on their values and experience.
☐ Recognize the ways science and technology have changed their lives in the past by changing the coping skills available to them.
☐ Possess a sense of custodianship (collective responsibility for the environment over a period of time).
☐ Recognize that science will not provide "magic" solutions or easy answers. Instead, the use of hard work and the processes of science are required to "resolve" rather than "solve" many problems.

Goal Cluster III: Academic Preparation

Students will:

☐ Develop an understanding of information and concepts from a wide variety of topics selected from the life, earth, and physical sciences. There is no set of basic topics for elementary science instruction.

  1. This variety of topics may be used to help develop the skills in generating, categorizing, quantifying, and interpreting information from an environment.
  2. This variety of topics may be used for the sole reason that they are interesting to students at a particular age.

Goal Cluster IV: Career Education/Awareness

Students will:

☐ Recognize that scientists and technicians are people with personal and human characteristics. (Teachers should use biographical sketches, personal knowledge, etc.)
☐ Observe both sexes, minorities, and handicapped persons represented in the written materials to encourage equal access to science-related careers.

HOW CAN I USE OBJECTIVES?

Since science will be only one of the subjects you teach, you may ask, "How can I use the above objectives in my teaching?'' Every time you select things for your students to learn, you are setting objectives. These objectives could be for learning science content, practicing process skills, or developing and/or strengthening attitudes and values.

How do you get ideas for your objectives? Your science curriculum or textbook teachers' manual will supply some; you may pick some from this textbook. Regardless where you get them, you must pick those most applicable to your particular students and to what *you* want for them. *You* will be the only one who has enough information about your students to define the precise objectives prescribed for their needs, levels of maturation, and interests, as well as for their cultural and social environments.

How Do Goals and Objectives Differ?

Many science educators distinguish between goals and objectives. *Goals* give direction to the people who plan and write science programs, courses, or curricular guides. Goals are written *broadly,* often in such terms as "to understand," "to appreciate," "to know," etc. The Project Synthesis four major goal clusters are examples of broad goals. *Objectives* are usually specific and may be more useful for you working directly with children. Objectives are often written *behaviorally,* but the use of behavioral objectives in science education is controversial.

The antagonists of the behavioral-objective movement argue that prescribing ends in advance limits the teacher's freedom moving through an activity as his or her instincts dictate would be most desirable. In other words, this group believes that defining behavioral objectives constitutes a closed system, preventing creative teaching. They also believe it is difficult, if not impossible, to measure truly valuable human objectives and that teachers will tend to write trite ones because they are easier to assess.

How Can Behavioral Objectives Help Me?

Behavioral objectives are those objectives stated in terms of an *observable* behavior that a student will be able to perform after having completed the learning period. Although identifying observable behaviors as objectives is useful, you should know some of the limitations. J. Myron Atkins, speaking for many science educators, has these reservations:[4]

1. Not all goals and objectives are easily identified.
2. Behavioral objectives may limit the range of exploration.
3. Instructional priorities must be flexible.
4. Goals should come first—they are not ways of measuring behavior.

Martin Haberman, while recognizing the advantages of using behavioral objectives, suggests these additional limitations:[5]

1. The most powerful element in the process of schooling is *social* interaction, not content.
2. The interrelationships of content are *internal* as well as external. Pupils organize content psychologically as well as logically.
3. Skills become overemphasized, generalizations are undervalued.
4. All content does not fit the behavioral approach.

Writing Behavioral Objectives

Suggestions for writing cognitive behavioral objectives include: (1) define your goals; (2) select content you think will contribute to those goals; (3) write a tentative objective; and (4) evaluate and modify the objectives. The following sample is a guide in writing behavioral objectives.

The student should be able to:

1. Hypothesize what will happen to a slug when placed in salt water (hypertonic solution).
2. Design an experiment to determine whether coffee or tea retains heat better.
3. Infer that slight environmental changes may cause the death of certain organisms, for example, the slug.

The objectives below are poorly written.

1. The student should circle the numeral representing the number of triangles in a given diagram.

2. The student should join two sets by drawing a single loop around them.
3. The student should indicate the number of objects in each of two sets.

Compare these two sets of objectives. Why is the second set in a poorer format than the first? Note that the phrase "the student should be able to" is written only once in the first set, but the second set repeats the statement. This forces the reader to read the same expression several times. Using the statement once economizes the reader's time.

Note also that the *action* verbs *hypothesize, design,* and *infer* are underlined in the first set. It is our experience that placing the action verb first and underlining it defines the behavior more accurately. You, as a result, are usually able to determine more easily and quickly if a statement is in behavioral terms. Compare the following objectives:

	Type of Objective
1. <u>Defines</u> seriation operationally	Science process
2. <u>Understands</u> the law of conservation of weight	Science content
3. <u>Knows</u> how to use it	Science content
4. <u>Identifies</u> brine shrimp	Science content

Which of these objectives are written behaviorally? How does the underlining help you identify the behavior? Note the use of *understand* and *know*. These are not cognitive action verbs that define in observational terms what the student is to demonstrate after learning. How would you change these to make them behavioral objectives?

The above examples contain both science content and science process objectives. Beginning teachers tend to devote their total attention to science content objectives. Try to include both types of objectives.

Several funded science curriculum projects have written behavioral objectives for their material. Chapter 9 discusses some of these programs.

Action verbs. The key to writing behavioral objectives is to use an action verb at the beginning of the statement. You may observe the performance of a direction containing an action verb. However, not all verbs indicate observable action. The word *understand* above, for example, is a verb but you cannot determine whether someone understands something unless you have the person perform actions such as state, describe, write, diagram, or draw. Verbs used to write behavioral objectives, therefore, should be of the *observable* type.

Examples of general action verbs are *name, state, describe, identify,* and *explain.* Examples of science action verbs are *classify, compute, organize, measure,* and *hypothesize.*

IMPLICATIONS OF GOALS AND OBJECTIVES FOR YOUR SCIENCE TEACHING

More than at any other time in history, today's schools are being held accountable. *Accountability* assumes that the public is capable of understanding education, if it is given the necessary information. We as teachers must justify to the public our specific goals and objectives, explain how we intend to teach and evaluate the results, and explain how we plan to use these results and professional judgments to improve our science programs.

Once your goals and objectives are specifically stated, how do you assess the extent to which your students are reaching those goals? How will you use your observed evaluations and results to continually improve your teaching? Benjamin Bloom has suggested that we arrange all educational objectives into three large categories or *domains.*

1. *Cognitive Domain*—recalling previously learned knowledge
2. *Affective Domain*—interests, appreciations, attitudes, values
3. *Psychomotor Domain*—motor and manipulative skills

Pages 49–73 in this chapter show how the goals in Clusters I–III fall into Bloom's three domains.

Evaluating Your Science Goals and Objectives

The rest of this chapter will provide practical suggestions on implementing evaluation devices for Bloom's three domains and specific directions on how to use them most effectively. As you read these evaluation suggestions, please keep these important ideas concerning evaluation in mind.

1. A *variety* of evaluation techniques, instruments, and procedures is necessary to understand and display what each student has learned.
2. Materials and processes of evaluation are to be so developed and utilized that they are integral to, not apart from, the other learning processes in a course.
3. Evaluation procedures are most effective when students and teachers work together in their development and implementation. Evaluation should provide students and teachers with opportunities to summarize and interpret what they have accomplished. It should not be restricted to securing data for grading.
4. Planning, judging, and revising materials and procedures for evaluation is most effectively accomplished when students and teachers work together to improve their quality.
5. Quality of thinking, development of competencies in criticism and evaluation, and reflection upon and integration of learning will take priority over moving on to new subject areas whenever these alternatives are in contention for class time.[6]

ASSESSING INDIVIDUAL PROGRESS

Stated simply, your teaching consists of three basic elements.

1. You decide *what* you will teach: science content, processes, value systems, or a particular science program.
2. You are concerned with *how* you teach: physical environment and intellectual atmosphere, teaching methods, science materials and equipment, *etc.*
3. Finally, you need to know *how well* you have taught and how well your students have learned.

Item 3 means you may need to change your teaching practices and procedures.

The roles and procedures for evaluation have changed gradually to match the corresponding shifts in emphases of the new science programs. You now need newer and more relevant techniques for assessing your pupils' progress in acquiring science content, skills in scientific processes or Piagetian operations, and values clarification skills. You should also be interested in self-evaluation and in assessing your effectiveness in the classroom. This chapter looks mainly at teacher/learner interaction.

Continuous and Cumulative Evaluation

Although the terms *measurement* and *evaluation* are similar, they are not synonymous. *Measurement* usually involves collecting information about your students through tests, checklists, worksheets, and so on. Very often, *measurement* (as the term connotates in mathematics) involves a numerical score or other reading.

On the other hand, *evaluation* is a broader concept. It involves your professional judgment, which is based on a variety of data such as measurement, your feelings and observations, and other information you gather from the learning environment. Evaluation is not merely a device you use at the *end* of a science lesson or unit of study. Instead, you need to use evaluation minute by minute throughout all of your teaching. You can accomplish much evaluation by judicious and effective questioning and sensitive listening. Continuous evaluation will help you quickly spot which science areas your students have been exposed to previously.

Diagnostic Evaluation

Evaluation procedures can supply you with a lot of diagnostic data about individual children in your class. Such procedures can help you identify a child's science strengths, weaknesses, and interests. This information will indicate how well children work alone or in groups, with your direct assistance or on their own, with a variety of sensory devices (filmstrips, films, audiotapes, and so on) or by reading. By using a measurement device and testing the children *before* you start your teaching, you can determine what specific experiences will best encourage their science progress. Diagnostic data help you adjust the learning to your children's individual differences.

Once the learning is under way, it becomes your responsibility to find out how well the children are doing with the learning activities you have prescribed as a result of your diagnosis. Your teaching/learning model is very much like the physician's endless loop model.

Research has shown that you can increase content achievement in your students by giving more diagnostic tests corresponding to your learning objectives.[7] Recent findings by R. Fiel and James Okey are consistent with those obtained at different grades and in different subjects.[8] It was also found that if you follow your diagnostic testing with reteaching and student restudying, you will get significant increases in achievement, even among students who have low aptitude.[9]

Evaluation as Achievement Appraisal

Evaluation techniques give you insights into how well your students are learning the science content and processes you planned for them through diagnostic devices. By skillfully using these achievement data with your students, increased interest and motivation can be provided by

1. Making children *active* partners in the teaching/learning act, rather than the traditional, passive absorbers of information.
2. Inviting children to set realistic goals and providing information to both you and them concerning their progress toward these goals.

3. Showing children that progress has been made, no matter how small, to help them attain satisfaction as well as a desire to continue learning.
4. Guiding children to become increasingly self-directed as they put into perspective where they were, are, and should be in the future.
5. Showing children that an adult really cares about their progress.

There is much evidence that how you interpret evaluation results to your students affects their future achievement. The way you relate the results of measurement and evaluation to your students affects their self-ratings and estimates of self-perceptions. Show children how well they are doing, and they will strive to do well on the next task. Remember: *"Success breeds success. Failure breeds more failure."*

How Evaluation Helps You Group Children

Evaluation gives you sound evidence about the variations in your students' achievement. Such data from evaluation can be used to identify skill needs and strengths or weaknesses of your students, for individualizing your teaching, and for supplying enrichment activities.

Groups can be based temporarily on skills or needs and then dissolved or rearranged for different needs or skills. Evaluation data can also be used for setting up groups of "special" children, intellectually or artistically gifted, physically or emotionally handicapped, and so on. Tests that identify gifted elementary children with outstanding science talents have been developed and validated by Gerald Lesser, Frederick Davis, and Lucille Nakemow at Hunter College in New York City.[10] Many educators feel we should do more than we have in the past for our "special" children. In fact, legislation has been passed in many states making it mandatory that we provide programs geared especially for their needs and interests. We in science education, more than *ever* before, will be required to show what kinds of programs we are providing for *all* children and how well our students are learning from these programs. We will need more sophisticated means of evaluation so we may communicate how well our students are learning science.

How Evaluation Helps You Communicate to the Public

Evaluation can provide you with the raw data you need to report to parents, school boards, and the community at large. Good communication between you and your students' parents helps supply the best possible learning experiences for your students. By having good evaluative procedures and solid information upon which to make interpretations to your community, you are better able to handle questions and criticisms of your science program intelligently. You will be better equipped to communicate your objectives and achievements in the science program with such information. Through adequate science evaluation, administrators also will be provided with valid information to make *their* judgments and recommendations to school boards of education. Administrators need such data to support your efforts. With the millions of dollars and countless hours being spent on science programs, communities deserve to know the effectiveness of the programs they support. The "back-to-basics" movement in some communities means, unfortunately, "an across-the-board deemphasis of science education from kindergarten through high school." Some school systems have cut science programs to transfer additional funds into politically acceptable areas of education: reading and language arts.[11]

Our objectives and our evaluation techniques, as well as our communication of them to the public, must be specific, in concrete, unambiguous terms. Keep in mind the words of noted science writer Isaac Asimov, speaking before the annual convention of the National Science Teachers Association, in Washington, D.C. in 1977: "Science must fight to maintain its honor. We must reach out to the public. We must be proselytizers."

Figure 3–1 shows the many levels your evaluation can take. *One* of the elements of instruc-

tion, it helps you diagnose, prescribe, and modify your instruction, and communicate to students and your public accurately.

COGNITIVE DOMAIN

The cognitive domain contains the behaviors associated with scientific products and processes in your science program. This area receives major emphasis in science education today, although many educators want to increase activities involving science processes, Piagetian types of reasoning, and affective domain objectives, as indicated in chapter 2. Emphasis today, however, is still on knowing how to apply scientific knowledge.

Studies[12] have shown that most tests given by teachers require only the *lowest* form of the cognitive domain: *the recall of knowledge.* These low-level objectives solicit students' knowledge and comprehension of scientific facts, concepts, and principles. Bloom believes children must know these things if they are to go to the higher levels of thinking: application, analysis, synthesis, and evaluation. Following are practical evaluation devices to assist you in evaluating your students' mastery of these higher thinking processes.

Testing Scientific Knowledge: Products

Over the years, teachers and schools have stressed the area of knowledge and comprehension in the evaluation of teaching/learning in their science programs. Historically, because of this emphasis, many helpful techniques for evaluation of knowledge have been tried. These include

1. Tape recordings of discussions and question-and-answer sessions
2. Teacher conversations
3. Anecdotal record keeping
4. Teacher-pupil interviews

Unfortunately these techniques are time-consuming and laborious. Most teachers, although highly motivated and dedicated, have difficulty fitting such techniques into their already over-

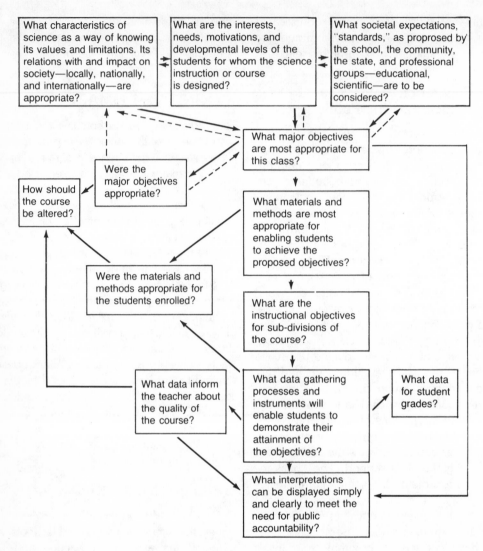

FIGURE 3-1

A conceptualization of the interrelations of the complex of factors in classroom evaluation. (Dotted lines indicate feedback.)

James T. Robinson, "A Critical Look at Grading and Evaluation Practices," *What Research Says to the Science Teacher, Vol. 2* (Washington, D.C.: National Science Teachers Association, 1979), Mary Budd Rowe, Editor, p. 3.

crowded school day. Most elementary school teachers rely more on written tests as their staple in evaluation. This book concentrates on techniques for improving your written evaluation devices. Others are presented too, so you may see how they might fit into your evaluation program.

Tape recorders. An excellent and easy device to use is the tape recorder. This is also the simplest means of assessing your students' accuracy in observation of objects and events. The tape recorder can be used even if you teach in a nursery, preschool, or kindergarten. Cassette audiorecorders are relatively inexpensive and easy enough for the youngest child to operate. They are generally durable and can take abuse. You can tape-record science situations and questions; children can then listen to the tape, stop where instructed, and perform

the required tasks using materials you supply with the tape recording.

Another practical use of audiotapes is taping questions for tests for children who might have difficulty reading them. This has been found to be of exceptional value also for presenting materials to blind and visually handicapped students. If you have such children in your class, tape-record your questions and have the children respond to the questions either by *their* recording of *their* answers on the tape or by working with a classmate.

Occasionally, you may want to audiotape your class discussions so you and your class can evaluate them. Part of the audiotaped class discussion can be *your* self-evaluation, perhaps consisting of these questions you have about your questioning techniques (as discussed in chapter 6).

☐ What cognitive processes and operations did I try to develop?

☐ How much time was involved in teacher talk compared with student talk?

☐ If I were to conduct this discussion again, how would I modify *my* behavior?

☐ How many of my questions did *I* answer?

☐ In how many situations did I *not* give sufficient wait-time after a question?

☐ What reasoning-types of questions did I use?

Beginning with a short segment of one of your class discussions (about 15 minutes would be sufficient), you might concentrate one time on how you open or structure the lesson. In subsequent recordings, you could focus on student responses or other aspects of the class discussion.

For further information on how to use the audiotape recorder in evaluating your science program, the following references are recommended:

☐ John Bullard and Calvin E. Mether, *Audiovisual Fundamentals* (Dubuque, Ia.: Wm. C. Brown Company, Publishers, 1974).

☐ John B. Haney, *Educational Communications and Technology* (Dubuque, Ia.: Wm. C. Brown Company, Publishers, 1975).

☐ Ed Minor and Harvey R. Frye, *Techniques for Producing Visual Instructional Media* (New York: McGraw-Hill Book Co., 1977).

☐ Herbert E. Scuorzo, *Practical Audiovisual Handbook for Teachers* (Englewood Cliffs, N.J.: Prentice-Hall, 1967).

Record keeping. Another simple way for you to informally assess your students' accuracy of objects and events is to keep records of their actions. Records are notations about events or observations children put into some form for future use in their studies. Figure 3–2 shows a list of the types of science records children might compile. Mary Clare Petty reveals in that list how children can show you their observational accuracy. For instance, for "Pictures and Symbols," one of your students could make a simple drawing of the sun on a calendar to indicate that he or she has an accurate observation of the day's weather. How might *you* use that chart in your own science program evaluation? What other types of science record keeping can you add that are not listed in figure 3–2?

Robert Holtz suggests other ways of keeping records and communicating children's progress in science. He recommends that teachers focus on the four areas of evaluation, shown in figure 3–3.

Entries can be made in the appropriate boxes to record when the task was completed.

FIGURE 3–2
Types of science records

Labels and Lists	of collections, specimens, parts of plants, parts of diagrams . . . of birds, plants, shrubs in community or on school grounds, materials needed for experiment, characteristics of insects, objectives, or purposes. . . . Lists may be very simple or relatively highly organized, showing classifications and/or relationships. . . .
Pictures and Symbols	of smiling suns, rotund snowmen on weather records, pictures of parts of plants we eat, drawing of "signs" of winter or spring. . . .
Diagrams	of parts of a simple machine, location of trees in park, plans for a spring garden, relative size of planets, set-up of apparatus for an experiment. . . . Diagrams may be copies or original drawings.
Graphs	of numerically expressed data: rainfall, temperature, relationship of height and weight, proportion of different gases in air, a balanced diet. . . . Use of line graphs, bar graphs, circle graphs, and pictographs should be developed.
Tables and Charts	of information about geologic eras, or the force needed to lift a weight with three different arrangements of pulleys, or the description of temperature zones.
Records of Sequence	of care and development of small animals, or development of eggs in incubator, growth of plants used in experiment, observations of changes in moon over period of weeks, water level in dishes during evaporation studies. . . .
Simple Memoranda	of details about care of pets or plants in the classroom, plans about future activities, responsibilities accepted, ideas and theories to be checked later. The memoranda may be incorporated later into more complex forms of records; they insure accuracy of recall and minimize oversight of significant information at a later date.
Records of Raw Data of Observations	of elements of time, selection of appropriate units of measure, approximate nature of all measurements, weights pulled by pulleys, length of time candles burn in containers of different sizes, measurements of the same surface obtained by different children, temperature at which they find water boils. . . . *Children must be encouraged to record raw data they obtain and not what they believe these data should be.*
Narrative and Descriptive Records	of accounts by the class, with teacher serving as "secretary," following a trip to a zoo, visit to a resource person, a discussion stimulated by an article in the newspaper. . . . These reports are not "unscientific" and can stimulate interest, raise questions, and help in identification of valuable scientific problems for study.
Tape Recordings	of use for narrative and descriptive records. Tape recordings allow more freedom to the children, who can concentrate better on *what*

they have to say. Playback may be followed by discussions and lead to questions such as: "Why did we say that?" "What is wrong with this conclusion?" "Is this a reasonable statement?" Recordings may be used to explain diagrams or models, supplement pictures and drawings. . . .

Reports in Three Dimensions of models of cross section of earth's crust, of an oil well, the solar system, collections of leaves and bark, displays of seeds in different stages of germination. . . . These are best used when children have a major interest in sharing information with others. Three-dimensional reports make concepts more vivid, accurate, and meaningful.

Formal Reports of Experiments of actual results obtained by the children in their experiments. Experience with formal reporting makes for "scientific literacy" and prepares the students for the type of records expected of high school students.

Source: Mary Clare Petty, *How to Record and Use Data in Elementary School Science* (Washington, D.C.: National Science Teachers Association, 1965), p. 4.

In addition, you can use this form as a basis for parent-teacher and student-teacher conferences, and/or as a reporting card using a rating scale for each of the topics:

1. Outstanding work
2. Improvement shown
3. Works up to ability
4. Improvement needed

This "teacher evaluation list" contains *specifics;* you can add many others. Being able to form such a list is vital if you are to make your evaluation of nontest items tangible and concrete, especially to parents and other non-professional educators.

Evaluating your students' recall. You can devise simple tests to discover your students' knowledge of terminology and specific facts. First, determine the specific observable behavioral objective, then prepare the test. Two examples are

Behavioral Objective:

To identify whether students can define technical terms by giving their properties, relations, or attributes.

A volt is a unit of:
 A. weight
 B. force
 C. distance
 D. work
 E. volume

Behavioral Objective:

To identify whether students can recall terms, events, discoveries, and reactions.

Which of the following types of waves can travel through a vacuum?
 A. sound
 B. light
 C. electromagnetic
 D. A and B
 E. B and C

These evaluation devices are termed *recall tests.* As the name implies, recall questions ask your students to bring back into their consciousness information they explored in the past. Psychologists have found that people associate items with other items and rarely, if ever, completely isolate them. The ways in which we associate isolated items is still a mystery. Even tests of isolation, such as the inkblot designs used in the Rorschach tests, evoke widely divergent responses. This is due to the unique backgrounds, perceptions, and formed associations of individuals. Testing recall with

Teacher's Evaluation List

	1	2	3	4
I. *Tests*				
II. *Experiments*				
1. Is able to recognize and solve problems.				
2. Uses a variety of sources in searching for information.				
3. Makes careful observations and takes notes and records data carefully.				
4. Forms intelligent hypotheses.				
5. Is able to detect similarities and differences, discrepancies and inconsistencies.				
6. Shows open-mindedness in pursuit of solutions to problems.				
7. Is able to organize information after bringing together all data collected.				
8. Works effectively with other students.				
III. *Projects*				
1. Uses originality in planning a project.				
2. Is able to organize material.				
3. Is able to complete an activity once begun.				
4. Is aware of scientific principles involved in the chosen project.				
IV. *Scientific Interests*				
1. Extends interest independently. (Home experiments, brings things for the science corner, extra readings, etc.)				
2. During discussions, is able to offer own ideas and generalize about what has been learned.				
3. Asks thoughtful questions related to the material being studied.				
V. *Comments*				

FIGURE 3–3
Teacher's evaluation list

Source: Modified from materials in Robert E. Holtz, "More Than a Letter Grade." Reproduced with permission by *Science and Children* 14, no. 1 (September 1976), p. 23. Copyright 1976 by the National Science Teachers Association, 1742 Connecticut Avenue, N.W., Washington, D.C. 20009.

children thus becomes a problem of framing your questions to stimulate the remembrance of situations in which the intended information occurred. One of the best ways to do this is to use pictures, especially if you are working with younger children.

Picture tests for knowledge of classification. Picture tests can be used for the more complex aspects of knowledge such as classification, methodology, principles, abstractions, generalizations, and theories. Imagine showing a series of slides on a screen and asking questions using a tape recorder. In the latter case, all the students have to do is identify the right diagram.

Researchers found that the science knowledge test showed expectedly strong dependence on reading; however, when the students were given the *Pictorial-Aural Inventory of Science,* they showed no significant differences in mean scores between good-reading student groups and the poor-reading students. The implication of this research to science is that you must guard against overemphasizing reading-dependent tests. All teachers have students who clearly understand and contribute in class discussions, only to flunk a paper-pencil test; the use of more *pictorial* evaluation devices may remedy this. With practice, you will soon develop your skill in preparing these devices and gain better insights into whether you are truly evaluating your behavioral objectives. For additional information about Finkelstein and Hammill's research, you should read this four-page abstract: Leonard B. Finkelstein and Donald D. Hammill, "A Reading-free Science Test," *The Elementary School Journal,* October 1969, pp. 34–37.

Figure 3–4 is an example of a pictorial test of knowledge of classification. The behavioral objective is to observe whether the student can classify things on the basis of whether they sink or float in water.

Even though the pictorial test shown in figure 3–4 has a minimum of words and uses pictures for reinforcement, some children may still find it too difficult. For these children, you can make *wordless* pictorial tests. Either you or your students can get pictures from magazines or you can take a series of still pictures of some scientific event. As in the example, you might take pictures of a melting snowman and *verbally* ask the children questions as you show them the pictures.[13]

Which aspect of Bloom's cognitive domain does the snowman pictorial riddle evaluate? What observable behavioral objective is being tested? The test is intended to determine the children's knowledge of trends and sequences. What are other ways of testing your students' knowledge of scientific principles?

Matching tests. Matching tests, as used by teachers, usually test only for a low level of objectives: recall. They should be used sparingly. Matching tests also present several problems:

1. Children are asked to put things into pigeonholes that might not be of the same kind of classification as their thinking.
2. The tests are not always indicative of the student's ability to perceive deeper meanings or relationships.
3. If an even number of items and matching answers are presented, students will get *two* incorrect answers for each one answer that is wrong.

To overcome item 1, you might have the children in the upper elementary grades make up their own matching tests following a science lesson. For item 3, you should always have *more* responses (answers) than premises (items to be matched).

Multiple-choice tests. Multiple-choice testing is another way to evaluate your students' understanding of scientific principles and concepts and in some ways is better than the matching test. Here is a sample of a multiple-choice test:

> If you wanted to get a top to spin a long time, which of the following would you do and why? Would you spin it:
>
> a. Under water
> b. On a syrup-covered surface
> c. On a thin, oil-covered surface
> d. On sand

To improve your multiple-choice tests, keep these things in mind:

1. They have **three** parts:
   a. *Stem:* presenting task to your students
   b. *Distractors:* incorrect responses
   c. *Correct response*
2. Be sure your stem asks a direct question.
3. Check to see if you have one correct response.
4. Try to keep your responses (both distractors and correct response) to four. More responses are unwieldy, and fewer make it almost a true or false test.
5. Avoid "all of the above" or "none of the above," as these responses may confuse some children.

What differences do you see in these 3 pictures?
Which do you think will happen first? Second?
   Last?
Why do you think the snowman is changing?

Test each object in the water.		Test each object in the water.	
Circle the word *floats* if your object floats in water.		Circle the word *floats* if your object floats in water.	
Circle the word *sinks* if your object sinks in water.		Circle the word *sinks* if your object sinks in water.	
rock — floats sinks	scallop shell — floats sinks	rubber band — floats sinks	crayon — floats sinks
button — floats sinks	bean — floats sinks	plastic spaghetti — floats sinks	paper clip — floats sinks
piece of metal — floats sinks	piece of wood — floats sinks 17	sugar cube — floats sinks	bottle cap — floats sinks 18

FIGURE 3–4

Source: These exercises are reproduced by permission of Science Curriculum Improvement Study, *Material Objects Teacher's Guide* (Chicago: Rand McNally & Co., 1970), pp. 72 and 73.

Crossword puzzles. Another technique for evaluating children's knowledge of specifics and terminology is the crossword puzzle. Generally, children in the primary grades have limited reading vocabularies, and primary grade teachers have made simple crossword puzzles using words from primary reading lists. Intermediate and upper grade teachers find children respond favorably to science crossword puzzles. In fact, children like to create their own puzzles at the conclusion of a science study. A student teacher wrote the puzzle in figure 3–5 for her fourth grade.

All of these illustrations of testing devices are limited to Bloom's simplest level of thinking—knowledge. This level is equated with scientific *products.* Let us examine now the higher levels of thinking.

Testing Scientific and Piagetian Understanding Processes

Bloom's next five levels of thinking enter the realm of testing children's understanding of the thinking processes: comprehension, application, analysis, synthesis, and evaluation. The scientific processes we are really trying to evaluate are the children's abilities to

1. *Translate* major ideas into their own words.
2. *Interpret* the relationships among major ideas.
3. *Extrapolate,* or go beyond, data to implications of major ideas.
4. *Apply* their knowledge and understanding to the solutions of new problems in new situations.
5. *Analyze* or break an idea into its parts and show that they understand their relationship.
6. *Synthesize* or put elements together to form a new pattern and produce a unique communication, plan, or set of abstract relations.
7. *Evaluate* or make judgments based on evidence.

Many possible testing devices are available to assess your students' levels of process thinking.

Essay tests: translation. The use of essays in science is a two-headed proposition. Like all testing devices, the essay presents many serious disadvantages along with many positive evaluative advantages. This brief summary gives some advantages and disadvantages of the essay test.

1. It shows how well the student is able to organize and present ideas, *but* scoring is very subjective due to a lack of set answers.
2. It shows varying degrees of correctness, since there is not only a right or wrong answer, *but* scoring requires excessive time.
3. It tests ability to analyze problems using pertinent information and to arrive at generalizations or conclusions, *but* scoring is influenced by spelling, handwriting, sentence structure, and other extraneous items.
4. It gets to deeper meanings, reasoning, and interrelationships rather than isolated bits of factual materials, *but* questions usually are either ambiguous or obvious.

To offset the disadvantages of the essay test, you must carefully consider the construction of each essay question. You should word the question so your pupil will be limited as much as possible to the concepts being tested. For instance, for junior high or middle school level, it is better to use

If you moved to Greenland, how would the days and nights differ from where you live now? How would the seasons differ?

than

Discuss the differences between the places in the world in relation to their days and nights throughout the seasons.

The second question is much too broad and does not give your pupil direction to know what you expect.

With a fourth-grade student, you might ask this question for an essay-type test.

How is your life affected by the shorter daylight hours in winter? How do you think animals in your area are also affected?

DOWN

1. The planet on which we live.
2. When the sun shines.
3. The sun rises in the _____.
4. The hot time of the year.
7. When we see the stars.
9. When the sun is straight over your head.

ACROSS

4. Twinkle, twinkle little _____.
5. The earth is a _____.
6. The man in the _____.
8. The time of the year when it snows.
10. The yellow ball that shines in the daytime.
11. The sun sets in the _____.

Note: Words to be found in a crossword puzzle may be placed in a list below the puzzle, especially for primary grade children or those who have limited reading vocabularies:

Earth	day	east	summer
night	noon	star	planet
winter	sun	west	

FIGURE 3–5

You will be able successfully to overcome or minimize the shortcomings of excessive subjectivity in scoring essay-type questions by preparing a scoring guide beforehand and by scoring each question separately. If a list of the important ideas you expect is made before scoring, there is less chance for indecision while scoring.

You should be flexible and open-minded in setting up the important ideas you will accept as answers for an essay. There may be valid student ideas that you have not considered. You should also give your students an explanation of your scoring so they can benefit from the test and use it for a further learning experience. An example of an essay to test your students' ability to translate scientific concepts into their own words, along with an appropriate behavioral objective, might be

Behavioral Objective:

To determine whether students are able to state a scientific principle in their own words

In one paragraph, in your own words, explain how oil helps make it possible for things to move more easily.

How children can apply previous ideas? In Bloom's category "Application," students use previously acquired knowledge and comprehension to solve problems in situations new or uniquely different from those to which they were previously exposed. In essence, we are asking if children understand the elements of a particular idea well enough to apply them in another context. The teacher might use the following kind of evaluation activity to test this.

Now that we have studied about heat and thermal energy for some time, see if you can apply your understandings to these new situations:

1. According to *your* understanding of ENERGY SOURCE and ENERGY SINK, why is this common statement *inaccurate:* Close the door, you're letting in the cold.

2. How would you correct the above statement to make it accurate?
3. Using the above ideas, how would you account for a person getting a bad *burn* if he touches dry ice?

Assessing analysis skills. Students are asked to reduce ideas into their component parts in Bloom's category "Analysis." They are also asked to show they understand the relationship of the component parts. Although this category appears very similar to the previous one on interpretation and application, these differences exist.

1. Interpretation and application. Emphasis is on using *subject matter* to arrive at conclusions.
2. Analysis. There is concern for subject matter, but students must also be conscious of the intellectual processes they are using and know the rules for reaching valid conclusions.

Cartoons, graphs, pictures, and other nonverbal forms offer the teacher an opportunity to evaluate the learners' ability to put ideas into their own words and thoughts. An example might be to ask children if they can see the artist's purpose for drawing the cartoon below.

"According to the charts, George, you're going to have to lose some of that extra weight."

The cartoon illustrates that

1. People in the United States tend to be fatter than other people in the world.
2. The doctor doesn't practice what he preaches.
3. The doctor was being funny.
4. This person hasn't been watching weight charts closely enough.

Testing analysis of elements. Here you would be testing to see if your students can break down ideas into their parts and show the relationships. The examples in figure 3–6 ask your students to separate the elements of *observations* from *inferences*. A more advanced or complex example of an inference assessment device requiring good spatial relation ability, probably for ages 10 to 12, is shown in the second drawing.

Testing your students' analysis of relationships (Piagetian type of operational ability). Figure 3–7 can help you test your students' perceptions of cause-effect relationships.

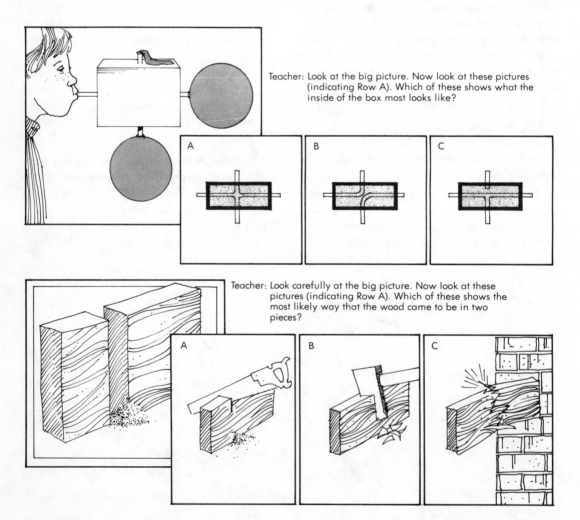

Teacher: Look at the big picture. Now look at these pictures (indicating Row A). Which of these shows what the inside of the box most looks like?

Teacher: Look carefully at the big picture. Now look at these pictures (indicating Row A). Which of these shows the most likely way that the wood came to be in two pieces?

FIGURE 3–6

Source: Loretta L. Molitar, "Why? 'Cause It's 'Sposed to." Reproduced with permission by *Science and Children* 13, no. 3 (November/December 1975), p. 18. Copyright 1975 by The National Science Teachers Association, 1742 Connecticut Avenue, N.W., Washington, D.C. 20009.

PRETEST AND POSTTEST FOR TIPPING AND BALANCE.

Before you begin this kit please answer these questions on your own.

Your first and last name _____
Date _____
Classroom number _____
Grade _____
Your age _____

Board ⟶ ☐⟵ Chip

1. When the board above does not tip to one side or another, it is said to be _____.

2. Circle the triangle (△) above which will balance the board and chip.

3. What is this called? _____
4. With a balance stick set up like the picture below.

7 chips will balance _____ chips.

5. Another name for a "balancer" is a _____ .

6. Show how you would balance this stick by adding chips.

7. Circle the stick that is balanced.

8. To weigh things on a balance scale, you must balance the empty scale first.
This is true [ ]
This is false [ ]

9. It is not possible to balance 2 chips with one chip.
This is true [ ]
This is false [ ]

10. Circle the stick that is balanced.

Turn this sheet in to your teacher.

FIGURE 3–7

Source: Joseph Abruscato and Douglas Varney, "Kits for Less Than Fifty Cents." Reproduced with permission by *Science and Children* 13, no. 1 (September 1975), p. 13. Copyright 1975 by The National Science Teachers Association, 1742 Connecticut Avenue, N.W., Washington, D.C. 20009.

Testing synthesis. Unlike analysis (which breaks a whole into its parts), *synthesis* asks your students to put parts together, to make patterns that are new to them. Bloom divides these higher creative-thinking processes into three subcategories.

1. Production of a unique communication
2. Production of a plan or proposed set of operations
3. Derivation of a set of abstract relations

Here are some ways to find out your students' perceptions in synthesis using open-ended or divergent questions from situations common to most of your students' lives.

1. *Production of a unique communication.* The teacher might structure this type of question: "We have just come back from a trip to our city's water purification plant. For homework tonight, write your answers to these questions so we can discuss them tomorrow."

I agree with the water commissioner that big industries in our town are polluting our waters because. . . .

I disagree with the water commissioner that little can be done to correct the pollution because. . . .

Older students could address themselves to local situations such as

High school students should have a say in deciding dress rule regulations because. . . .
A request to build an atomic power plant outside the city should not be granted because. . . .

2. *Production of a plan or proposed set of operations.* Here we ask students to move from "cookbook experiences" where everything is planned out for them. They are asked to devise other ways of investigating by questions such as

We just finished studying about static electricity and ways of producing and controlling it. Use that information to answer:
Why do you get a "shock" every time you slide across the plastic seatcovers in your parents' car? How would you devise ways to prevent the shock?

3. *Derivation of a set of abstract relations.* Learners are encouraged to formulate hy-

potheses to explain elements of phenomena they analyze. Help them learn how to ask the "right" kinds of questions with exercises such as

We are on a class picnic and field day. As the bus stops at the park, three volunteers go to find us a good picnic spot. They all come back excited about their finds for the spot. What questions would you ask them to decide which spot to pick?

Testing students' evaluation of data. Bloom's highest order of cognitive domain is the evaluation stage of learning. Your students are asked to blend knowledge, comprehension, analysis, and synthesis to perform two kinds of judgments.

1. Judgments in terms of *internal* evidence (set up their own standards of values)
2. Judgments in terms of *external* criteria (determine how closely ideas and phenomena meet the standards or values above)

You can use these techniques to discover your students' skills at evaluating data on the above two criteria.

AFFECTIVE DOMAIN

Cognitive domain dealt with knowledge and intellectual understandings. *Affective domain* deals with feelings, emotions, interests, attitudes, values, and appreciations. It deals with how your students are affected by their learning, as well as how their feelings affect their learning.

Until recently, science education has done relatively little to include these objectives in its teaching and evaluation. Now more science educators are beginning to see how important it is for children to build positive social value systems while acquiring scientific knowledge and processes. Chapter 4 looks at the place of the affective domain in science education and suggests how you might use it to teach science. Additional techniques are briefly presented here. For greater detail, you are urged to read the following book and use the media pak that

accompanies it, especially chapters 7 and 8, "Questioning for Values and the Affective Domain" and "How to Write Cognitive Domain Questions": Arthur A. Carin and Robert B. Sund, *Creative Questioning and Sensitive Listening Techniques: A Self-concept Approach,* 2nd ed. (Columbus, Ohio: Charles E. Merrill Publishing Co., 1978).

Determining Your Students' Scientific Attitudes

One of the best ways of evaluating your students' attitudes is to observe the children directly as they work and play with other children, and not only while you are teaching science.

Checklists can help you organize and record observations of your students' affective domain attitudes and behaviors. Bloom divides the "affective domain" into five subcategories.

1. Receiving: student's sensitivity to stimuli and phenomena
2. Responding: student does something about the stimuli
3. Valuing: student develops criteria of worth for things, phenomena, and behaviors
4. Organization: student begins formulation of a value system
5. Characterization by a value system: student internalizes value system

These five subcategories of affective domain are described by most nonprofessionals as students' interests, appreciations, attitudes, values, and adjustments.

Leopold Klopfer prepared a grid to show how Bloom's affective domain corresponds to science phenomena. In figure 3–8, the vertical axis lists phenomena toward which some affective behavior by your students is sought. The phenomena are grouped into four divisions: events in the natural world, activities, science, and inquiry. The horizontal axis contains Bloom's affective domain subdivisions. By using this grid as a foundation, you can develop a checklist to observe and record your students' affective behaviors. You can see how to make such a checklist by looking at figure

PHENOMENA	A.O. Receiving			B.O. Responding			C.O. Valuing			D.O. Organization		E.O. Characterization: by a value complex	
	Awareness	Willingness to Receive	Controlled or Selected Attention	Acquiescence in Responding	Willingness to Respond	Satisfaction in Response	Acceptance of a Value	Preference for a Value	Commitment	Conceptualization of a Value	Organization of a Value System	Generalized Set	Characterization
	A1	A2	A3	B1	B2	B3	C1	C2	C3	D1	D2	E1	E2
1.0 Events in the natural world 1.1 Biological events 1.2 Physical events													
2.0 Activities 2.1 Informal (generally outside of school) 2.11 science activities 2.12 science-related activities 2.2 Formalized science learning activities in school													
3.0 Science 3.1 Science as a source of knowledge about the natural world 3.11 science in general 3.12 any content area in science 3.2 Science as enterprise organized to gain understanding of natural world 3.3 Science in its interrelationships with society 3.4 Scientists as people													
4.0 Inquiry 4.1 Processes of scientific inquiry 4.2 Scientific inquiry as a way of thought 4.3 Inquiry as a way of thought 4.31 in association with phenomena and problems in science 4.32 in association with phenomena and problems not in science													

FIGURE 3–8

The affective domain in relation to science education.

Source: Leopold E. Klopfer, "A Structure for the Affective Domain in Relation to Science Education," *Science Education* 60. Reprinted by permission of John Wiley & Sons, Inc. (July–September 1976), pp. 299–312.

3–9. You can develop any observable behavioral objectives that suit the purposes for your checklist.

Discovering Your Students' Feelings

Another way you might assess your students' feelings is with a "forced-choice continuum." Figure 3–10 shows such a device using the theme, "Science is. . . ." Try to make one yourself using themes such as:

Building atomic power plants is. . . .
Being a vegetarian is. . . .
Scientists should. . . .

Make certain you have the two extremes of each idea you use. Older children could be asked to make their own forced-choice con-

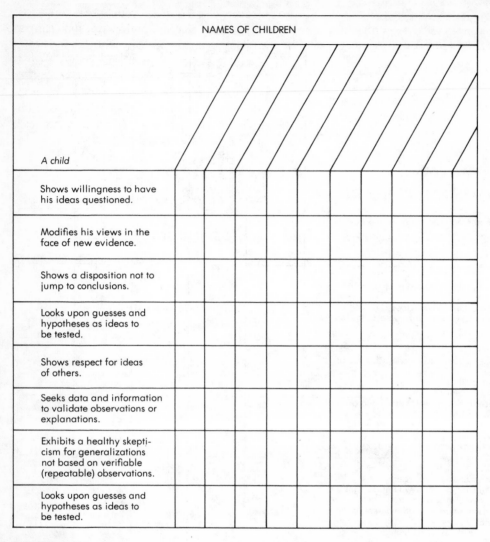

NAMES OF CHILDREN

A child									
Shows willingness to have his ideas questioned.									
Modifies his views in the face of new evidence.									
Shows a disposition not to jump to conclusions.									
Looks upon guesses and hypotheses as ideas to be tested.									
Shows respect for ideas of others.									
Seeks data and information to validate observations or explanations.									
Exhibits a healthy skepticism for generalizations not based on verifiable (repeatable) observations.									
Looks upon guesses and hypotheses as ideas to be tested.									

FIGURE 3-9
Checklist for scientific attitudes.

Source: Paul E. Blackwood and T. R. Porter, *Evaluating Science Learning in the Elementary School* (Washington, D.C.: National Science Teachers Association, 1968), p. 7.

tinuum, either individually or in small groups, for the other children to respond to.

Another tool to discover your students' feelings about controversial topics is the "values continuum." For a detailed description, see chapter 4.

Assessing Your Students' Values

The following are thought-provoking questions students may tackle either individually or in small groups of their own choosing. The questions are intended to stimulate values-related responses. Therefore, students may want to jot down or explicitly mention what beliefs or values they are protecting or holding. The questions deal with a topic that makes many people anxious and, yet, is so conscientiously avoided—death.

When have you seen a dead bird?
How did you feel about it?

What might have caused it to die?
What happens to living things when they die?
What other things have you seen that died?

Many more affective domain techniques and instruments are available to you in chapter 4, if you are interested in finding out about your students' affective learning. Easily administered and scored tests for this area can be found in appendix B.

PSYCHOMOTOR DOMAIN

The *psychomotor domain* emphasizes muscular or motor skills or manipulation of materials of the kinds currently used in most "doing" or hands-on science programs. Bloom and his associates did not prepare a taxonomy for the psychomotor domain as they did for the cognitive and affective domains, but Elizabeth Simpson has put such a taxonomy together.[14]

There are many situations in your science program for evaluating your students' manip-

ulative skills. To make your assessment more behaviorally objective and specific, you can use an "observation checklist" and "rating scales of performance." Figure 3–11 shows a structured teacher observational checklist to assess your students' ability to use a microscope properly. Notice the use of specific behavioral objectives instead of broad, nebulous goals, such as "can use microscope effectively."

EVALUATION TIPS FOR TEACHERS

1. Identify your objectives clearly.

Avoid objectives that are vague, nebulous, or too broad.

2. Whenever possible, write your objectives in specific, observable terms.

Emphasize objectives you can phrase in human

FIGURE 3–10
Forced-choice continuum.

Source: Albert F. Eiss and Mary Blatt Harbeck, *Behavioral Objectives in the Affective Domain* (Washington, D.C.: National Science Teachers Association, 1969), p. 20.

Directions
Please place a check *anywhere* along the continuum of each of the two opposing words on a line to show how YOU feel about science.

SCIENCE IS

whee	yetch!
theoretical	practical
inconvenient	convenient
complex	simple
wide	narrow
easy	troublesome
unnecessary	basic
dull	emotional
efficient	inefficient
universal	limited
outgoing	ingrown
broadly interpretive	dogmatic
imaginative	unimaginative
interesting	uninteresting
objective	subjective
clear	fuzzy
useful	harmful
good	bad
exciting	boring

<table>
<tr><td colspan="2" align="center">*The Schema for Classifying Educational Objectives in the Psychomotor Domain*</td></tr>
<tr><td>Perception</td><td>Sensory cues that guide action for a particular motor activity (seeing, hearing, and so on)</td></tr>
<tr><td>Set</td><td>Preparatory adjustment or readiness for a particular kind of action or experience (mental, physical, emotional set)</td></tr>
<tr><td>Guided response</td><td>Overt behavioral act under the guidance of a teacher or in response to self-evaluation (imitation, trial and error)</td></tr>
<tr><td>Mechanism</td><td>Learned response becoming habitual</td></tr>
<tr><td>Complex overt response</td><td>Individual performing a motor act considered complex with skill, smoothly and efficiently</td></tr>
<tr><td>Adaptation</td><td>Altering motor activities to meet the demands of new problematic situations</td></tr>
<tr><td>Origination</td><td>Creating new motor skills or ways of manipulating materials out of understanding, abilities, skills</td></tr>
</table>

Here are some examples of educational objectives in science for the psychomotor domain.

<table>
<tr><td>*Psychomotor Domain*</td><td>*Science Example Involving Plants*</td></tr>
<tr><td>Perception</td><td>Recognition of different sizes of plants as a prerequisite to nonnumerical or numerical measurement</td></tr>
<tr><td>Set</td><td>Knowledge of bigger-than, smaller-than, inches or millimeters, and so on</td></tr>
<tr><td>Guided response</td><td>Imitation of procedures for using meter stick to measure plant growth, presented by teacher</td></tr>
<tr><td>Mechanism</td><td>Ability to measure growth of plants over a period of two weeks by himself or herself</td></tr>
<tr><td>Complex overt response</td><td>Measuring and recording daily meter stick readings of plants on graph paper</td></tr>
<tr><td>Adaptation</td><td>Adapting the measuring skills to another aspect of plant growth, that is, measuring precisely the amount of water given at set periods</td></tr>
</table>

behavior. The following objectives are specific, capable of being observed and therefore evaluated, and varied.

Behavioral Objective:

To determine if student can read an alcohol thermometer

Behavioral Objective:

To determine if student can identify parts of a flower

Behavioral Objective:

To determine if student can analyze, experiment, and suggest alternate plans for possible solutions to a problem

---

3. Determine content, methods, materials, and type of evaluation for achieving and assessing your behavioral objectives.

A format for organizing your planning for teaching and evaluating science is on page 69.[15]

4. Select a variety of evaluation devices.

Avoid overdependency on one type of testing device. Include a wide range of tests and other evaluative devices such as:

1. Essay
2. Short answer
3. Fill-in (avoid)
4. True/false
5. Multiple choice
6. Matching (minimal use)
7. Crossword puzzle
8. Picture tests
9. Situational
10. Performance or motor
11. Checklist
12. Student self-evaluation
13. Others

CHECKLIST OR RATING SCALE—USE OF MICROSCOPE

Behavioral Objectives	Always	Sometimes	Never
Is careful in handling microscope.			
Cleans lenses properly.			
Focuses instrument properly.			
Prepares slides correctly.			
Arranges mirror for correct amount of light.			

FIGURE 3–11

Source: From Harold E. Tannenbaum, Nathan Stillman, and Albert Piltz, *Science Education for Elementary School Teachers,* 2d ed. (Boston: Allyn and Bacon, 1965), p. 270. Copyright © 1965, by Allyn and Bacon, Inc., Boston. Used with permission.

TEACHER OBSERVATIONAL CHECKLIST (for figure 3–11)

Behavioral Objectives:

1. Handle the instrument with great care. Clean the lenses only with "lens tissue" or with a soft, clean cloth.
2. Never focus the microscope downward toward the slide. Always move the objective downward while the eye is away from the eyepiece and then focus the microscope upward with the eye looking through the microscope.
3. Arrange the mirror for optimum amount of light. Too much light is quite as unsatisfactory as too little light.
4. Prepare materials for observation using the techniques most appropriate to the things being examined; comparatively large materials (minute crustacea, for example) require either depression slides or bridge arrangements so that they are not crushed; smaller items can simply be covered with a cover slip.

5. Make your tests and other evaluative devices test what you taught.

Test only those things to which your students were exposed or can reasonably be expected to project into relatively similar situations.

6. Evaluate and test often and have your students participate in the results.

Your students should be evaluated continually. This can help them lessen their anxiety and fear of tests, especially if the results are used for instruction instead of punishment. You should stress that testing is one step along the path to learning and not the end of the journey.

7. Your tests should show what you value in science teaching.

Your students will follow your lead. If you stress memorization or recall in your tests, they will memorize. If process and higher cognitive levels of thinking are important to you, make certain your tests reflect these criteria.

Format for Organizing Planning

Objective	Methods and Materials	Type of Evaluation
The ability to record and interpret temperature data from information gathered using outdoor thermometers.	Make simple bar graphs of the daily temperature as found at noon in the shade next to the building. Use the graphs to find significant temperature information: make comparisons among the days studied and also among readings made by different children. Have sufficient supply of outdoor thermometers so that variations in readings can be observed. Have necessary graph grids prepared so that each child has appropriate equipment.	Examine the charts prepared by each child. Does the chart show that the child can make an accurate and understandable table of data? Written questions to be answered by individual children, each using his own chart: Which day was hottest? Which day was coldest? On which two days was the temperature about the same at noon?

Look at the following behavioral objectives[16] and write the best type of evaluative device to use with that goal in the spaces in front of each number below.

Evaluative Devices

a. Checklist for product (observation of learner's reports, written work, graphs, artwork, and so on)
b. Paper-pencil test
c. Self-report (learner self-evaluates work)
d. Checklist for observation of learner

Science Behavioral Objectives—
The Child Will

_____ **1.** Be able to follow the sequence of instruction
_____ **2.** Measure and record plant growth over two weeks to show accuracy and correct graphing
_____ **3.** Use a particular method in setting up his or her experiments of solving problems
_____ **4.** Be able to solve problems
_____ **5.** Read orally in sharing his or her findings with classmates with proper inflection and enthusiasm
_____ **6.** Be able to read accurately and recognize subtleties, tone, and mood set by the author
_____ **7.** Read a variety of books in the research part of his or her science studies
_____ **8.** Willingly and enthusiastically engage in science experiments and other hands-on activities
_____ **9.** Wait his or her turn when working in a group
_____**10.** Do his or her science homework before watching TV at home

You can check your written answers in appendix L.

8. Continually evaluate your evaluation.

Scrutinize your testing and revise your tests as a result of your students' responses to them. Invite your students' comments on your tests and even have them try writing tests. Suggest that they make self-evaluations, such as

Mark a B below for what you knew _before_ about the science topics we studied. Mark an A for what you knew _after_ the study.

Science Topics

volcanoes	1	② B	3	④ A	5
floods	① B	2	3	④ A	5
weather	1	2	③ B	4	⑤ A

1 = knew little
5 = knew a lot

9. Continue your own self-evaluation.

Teachers today are professionally committed to improving the learning of all children. You probably believe "children _do_ fail to learn. They can only assimilate what their minds are ready to learn." Therefore, do not blame the children or yourself if not all of them do well on some evaluative measures. Use the situation to look closer at your students. At the same time, look more introspectively at your own teaching to examine the impact of your goals, methods of teaching, and evaluation techniques. Such self-evaluation will probably make you more effective with the "culturally deprived" or "handicapped." Evaluation will help you grow as a person and a teacher. It will help you see the individual differences and uniquenesses of your students with clearer and more sensitive vision. Because learning to use evaluation effectively will help you become a better teacher, it is clearly worth the effort.

SUMMARY

The basic goals and objectives of science in the elementary schools include the processes of modern science. Our major goal in science education is to develop scientifically literate people who can think critically.

Presently, there is a controversy about determining the way objectives for elementary science should be written. Some educators believe objectives should be written in behavioral terms, others think these terms limit the teacher and contribute to trivial goals. Regardless, most states have established some form of accountability system. In most cases, teachers are required to write and evaluate behavioral objectives. You, therefore, must become aware of the advantages and disadvantages of writing them and learn to construct significant and relevant ones.

Many science curriculum projects outline their objectives in behavioral terms to assist teachers. These include not only science content concepts but science process concepts as well.

Behavioral objectives are written so their achievement may be observed.

Pressure has increased from diverse segments of our society for greater "accountability" of the public schools for the learning of children. This has resulted in increased interest and activity in the evaluation of science programs.

Individual schools and school districts want to know how good their science programs are. They must have this information to determine which programs to continue, drop, or modify, as well as to help them communicate to the public financing the schools through taxes.

Teachers use evaluation as a continuous and all-encompassing part of their science programs. It is part of diagnosing children's learning needs, prescribing what learning activities are needed, and determining a learner's progress, so additional learning activities can be planned.

Behavioral objectives should be the basis for teaching/learning/evaluating activities whenever feasible, in spite of some of the limitations noted. Bloom's categories of behavioral objectives are cognitive, affective, and psychomotor. Cognitive behavioral objectives refer to remembering knowledge previously learned and being able to apply it to solve problems. Affective objectives refer to interests, attitudes, and values. Psychomotor objectives refer to muscular and manipulative skills.

This chapter suggests techniques for testing scientific knowledge. Among these are audiotape recordings, record keeping, multiple-choice tests, picture tests, matching tests, and crossword puzzles. You can test higher thinking with cartoon tests, pictorial-sequence tests, essays, interpretation tests, story situation analysis tests, application of knowledge tests, and evaluation of evidence tests. Affective domain objectives are more difficult to assess. Several ways to discover your students' attitudes and interests are the teacher checklist, forced-choice continuum, and situational tests. The psychomotor objectives have not been as extensively developed as the cognitive and affective domain objectives. They can be evaluated by the teacher observational checklist, rating scales, and performance tests.

SELF-EVALUATION AND FURTHER STUDY

1. Why do you think teachers generally give more attention to the development of cognitive parts of learning?
2. What do you think are the advantages and disadvantages of writing specific performance behavioral objectives?
3. Select ten cognitive performance behavioral objectives for your class. Write them using the action verbs presented in this chapter. Make sure they are *observable* behaviors.
4. Write five affective behavioral objectives. Pick a science topic for study by your class this year. Organize the study from a multidimensional approach as described in this chapter. Show specifically the kinds of possible activities for each of the curricular areas.
5. If you were to write five of the most important objectives for a year's science teaching, what would they be and why?
6. Develop an evaluative device to assess your students' scientific content, concepts, or principles for a science area you are studying.
7. Pick several hands-on science activities in which children handle science equipment and apparatus. Construct devices to record their psychomotor skills, using the types of devices mentioned in this chapter.
8. Using magazine pictures or photographs you or your students take, construct pictorial tests or help your students make their own.
9. Encourage your students to work either individually or in small groups to make their own science crossword puzzles, after one of your science studies.
10. Work with a group of students in a science area and devise ways of evaluating your and their work cooperatively. Have your students prepare a variety of tests, such as the picture type, administer and score them, and share the results with their peers. When they have completed this work, evaluate the evaluation with your students.
11. Audiotape a test especially for children who cannot take a written one (nonreaders, preschool and nursery, children, the blind or visually impaired).

ENDNOTES

1. Rockefeller Foundation, *The Humanities in American Life: Report of the Commission on the Humanities* (Berkeley, California: University of California Press, 1980).
2. Robert E. Yager, "Editor's Corner," *The Science Teacher,* 49, no. 6 (September 1982), pp. 10–11.
3. Harold Pratt, et al., "Science Education in the Elementary School," in Norris C. Harms and Robert E. Yager, *What Research Says to the Science Teacher,* Vol. 3 (Washington, D.C.: National Science Teachers Association, 1981), pp. 75–76.
4. J. Myron Atkins, "Behavioral Objectives in Curriculum Design: A Cautionary Note," *The Science Teacher* 35 (May 1968), pp. 27–30.

5. Martin Haberman, "Behavioral Objectives Bandwagon or Break-through," *Journal of Teacher Education* 19, no. 1 (Spring 1968), pp. 92–93.
6. James T. Robinson, "A Critical Look at Grading and Evaluation Practices," *What Research Says to the Science Teacher,* Vol. 2 (Washington, D.C.: National Science Teachers Association, 1979), p. 9.
7. James R. Okey, "Diagnostic Testing Pays Off," *The Science Teacher* 43, no. 7 (October 1976), p. 27.
8. R. Fiel and James Okey, "The Effects of Formative Evaluation and Remediation on Mastery of Intellectual Skills," *Journal of Educational Research* 68 (1975), pp. 253–55.
9. C. Burrows and James Okey, "The Effects of a Mastery Learning Strategy on Achievement" (Paper read at the American Educational Research Association Meeting, Washington, D.C., March 1975); J. Nazzaro, J. Todorov, and J. Nazzaro, "Student Ability and Individualized Instruction," *Journal of College Science Teaching* 2 (December 1972), pp. 29–30.
10. Gerald Lesser, Frederick B. Davis, and Lucille Nakemow, "The Identification of Gifted Elementary School Children with Exceptional Scientific Talent," *Educational and Psychological Measurements* 22 (Summer 1962), pp. 349–64.
11. R. C. Newell, "Can Science Survive?—A Shocking Report on Science Education in America's Schools," *American Teacher,* October 1978, p. 26.
12. Edwin B. Kurtz, Jr., "Help Stamp out Non-Behavioral Objectives," *The Science Teacher* (January 1965), pp. 31–32; David E. Newton, "The Problem Solving Approach—Fact or Fancy?" *School Science and Mathematics* 61 (November 1961), pp. 619–22; William B. Reiner, "Meeting the Challenge of Recent Developments in Science in Assessing the Objectives of Modern Instruction," *School Science and Mathematics* 66 (April 1966), pp. 335–41.
13. For information on how you can make and use photographs in your evaluation, see John L. Debes, "Photography and the Intellect," *The Science Teacher* 43, no. 8 (November 1976), pp. 26–27.
14. Elizabeth J. Simpson, "The Classification of Educational Objectives in the Psychomotor Domain," in *The Psychomotor Domain—A Resource Book for Media Specialists* (Washington, D.C.: Gryphon House, 1972), pp. 43–56.
15. Harold E. Tannenbaum, Nathan Stillman, and Albert Piltz, *Science Education for Elementary School Teachers,* 2nd ed. (Boston: Allyn and Bacon, 1965), p. 270. Copyright © 1965, by Allyn and Bacon, Inc., Boston. Used with permission.
16. Modified from materials found in John D. McNeil, *Designing Curriculum: Self-Instructional Modules* (Boston: Little, Brown and Co., 1976), pp. 118–20.

4

The Role of
Human Values
in Science Teaching

> "The *active* involvement of students in dealing with science/society issues will not only eventually determine the outcomes of these problems, but will be a driving force in the successful solutions of problems that will arise in the future." (Charles R. Coble and Dale R. Rice, "Rekindling Scientific Curiosity," *The Science Teacher,* 50, no. 2 [February 1983], p. 50.)

Y ou know about modern science, how children learn, and how to set goals and evaluate progress in science education. This chapter investigates the reasons why we have shied away from humanistic aspects and how you can make them vital parts of your science teaching. To discover how to do this, we must look to the relationships among science, human values, society, or culture, our views of ecology, and human creativity.

WHY ARE WE PROFESSIONALLY TIMID?

Traditionally, elementary school teachers who teach science have emphasized the *cognitive* parts of science; they have stressed knowledge, comprehension, and the application of concepts and principles. However, they have forgotten that science is dynamic and that scientists have emotions, biases, values, and attitudes. Occasionally, scientists make decisions based not only on what they *know* but on what they *feel*. Although we know a lot about the *affective* domain, we have not incorporated this knowledge into our science programs. The affective domain deals with attitudes, interests, appreciations, values, and motivation. A. F. Eiss and M. B. Harbeck underscore the importance of the affective domain in figure 4–1 and in this statement.

The affective domain is central to every part of the learning and evaluation process. It begins with the threshold of consciousness, where awareness of the stimulus initiates the learning process. It provides the threshold for evaluation, where willingness to respond is the basis for psychomotor responses, without which no evaluation of the learning process can take place. It includes values and value systems that provide the basis for continued learning and for most of an individual's overt behaviors. It provides the bridge between the stimulus and the cognitive and the psychomotor aspects of an individual's personality.[1]

Look at Eiss and Harbeck's model (figure 4–1) of interrelationships among the cognitive, affective, and psychomotor (actions) domains. See how all initial sensory input may enter the subconscious; interact with the affective, cognitive, and psychomotor; and exist as overt behavior, which is then fed back into the system.

If educators have known about the influence of the affective domain on learning from researchers such as Benjamin Bloom and his associates Jean Piaget and Carl Rogers, why have some science teachers avoided or ignored it? Howard Birnie gives these reasons:[2]

1. Because entering the world of personal values is seen as indoctrination or brainwashing.
2. Because our methods and materials have been ineffective in reaching affective goals.

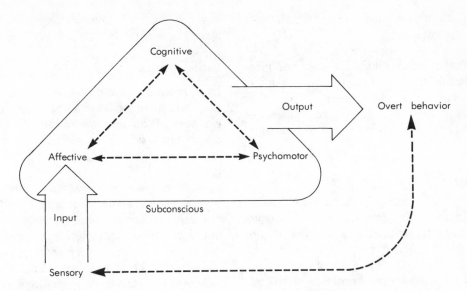

FIGURE 4-1

Source: A. F. Eiss and Mary B. Harbeck, *Behavioral Objectives in the Affective Domain* (Washington, D.C.: National Science Teachers Association, 1969), p. 4.

3. Because we do not have evaluation techniques and instruments to tell us whether or not we have been successful in achieving affective outcomes.
4. Because we believe that behavior is the only thing that really matters in education; that affect is an unfit subject for scientific study.
5. Because we have assumed that there is a direct relationship between knowing and behavior (that, for example, the child can list endangered species and will, therefore, be concerned with their survival).

THE IMPORTANCE OF AFFECTIVE QUALITIES

If we as teachers believe that scientists are really the same as we are in many respects, it will help us see the proper place of the affective domain in science. Crocker and Nay have compiled an inventory of the affective attributes of scientists.[3] It is revealing that the reasons men and women initially become scientists involve affective things such as *excitement* with natural phenomena and *pride* in contributing to knowledge and human welfare. In their actual work as scientists, their affective

attributes are also shaped by the nature of science itself. For instance, people who like and feel comfortable with the nature of scientific work (patience, precision, flexibility, tolerance, and so on) will be attracted to it and will be successful.

Cultural Values Influence Feelings and Attitudes

Part of what we are and how we feel about the world is distilled from the people who surround and influence us from our earliest years. We are part of a culture and its value system. If what you do in science in your classroom is not compatible with the values of your students' cultural group, they may reject what you are trying to do. However, the school has traditionally been one of the most important institutions for transmitting mainstream culture to children, and, usually, the longer children stay in school and the more they learn and are "aculturized," the less likely they are to reject new ideas. In part, this may occur because teachers begin to recognize differences between their own and their students' cultural values. At the same time, teachers may become more flexible, tolerant, and supportive of cultural differences and help their students bridge the gaps.

Remember, cultures are continually changing. What is *your* cultural background? How can you find out? How can you use this information in your science teaching? What other affective information about your students is important to know for your science teaching?

LEARNING

How your students *feel* about science may be more important to their achievement in science than any other variable. Benjamin Bloom found this in studying data from children in 17 countries.[4] He said the amount of learning in a science classroom related positively to the initial interest and attitudes children brought to the classroom. It is interesting also that this relationship is cumulative; that is, success breeds success. As children develop more positive attitudes and interests in science, their achievement increases. One of the variables affecting children's attitudes toward science, or school in general, is their own self-concepts.

Self-Concept

Even more important than feelings about science and school, but influencing them greatly, is a person's attitude toward self. We all build up (or break down) our self-concepts by contact with parents, friends, teachers, tests, grades, etc.

How we greet each new situation is colored by how we feel about the situation from previous experiences with similar situations and by our own self-concepts. Research has shown a definite connection between children's feelings about self and how they learn. Your students' self-concepts affect the way they view *you* and indeed your very teaching acts. It was found that even simple teaching acts, intended by teachers to be positive and helpful to learners, may be seen by the students as threatening, hostile, and negative. Such predetermined perception occurs because of the students' previ-

ous experiences and the self-concepts they bring to the classroom.[5]

Children with *positive* self-concepts tend to have fewer learning problems and view teaching and learning in *positive* ways. They approach new learning situations more eagerly and with greater assurance than children with negative self-concepts. Even very young children say things such as, "I'm not very good at reading." More seriously, they go around with drooping heads, saying, "I'm dumb and not very good." Children often have a difficult time separating the first part of this statement from the second.

Self. The technique you can use to discover and modify your students' feelings about self and teaching/learning is the *story situation device.* You can write stories of everyday classroom situations and see how the children respond to them.

Here is a sample of such a story with open-ended questions to elicit students' feelings about their teacher and the child in the story. It was found that children empathize and project their feelings to Johnny.

A fifth grade class was working on their times tables and teacher was walking around the room helping children. When the teacher came to Johnny's place, she said:

Teacher: Did you get your special assignment done?

Johnny: You mean counting by 8's? I wrote by 8's up to 96.

Teacher: That's wonderful. Can you say them right off to 64?

Johnny: 8, 16, 24, 31—uh 33? No—32.

Teacher: Yes—32. You didn't work on them, did you?

* * * * *

Question: What do you think Johnny thought when the teacher first stopped at his desk?

Question: How would you feel if you were Johnny?[6]

Even the common situation depicted above evoked strong feelings in the children as shown by statements such as, "She didn't believe he did his work."; "Teachers don't trust kids."; "I hate teachers, 'cause they think you're always ripping them off by not doing your work." If your students react with such strong feelings to relatively emotion-free situations, how might they react to

☐ A snake brought into class?
☐ Turning over a decaying log in the woods on a field trip?
☐ A sudden thunderstorm?
☐ Discovery of dead guppies in your classroom aquarium?
☐ Children laughing at a stutterer?

Remember that each child is different and will react differently depending on whether he or she has a strong or weak self-concept.

CLASSROOM ENVIRONMENT AND SCIENCE LEARNING

What are specific things you can do to modify the self-concepts of your students? How can

you reinforce the positive self-concepts your students already have, and help them build new, more positive self-concepts? How can you increase the interest and motivation of your students in science?

Obviously, *you* are the key element in your classroom environment. Knowing that your students' feelings have great impact on what, how, and how much they will learn in your science program should make you alert to the atmosphere you establish. One of the most important elements of your classroom is what you expect from your students (teacher expectation) and how you convey this to them.

The Self-Fulfilling Prophecy

Robert Travers emphasized the "power" of a teacher over self-concept formation and the learning of students with this statement.

> One can be fairly sure that the feelings of the teacher toward the children will influence his behavior in the classroom, and that the children will respond to the behavior thus solicited.[7]

What this says is that if you tell children often enough that they are either bright or dumb, they will live up to the name. This is called the *self-fulfilling prophecy.*

One of the most significant and controversial research studies to point out the self-fulfilling tendency was done by Robert Rosenthal and L. Jacobson. Even their book title, *Pygmalion in the Classroom: Teacher Expectation and Pupils' Intellectual Development,* conveys the impact of teacher expectation. The researchers randomly selected 20 percent of a large student sample and told teachers these students had scored very highly on I. Q. tests. Teachers were asked to observe these students closely as they were likely to "bloom" intellectually. In later testing of the whole sample, it was found that the students randomly labeled "very bright" scored significantly higher I.Q.'s than the other students. The conclusion was that teachers probably communicated to them that they

were "very bright" and the students in return obliged their teachers with better achievement.[8]

Other studies found evidence that teachers have lower expectations for minority (or nonwhite) students than they do for whites.[9] This probably influences the kinds of instruction some minority students get and may ultimately affect their self-concepts.

Using the self-fulfilling prophecy in science teaching: humanism. You will find that using the self-fulfilling prophecy can be an effective positive element in your classroom atmosphere. Most classes have a whole range of achievers from low to "average" to high, with as wide a range in positive and negative self-concepts, interests, and motivation. Goals and level of work should be appropriate to the level of each child. Also, each child should be given the feeling that he or she is an integral part of the whole class. Science hands-on activities have an advantage here because they involve several talents and not just verbal ones. All students are more likely, therefore, to contribute from this large talent pool, and they receive as a consequence a positive self-worth. Sometimes the best science experimenters may be relatively poor readers. In science, these students get their time to shine as very valuable persons. Avoid giving the impression to children that they are members of some group (minority) that must be tolerated for the year. Real or imagined discrimination causes children to strike back in many hostile ways. They then become "discipline" problems.

Relating to children in ways that show respect for them as individuals with rights is called *humanistic thinking.* In humanistic teaching, each person is expected to learn to respect the rights of all others. Furthermore, everyone (teachers, children, administrators, custodians, bus drivers, and so on) in the school tries to be aware of how the other people feel. Their likes, dislikes, fears, and hopes are taken into account. As Mario Fantini, the humanistic educator, put it: "A humanist is not someone who is preoccupied with himself. He is rather more likely to be concerned with the welfare of others."[10]

There are many practical things you can do in your classroom to make it more humanistic. One is to explore the feelings of your students.

EXPLORING FEELINGS

Hilda Taba devised techniques and carried out research about strategies for the social studies curriculum that are relevant to humanistic science discovery teaching and learning. The two strategies most appropriate are "Exploring Feelings" and "Interpersonal Problem Solving."[11] (See Chapter 11 for more information about Taba's strategies.)

In "Exploring Feelings," Taba involved students in sensing their own and others' feelings. By doing this they learn better how others perceive a situation. Students also learn to understand their own emotions. The strategy is devised so that students do not feel threatened if asked what their values are about some topic, such as mercy killing of deer or wild horses. Instead, a situation is provided and students are encouraged to explore and react to it. This method is especially appropriate to the environmental sciences. The interpersonal problem-solving strategy uses this technique.

1. Social problem involving interpersonal conflict is presented.
2. Students are asked to relate their similar experiences.
3. Students then propose solutions and defend them.
4. Students evaluate proposed solutions and explore alternatives.

Lawrence Kohlberg's theory of six stages of moral development also uses a hypothetical or factual value dilemma story, which is then discussed in small groups.[12]

Taba and her associates pointed out a danger in using this strategy. Students, because of their own egocentricity, may not proceed to the higher levels of exploring criteria and alternatives in making judgments. This possibility can be overcome if you move the group to the other steps in the strategy. An example of an interpersonal problem-solving situation in science might consist of the pro's and con's of building a dam or atomic energy plant near a populated area.

Using Feelings in Science Teaching

How can you use the information about feelings to make your science teaching more humanistic and effective for your students? Many students show us that children work better and learn more when they believe their teachers care about them. Caring is not related only to academic achievement. Children respond best when teachers "make them feel good." When interviewed, children volunteered that they worked harder and learned more from teachers who cared about their feelings.[13] In our own lives, we probably have examples that highlight this tendency for us. A pat on the back, a friendly word of encouragement, or the recognition that "you're really trying hard today, Jamie," goes a long way.

Also, this fact reinforces the studies described earlier concerning self-concept and its relationship to academic success.

HUMAN VALUES AND THE WHOLE BRAIN

Just as people's feelings, attitudes, cultural values, and other *affective domain* qualities influence their learning, so do the different parts of the brain. Recent research has revealed insights into the brain's complex functioning. One of these researchers, Virginia Johnson, now believes that the right and left sides of the brain are involved with different aspects of thought. Figure 4–2 shows that the two hemi-

FIGURE 4–2

Information perceived by the human brain

D. J. Coulter in Virginia R. Johnson, "Myelin and Maturation: A Fresh Look at Piaget," *The Science Teacher,* vol. 49, no. 3 (March 1982), p. 43.

Right hemisphere spatial, holistic, pictorial, and nonverbally oriented	*Left hemisphere* linear, time-related, and sequential functions
1. visual images—pictures	**1.** abstract symbols

2. language—verbal
   a. expression
     tone
     intonation
   b. body language
     gestures
     facial expression
   c. logos—pictorial symbols
	2. language—verbal
	   a. alphabet
	     words (spelling)
	     sentences (syntax)
	   b. reading
	     speaking
	     writing

3. language—mathematical
   a. spatial
     shapes
   b. geometry
     shapes—relationships
   c. patterns
   d. relationships
	3. language—mathematical
	   a. numerals
	     operations (basic facts)
	   b. computation
	     addition, subtraction,
	     multiplication, division

4. creativity	**4.** logic
5. melody	**5.** rhythm

6. time—cyclical
   a. seasons
	6. linear time
	   a. seconds—minutes—hours
	     —days—weeks—years

7. functions	**7.** definitions
8. images—pictures	**8.** labels

spheres develop differing, but complementary, abilities.

Left Cerebral Hemisphere

Figure 4–2 reveals that the *left* cerebral hemisphere functions mainly in relating things in time, performing acoustic analysis, decoding speech, and interpreting sequential or linear data such as mathematical computation, written language, and *logical* thinking. Reasoning, mathematics, and words in sentences are linear since they have to possess a certain order to make sense. This linear function underlines much of our verbal activities. The left hemisphere enables you to perform the operations of language and sequential logical functions. Thus, it might be referred to as the *temporal* or *time-oriented* linear hemisphere.

Right Cerebral Hemisphere

The *right* hemisphere of the brain differs from the left in that it operates in a more holistic manner. Sensing and simultaneous processing of information are major functions of this hemisphere. When you look at a room, a television screen, a scene in nature, or a group of people, you sense everything simultaneously. The right hemisphere is able to do this because it is the center for visual and spatial interpretations. It also plays a major role in dreams, daydreams, fantasies, musical abilities, body movement such as dancing and athletics, and intuitive creativity. It might be thought of as the visual, spatial, sensual, and intuitive hemisphere.

Figure 4-3 highlights the differences between the two hemispheres.

KINDS OF CEREBRAL DOMINANCE

There are two kinds of dominance: physical and cerebral. Physical dominance correlates highly with cerebral dominance. This means that a person who is right-handed is more likely to be left cerebrally dominant than one who is left-handed. A left physically dominant person is more likely to be right cerebrally dominant. However, many left-handed individuals are also left cerebrally dominant.

Determining Your Brain Hemispheric Learning Preference

To get an approximation of your cerebral learning brain preference, score yourself on each task described in figure 4–4.

Interpretation of your score. If you marked significantly more *odd-numbered items,* this suggests you are *right cerebrally* dominant. If you marked significantly more *even-numbered items,* you are more likely to be *left cerebrally* dominant. If you marked approximately half even and odd, you are *mixed cerebrally* dominant.

It is not important that the above evaluation be accurate for you, but it is important that as a teacher you realize there are different cerebrally hemispherically oriented individuals in your class. Left and mixed cerebrally dominant students are more likely to enjoy and be successful at performing linear activities such as using mathematics, working on equations, and writing laboratory summaries. Right cerebrally dominant students are more likely to become involved in sensitive observations of some phenomena in the environment, in artistic or musical activities, in performing fantasies, in learning through body movement, and in using intuitive creativity.

American society rewards left lateralization. Our society mainly rewards left hemispheric functions. Dr. Thomas H. Budzynski of the Department of Psychiatry at the University of Colorado Medical School and Biofeedback Institute says, "There is a growing feeling that perhaps our technologically oriented Western culture has selectively favored one cognitive mode over the other."[14] This is evident in the professions to which we assign high status: lawyers, doctors, business executives. But we all lose when we devalue artists, poets, dancers, and musicians. By doing so, we also fail to value our own abilities to create, dance, sing, write, and be poetic and artistic. As a consequence, many people in our culture believe they are not capable of being creative. We need to assert and respect all of our human abilities so the brain's hemispheric suppressed potential is freed.

IMPLICATIONS OF AFFECTIVE DOMAIN, SOCIETY, AND RIGHT-BRAIN/LEFT-BRAIN FOR TEACHING SCIENCE

Broaden Your Students' Science Horizons

When you sensitize your students to their own and others' feelings, their perceptions are broadened. Society needs scientifically literate

FIGURE 4-3
Information-processing systems of the human brain

D. J. Coulter in Virginia R. Johnson, "Myelin and Maturation: A Fresh Look at Piaget," *The Science Teacher*, vol 49, no. 3 (March 1982), p. 43.

Right hemisphere	Left hemisphere
intuitive	logical
holistic	sequential
divergent	convergent
inclusive	exclusive
synthesizing	analyzing
multiple implications	either/or
creative	decision making—right or wrong
consequences of decisions	

Select 10 items from the following list that you excel at and value highly. Place the number of the items (odd or even) in each of the spaces provided.

1. Making analogies
2. Analyzing
3. Undertaking an artistic endeavor
4. Classifying
5. Perceiving color and images
6. Criticizing
7. Being creative
8. Thinking logically
9. Designing
10. Reasoning mathematically
11. Daydreaming
12. Ordering—placing things in order or keeping an ordered environment
13. Dancing
14. Organizing
15. Using intuition
16. Outlining
17. Using imagination

18. Planning
19. Inventing
20. Reading
21. Making metaphors or similes
22. Spelling
23. Working with music
24. Reasoning scientifically
25. Working with poetry
26. Verbalizing main ideas
27. Doing puzzles
28. Doing expository writing
29. Engaging in athletic activity such as tennis

When you are finished, total your score as follows:

Number of even ___4___

Number of odd ___5___

FIGURE 4-4
Hemispheric preference survey

THOUGHT AND MEMORY

The cerebral cortex is the area of memory storage. Sensations are stored here and voluntary actions are begun. This area of the brain is involved when the child draws a soccer play and shares his experiences with his teammate.

SENSE INTEGRATION

The thalamus works with the cerebral cortex to integrate messages from the sense organs such as the eyes and ears. Thus, the kicker is able to interpret how he sees his teammate, and involve other centers to react to where he should kick the ball for the teammate to score. She responds to sight and hearing the child call his name.

EMOTION

The limbic system, buried deep within the brain, is involved in emotional reactions and control. The sensation of fear, caused by the dog running at the soccer player, involves this area of the brain.

MUSCULAR COORDINATION

The cerebellum acts in coordination by sending messages to the cerebral cortex for "awareness". Messages are also sent to muscles of the body. Coordination required to kick the soccerball is controlled by the cerebellum.

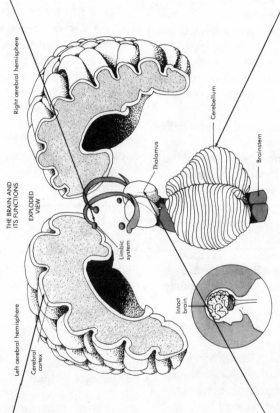

THE BRAIN AND ITS FUNCTIONS

EXPLODED VIEW

Left cerebral hemisphere

Right cerebral hemisphere

Cerebral cortex

Limbic system

Thalamus

Cerebellum

Brainstem

Intact brain

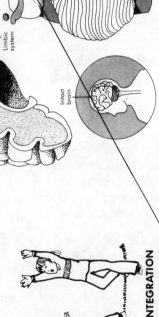

FIGURE 4-5

85

citizens capable of making *humanistic* decisions about a host of social, economic, political, and technological problems. The National Science Teachers Association recognized this need in its position paper, which says in part[15]

Program Characteristics

Program characteristics viewed as desirable to produce student outcomes above include: (italics mine)

☐ Genuine alternatives should *exist* so that real *decisions* can be made, real problems solved, and the consequences known or experienced.

☐ The problems presented to students should be *definable,* possible to accomplish, and should grow out of *first-hand* experience.

☐ Students should be *actively* involved in gathering data.

☐ Information that is presented should be clearly articulated through *alternative* modes; e.g., books, films, "hands-on" experiences, etc.

☐ Information transmitted should be as *appropriate* as possible for the age level of the student and reflect how it is developed.

☐ Science programs should be *interdisciplinary* in nature (involving areas other than science).

One way you can make your students aware of, and participate in, societal-oriented science, is to integrate or coordinate your science teaching with other subjects, such as social studies and mathematics. Some educators call this *holistic* teaching, which is introduced here and discussed more thoroughly in chapter 12.

Integrating Science Education With Other Subjects: Using the Holistic Approach

Integrating science, affective domain, values, and society should help your students become "truer, kinder, gentler, warmer, humbler, firmer, stronger and wiser."[16] Alvin Toffler in *Future Shock* stresses the need for new arrangements of subject matter for solving the world's problems: "Tomorrow's schools must . . . teach not merely data, but ways to manipulate it. Students must learn how to discard old ideas, how and when to replace them."[17]

One approach to combining or integrating science education with other areas of the elementary school curriculum is called the *holistic approach to science education.* Holistic science education takes children's interests and concerns as the starting point. Children are naturally very interested in science. Interest, or high motivation, is a powerful force in learning. No doubt you have noticed in your own class that high student motivation can often compensate for a lack of specific skills. Research has shown that high interest can overcome as much as a two-year reading deficiency.[18] Chapters 12 and 13 explore the integration and correlation of other curricular areas (social studies, math, language arts, and so on) with elementary science education, offering practical suggestions.

Science is a multidimensional study in which each dimension relates to each other dimension, as shown in figure 4–6. Notice that science is a distinct and identifiable discipline interacting with many curricular dimensions. You can select the dimension or curricular area that matches a particular student's interests most closely as the starting point for that student. You might start one student with a mathematical aspect of your selected science study, and another in the arts. You want to motivate each child to maximize learning. Once you do this, students will naturally move through your instructional program toward the center of figure 4–6, where all aspects of your science study merge. The "Study of Environment from Multidimensional Perspectives" on page 87 is an example of how this process might work in a study of the classroom, school, and the school grounds environment. See also the materials on a thematic approach to science teaching in chapter 10, "How Can You Mainstream and Individualize Science for All Your Children?"

To have maximum value and relevance to children, your science teaching should be interdisciplinary and related to the everyday life and activities of your students. One topic for selection might be energy education. Notice how David Kuhn treated energy education as an

FIGURE 4-6   HOLISTIC APPROACH TO ELEMENTARY SCHOOL SCIENCE

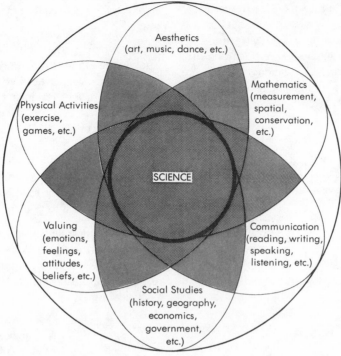

Study of Environment from Multidimensional Perspectives

Student Interest Starting Point	*Possible Kinds of Activities*
Aesthetics (arts, music, dance)	Find and collect fallen objects and make a collage or three-dimensional artwork.
Mathematics	Measure the perimeter of the ball field.
Communication (reading, writing, speaking, listening, and so on)	Make a list of opposite word pairs (hard-soft, rough-smooth, and so on) and find objects that are represented by these word pairs.
Social studies (history, geography, economics, government)	What was on this land before our school was built? Who owned the land? How did the school board get the land?
Physical activities (exercise, games, and so on)	How are the open spaces of our fields used for exercise and games?
Valuing activities (feelings, attitudes, beliefs, and so on)	Walk in pairs, one blindfolded, the other leading. What things were you aware of blindfolded? When (if at all) did you start to feel comfortable blindfolded? Why?

Source: Modified from Hans O. Andersen, "The Holistic Approach to Science Education," *The Science Teacher* 45, no. 1 (January 1978): 27–28.

---

interdisciplinary, relevant, attitudinally aware, and future-oriented study in a recent *Science Teacher* article.[19]

1. *Energy education should be interdisciplinary.* It should branch into *every* area of curriculum including social studies, language arts, mathematics and art.

2. *Energy education should relate to the everyday life of children.* Concepts such as insulators and conductors take on much more meaning when related to the problems of insulating a school or home. More broadly, you can look at the social implications of tax hikes on gas-guzzling autos.

3. *Energy education should consider attitudes, values, and decision making.* There are both cognitive and affective levels in energy education.

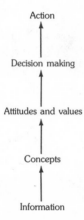

Action

↑

Decision making

↑

Attitudes and values

↑

Concepts

↑

Information

Values clarification techniques, simulation exercises, and the analyzing of advertising are useful in this area and are explored in the section "Science Teaching and Values Clarification."

4. *Energy education should be future-oriented and stress alternatives.* Help your students to see that *many* futures are possible and decisions made now will affect both their lives and those of generations to come. Stressing the futuristic element of energy education helps students realize the importance of being flexible and adaptable. Give children many opportunities to develop alternatives. As Sidney Simon, proponent of values clarification, put it, "Much of the time we make our decisions and live our lives without looking at *all* the possible alternatives."[20]

Encourage full discussion of all facets of energy-related issues, such as nuclear energy and possible government rationing of fuel. Avoid inflicting your personal views on students. They should gather information, explore their own values, and make their own decisions.

SCIENCE TEACHING AND VALUES CLARIFICATION

Our technological, social, economic, and scientific problems cannot be solved by cognitive knowledge alone. We cannot approach issues loaded with values as if they have absolute answers. Through science teaching, you can help students become aware of the consequences of certain choices they might propose. If you avoid questions dealing with values, it simply means they will be dealt with elsewhere, probably in a setting where there is no input from science. Here are some practical strategies to infuse values into your science teaching.

1. Try to add *real societal issues and controversies including values* to your science teaching. Robert E. Yager and his associates support this idea and recommend the following:

> Certainly issue-centered science programs for the '80s will be radically different from those of earlier years. A focus on social issues can directly involve students in decision making, problem solving, and cooperation with one another. Research suggests that this approach in science instruction can effectively make science more interesting and more valuable to all students.[21]

The authors also present examples of modules, minicourses, challenges, and packets with an issue-centered approach to teaching (see table 4–1).

2. Include materials relating to your *students'* lives and how they *feel* about those materials. For a long time, we have largely been indifferent to our students' feelings. "It's easy to convince people that children need to learn the alphabet and numbers. . . . How do we help people to realize that what really matters . . . is how a person's inner life finally puts together the alphabet and numbers of his outer life. What really matters is whether he uses the alphabet for the declaration of war or for the description of a sunrise, his numbers for the final count at Buchenwald or for the specifics of a brand new bridge."[22]

TABLE 4–1
Examples of modules, minicourses, challenges, and packets with an issue-centered approach to science (with sources)

Unified Science and Mathematics for the Elementary School (USMES)	Outdoor Biology Instructional Strategies (OBIS)
(Durham, NC: Moore Publishing Co., 1973)	(Nashua, NH: Delta Education, 1974)
Pedestrian Crossing	Natural Recycling in Soil
Lunch Lines	Litter Critters
Eating in School	Adaptation-Predator-Prey
Consumer Research	Hopper Herding
Mass Communication	What Lives Here?
Individualized Science Instruction System (ISIS)	**Human Science Program (HSP)**
(Lexington, MA: Ginn and Co., 1973)	(Batavia, IL: C and F Associates, 1975)
Packaging Passengers	Blood Pressure
Household Energy	Interrelationships with Environment
Heart Attack	Ways of Knowing
Fossil Fuels	Feeling Fit
Ways We Learn	Kidney Machines
Health Activities Project (HAP)	**Science 5/13 (Sc 5/13)**
(Northbrook, IL: Hubbard, 1976)	(London, England: Macdonald Educational, 1972)
Breathing Fitness	
Growth Trends	Cooking Things
Consumer's Choice	Science from Toys
Madison Avenue	The Shaping of Metals
Lunchtime	Wintry Things

Source: Robert E. Yager et al., "Science Attuned to Social Issues: Challenge for the '80s," *The Science Teacher*, 48, no. 9 (December 1981), pp. 13–14.

3. *Begin to think in terms of affective behavior* for your students in addition to cognitive behavior with which you are probably more familiar and comfortable. Focus upon their *covert* and *overt* affective behaviors.

4. *Integrate values clarification activities* into all your science teaching and other subjects when applicable. Table 4–2 is an example of how to integrate values clarification into biology or living sciences from elementary to high school. It is important for you to survey the science topics you will investigate this year and do the same for them.

5. *Present all of your subject areas so your students investigate content and issues on these three levels:*
   a. Facts   **b.** Concepts   **c.** Values

6. *Whenever possible, try to involve your students in peer group value-oriented activities,* instead of letting them always rely on *you* or some other adult authority.[23] However, you must be careful how you do this, because the peer group may decide upon antisocial actions based upon their immature or deviant ideas. Lawrence Kohlberg, unlike Sidney Simon, believes that you (as an adult leader) should interject questions that are slightly higher ethically than the level the children are on. One way to do this is to divide your class into groups of four or five students. Present a social problem or dilemma (such as "Should an atomic energy power plant be constructed near populated areas where the power is needed most?") to discuss and resolve. Jean Piaget and Lawrence

TABLE 4–2
Selection and sequencing of biologic content and related social issues

Biologic Content	Social Issue
1. Flow of matter and energy	1. Should solid refuse be disposed of in landfills?
2. Relationship of organisms to each other and their environment	2. Should we continue the use of pesticides to control agricultural pests?
3. Population growth and regulation	3. Should the human race be considered too populous?
4. Succession	4. Should we continue the use of strip mining?
5. Cellular structure and diffusion	5. Should abortions be allowed?
6. Foods and respiration	6. Should Americans question the nutrition of the foods they eat?
7. Cellular multiplication	7. Should drugs that cause chromosomal damage be allowed?
8. Synthesis of carbohydrates and proteins	8. Should food shortage be allowed to control the size of the human population?
9. Gamete formation	9. Should we allow the use of mutagenic agents?
10. Mendelian laws	10. Should geneticists be allowed to alter the genes of people?
11. Natural selection	11. Should the minority have rights over a majority when the minority's health is involved?
12. Reproduction	12. Should we allow venereal disease to eliminate behavioral deviants?
13. Development	13. Should society retain all congenitally defective persons at home?
14. Plants: classification and structure	14. Should we allow humans' technologic progress to continue the destruction of natural plant life?
15. Animals: classification and structure	15. Should we be aware of how we determine when we die?
16. New Bubbleton's budget	16. Should biologic principles form the basis of a community's resolution of its social issues?

Kohlberg both stress group participation to provide social conflict and interaction. Social interaction provides opportunities for individuals to perceive situations from different perspectives. See the suggestions by Hilda Taba and Lawrence Kohlberg earlier in this chapter on how to do this.

a. Encourage your students to play *moral games,* where they take different roles. Ask them to make decisions that anyone can live by—justice.

b. Have your students consider situations where there are moral breakdowns (lynching, vandalism, rioting, and so on) and discuss how such things could be prevented.

c. Encourage your students to think and share their ideas on how the discussion relates to *their* behavior in class, school, and the community.

d. Use real as well as contrived conflicts, such as, "In what ways can we treat each other in this class to make everyone feel more comfortable, welcome, and wanted and contribute to everyone else's and our own growth as people?"

e. Avoid imposing *your* ethical principles on your students.[24]

7. *Experiment making "values sheets"* for use with upper elementary children. You can help your students clarify their values with a sheet like this, inspired by Sidney Simon:

Ecology and Its Implications

In Malaysia recently, in an effort to kill off mosquitoes, American technologists sprayed woods and swamplands with DDT. Result? Cockroaches which ate poisoned mosquitoes were so slowed in their reactions that they could be eaten by a variety of tree-climbing lizards. The lizards, which sickened in turn, could be eaten by cats, which promptly died of insecticide poisoning. The cats having died, the rat population began to increase; as rats multiplied, so did fleas: hence, the rapid spread of bubonic plague in Malaysia. But this is not all. The tree-climbing lizards, having died, could no longer eat an insect which consumed the straw thatching of the natives' huts. So as

Malaysians died of plague, their roofs literally caved in above their heads.[25]

Questions to think and write about:

a. Write your reaction to the above paragraph.

b. How can this happening possibly affect *your* life?

c. List some things *you* did in the past that might have broken the delicate balance of nature.

d. What changes have *you* made in *your* life because you are more aware of ecology?

8. *Become familiar with the "values continuum."* The values continuum is a very adaptable activity that can help your students explore most values-laden issues. To begin, you and/or your students identify any issue for discussion. Then draw a long line on the chalkboard, floor, or playground, and describe the two extreme positions. For example, if the issue concerned how children select their food, the values continuum might look like the figure below.

Then ask your students to indicate where *they* stand on the continuum. You can handle this in several ways.

a. Have your students write out on a sheet of paper where they stand and ask for volunteers to mark in their positions on the chalkboard. (By having them write their positions first, you can minimize peer group pressure.)

b. Have your students write their names on pieces of paper and ask volunteers

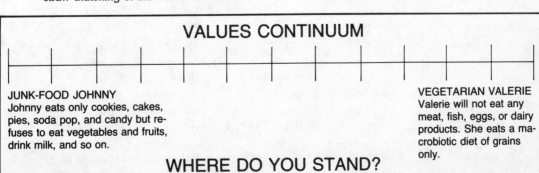

VALUES CONTINUUM

JUNK-FOOD JOHNNY
Johnny eats only cookies, cakes, pies, soda pop, and candy but refuses to eat vegetables and fruits, drink milk, and so on.

VEGETARIAN VALERIE
Valerie will not eat any meat, fish, eggs, or dairy products. She eats a macrobiotic diet of grains only.

WHERE DO YOU STAND?

to tape their names at the appropriate point on the values continuum.

c. Have your students stand at the point on a line drawn on the floor of your classroom that corresponds to their stand on the issue.

After your students have taken a stand on the continuum, allow sufficient time for discussion. You could suggest that students discuss their choices either with people who are next to them on the continuum or with those who are at the opposite extreme from them. The purpose of this activity is to show that many of the values issues we face do not involve simply either/or, black/white, or yes/no choices. Neither are there "right" or "wrong" answers on a values continuum. The values continuum gives your students an opportunity to hear and consider alternatives.

9. *Approach science so your students see it as nonviolent, noncoercive, and nonmanipulative.* Everett Mendelsohn reminds us that

> We know that we spend many more dollars for the military than for social good. By default, then, we have been willing to take part in the construction of tools of violence. What if we were to insist that the dollars and the knowledge be redirected? The physician is under conscious and explicit oath not to construct substances harmful to human life.

What if the same were required of scientists? What would we not be doing now? What might we be doing?[26]

10. Use *comparisons* in your science teaching to stimulate your students' *right cerebral creative processes.* A simile is a figure of speech in which one thing is likened to another: "Parched earth has the wrinkle of an old man's face." You can help your students' *intuitive* processes by giving them practice in using comparisons. Scientists often get insights into how to solve problems by making interesting comparisons in their minds. There is a lesson using several types of comparisons in figure 4–7 for a study of rocks. Some other types of comparisons you could use in your science teaching are listed here.

Comparisons

Type	Format	Examples
1. Simple	What is _____ like?	What is a rock like?
2. Direct	How is _____ like _____?	How is a rock like a cake?
3. Personal	How would it feel to be a _____?	How would it feel to be a rock?
4. Unlike	What is _____ not like?	What is a rock not like?
5. Conflicting couplet	Form two-word paradoxes.	For example, gentle rock, morose smile.
6. Opposing simile	A _____ is like _____ but not like _____.	A rock is like cake but not like _____.
7. Symbolic	Make symbols to represent concepts.	For example, ✚ ♀ 🕊 ☺

1. *What is* a rock like?

   Answers:
   Cheese
   Iron
   Heads
   Coconut

2. *How is* a rock like:
   Cheese
   Iron

   Heads
   Coconut

   Answers:
   Color, holes, texture
   Heavy, solid, rough, dense, cold, sharp, strong, hard
   Dense, heavy, layered, ugly, bumpy, varied
   Flaky, white, geode

3. *How would it feel* to be:
   A rock
   Cheese
   Iron
   Coconut

   Answers:
   Cold, peaceful, lonely, stiff, durable
   Soft, tasty, useful
   Heavy, strong, lusty, supportive
   Hard, round, grainy

4. How is a rock unlike _____?
   A coconut
   An orange
   Plastic
   A balloon

   Answers:
   Usually inorganic
   Doesn't become moldy
   Doesn't float
   Isn't transparent

5. Student creative phase:
   Use these words on the right side of the page to write a poem or essay about rocks.

FIGURE 4–7
Science lesson using several types of comparisons

11. *Have your children engage in body movements in your science teaching.* Brain research shows that one of the best ways to learn is through enactive involvement, which incorporates more *right* hemispheric response. To help students learn the meaning of the word *force,* you can talk about it, spell it out on the board, and define it, but some children will still not understand it. How much better it is to have children push or pull another child and then tell them that a force is a "push or pull." Here is how to use large muscle movement for right hemispheric learning in your science teaching.

☐ Play *Let's Pretend:* being fish, butterflies, trees, etc. and moving like them.

☐ Stand up and show that you're a candle burning slowly, a tree being blown by a gentle and then a strong wind, wallpaper becoming unglued, etc.

☐ Play *Hunter and Prey:* ways animals must adapt to survive.

☐ Play *Changing States of Matter:* "You're an ice cube and starting to melt."

☐ Move like a gear: have four students stand together in a circle and work out how they will move like gears.

☐ Make a fun machine: demonstrate some moving part of a machine.

SUMMARY

We need to be concerned in our science teaching with humanism as well as cognitive learning. Reasons why we science teachers avoid the affective domain (feelings) have been explored in this chapter. Interrelationships between the affective and cognitive domains have been investigated for the implications for our teaching.

An inventory of the affective attributes of scientists revealed that scientists are initially motivated to choose science for a career because of affective things such as *excitement*

with natural phenomena and *pride* in contributing to knowledge and human welfare. The inventory also looked at scientists' interests, attitudes, appreciations, values, beliefs, and other affective elements.

We teachers have belief systems, and ways of looking at our own systems have been presented. Finding ways to discover and use the knowledge of our students' cultural values and their attitudes toward science and themselves (called self-concept) is vital. Self-concept is one of the most powerful influences on your students' achievement in science.

Humanistic science teaching means relating to your students in ways that show respect for them as individuals with rights. Ways for you to explore feelings with children have been shown, as well as how to use these feelings in your science teaching. Specifics of how to use teacher empathy to improve your students' science learning have also been described in this chapter.

Leaders in education state that modern education should be holistic. This means that both cerebral hemispheres of the brain should be involved in the learning process. American schools have traditionally emphasized left cerebral types of learning. Therefore, we have emphasized right brain creative activities in this chapter.

Your science teaching should integrate science with other areas of the curriculum.

Values clarification helps your students evaluate alternative approaches to problem solving. In these activities, you should use real, basic societal issues and controversies, including values. Materials related to your students' lives and how they feel about these materials should be included.

You should become familiar with affective behavior in the same way you have with cognitive behavior. Integrate values clarification activities into all your science and other subjects on three levels: facts, concepts, and values. Examples in biological and living science have been given. Try to use a peer group as the source of value-oriented facts instead of *you* or another adult authority.

Experiment with values clarification activities such as values sheets and the values continuum. Creativity involves both right and left cerebral activity. The intuitive phase is mainly done in the right cerebrum. The working out of the intuitive idea requires much left hemispheric productivity.

The production of comparison, body movement for conceptualizing, and guided imagination or fantasy all require right hemispheric brain activity. Answering questions about these things and responding to them involves both parts of the brain, thereby requiring more holistic student responses.

SELF-EVALUATION AND FURTHER STUDY

1. Plan and present two lessons using an *affective* or *values-laden* frame of reference in the manner presented in this chapter.
2. Write *five affective* behavioral objectives.
3. Pick a science topic for study by your class this year. Organize the study from a multidimensional approach as described in this chapter. Show specifically the kinds of possible activities for each of the curricular areas.
4. Develop a values sheet and a values continuum for your class on a controversial issue.
5. Pick one of your science topics and plan to teach it on the facts, concepts, and values levels using the biology example as your model.
6. How do *you* relate to "bright" students? "Slow learners"? "Discipline problems"? Look over the list of students with whom you work and write down how you feel about them, which ones you prefer or dislike and why, and how you react (specific actions) to them in your classroom.
7. Obtain further information about the *School Situation Perception Test* and use it with a group of children to discover *their* perceptions of *your* reading.
8. Prepare several types (simple, direct, and so on) of metaphorical questions that you could use in teaching science.
9. Make some metaphorical types of lessons as indicated in this chapter.
10. Write some science movement types of activities and try them out either in microteaching or in a classroom. Evaluate them.

ENDNOTES

1. A. F. Eiss and Mary B. Harbeck, *Behavioral Objectives in the Affective Domain* (Washington, D.C.: National Science Teachers Association, 1969), p. 4.
2. Howard H. Birnie, "Identifying Affective Goals in Science Education," *The Science Teacher* 45, no. 9 (December 1978): 29.
3. Robert K. Crocker and M. A. Nay, "Science Teaching and the Affective Attributes of Scientists," *Science Education* 54 (1970): 59–67.
4. Benjamin S. Bloom, *Human Characteristics and School Learning* (New York: McGraw-Hill Book Co., 1976).
5. Arthur A. Carin, "Children's Perceptions of Selected Teaching Acts" (Ph.D. diss., University of Utah. Salt Lake City, Utah, 1958). Jean

Piaget sees intelligence as the building of experiences on each other, forming ever more complex structures of schemas. Sensory experiences are vital in Piaget's view of development. For further information, see Jean Piaget, *The Grasp of Consciousness* (Cambridge: Harvard University Press, 1976); _____, *The Development of Cognitive Structures* (New York: Viking Press, 1977); _____, *The Origins of the Idea of Chance in the Child* (New York: W. W. Norton & Co., 1976).

6. Sample story from *School Situation Perception Test,* by Arthur A. Carin and Marie Hughes. All rights reserved. Further information may be obtained from Arthur Carin, Queens College of City University of New York, Flushing, N.Y. 11367.

7. Robert M. W. Travers and Jacqueline Dillon, *The Making of a Teacher* (New York: Macmillan Publishing Co., 1975), p. 32.

8. Robert R. Rosenthal and L. Jacobson, *Pygmalion in the Classroom: Teacher Expectations and Pupils' Intellectual Development* (New York: Holt, Rinehart & Winston, 1968). This study has been criticized for certain design and statistical weaknesses, and further replications failed to confirm the results. For additional information on this controversy, see P. E. Vernon, "Environment and Intelligence" in *Piaget, Psychology and Education,* ed. Ved. P. Varma and Phillip Williams (Itasca, Ill.: F. E. Peacock Publishers, 1970).

9. T. J. Adenkia and G. L. Berry, "Teacher's Attitudes Toward the Education of the Black Child," *Education* 97 (1976): 102–14; Robert A. Altman and P. O. Snyder, *The Minority Student on Campus: Expectations and Possibilities* (Boulder, Colo.: Western Interstate Commission for Higher Education, 1971).

10. Mario Fantini, "Humanizing the Humanism Movement," *Phi Delta Kappan,* February 1974, p. 402.

11. For a more detailed explanation of these strategies, see Hilda Taba et al., *A Teacher's Handbook for Elementary School Studies—An Inductive Approach,* 2nd ed. (Reading, Mass.: Addison-Wesley Publishing Co., 1971).

12. For additional information, see Lawrence Kohlberg, "Moral Development and the New Social Studies," *Social Education* 27, no. 5 (May 1973): 369–75.

13. Mary Budd Rowe, "Teachers Who Care," *The Science Teacher* 44, no. 5 (1977): 37–38.

14. Thomas H. Budzynski, "Biofeedback and Twilight, States of Consciousness," *Consciousness & Self Regulation,* vol. 1, no. 76 (New York: Plenum Publishing Co., 1976), p. 382.

15. Harold Pratt et al., "Science Education in the Elementary School," in Norris C. Harms and Roger E. Yager, *What Research Says to the Science Teacher, Vol. 3* (Washington, D.C.: National Science Teachers Association, 1981), pp. 76–77.

16. Paul F. Brandwein, "Convention '78 Revisited" (Address given at the National Science Teachers Association's 26th Annual National Convention in Washington, D.C.), *The Science Teacher* 45, no. 5 (May 1978), p. 30.

17. Alvin Toffler, *Future Shock* (New York: Bantam Books, 1970), p. 414.

18. T. H. Estes and J. L. Vaughan, "Reading Interest and Comprehension: Implications," *Reading Teacher,* no. 27 (November 1973): pp. 149–53.

19. The authors are indebted to this article for the materials included here: David J. Kuhn, "Teaching the Energy Lesson," *The Science Teacher* 45, no. 6 (September 1978): pp. 32–35.
20. Sidney Simon, Leland W. Howe, and Howard Kirshenbaum, *Values Clarification: A Handbook of Practical Strategies for Teachers and Students* (New York: Hart Publishing Co., 1972), p. 5.
21. Robert E. Yager et al., "Science Attuned to Social Issues: Challenge for the '80s," *The Science Teacher* 48, no. 9 (December 1981), pp. 13–14.
22. Neil Postman and Charles Weingartner, *The School Book—For People Who Want to Know What All the Hollering Is About* (New York: Delacorte Press, 1973), p. 128.
23. It is a well-known trait of young people that they tend to reject value-oriented facts when they are presented by parents, teachers, or other "authority figures." Coming from adults, such material is considered to be "preaching." In contrast, the same ideas are likely to be accepted without prejudice when the source is a peer or peer group. For an excellent short description of the application of this peer technique to the structuring of antismoking education in Quincy, Massachusetts, by lecture-demonstrations of high school students, the reader is urged to see William H. O'Kane, "Peer Group Presents Value-Oriented Concepts," *The Science Teacher* 37, no. 9 (December 1970), pp. 17–18.
24. For an excellent resource of specific techniques for helping your students with moral development, see Ronald E. Galbraith and Thomas M. Jones, *Teaching Strategies for Moral Dilemmas: An Application of Kohlberg's Theory of Moral Development to the Social Studies Classroom* (Pittsburgh, Pa.: Carnegie-Mellon University, Social Studies Curriculum Center, 1971); Richard H. Hersch, Diana Pritchard Paolitto, and Joseph Reimer, *Promoting Moral Growth—From Piaget to Kohlberg* (New York: Longman, 1979); Hersch, John Miller, and G. Fielding, *Models of Moral Education* (New York: Longman, 1979).
25. Peter A. Gunter, North Texas University, writing in *The Living Wilderness* (Spring 1970).
26. Everett Mendelsohn, "Values and Science: A Critical Reassessment," *The Science Teacher* 43, no. 9 (January 1976), p. 23.

5

Why Teach Science Through Guided Discovery?

Your approach to teaching science should grow out of what you know about the processes and products of science, how your children learn best, what your goals and objectives in science teaching are, and how you *feel* about the relationship of science, human values, and your concern for the environment.

NO BEST WAY TO TEACH SCIENCE TO ALL CHILDREN

Because each of your children is unique, there is no *one* best way to teach everyone. Generally, there are three types of science-teaching strategies: exposition (telling), guided discovery, and inquiry discovery. One of the most important differences between the three teaching strategies is the roles of teacher and student (see figure 5–1). *Exposition* is the end of the continuum where the *teacher* dominates, with students passive. On the other extreme is *inquiry*, or *free discovery*, where *students* are most active and the teacher facilitates the development of the student's skills. In the middle is *guided discovery*, combining both strategies.

Exposition Science Teaching

The teacher is the primary focus in expository science teaching; you are the "doer," while your students (you hope) are participating *mentally*. There are times when you will find it appropriate to present information to your children directly. Some of the ways to do this are

1. telling them
2. demonstrating using scientific apparatus
3. carrying on a discussion
4. reading to children
5. showing them a film, filmstrip, slides, or TV presentation
6. having a resource person present something to them

David Ausubel calls this *reception* teaching. In reception teaching, knowledge to be learned is presented, and the teacher defines concepts for the student.[1] If the new knowledge is linked to relevant existing concepts in the learner's cognitive structure, *meaningful* learning occurs. *Rote* learning takes place when new knowledge is arbitrarily incorporated into cognitive structure. Whether the new information you present is meaningful or rote learning for your children depends on how relevant you make it for them and how well it matches their level of cognitive development. This example shows how important it is to know how much your children know *before* you present any scientific concepts to them.

100

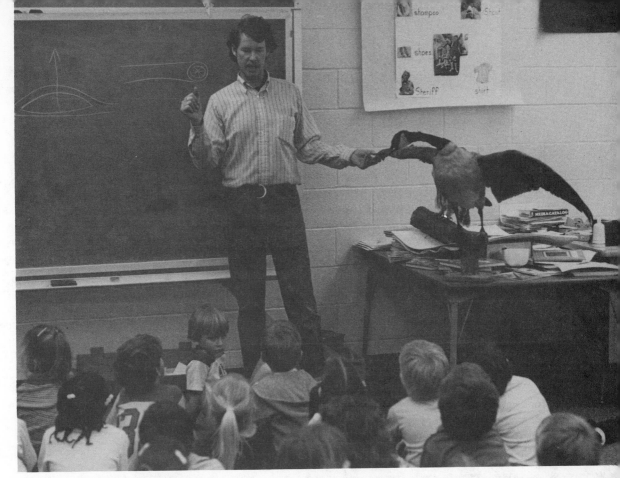

. . . we can define diffusion as "The movement of a substance from a region of higher concentration to a region of lower concentration due to random molecular motion." However, the student who does not already have concepts of "concentration" and "random molecular motion" cannot learn this definition meaningfully and must resort to rote learning. Typically, students have some *limited* development of these concepts and thus are capable of meaningfully learning the definition to some extent.[2]

According to Ausubel, reception learning of concepts is the foundation upon which higher learning builds. Without it, there cannot be discovery or inquiry learning.

Teaching strategy	EXPOSITION	GUIDED DISCOVERY	INQUIRY OR FREE DISCOVERY
Teacher role	Active/Dominate	Active/Facilitator	Facilitator
Student role	Passive or Active	Active	Active

$\longleftrightarrow$

FIGURE 5–1
Science-teaching strategies continuum

Inquiry or Free Discovery Learning

On the other side of the teaching-strategies continuum is inquiry or free discovery. Inquiry teaching structures teaching strategies so that students develop their abilities to manipulate and process information from a variety of sources: academic, social, and experiential. In inquiry, students identify problems, generate hypotheses or possible answers, test these hypotheses in the light of available data, and attempt to apply their conclusions to new data, new problems, or new situations. Inquiry focuses upon *how* students process data (processes) rather than *what* they process (products). Two educators summarize inquiry this way.

> In an educational context, inquiry is both a noun and a verb—both an act and a *process* . . . inquiry is a learning process, a way in which students and adults can go about solving problems or processing information.[3]

It is unlikely that teachers will encounter many (if any) children who can engage in this very advanced mental strategy; Piaget's evidence about children's development (presented in chapter 2) tells us such children are rare. And yet, inquiry processing is one of the goals of science teaching. We can combine some of these processes with exposition teaching to develop a learning strategy called *guided* discovery, which is appropriate for elementary children.

Guided Discovery Teaching/ Learning

Guided discovery science teaching blends teacher-centered and student-centered techniques. Figure 5–2 illustrates the relationships that may exist between the amount of teacher dominance and children's age and/or mental development, as well as the relationship between children's mastery of science concepts

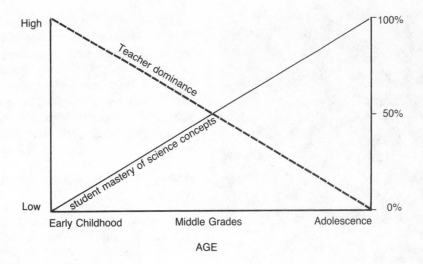

FIGURE 5–2
Interrelationships between children's age, science concept development and teacher dominance in science teaching

and their ability to engage in discovery learning, either guided or free. The younger the children, the more you must present information and guide them; the older the children, the less you present, the more they will initiate work with you as a facilitator, resource person, and encourager.

This text emphasizes guided discovery, not because it is the only way to teach, but for three important reasons. First, more of us are familiar and comfortable with expository teaching because it was used almost exclusively in our own education. Second, if we want our children to be scientifically literate and able to solve problems, they must actually participate at their appropriate level in these activities with your assistance. (Expository teaching *is* important and will be discussed in chapter 8 on classroom management and science teaching.) Guided discovery with young children may lead to free discovery or inquiry in adolescence and adulthood. Third, guided discovery teaching will broaden your repertoire of teaching strategies to meet the diverse levels of the children you teach.

GUIDED DISCOVERY TEACHING

Teaching Learners to Learn

Guided discovery teaching/learning tries to help students learn to learn. Guided discovery helps them acquire knowledge that is uniquely their own because they discovered it themselves. Guided discovery is *not* restricted to finding something entirely new to the world such as an invention (television) or theory (heliocentric view of the universe). It is a matter of internally rearranging data so your students can go beyond the data to form concepts new to *them*. Guided discovery involves finding the meanings, organization, and structure of ideas. Robert Karplus and Herbert Thier, co-developers of the Science Curriculum Improvement Study (SCIS), described this aspect of discovery in this way: "A discovery is the recognition of a relationship between an idea and an observation, or between two ideas, or between two observations."[4]

Discovery teaching is not new. The ancient Greek philosopher Socrates, with his question-

ing style, used a discovery, nontelling approach to learning. More recently, John Dewey, the main spokesman for progressive education in the 1930s, advocated that children should "learn by doing," rather than be lectured to. Jean Piaget and Jerome Bruner, former Harvard psychologist, were responsible for a sharply increased interest in learning by discovery in the middle 1960s.

Advantages of Guided Discovery

Jerome Bruner, instrumental in leading the movement toward discovery teaching, outlines four reasons for using this approach.[5]

1. Intellectual potency
2. Intrinsic rather than extrinsic motives
3. Learning the heuristics of discovery
4. Conservation of memory

By *intellectual potency,* Bruner means an individual learns and develops his mind only by using it. He believes, as a consequence of succeeding at discovery, the student receives a satisfying intellectual thrill—an intrinsic or self-satisfying reward. Teachers often give extrinsic rewards (A's, for example), but if they want students to learn for the fun of it, they have to devise instructional systems that offer students intrinsic satisfaction. Bruner emphasizes that *the only way a person learns the techniques of*

making discoveries is to have opportunities to discover. Through guided discovering, a student slowly learns how to organize and carry out investigations. One of the greatest payoffs of the guided discovery approach is that it aids better memory retention. Something a student discovers independently is remembered but concepts he or she is told can be quickly forgotten.

Shifting Students from Extrinsic to Intrinsic Motivation

Learning may occur in response to some reward; children may also be motivated to learn to avoid failure. These two types of motivation may become a pattern, where children seek cues about how to conform to what is expected of them. In your class, the children may spend the first few days finding out what it is *you* want, so they can please you. David Reisman, renowned sociologist, explained this by saying: ". . . mental life moves from a state of *outer-directedness* in which the fortuity of stimuli and reinforcement are crucial to a state of *inner-directedness,* in which the growth and maintenance of mastery becomes central and dominant."

Reisman's outer-directedness means that children are doing things for *us.* They want *our* praise and want to avoid *our* wrath. This works against our goals in science education. It makes the children dependent on an authority for rewards, motivation, and constant directions.

Guided discovery helps students become more autonomous, self-directed, and responsible for their own learning. Your students will become more self-motivated when they approach learning by discovering something themselves, rather than hearing about it. They learn to carry out their activities with the autonomy of self-reward. More properly, you can say the reward is the discovery itself. Children learn to manipulate their environment more actively. They achieve gratification from coping with problems.

Extrinsic motivation has little or no relationship to the act of learning. Intrinsic rewards are personal, vary widely from person to person, and are directly connected to obvious external incentives. Here is an example of the differences between extrinsic and intrinsic motivation.

A "Peanuts" cartoon of a few years ago expresses the difference quite clearly. Schroeder is seated at a piano and he says to Lucy, "I'm trying to learn to play all of the Beethoven sonatas." Lucy replies, "Gee, if you do learn to play them all, what will you win?" Indignantly Schroeder responds, "I won't *win* anything!" Disgusted, Lucy walks away saying, "You won't? What's the sense in doing something if you don't win a prize?"[6]

Research has shown that extrinsic motivation is more efficient in terms of the relative amount of time spent in learning the task, skill, or knowledge. However, information learned by intrinsic motivation is retained longer.[7]

J. Richard Suchman, one of the leading proponents of discovery learning, believes the very nature of discovery learning provides an environment free of extrinsic motivation. By discovery-oriented teaching, you are more likely to provide a nonpunitive, stimulating atmosphere where children engage in learning because it is fun, interesting, and self-rewarding. Your job is to act as a *facilitator* and provide your students with an environment responsive to their needs. Try to shed yourself of the view of the teacher as a dispenser of information and rewards. Give your students an opportunity to try things without fear of *your* (external) rewards or punishments.

Learning the Heuristics of Discovery

As John Dewey said, "We learn by doing and reflecting on what we do." There is a great deal of evidence from psychology and other sources indicating that learning is not a passive process. Jerome Bruner put it this way: ". . . the student is not a bench-bound listener, but should be actively involved in the learning process."[8]

The child must be *actively* involved in learning. But sometimes people misinterpret this concept and limit activity to manual or manipulative activities. Children can be *actively* involved by listening, speaking, reading, seeing, and thinking, if their minds are acting on what is being learned. Your job is to find ways of getting the learner actively involved in whatever activities are presented. Piaget has said there is no learning without action. It is only through the exercise of problem solving that your students will learn the heuristics of discovery (learning how to learn). The more they are involved in solving problems, the more likely they are to learn to generalize what they have learned into a style of discovery that serves them best.

The Aid to Memory Processing

The human mind has often been compared to an extremely complicated computer; the biggest problem of this human computer is not the storage but the *retrieval* of data. Psychologists and learning researchers believe the key to retrieval is organization. In simpler terms, this means knowing what information to find and how to get it. Research indicates that any organization of information that reduces the complexity of material by putting it in a pattern *the learner* has constructed will make that material easier to retrieve. Material that is organized in terms of the learner's *own* interests and uniqueness has the best chance of being accessible in memory. You probably can think of something you learned by setting up a system that worked for you. Do you remember high school or college science classes where your teacher tried to help you remember something by association, for example, remembering the colors of the spectrum by saying ROY G. BIV? The best kind of system is one a person invents personally, but we should still show our students how other people remember and structure things. The very attitudes and activities that characterize figuring out or discovering things for oneself also seem to have the effect of making material readily retrievable in the learner's memory.

Psychologists call this *transfer of training*. There is little evidence that learning one subject will enhance mastery in another subject. But teachers used to believe that it would, and they taught Latin to "train the mind," make the learner more logical, and improve the learning of English. It just did not work that way. For the transfer of training to be most effective, two factors must be at work.

1. Positive transfer of training will take place if there is a similarity between subjects. The closer the similarity of the subjects, the better the chance of a transfer of training.
2. Positive transfer of training will take place if there is a learning of principles or techniques in the first situation that can be usefully applied to the second situation.

If you want your students to be problem solvers, learn by discovery, and do things for themselves, you must give them practice in all of these things. The more they solve problems with your guidance, the greater will be the chances that transfer of training will find its way into new situations.

Discovery Learning Research

Although more research in the area is needed, there is evidence that discovery learning is effective. In a conference on learning by discovery, the research on discovery was summarized as follows: "In the published studies, guided discovery treatments generally have done well both at the level of immediate learning and later transfer."[9]

One of the best studies of discovery teaching was a three-year longitudinal investigation to see what differences (if any) this type of teaching made on the students' learning behaviors. Investigators at Carnegie-Mellon University found that a discovery-oriented social studies curriculum increased the students' abilities to inquire about human affairs significantly more than a program using nondiscovery materials.[10] This study was important since it showed that discovery teaching over a three-year period does make individuals better learners. The implications for science teaching are numerous. If you are interested in the results of additional research on discovery learning, read the articles and books listed in endnotes 11, 12, and 13.

In another study, T. E. Allen found that "discipline problems" from "troublemakers"

were significantly reduced in science classrooms where the teachers were nondirective and nonauthoritarian, and where student opportunity to select and explore alternatives was increased.[11]

Discovery vs. Structure

Edmund Amidon and N. A. Flanders found in their study that highly anxious children functioned better in student-centered classrooms. These classrooms had less structure and teachers gave fewer directions.[12] Carl Rogers also cites case studies of teachers who have used the discovery approach at the elementary, high school, and college levels with much success.[13]

How Guided Discovery Learning Builds Self-Concepts

We all have self-concepts. If our self-concepts are positive, these things happen.

☐ We feel psychologically secure.
☐ We are open to new experiences.
☐ We are willing to take chances and explore.
☐ We tolerate minor failures relatively well.
☐ We are more creative.
☐ We are generally in good mental health.
☐ We eventually become fully functioning individuals.

Part of the task of becoming a better person is building a positive self-concept. We can help children do this by actively involving them in their learning. Through *active* involvement, children are more likely to work up to their potential and gain insights into their "self." Guided discovery teaching provides opportunities for greater involvement, giving children more chance to gain insights and better develop their self-concepts.

Your Students' Expectancy and Guided Discovery

Your students' self-concepts are directly related to their expectancy levels. That is, your students have certain ideas about how they can or cannot accomplish a task on their own. Many children, unfortunately, have learned (or accepted) low expectancy levels for themselves, characterized by statements like

I can't do math problems.
Boy, am I dumb.
Science is one subject I never could do.
Forget it, I couldn't do that if my life
depended on it.

It is a vicious cycle: low expectancy levels lead to high anxiety, and high anxiety leads to further lowering of expectancy levels. In fact, the overwhelming weight of research has found that a high anxiety level generally accompanies poor student performance.[14] In addition, highly anxious children tend to lack self-confidence, curiosity, and adventurousness.[15]

It has been found, however, that children in discovery-oriented classrooms learn to think and function more autonomously. From having had many successful experiences in using and being encouraged to use their investigative talents, these children learn

I can work things out for myself.
Mrs. Orkand, can I try to do that, please?
Let me try doing it.
I am a valuable person.

Time to Learn Properly

Teachers sometimes try to rush or short-circuit learning. They think they can drastically cut the time it takes for students to learn something. However, students need adequate time to think, reason out, and gain insights into the concepts, principles, and skills in science. It takes time for students to act on things in their minds for *meaningful learning.* The learning process may seem meaningful to teachers, but unless it becomes meaningful to the learner, it is all for naught.

Piaget believes there is no true learning unless the child has time to assimilate and accommodate what he or she encounters in the environment. Unless this happens, you and your students are involved in what Piaget calls *pseudolearning,* parroting an explanation without a real change in mental awareness about a subject.

Look at figure 5–3 and think about the many ways that activity-oriented discovery science teaching is better than teaching that merely tells about science.

IMPLICATIONS FOR YOUR TEACHING

This section will discuss some practical ways to use guided teaching in your classroom. How much structure to provide in guided discovery activities is probably one of your first concerns.

How Much Guidance in Guided Discovery?

Guided discovery teaching is not the laissez-faire, "Children, do what you want and you'll learn" approach. You should have enough structure to insure that students use their minds to discover science concepts and principles. You should have some broad objectives in mind and your classroom activities should guide your students toward these objectives. However, some of the time you have to refrain from *telling* children what you want them to learn or they will merely memorize.

You have to present a *variety* of activities so the children build a storehouse of sensory observations from which verbal (and eventually written) symbols are "invented" by the teacher. Robert Karplus and his associates, developers of the Science Curriculum Improvement Study (SCIS), emphasize this point by stressing three stages of the learning cycle. (See the chart on page 109.)

For instance, at the preschool or primary level, give your students an assortment of buttons and ask them to group them any way they want. You can *guide* them to discover the buttons' characteristics or properties, which Karplus calls *exploration.* Without *telling* the children that buttons can be grouped according to their color, shape, texture, size, or kinds of materials (properties), you can ask, "What do all of Alice's buttons have in common?" or "What is alike in all of the buttons Harry grouped together?" Following this, say something like, "When you put the buttons together

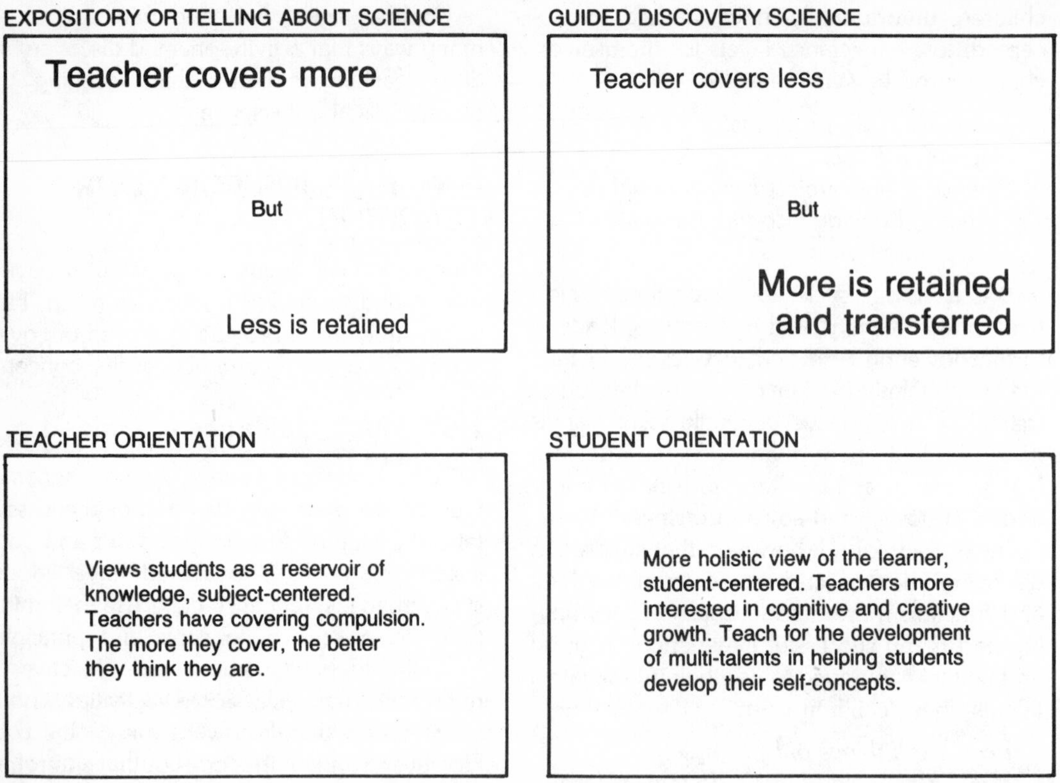

EXPOSITORY OR TELLING ABOUT SCIENCE

Teacher covers more

But

Less is retained

GUIDED DISCOVERY SCIENCE

Teacher covers less

But

More is retained and transferred

TEACHER ORIENTATION

Views students as a reservoir of knowledge, subject-centered. Teachers have covering compulsion. The more they cover, the better they think they are.

STUDENT ORIENTATION

More holistic view of the learner, student-centered. Teachers more interested in cognitive and creative growth. Teach for the development of multi-talents in helping students develop their self-concepts.

FIGURE 5–3
Attributes of expository science and guided discovery science

Source: Reproduced with permission by *Science and Children,* April 1977. Copyright by the National Science Teachers Association, 1742 Connecticut Avenue, N.W., Washington, D.C. 20009.

by their color, shape, how they feel, etc., scientists say you are grouping by properties" (Karplus' *invention* stage). Give the children a variety of seeds and ask, "How can we now group these seeds by their properties?" This gives children an opportunity to apply what they learned in exploration and invention stages to new situations (in Karplus' terminology, the *discovery* stage). By being involved in all these activities, children slowly build in their minds what Piaget calls *physical knowledge.*

IMPORTANCE OF "LABORATORY" ACTIVITIES IN GUIDED DISCOVERY SCIENCE TEACHING

The 1981 Board of Directors of the National Science Teachers Association unanimously en-dorsed the necessity of laboratory experiences for teaching and learning science. For the elementary school science program this means hands-on experiences emphasizing science process skills of observing, measuring, recording, classifying, interpreting data, inferring, predicting, investigating, and making models. Hands-on experiences, if properly guided by the teacher, can provide practice in thinking and reasoning. Darrell Phillips summarizes the place of hands-on activities in guided discovery learning.

The individual's construction of the tools of thought (i.e., Piaget's operations and operational structures) are abstracted from actions on objects. In essence, without action on objects, there can be no abstraction, operations, or structures. Teaching science as a reading lesson, a "cookbook" lab, or an

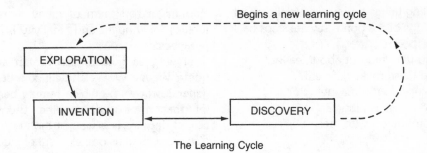

The Learning Cycle

exercise in memorization inhibits the development of reasoning. . . . Teachers must offer *sciencing* (active exploration and discovery of relationships) as opposed to school *science* (passive mimicking and memorization).[17]

Elementary school children are in a formative stage of mental development, which requires actions on objects for the development of reasoning. What you must supply during these vital growth years is a variety of hands-on activities in which your children manipulate objects, are helped to see relationships, and draw conclusions. Refer to chapter 2, dealing with hemispheric brain functions, to review the importance of laboratory or hands-on science activities for intellectual development of elementary school children.

Practicing Guided Discovery Activities

If you and your students have not had experience in learning through discovery, you may need more structure, initially, in your lessons. After you both have gained some experience in how to carry out discovery investigations, you will be able to work with less structure.

This text uses *guided* discovery activities. However, you will reach a point in your teaching where you will be more comfortable with the discovery approach. At that point, you will probably want to use more of the *less structured* discovery activities.

With guided science discovery lessons, you will outline much of the planning. Your students, for example, probably will not originate the problem; you will be guiding them on how to set up and record the data. Later, however, you will probably have the students originate

problems, determine how to resolve them, collect data, communicate their findings, and so on.

Chapter 7 shows you how to create and give discovery laboratory lessons. As you become more experienced with this method, you will develop your own discovery techniques.

LESS STRUCTURED GUIDED DISCOVERY

Another way you can guide your students' discovery is through *less* structured activities. This differs from guided discovery in that you only present the problem and then invite your students to observe, explore, and/or work out procedures for resolving it.

If you are a primary or lower elementary grade teacher, you will probably find this approach more useful. Upper elementary teachers may also find it useful and, in addition, may have the students outline investigative procedures for designing and carrying out their own experiments.

In less structured guided discovery, either you or your students may pose a problem. You provide the materials or the setting for resolving it. Give your students a lot of freedom to solve the problem(s). Here are some problems you might suggest to the children (if they do not pose them by themselves) for involving them in less structured guided discovery activities.

(Primary Level—Mainly Exploratory)

1. What do you notice about fish in the aquarium?
2. What did you find out about the butterflies?
3. In what ways could you group these different things?

4. What living things do you see in the pond, on the edge of the pond, several steps back from the pond?
5. What did you find out about leaves?
6. How are these rocks different?
7. What things do the magnets do?
8. What do magnets attract?
9. What can you do with these objects?

(Upper Elementary—Exploratory; Devising and Carrying Out Experiments)

1. How would you determine the effects of DDT on water snails?
2. What effect does temperature have on the sprouting of seeds?
3. What are all the ways you can get the light bulb to light using the wire and batteries?
4. What types of things stimulate the worms?
5. What affects the swing of pendulums?
6. What is the fastest way to get beans to sprout?
7. How could you determine whether this water is polluted?

Encourage your students to attack similar problems on their own or in small groups. You should set yourself up as a *resource person.* Give only enough aid to insure that the children do not become overly frustrated, experience undue failure, and give up. The assistance you give should be in the form of questions to guide students' thinking about possible investigative procedures. For example, ask the children questions that help them to sense the direction for solving a problem rather than *tell* them what to do. In a problem where children are studying what affects the movements of earthworms, you might ask, "What effect do you think light might have on the movements of earthworms? How could you find that out?" Questions like these, asked at the right time, may stimulate the students to become more involved in their creative investigation. Contrast this approach with that of a teacher who says, "Study earthworms and find out their characteristics and what things affect them." This statement might limit your students' investigation to the physical appearance of worms.

You might rob them of many more opportunities for thought and creativity in their approaches.

How does guided discovery relate to inquiry? Wayne W. Welch defined inquiry as "a general process by which human beings seek information or understanding. Broadly conceived, inquiry is a way of thought." Guided discovery, then, is one element of inquiry. This article discusses the difference: Wayne W. Welch, "Inquiry in School Science," in *What Research Says to the Science Teacher, Volume 3,* Norris C. Harms and Robert E. Yager, editors (Washington, D.C.: National Science Teachers Association, 1981), pp. 53–64.

Free Discovery, or Inquiry, Activities

After the students, over many years, have been exposed to numerous guided discovery science studies, have learned how to attack scientific problems (processes of science), have gained sufficient cognitive science knowledge (products of science), and have performed less structured discovery activities, they may be ready for *free* discovery, or inquiry, activities. Only you can tell if your students are ready. These free discovery activities will differ from the guided or less structured discovery activities in that your *students* will identify or originate what problems *they* would like to study. Usually this occurs in upper elementary grades, but you should be alert at the lower grades for children who are ready for free discovery activities because of their experiences, abilities, interests, and skill development.

Here are some questions to ask to see if your students are ready to use the free discovery, or inquiry, approach.

1. If you were the teacher of this class and you were going to select the most exciting things to investigate this term, what would they be?
2. What are some problems related to our community that you would like to study?
3. Now that you have studied, for example, salts, algae, light, heat, pollution, animal be-

haviors, and so on, what problems can you come up with that you would like to investigate individually or in teams?

4. Now that you have finished this experiment, what other experiments can you think of and which of them would you like to do?

5. When you see problems in the community, for example, pollution, or when you discover some problem related to science that you would like to discuss, bring it to our attention in class.

6. What kind of science fiction story would you like to write?

SUMMARY

No one method of teaching science is best for all children, all of the time, under all circumstances. The three ways to approach teaching are expository (telling), guided discovery, and free discovery, or inquiry. This text advocates guided discovery science teaching/learning because this method incorporates the best of what we know about the processes and products of science, how children learn best at this age, the goals and objectives of science, and the relationships among science, humanism, our values, and our concerns for the environment.

Discovery is the process by which the learner uses the mind in logical and mathematical ways to organize and internalize concepts and principles of the world. The learner is guided to learn to learn, which is called *heuristics*. John Dewey fostered the idea of "learning by doing" and then reflecting upon what was done. The research of Jean Piaget and Jerome Bruner renewed interest in discovery learning.

Some of the advantages of guided discovery learning are that the students learn how to learn, learning becomes self-rewarding, self-motivational and is more easily transferable, it minimizes or avoids rote memory, and learners become more responsible for their own learning.

Guided discovery activities may have three elements: exploration, invention, and discovery. Hands-on experiences are extremely important at the elementary school level according to Piaget's operations and operational structures; they are also important because children need to react to objects to develop reasoning.

The amount of structure you supply depends on your children's level of development and experiences with sciencing. Guided discovery teaching has more structure than free discovery or inquiry. In guided discovery teaching, you provide a great deal of guidance and direction. You provide the problems, materials and equipment, but encourage your students to work out the procedures for solving the problems themselves. The format for guided discovery lessons used in this text includes

☐ Setting the problems (in question format)
☐ Grade level and science area to be investigated
☐ What do I want children to discover?
☐ What will I need?
☐ What will we discuss *before* doing the activity?
☐ What will the children do?
☐ What must I know?
☐ How will children use (or apply) what they discover?

In less structured discovery activity, you pose the problem and provide the materials or setting; the children have a lot of freedom in solving the problems. You function mainly as a resource person and give only enough aid to keep your children moving toward the solution.

Free discovery or inquiry activities are usually for older, more experienced children in upper elementary or junior high school grades. In this approach, children identify or originate what they would like to study.

SELF-EVALUATION AND FURTHER STUDY

1. How would you define the differences between guided, less structured, and free discovery or inquiry teaching/learning? Give an example of each.
2. Read the following (or other) articles on discovery learning and discuss what you think are the best aspects of learning by discovery.

   ☐ Wayne W. Welch, "Inquiry in School Science," in *What Research Says to the Science Teacher, Volume 3,* in Norris C. Harms and Robert E. Yager, editors (Washington, D.C.: National Science Teachers Association, 1981), pp. 53–64.

   ☐ Joseph D. Novak, "Implications for Teaching of Research on Learning," in *What Research Says to the Science Teacher, volume 2,* Mary Budd Rowe, editor (Washington, D.C.: National Science Teachers Association, 1979), pp. 68–79.

3. Hands-on or laboratory activities are very important in the guided discovery approach to teaching science. Read these articles and summarize the advantages (and any disadvantages) of this approach to science teaching.

   ☐ Harry McAnarney, "Wanted: A More Appropriate Use of Hands-on Science," *Science and Children,* 17, no. 7 (April 1980), p. 15.

   ☐ Gerald F. Consuegra, "Strategies for Teaching Elementary and Junior High Students," *Science and Children,* 17, no. 7, (April 1980), pp. 29–30.

   ☐ Kathleen M. Donnellan, "A Rationale for the Laboratory in Preschool/Elementary Programs: A Position of the NSTA Preschool and Elementary Division," in Robert E. Yager et al., "Science Activities Are Central to Science Education in the Elementary School," *Science and Children,* 19, no. 2 (October 1981), p. 42.

   ☐ Ted Bredderman, "What Research Says: Activity Science—The Evidence Shows It Matters," *Science and Children,* 20, no. 1 (September 1982), pp. 39–41.

4. Why is guided discovery learning more transferable and longer lasting than exposition or learning by rote? Use these resources and any others you feel document your case.

   ☐ M. C. Linn et al., "Teaching Children to Control Variables: Investigations of a Free Choice Environment," *Journal of Research in Science Teaching,* 14 (1977), pp. 249–255.

   ☐ Joseph D. Novak, "Understanding the Learning Process and Effectiveness of Teaching Methods in the Classroom, Laboratory, and Field," *Science Education,* 60 (1976), pp. 493–512.

   ☐ L. J. Cronback and R. E. Snow, *Aptitudes and Instructional Strategies: A Handbook for Research on Interactions* (New York: Irvington Publishers, 1977).

5. Why is it important for children to have what David Ausubel calls "meaningful *reception* teaching/learnings" *before* guided discovery experiences can be presented to them?
6. Select a science problem and prepare a series of guided, less structured or free discovery or inquiry approach activities. Use the activities in the back of this textbook or make your own.
7. What are some intrinsic motivational drives you as a teacher might use to have your students move toward greater independence?

8. How would you use guided discovery teaching to help your children build more positive self-concepts? Give some examples.
9. What do you think are the relationships among guided, less structured, and free discovery or inquiry teaching/learning? Use diagrams, drawings, or any other visual or graphic materials.
10. In what ways might discovery science teaching contribute to *your* self-concept and why?
11. Write a brief essay to convince one of your colleagues or fellow students of the advantages of guided discovery science teaching/learning for elementary school children. Document your statements.

ENDNOTES

1. David Ausubel et al., *Educational Psychology: A Cognitive View,* Second Edition (New York: Holt, Rinehart & Winston, 1978).
2. Joseph D. Novak, "Implications for Teaching of Research on Learning," *What Research Says to the Science Teacher, Vol. 2,* Mary Budd Rowe, Editor (Washington, D.C.: National Science Teachers Association, 1979), p. 70.
3. David A. Welton and John T. Mallan, *Children and Their World: Strategies for Teaching Social Studies,* Second Edition (Hopewell, New Jersey, 1981), p. 182.
4. Robert Karplus and Herbert D. Thier, *A New Look at Elementary School Science* (Chicago: Rand McNally & Co., 1967), p. 40.
5. Jerome Bruner, "The Act of Discovery," *Harvard Educational Review* 31 (Winter 1961): pp. 21–32.
6. Barry A. Kaufman, "Psychological Implications of Discovery Learning in Science," *Science Education* 55, no. 1 (1971): p. 79. Reprinted by permission of John Wiley & Sons, Inc.
7. Lee S. Shulman, "Psychological Controversies in the Teaching of Science and Mathematics," *The Science Teacher* 35 (September 1968), pp. 34 ff.
8. Bruner, "The Act of Discovery," p. 26.
9. Shulman, "Psychological Controversies," p. 90.
10. John M. Good, John U. Forley, and Edwin Fenton, "Developing Inquiry Skills with an Experimental Social Studies Curriculum," *The Journal of Educational Research* 63, no. 1 (September 1969), p. 35.
11. T. E. Allen, "A Study of the Behaviors of Two Groups of Disruptive Children When Taught with Contrasting Strategies: Directive vs. Non-directive Teaching" (Ph.D. diss., The Florida State University, 1976).
12. Edmund Amidon and N. A. Flanders, "The Effects of Direct and Indirect Teacher Influence on Dependent-Prone Students Learning Geometry," in *Interaction Analysis: Theory, Research, and Application,* ed. Edmund Amidon and John B. Hough (Reading, Mass.: Addison-Wesley, 1967), pp. 210–16.
13. Carl Rogers, *Freedom to Learn* (Columbus, Ohio: Charles E. Merrill Publishing Co., 1969).
14. E. Gaudry and C. D. Spielberger, *Anxiety and Educational Achievement* (New York: John Wiley & Sons Australasia Pty. Ltd., 1971).
15. For an excellent chapter on the effects of various teaching strategies on learning science, you are directed to James A. Shymansky, "How Teaching

Strategies Affect Students: Implications for Teaching Science," in *What Research Says to the Science Teacher,* ed. Mary Budd Rowe (Washington, D.C.: National Science Teachers Association, 1978), pp. 31–39.

16. Chester A. Lawson et al., *Organisms (level 1) Teacher's Guide* (Chicago, Ill.: Rand McNally & Co., 1978), p. XVIII.

17. Darrell G. Phillips, "The Importance of Laboratory (Hands-On) Experience in Science in the Elementary School: A Research Prospective," in "Science Activities Are Central to Science Education in the Elementary School," Robert E. Yager et al., *Science and Children,* vol. 19, no. 2 (October 1981), p. 43.

6

How Can You Improve Your Questioning and Listening Skills?

"The use of both convergent and divergent questions by teachers obviously is called for in the learning process, but the closed question, because it is expedient and traditional, has been overused. The risks for the teacher who practices divergent question-asking should not be underestimated: an open-ended question can alter the day's schedule, spark discussions on topics the teacher may not be prepared for, and shift the teacher's role from guardian of known answers to stimulator of productive (and often surprising) thinking. But they are risks well worth taking." (Carol L. Schichter, "The Answer is in the Question," *Science and Children,* 20, no. 5 [February 1983], p. 10.)

The essence of guided discovery science teaching is *good questioning.* Teachers who practice the ideas in this chapter are more satisfied with their work. They can even modify their personal behavior, becoming less manipulative and more facilitative.

IDENTIFYING GOOD QUESTIONS

You probably know more about asking questions than you might expect. To test yourself, look at the questions in figure 6–1. Rate them according to whether you think you think they stimulate high or low levels of children's thinking. Explain *why.* Write your answers down before going on to the next part of this chapter. Now, answer several questions about the questions in figure 6–1. Write down your answers and refer to them again after you complete this chapter.

Questions for Figure 6–1

1. Which three questions are the *best* to ask? Why?
2. Which questions require the student to *evaluate* something?
3. Which questions allow only a *few* responses?
4. Which questions encourage *many* responses?
5. Which questions require the student to mainly *observe*?
6. Which questions require the students to formulate *operational definitions*?
7. Which questions require the student to mainly *classify*?
8. Which questions require the student to demonstrate *experimental* procedure?
9. Which questions require the student to *hypothesize*?
10. How would you group or *classify* most of the questions?

DIFFERENT QUESTIONS FOR DIFFERENT PURPOSES

Educators have developed classification systems for questions; here are four to help you evaluate your questions and serve as a guide.

1. convergent and divergent
2. Bloom's taxonomy
3. critical thinking
4. multiple talents

	HIGH LEVEL	LOW LEVEL

1. Which tree is taller?

2. Does the heat of the candle affect the air in the jar?

3. What do you think will happen if you add cold coffee to the water with the brine shrimp?

4. If you were going to design an experiment to show, for example, the effects of cigarette smoke on an animal or plant, what would you do?

5. How would you group these objects?

6. Can you tell which of these metals was influenced by the magnet?

7. What did you notice about how the flies in the jar behaved when half of it was covered with black paper?

8. Which of these things are metals and which are not?

9. What do you conclude from the experiment?

FIGURE 6–1

Whenever you use questions, you should evaluate them according to one or more of these four classification systems. This will improve the quality and variety of your questions significantly.

CONVERGENT AND DIVERGENT QUESTIONS

One of the simplest ways to classify questions is to determine whether they are convergent or divergent. *Convergent questions* are those that have only a few responses. They are also called *closed-ended* questions and may be thought of schematically as

Question ⎯⎯⎯ answer.

Divergent questions, on the other hand, are those that encourage a broader range of responses. They are often referred to as *open-ended* questions:

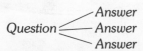

Convergent and divergent questions differ in the type of thinking they stimulate in children,

but both are legitimate and useful in science education.

Convergent Questions

In a guided discovery-oriented science program, it is generally desirable to start with very convergent questions (especially in the primary grades) and move toward more divergent ones later on. Convergent questions serve many purposes. In the pictorial riddle diagram in figure 6–2, an insect walking on water and a

Convergent Question	Purpose
What objects are in the riddle picture?	observation
Describe what is happening in dish #1.	description
Name the objects in dish #2.	observation/recall
Which dish has the insect?	observation/recall
How are dish #1 and #2 alike?	observation/ comparison
How are dish #1 and #2 different?	observation/ comparison

117

needle floating on water, the student is presented with a *discrepant* event. A discrepant event is one in which there is an inconsistency between what can reasonably be expected to happen in a given situation and what is depicted as happening.

Use convergent questions to guide the learner and to evaluate what he or she sees, knows or feels about the event.

Convergent questions help direct the learner's attention to specific objects or events. They also sharpen the student's recall or memory faculties. These questions help you evaluate students' observational and recall skills, and allow you to adjust your teaching to present ideas again, present new ideas, or go back to less complicated ideas.

Although a balance between convergent and divergent questioning is desirable, studies have shown that approximately 70–80 percent of the questions asked by teachers require only simple recall answers.[1] Convergent questions are necessary to provide children with skills and concepts to help them move to higher levels of learning, where they can benefit from divergent or open-ended questioning.

Divergent Questions

Using divergent questions will broaden and deepen your students' responses and involve them in thinking creatively and critically. Divergent questions stimulate children to become better observers and organizers of the objects and events you present. Many of these questions guide children in discovering things for themselves, help them to see interrelationships, and make hypotheses or draw conclusions from the data.

Here are some divergent questions you might ask about the two dishes in figure 6–2.

Divergent Question	*Purpose*
What things can you say about these pictures?	drawing inference
Under what conditions could this be possible?	hypothesizing
How could you go about showing the scientific principles involved in this riddle?	organizing data/ experimentation
What causes the needle and the insect to "float"?	hypothesizing
Under what conditions would both the needle and the insect sink?	hypothesizing
Set up an experiment to show the above.	organizing data/ experimentation

How much more stimulating for students to start with any of the above open-ended questions, instead of initially asking them, "Does surface tension affect how an object floats?" The latter statement asks children to guess what is in your head, while the former allows them more freedom to use their minds.

It is very important for you as a science teacher (or as a teacher of social studies, read-

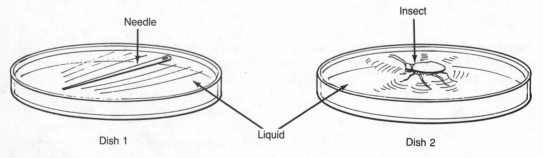

FIGURE 6–2
Pictorial riddle

ing, mathematics, or the other subjects in a self-contained elementary school curriculum) to

1. be able to identify the differences between convergent and divergent questions
2. be able to quickly write good convergent and divergent questions
3. know when it is appropriate and desirable to use both
4. become familiar and comfortable enough with both kinds of questions to increase the percentage of divergent questions you are using

Table 6–1 shows that even a *slight* increase in the percentage of divergent questions yields a *large* increase in divergent productivity by students; a larger number of students respond and their responses are deeper. The deeper responses, in turn, stimulate further discussion among the children.

Read the questions in figure 6–3 and classify them in the left margin as divergent or convergent. Then, respond to these questions about figure 6–3.

1. Which questions are the most divergent?
2. What answers are possible for these questions?
3. What words start these sentences?
4. How would you change the questions to make them more divergent?

Work on this before going on and check your answers on page 132.

Figure 6–4 analyzes a guided discovery discussion about shadows. Notice how the teacher uses a variety of questions to guide students in developing concepts and skills.

A Guide to Help You Use More Divergent Questions

To learn to write and ask better questions, here are guidelines.

1. Avoid questions that can be answered by *yes* or *no*.

TABLE 6–1
Divergent teacher questions stimulate divergent student responses

Source: Arthur Carin and Robert B. Sund, *Creative Questioning and Sensitive Listening Techniques—A Self-Concept Approach* (Columbus, Ohio: Charles E. Merrill Publishing Company, 1978), p. 215.

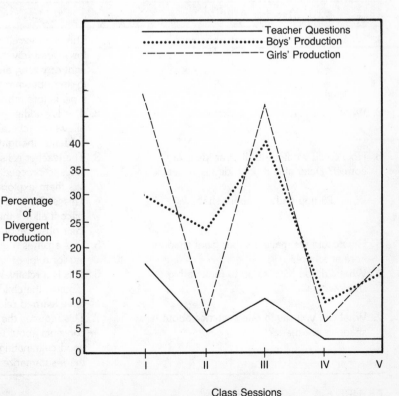

Class Sessions

Divergent/Convergent Classification of Questions	
_____ D _____	1. What do you think I am going to do with this material?
_____ D _____	2. What conclusions can you make from the data?
_____ C _____	3. Can anything else be done to improve the design?
_____ C _____	4. Is baking powder a producer of a gas?
_____ C _____	5. Do you think heat caused the plant to wilt?
_____ C _____	6. Which of these animals would you like to be and why?
_____ D _____	7. What can you tell me about pollution in this area from the photograph?
_____ C _____	8. Would you say you have sufficient information to come to that conclusion?
_____ D _____	9. What ways can you make the lights burn with the wire, switch, and battery?
_____ D _____	10. What things can you tell me about the world during the time of the dinosaurs?

FIGURE 6-3

Teacher Asks:	Analysis
1. What can you tell me about shadows?	1. This is an excellent question because it allows for several (divergent) responses. There is no right or wrong answer and the teacher is able to find out what the children know about the topic before introducing the rest of the lesson.
2. What ways can you make shadows?	2. This is another good question since it still allows for several answers while focusing the students' thoughts on the topic.
3. How could we find out if your ideas are correct? Determine if your idea is correct.	3. The teacher asks the children to consider some ways to proceed with an experiment and then lets them explore.
4. What did you find out about shadows?	4. This is also a relatively divergent question since it allows the children to share several of their observations and conclusions.
5. How could we make a super giant shadow here at school?	5. This again is a good divergent question allowing for a lot of creative input by the children.
6. What did you have to do to make a big shadow?	6. This is a relatively convergent question that requires the children to focus on what they have learned related to producing shadows.
7. What can you say in one sentence about how shadows are made?	7. This requires the children to construct mental concepts about what they have learned. It is a good culminating question because it helps them summarize their learning experiences.

FIGURE 6-4
A guided discovery discussion about shadows

2. Look at the words that start your questions because they often dictate the style of the answer.
3. Questions that begin with *do, did, are, is, can, will, would,* and *should* require a *yes* or *no* response.
4. If *yes* or *no* questions must be used, you make them more divergent by adding *Why? How do you know? How might we find out? What makes you think so? What gives you that idea?* etc. Example: *Is baking powder a producer of gas? How might I set up an experiment to test my idea?*
5. Look for questions that ask children to discover conditions that could change objects or events, such as, *What can you do to the magnets to make them stronger?* or *What ways can you make the lights burn brighter with the wire, switch, and dry cell?*
6. Ask children questions that require them to discover and compare things, e.g., *In what places do we find mold in the summer?* or *Using these objects and the bowl of water, which objects do you think will sink and float?*

There are times when convergent questions focus children's attention to specifics and therefore have a legitimate place in your science teaching. But try to use more divergent questions; you will be pleased with the resultant higher level of responses.

OTHER WAYS OF CLASSIFYING QUESTIONS USING BLOOM'S TAXONOMY

Chapter three introduced Bloom's taxonomy of educational objectives. Bloom's taxonomy may be used to focus on levels of questioning related to levels of learning. The cognitive domain objectives could be organized in questions this way, from the highest level of difficulty, *evaluation,* to the lowest, *knowledge.*

Questions requiring responses from the higher levels of the taxonomy are more desirable, especially in the upper elementary grades, because answering them involves critical and creative thinking and indicates a deeper understanding of the concepts.

Return to figure 6–1 and classify the levels of the questions after looking at Bloom's taxonomy.

Preschool and primary teachers may have difficulty getting children to respond to these higher level questions. This is, in part, due to the children's lack of experience with the topic or insufficient cognitive development. These children are functioning at Piaget's preoperational and lower concrete operational levels of development.

USING CRITICAL-THINKING PROCESSES

Another way to classify questions is by critical-thinking processes.

Do Not Stop with the Right Answer

When asking questions to stimulate critical and creative thinking, *do not stop* the discussion when you get a correct answer; to do so stops the thinking of the children. Elicit other responses. Later you can return to the right answer and discuss it. When you do return to the correct answer, tell your students that their an-

Bloom's Cognitive Domain	Possible Questions
Evaluation	How may changes in population affect life in the year 2000?
Synthesis	Develop a plan that might avoid the negative consequences of nuclear energy electric plants.
Analysis	What things do all these animals have in common?
Application	Knowing what you know about heat, how would you get a lid off a jar that won't unscrew easily?
Comprehension	Define a lens operationally.
Knowledge	How many states produce oil?

Critical-Thinking Processes	Sample Questions
1. classifying	How would you group these buttons?
2. assuming	
3. predicting, hypothesizing (making good guesses)	What do you think will happen if more salt is added to the oceans each year?
4. inferring, interpreting data, or making conclusions	What conclusions can you make from the experiment information?
5. measuring	How much has the plant grown?
6. designing an investigation to solve a problem	How would you determine the effects of pollution on curb trees in our town?
7. observing	What do you observe about these animals?
8. graphing	How would you graph your findings?
9. reducing experimental error	How many measurements should be made in order to report accurate data?
10. evaluating	If you had only one heart to transplant for five patients, which type of person would you give it to and why?
11. analyzing	Based on the things we've done with magnets, what do you think causes short circuits and fires in our electrical systems at home?

swers are good and indicate a lot of thinking. Say, however, you would like to talk about one thing they said and then continue the discussion. Saying this shows the children that you prize their thinking first and the content next.

Using Questions to Discover Multitalent

Cognitive questions are not the only important ones. You should also ask talent-oriented questions to get to know your students better. You should not only determine talents, but help to manifest them. Some examples of talent-oriented questions are listed in figure 6–5.

DON'T BE IN A HURRY FOR ANSWERS TO QUESTIONS

Mary Budd Rowe found that teachers usually wait less than a second for a response from students after asking a question! These very brief intervals result in rote, verbatim memory

FIGURE 6–5
Questioning to discover talents

Question	Questioning for
1. Who is willing to draw a mural illustrating prehistoric life?	Artistic talent
2. Who wants to help organize the field trip?	Organizing talent
3. Who will write a short article for the school paper about the science fair?	Communicating talent
4. What ways could we produce something to convey to the rest of the school how exciting this topic or subject is?	Creative talent
5. Who would like to be on the welcoming committee and welcome our guests?	Social talent
6. Who would like to be in charge of planning our investigations in the community throughout the next few weeks?	Planning talent

recall, usually of textbook or teacher-made information. Further investigations revealed, however, that some teachers waited an average of three seconds.[2] What differences in responses do you think were found in the longer wait-times? Dr. Rowe found that teachers who waited three seconds or longer obtained greater speculation, conversation, and argument than those with shorter wait-times. She also found that when teachers are trained to wait more than three seconds on the average before responding, the following occurs:

1. The length of student response increases 400–800 percent.
2. The number of unsolicited but appropriate responses increases.
3. Failure to respond decreases.
4. Confidence of children increases.
5. The number of questions asked by students increases.
6. Slow students contribute more. Increase is from 1.5–37 percent.
7. The variety of types of responses increases. There is more reacting to each other, structuring of procedures, and soliciting. Speculative thinking increases as much as 700 percent.
8. Discipline problems decrease.

Dr. Rowe also found that teachers trained to prolong wait-time changed in their classroom behavior as indicated below.[3]

1. They exhibited more flexible types of responses.
2. The number and kinds of teacher questions changed.
3. Teacher expectations for student performance were modified. They were less likely to expect only the brighter students to reply and viewed their class as having fewer academically slower students.

Wait-Time 1 and Wait-Time 2

There are two types of wait-times. *Wait-time 1* is the initial wait-time when an instructor waits for the *first* response. *Wait-time 2* is the total time a teacher waits for a class to respond to the same question. Wait-time 2 may involve several minutes, particularly if the question asked requires critical or creative thinking. Of the two, Rowe believes wait-time 2 is more important for a teacher to develop. She found a 500 to 700 percent increase in student responses when teachers used it. The responses from the poorer academic students, furthermore, increased significantly with longer wait-time 2s.[4]

Untrained teachers wait less than a second for wait-time 1. Teachers untrained in questioning techniques discriminate against slower academic students. They wait only 0.9 seconds for the slow students to reply, but wait at least 1.2 seconds for the "top five" academically talented students to answer. There is some evidence that wait-time may vary in different cultures. Rowe states, for example, that Australian teachers wait only 0.5 seconds on an average before calling on a student.[5]

Try to have a wait-time of at least 5 seconds. Teachers who practice a wait-time of at least 3 seconds are less likely to discriminate favorably toward the academically superior students because they get more student participation. Teachers who have a wait-time average of 5 seconds or more get even greater participation and more creative responses from their students.

If students are to inquire deeper into a subject, instructors need to increase their wait-time tolerance so the learners have more opportunities to think, create, and fully demonstrate their human potential.

MAKING DISCUSSION STUDENT-CENTERED

There are two general patterns of class discussion. One pattern is called the *Ping-Pong pattern*. A teacher using this approach says something, a student responds, and the teacher says something else. Class discussions follow a teacher-student-teacher pattern.

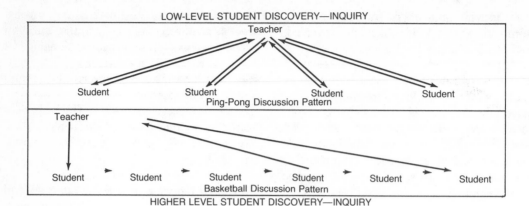

Teachers of discovery science lead discussions that are more like a *basketball-game pattern.* They say something and then there is a student-student-student-teacher-student interaction.

Teachers that direct basketball types of discussions use sufficient wait-times. When students respond, the teachers usually say nothing but look around the class to see if there are other students who might want to respond. These teachers are mainly traffic directors of the discussion. They point to whoever might speak so there is not more than one student talking at a time. They do not interject their thoughts until the students have finished their remarks. As a consequence, these teachers are more student-centered than the Ping-Pong discussion instructors.

Leading Better Guided Discovery Discussions

Do not give rewards during discovery discussions. Teachers traditionally have thought that giving positive verbal rewards facilitates class discussion. Recent research questions this procedure.[6] It indicates that rewarding students may, in fact, cause less student involvement. When teachers change their modes of response over several weeks so as not to give positive verbal rewards, the class participation begins to change. There is not only more student interaction, but a greater number of less academically able students participate. Those students, however, who are generally reward seekers may initially become somewhat disoriented. This is because they are not receiving their usual rewards. Nevertheless, after two or three weeks, they adapt to the new teacher behavior and become more autonomous.

Students apparently perceive subtle teacher behavior that suggests favoritism and a lack of fairness in the interaction process, preventing true democratic discourse. Teachers might find it helpful to make cassette tapes of their class discussions to evaluate how their expectations interfere with the discussion process. They should count how many praise words are used and determine which students receive them the most. Praise inappropriately used, particularly

125

with minority students, has been found to give them an unrealistic and distorted impression of their ability. This often causes problems when the students are advanced or try to enter college.[7]

Rewards are not always undesirable: "We all need strokes." The point of *not* giving rewards is to spark more speculative and critical thinking among your students, as well as to enable more involvement during group discussions. However, it is helpful to recognize the achievement of students during individual work or for performing well certain types of basic skills, especially if you make a point to recognize each student for specific things he or she has done well.[8]

A forceful book entitled *Try Giving Yourself Away*[9] documents the power of such recognition in changing the lives of individuals, making positive efforts to recognize and reward others for their kindness, humanism, and achievements. Teachers who try to look for good and value in every student and who inform them specifically and privately about these things are effective. They also are more likely to enjoy their teaching. This book documents how easy it is to look for something good to say to each individual, for example, when they come into class or in private discussions. Why don't more teachers make greater efforts to do this? There are even curriculum materials now that try to get teachers to do this more frequently. For example, in elementary school, writing "warm fuzzy" comments in which some psychological trait is recognized on a card for each student is a popular activity. Remember also, as Abraham Maslow, a prominent psychologist, indicated in his theory of human needs, that we all need to be recognized as valuable persons so our self-concepts continue to grow positively.

Provide halting time. *Halting time* is related to wait-time in that an instructor halts and waits for students to think, but the students do not answer questions. When teachers explain something that is relatively complex, they present some information and then stop, so students have time to see what the teachers have done and to think about it. The teachers then continue and may repeat this behavior several times. While stopping, they visually check with the class to see whether the students are with them. If they obtain positive indications that the students are following the explanation, they continue. If the students are not following, teachers may have to ask questions or retrace the work. Philosophers, when speaking, often demonstrate this technique. They make a statement, pause a few seconds for listeners to digest it, and then continue to the next point.

Avoid multiple questions. Avoid using multiple questions without giving students opportunities to respond. To ask multiple questions usually is to ignore wait-time. For example, "What causes do you think might have contributed to this situation? Which of these were important?" These questions in themselves are not bad, but when teachers run them together, they hinder the thinking processes of the children.

Avoid overreaction. Avoid overreacting to replies. For example, "That is terrific—fantastic thinking, George. Wow, what an answer!" This type of reaction may act as a constricting force because other children may think their ideas will not be so highly valued by the teacher.

Break constrictive thinking. Sometimes students become fixed on one aspect of a problem. Teachers then have to devise questions that will break the students out of their limited perceptual field. They might do this by asking the following:

> *What other factors might be contributing to . . . ?*
> *What other information are we given in this . . . ?*
> *What other interpretations are possible?*
> *What alternatives are there?*
> *What other things or ways are . . . ?*

Ask students to clarify material. A student may present a prolonged reply on material that is not easily understood by the other members of the class. The teacher may help to clarify this reply by saying

*You said it was similar. Similar in what
respect?*
*Please give an example to show where this
is occurring.*
What other examples are there?
What do you mean when you . . . ?

Guard against overgeneralizations. When
students make overgeneralizations, focus the
class's attention on these by asking questions
such as

You mean that is true for all . . . ?
*What in your investigations indicated that
this was true for all . . . ?*
*Where and under what conditions would
this be true?*

Ask students to summarize. Asking students
to summarize is particularly needed when the
concepts involved are abstract or vague, when
the student reply has been lengthy, or when
some investigations have taken a great deal of
time. The teacher might ask

*Briefly, please summarize what you have
just said.*
*Tell me in your own words what we have
learned.*
*What were the main ideas discussed
today?*
*What is the main point of what you are
saying?*

Amplify and pursue the thought. An instructor needs to act as a stimulus to keep the
discussion going. This can be done by having
students refocus, summarize, and consider alternatives, other forces, and factors that might
move the discussion to a higher level. This may
be done in the following ways

*I see you have come up with an answer.
How did you obtain it?*
*What evidence do you have that it is
correct?*
*You said that this animal behaved in this
manner. Why do you think that?*
*What effect do you think, for example,
polluting the stream will have?*

**Consider the emotional overtone of the ma-
terial.** Because of the children's backgrounds, many topics may have emotional
overtones. In discussions where this is the case,
the teacher must be particularly careful in
phrasing questions so as not to inhibit the rational responses of the children. For example,
in a class with a boy who was bitten by a snake,
it may be difficult for him not to become emotional if you ask questions about snakes.

Paraphrase what students say. Paraphrase
what the student has said when you are not
sure you understand the point, for example, "I
hear you say that. . . . Am I correct?" or when
you think other children may not have heard
the student's comment.

Use sensitive listening techniques. Krishna-
murti, an Indian philosopher, said that Americans do not truly listen. They are always judging, composing their thoughts, or preparing
salvos for reacting during the time a speaker is
discoursing. A person who truly listens in an
open, accepting, nonjudgmental way probably
is a rarity. Demonstrating poor listening skills is
undoubtedly related to how teachers perceive
their roles. If you see your function as being
mainly to develop or achieve some subject-
matter concept or principle, you naturally will
focus on its achievement. However, if you perceive your role as helping children develop,
you will tend to focus on the student as a
person first and on the content second. Listen
intently to what children have to say, and when
they have finished, and only then, formulate
questions and responses to help them make
discoveries and use their thought processes.
There can be no substitute for a teacher who is
primarily interested in people and really listens
to them.

How to Help Children Become Good Listeners

Children often do not achieve well because
they have not developed their listening abilities.
You, as a model of a good listener, can aid in
modifying this insufficiency. Listed below are

suggestions to help you improve your listening abilities. At first, you may have to use these suggestions consciously, but with time and practice, they will become a pattern of your normal conversational behavior.

Suggestions for Sensitive Listening Techniques

1. *Focus on the person and what he or she is saying.* Maintain eye contact with the speaker. Try not to evaluate what the speaker is saying until he or she has completed all statements.
2. *Do not take the discussion away from the children.* They are the ones who need to develop their minds.
3. *Give nonverbal signals* to show you are concerned and that you are listening by
   a. Eye contact
   b. Concerned posture, for example, body turned toward the child
   c. Appropriately smiling because the child is expressing himself or herself
   d. Nodding, to indicate understanding to the child
   e. Using gestures
4. *Develop silent-time.* This is similar to wait-time except that *silent-time* is time taken after a student apparently has finished speaking, before you reply. Silent-time prevents you from cutting off a child's statements and allows for others to interject their ideas without your interference. Calm silence also helps to indicate to the child and the class a trust in their abilities to think and make significant statements.
5. *Look for indicators* that children may want to say something, for example
   a. Raising their arms
   b. Rising up in their seats
   c. Eye contact with the teacher
   d. Glancing at you or the speaker with a meaningful expression
   e. Pressing their lips together like they are going to say something
   f. Mumbling
   When these signs occur, invite participation, for example, "John, is there something you would like to say?"

6. *Do not interrupt,* not even for clarificational reasons, until you are certain the child has completed his or her message.

Consider other things you need to work on to increase your listening ability. What are they? The other suggestions in this chapter should give you some help.

THE SECRET TO GOOD QUESTIONING

Asking Questions Appropriate to the Piagetian Level

As Piaget and other researchers have pointed out, there are significant differences between how primary and upper elementary children think. For this reason, in asking science questions for the elementary grades, you must adjust your questioning accordingly. Primary and lower elementary teachers should devote a great deal of attention to asking questions related to the following:

Primary and Lower Elementary

1. Observing.
2. Grouping and simple classification; for example, multiple classification, class inclusion.
3. Measuring.
4. Using number; for example, counting leaves, animals, and so on.
5. Placing objects in series or ordering them; for example, from small to large, short to tall, light to heavy, and so on.
6. Making inferences; for example, if the animals have no eyes, how is it that they don't run into things and hurt themselves?
7. Indicating time and space relations; for example, this is the same distance as this is.
8. Conserving substance, length, number, and area.
9. Reversibility.
10. Values; for example, learning to keep the environment clean.
11. Interpersonal relations; for example, learning to see things from other people's perspectives.
12. Predicting.

13. Making one-to-one correspondences; for example, for every one in this row there is one in that row.

Children in the upper elementary levels may be asked any questions related to the above areas when appropriate, plus those that follow.

Upper Elementary beyond Age 11

1. Formulating hypotheses.
2. Learning to control a variable; for example, this plant grew in the presence of light and this one did not.
3. Designing relatively sophisticated experiments.
4. Interpreting data from experiments.
5. Conservation of weight and volume.
6. Making operational definitions.
7. Constructing models (theories about natural phenomena); for example, molecules. (This probably should be limited to grades six to eight.)

In evaluating your questions, determine whether the children on the grade level you teach are cognitively able to answer them. In many cases, this may be difficult. The way to resolve this dilemma is to test your ideas in a classroom and note the children's responses; adapt your questions accordingly.

TYPES OF QUESTIONS TO USE

Listed below are examples of questions to use to get student reactions for various purposes.

General Questions to Involve Students in Investigations

1. What do you notice . . . , for example, this picture, equipment, the environment?
2. What will happen if . . . ?
3. If this is so, then . . . ?
4. This is so if and only if what? } (To be used only in upper elementary levels)

Questions to Stimulate Creative Responses

Use a Lot of "What-If" Questions:

1. What if you changed the size, shape, color of . . . ?

2. What if you added or took something away from the . . . ?
3. What if you were going to begin a better . . . what would you do?
4. What if different materials were used, what would happen?

Ask Future-Oriented Questions:

1. What will you look like in the future?
2. What things do you think will happen to our town in the future?
3. What would happen if we were to plant more trees around our school or in our park?
4. What kind of energy will you use in the future?

Use More "How-Would-You" Questions:

1. How would you design an investigation to find out about . . . ?
2. How would you, for example, improve the experiment?
3. How would you make something to . . . ?
4. How would you do it better?

Questions Inviting Students to Affirm Their Values Publicly

During the time students are in school, they develop values for life. Teachers, therefore, need to help them evolve values without imposing or moralizing. Listed below are questions to help students focus and clarify their values.

1. What valuable things have you learned today?
2. In what ways have you been successful today, this week, this year?
3. What makes you feel great about what we have been doing in science?
4. What makes you feel bad?
5. What do you think about, for example, what science does for society, pollution, or health?
6. How do you feel about this part of your work?
7. How did you come to this opinion?
8. What other conclusions could you have reached?

9. How do you think the other person sees the problem?
10. How do most people feel about that?
11. What have you done about, for example, keeping our environment clean?

Why Good Questioning Pays

Research indicates that teachers trained to ask better questions are able to construct them significantly better than those without specific training.[10] With this knowledge in mind, your task is to modify your questioning behavior, not only in teaching science but in other areas as well, to facilitate better learning and human development by your students. This is a great challenge.

SUMMARY

Basic to student-centered instruction is the teacher's ability to ask stimulating questions that facilitate creative, critical thinking and the manifestation of multiple talents. Discovery-oriented questions may be involved in all areas of teaching. Instructors may write questions before class but should remain flexible and adapt their teaching as dictated by student interaction. Before outlining questions, teachers should decide what talents, critical-thinking processes, and subject-matter objectives they hope to develop and the answers they think are appropriate.

Questions may be classified as convergent or divergent, according to Bloom's taxonomy, as critical-thinking processes, and/or by multiple talents. Divergent questions and those requiring more cognitive sophistication should be stressed. Multiple, emotionally overloaded questions and those answered by yes or no should be avoided.

The time a teacher waits for a response, called *wait-time,* is very important. Most teachers wait on an average less than one second. Five seconds' average wait-time results in more responses by slow learners, creative answers, complete sentences, questions, and suggestions for experiments.

The chapter has given suggestions for questions to involve students in investigations, stimulate creativity and clarify students' values.

Developing good listening skills will enhance your students' feelings toward you and your class. Focus on what the other person is saying. Don't interrupt or overreact. Do encourage other students to respond before you talk. Paraphrase, clarify, and draw out your students' answers.

Research indicates that teachers trained in questioning techniques change their questioning behavior in the classroom, asking more sensitive, creative, and science process questions.

Suggestions for Developing Better Questioning and Listening Skills

Several rules have been presented in this chapter.

1. Talk less but ask more.
2. Use some classification system to analyze your questions as a basis for improving them.
3. Use more divergent questions.
4. Avoid asking questions that can be answered only by yes or no.
5. Try to ask more questions that are higher on Bloom's taxonomy system.
6. Evaluate your questions for the critical-thinking processes the students require.
7. Ask more questions to discover multi-talents.
8. Do not stop the discussion with the right answer.
9. Increase wait-time 1 to at least 3 seconds.
10. Increase wait-time 2 to several minutes.
11. Lead more student-student-student basketball-type discussions.
12. Do not give rewards during a discussion.
13. Look for something good to say to individuals in private discussions.
14. Provide good halting times.
15. Avoid asking multiple questions.
16. Avoid overreaction.
17. Ask students to clarify material.
18. Guard against overgeneralizations.
19. Ask students to summarize.
20. Develop sensitive listening techniques.
21. Develop silent time.

22. Ask questions appropriate to the Piagetian level.

23. For creativity:
   a. Use a lot of "what-if" questions.
   b. Ask future-oriented questions.
   c. Use more "how-would-you" questions.

SELF-EVALUATION AND FURTHER STUDY

Evaluation Suggestions to Use in Microteaching or Teaching Students

1. Make a cassette tape recording of a pictorial riddle or discovery laboratory activity discussion you lead. Look in the index under these topics for ideas.

   Check each time you ask a question that is a convergent, yes or no type.

   Relisten to your tape and determine your average wait-time.
   Determine what you need to work on.

2. Lead a discussion where you try to get a basketball type of interaction. Evaluate how well you did. Determine by using a cassette recorder how many students you get to interact before you respond.

3. Try to improve your nonverbal indicators of sensitive listening. For example, face the person speaking, maintain better eye contact, smile more, nod your head, etc.

4. Work on getting students to listen more to each other. For example, have them paraphrase what has been said occasionally. Invite them to play "add on." (This is where one student says something about a topic and another student adds on to it with his or her ideas.)

5. Using a cassette recorder, evaluate how well you do on the suggestions listed on the preceding page in the Summary section.

Other Self-Evaluations

6. Observe or tape a conversation and classify the questions asked according to one of the four classificational systems suggested in this chapter.

7. Write some discussion questions and classify them according to Bloom's taxonomy, multiple talents, and science processes.

8. List as many words as possible that would require only yes or no answers when used as the first words of a sentence.

9. Return to the list of questions asked on page 120 and your answers and review them to see if you would like to alter any of your answers.

10. Read the booklet *Creative Questioning and Sensitive Listening Techniques—A Self-Concept Approach,* by Arthur Carin and Robert B. Sund (Charles E. Merrill Publishing Co., 1978). Prepare a list of things you need to work on to improve your questioning.

11. Lead a small discussion and have someone check your *wait-time, halting time,* and *silent-time* and how well you get students to talk to each other instead of to you.

12. Practice your listening and questioning ability on the points listed in this chapter several times in conversation. Rate yourself each time on a 1 to 5 point basis—1 being poor and 5, excellent.

ENDNOTES

1. Peter J. Belch, "The Question of Teacher's Questions," *Teaching Exceptional Children* (Winter 1975), p. 47.
2. Mary Budd Rowe, "Wait-Time and Rewards as Instructional Variables, Their Influence on Language, Logic, and Fate Control: Part One—Wait Time," *Journal of Research in Science Teaching,* 11, no. 2 (June 1974), pp. 81–94.
3. For more detailed analysis, see Mary Budd Rowe, "Wait-time and Rewards as Instructional Variables: Their Influence on Language, Logic and Fate Control" (Unpublished paper, University of Florida, Gainesville, Florida, 1972).
4. Mary Budd Rowe, "Using the Inquiry Method to Teach Basic Skills" (Address given at the National Association of Biology Teachers, Denver, Colorado, October 15, 1976).
5. Ibid.
6. Mary Budd Rowe, "Relation of Wait-Time and Rewards to the Development of Language, Logic, Fate Control: Part II Rewards," *Journal of Research in Science Teaching* 11, no. 4 (1974), pp. 291–308.
7. David L. Martin, "Your Praise Can Smother Learning," *Learning,* February 1977, p. 46.
8. Ibid., p. 48.
9. David Dunn, *Try Giving Yourself Away* (Englewood Cliffs, N.J.: Prentice-Hall, 1970).
10. Virginia M. Rogers, "Varying the Cognitive Levels of Classroom Questions in Elementary Social Studies: An Analysis of the Use of Questions by Student Teachers" (Ph.D. diss., The University of Texas, 1969). O. L. Davis, Jr. et al., *Studying the Cognitive Emphases of Teachers, Classroom Questions* (Austin, Tex.: The Research and Development Center for Teacher Education, 1969).

Answers to Convergent-Divergent Questions (Page 120)

1. Relatively divergent
2. Relatively divergent
3. Very convergent—only yes or no answer possible
4. Very convergent—only yes or no answer possible
5. Very convergent—only yes or no answer possible
6. Relatively convergent—answers possible depend on the number of animals
7. Divergent
8. Convergent—only yes or no answer possible
9. Divergent
10. Divergent

7

How Can You
Create and Give
Guided Discovery
Laboratory Lessons?

"Long periods of inactivity will kill science programs. Kids don't do anything except listen and read and read and listen. For variety, they answer questions at the end of chapters. The program is killed by lack of exercise—there are no opportunities for hands-on experiences. . . . Save your science program from atrophy by 'activating' your students. Concrete experiences are essential if students are to master scientific processes like observation, measurement, and investigation. Good elementary science programs ensure that kids are 'doing' science 40–60 percent of the time." (Kenneth R. Mechling and Donna L. Oliver, Who Is Killing Your Science Program? *Science and Children*, 21, no. 2 [October 1983], pp. 16–18.)

Previous chapters discussed the nature of science, goals and objectives of science education, how children grow and learn, and the importance of questioning in teaching children using a concrete, hands-on guided discovery approach. This chapter will look at how you can use this information to plan and conduct guided discovery lessons with your children.

TAILOR MATERIALS TO YOUR SPECIFIC CLASSROOM

There is an abundance of science resources for teaching science; in fact, there are so many that it is impossible for one person to know or use them all. Your problem will be to select and organize those things that fit your specific children, goals and objectives in science, and classroom setting. No curriculum has ever been designed that would fit all teachers or students. Therefore, you are the only one capable of selecting and supplementing the materials for your classroom. In addition, you will have to make some of the materials you need for teaching, because nothing exactly right exists.

After identifying goals and objectives for your class (either by a school-district, textbook, or commercial science curriculum), the next concern is organizing your thoughts into *teachable* lesson plans. This chapter will teach you how to write and use guided discovery science laboratory lessons. Of course, many other approaches to teaching are valid (e.g., exposition, reading about, field trips, audiovisual aids, etc.). Other chapters will show how to write and use different types of guided discovery lessons involving guided imagery, body movement, critical and creative thinking, metaphor, and so on.

It is important for you to write several lessons using the directions in this chapter. You will not learn to prepare guided discovery lessons by reading about them; actually preparing several will develop your creative potential.

SOURCES USEFUL IN WRITING AND USING SCIENCE LESSONS

If you do not have a good science background or are unfamiliar with teaching science, you may need some help to find activities and content appropriate to the interests and levels of your children. Outlined below are several sources to aid you in writing your own lessons.

For example, you may see an activity involving the effect of light on plants. Use the idea but design your own lesson using the guided discovery format, questions, and procedures. Once you are familiar with writing guided discovery lessons, you will see many opportunities for designing them from things within your own environment. Then you will be less dependent on outside resources. Here are some of the sources of ideas. See appendix B for more information on resources.

1. Elementary School Science Textbooks

Each textbook comes with a Teacher's Guide suggesting lessons to accompany the student's textbook. If these lessons are handled as *suggestions* instead of being used verbatim, they can be useful, especially to inexperienced teachers or student teachers. Harold Pratt and his associates reviewed textbooks and other published curriculum materials and categorized them in this way:[1]

Category A. (most frequently used text series: 22% primary classrooms, 40% intermediate)

☐ *Concepts in Science* (Brandwein)
☐ *Science: Understanding Your Environment* (Mallinson)
☐ *New Ludlow Science Program* (Smith)

Category B. (NSF funded programs: 8% of elementary classrooms)

☐ *Elementary Science Study*
☐ *Science Curriculum Improvement Study*
☐ *Science–A Process Approach*

Category C. ("New Generation" textbooks)

☐ *Ginn Science Program* (Atkin)
☐ *Elementary School Science* (Rockcastle)
☐ *Modular Activities Program in Science* (Berger et al.)
☐ *Elementary Science: Learning by Investigating* (ESLI)

2. Activities Presented in Various Parts of This Text

Also in Arthur A. Carin and Robert B. Sund, *Discovery Activities for Elementary Science* (Columbus, Ohio: Charles E. Merrill Publishing Co., 1980).

3. Science Textbooks for Teachers

☐ Glenn O. Blough and Julius Schwartz, *Elementary School Science and How to Teach It, sixth edition* (New York: Holt, Rinehart and Winston, 1979).
☐ Alfred DeVito and Gerald H. Krockover, *Creative Sciencing: A Practical Approach* (*vol. 1*) and *Ideas and Activities* (*vol. 2*) (Boston: Little, Brown, 1980).
☐ William K. Esler and Mary K. Esler, *Teaching Elementary Science, third edition* (Belmont, California: Wadsworth, 1981).
☐ Willard J. Jacobson and Abby Barry Bergman, *Science for Children* (Engelwood Cliffs, New Jersey: Prentice-Hall, 1980).
☐ Edward Victor, *Science for the Elementary School, fourth edition* (New York: Macmillan, 1980).

CREATING YOUR OWN LESSON PLANS

Do not let commercially prepared materials prevent you from designing your own lessons. Remember, if you use something *you* modified or made, you probably will do a much better job of teaching it than if you follow someone else's lessons. In this text there are many lessons. Never follow them like recipes. Always modify each lesson and adapt it in a way that *you* think will make it better. By so doing you will continually gain in your understanding, appreciation, and commitment for guided discovery learning. For example, an idea like using a candle for an experiment may come from some publication, but the way you design the activity using the candle is your own creativity. Keep your creative potential as a person alive, and write or modify all of the science lessons you use.

Using the Guided Discovery–Oriented Activities

Before writing discovery lessons of your own, you may wish to look over the guided discovery lessons from the major areas of science found in *Discovery Activities for Elementary Science* (Carin and Sund, 1980). If possible, teach some of them to your students. Do not use them verbatim but modify them to include your own creativity and teaching style. They are a valuable resource to use in constructing a science curriculum or for enriching a program. I know from working with thousands of teachers over the years that through giving several of these activities, in microteaching or working with children, teachers quickly learn how to teach by discovery. Once you know how to use and give guided discovery lessons of this type, it is relatively easy to construct similar lessons of your own.

WRITING AND USING GUIDED DISCOVERY LABORATORY LESSONS

Each guided discovery laboratory lesson in this text includes ten major parts, which are described below.

1. Age-Level Range or Group

To help you quickly and easily select discovery activities that are most appropriate for your group, the activities are organized by these age ranges and groups:

☐ Preschool
☐ Primary or lower elementary grades (kindergarten to third grade)
☐ Upper elementary grades (fourth to sixth grades)
☐ Middle or junior high school (sixth to eighth grades)

Grade levels are usually written as ranges because many of the guided discovery activities have been tested in *several* grades and found to work reasonably well in all of them. It depends upon how much depth you want to probe and the level at which your students are working.

Reminder: These are age *ranges* only. Because of the uniqueness of each class, only *you* can make a professional judgment about the suitability of any particular guided discovery activity and how it has to be modified to fit your class.

2. Science Topics

The broad topics of science in the guided discovery laboratory lessons in this text were recommended by Project Synthesis of the National Science Foundation in this manner:

Goal cluster III: academic preparation: Students will:

☐ Develop an understanding of information and concepts from a wide variety of topics selected from the life, earth and physical sciences. There is no set of basic topics for elementary science instruction.
☐ This variety of topics may be used to help develop the skills in generating, categorizing, quantifying and interpreting information from the environment.
☐ This variety of topics may be used for the sole reason that they are interesting to students at a particular age.[2]

Important note: No effort has been made to cover all concepts and principles embodied in an elementary science curriculum, since such a project would require an entire book for the activities alone. The guided discovery activities are organized along these three main sciences only as an aid for teachers in quickly locating a particular science topic:

☐ Living sciences
☐ Physical sciences
☐ Environmental sciences

3. Statement of Problem

The problem of each guided discovery activity is stated as a *divergent* question, for example, "What Causes the Seasons?" This helps you quickly select the *specific* area within one of the three sciences to present to your class.

4. What Do I Want Children to Discover?

The fourth question concerns the scientific principles and concepts children are to discover in doing the guided discovery activities outlined in each lesson. They are not exhaustive and others may be discovered by your students as a result of their backgrounds, your skill in guiding them, and other factors.

5. Science Processes

Scientific processes are listed at the left to show you the types of mental operations your students will be required to perform in each part of the guided discovery lesson.

6. What Will I Need?

The science supplies and equipment needed to perform the guided discovery activities are noted. Whenever possible, easily obtainable and nontechnical materials are suggested. For instance, instead of using a beaker (costly) for *nonheating* activity, a plastic tumbler may be suggested, or a pyrex baby nursing bottle may be suggested for a beaker that will be heated. Materials easily found in the immediate environment are stressed for two reasons:

☐ Most elementary schools do not have extensive science supplies or money to purchase them.

☐ It is important for children to see that the activities can be done with things easily available to *them*; hopefully, the children will replicate the activities at home. *Caution:* Please make it very clear that children should never use open flame or dangerous or unknown substances without adult supervision.

Important: Enlist your students' help in getting supplies and items needed for your guided discovery activities from *their* homes or environment. Besides saving you time, it will provide for greater involvement of the children in *their* discovery science activity.

7. What Will We Discuss?

Discussion questions are given for you to ask *before* your students start the guided discovery activities. The purpose of this section is to set the learning environment for the guided discovery activities that follow.

8. What Will Children Do?

The eighth question refers to the *pupil* discovery activities or investigations the children actively participate in, leading to their discovery of the concepts and principles listed under item 4 above.

9. How Will Children Use or Apply What They Discover?

Open-ended questions suggest to children additional investigations they might do to apply what they discover to new situations; for example, "On a cold day, why do you feel warm in the sunlight but very cold in the shade?" You should encourage students who are interested to attempt to answer these open-ended questions through further investigations. Many of the activities suggested by these questions can be done at home and need not take additional class time. These open-ended questions will also help children probe the *values* level of science as well as integrate other curricular subjects such as mathematics, social studies, and language arts.

10. What Must I Know?

Suggestions are given to you for guiding the children in their discoveries, and these things you must know to make the discoveries as meaningful as possible:

☐ *Teaching tips* to explain more complicated or involved parts of the guided discovery activity

☐ *Science content* (facts, concepts, principles, or theories) relevant to the guided discovery activity

☐ *Variables* in the guided discovery activity that can affect the outcomes, especially useful to you if "the experiment does not work"

Reminder: Some of the information in items 1 to 10 above is to be used by *you* and other parts by *your students*. Which ones are to be used and how can be determined only by *you*, the teacher. Some teachers using the guided discovery activities have duplicated these sections for children to use, mostly in the upper elementary or middle/junior high school grades:

> Statement of Problem
> What Will Children Do?
> How Will Children Use or Apply What
>   They Discover?

You have permission to reproduce those parts of the discovery activities that your students can use directly in your classroom. (*Caution:* They may *not* be further distributed or sold.) The rest of the above format you will find useful for your own background. In using it with primary grades (where a student may not read or read well enough) or in upper grades (where a student may not read well enough), you can read the appropriate sections to the students. Some teachers have even put the directions on cassette audiotapes for students to use by themselves.

The most important element in these discovery activities is for children to discover concepts through actual physical and mental participation in the activities. Do not tell the children beforehand what they should expect to find. This robs them of the joy of discovery.

A SAMPLE GUIDED DISCOVERY LABORATORY LESSON

Figure 7–1 is a sample of a guided discovery laboratory lesson. Notice that certain activities are mainly for teachers and others are essentially the concrete "hands-on and react" sections for students. Go over figure 7–1 carefully; study the format and the nature of the questions to gain a good idea of how to make your own guided discovery laboratory lessons.

How to Write Better Discovery Lessons Than You Can Buy

The following list gives the steps for creating your own laboratory activities. In following this

procedure, you will not only be able to make better lessons but also be able to modify almost any science activities and improve them. In writing your own lessons, be sure to apply what you have learned about questioning, particularly stressing those questions of a *divergent* nature.

1. Decide what concepts and/or principles you want to teach and state the problem in the form of a question.
2. In determining the grade level, indicate a *range* of grades for each lesson.
3. List the specific science content concepts and principles that are related to the problem and that you want the children to discover.
4. Leave space for a list of materials but do not fill in this section until you have completed writing the activity section.
5. Write questions that will set the stage of the lesson.
6. Consult science source books, science curriculums, or elementary science texts or look around you for ideas to use. This part of the lesson is given to the children in writing if they are able to read or orally if they cannot.
   a. Design the activities so the children will be involved in hands-on activities and science processes.
   b. After roughly outlining the activity, write the first step of the activity sheet, in which you tell the students to *collect the material* they will need.
   c. Ask how they would use the equipment to find an answer to the problem.
   d. Write a question asking what they think will happen if a certain procedure of investigation is used.
   e. Tell the children to perform the procedure and observe what happens to test their hypotheses.
   f. Ask the children to record what they observe. Strive to have them use mathematics in measuring and graphing where possible.
   g. Ask them to interpret or make inferences about the data they collected.

7. Reread your statements and compare them with these thinking processes: comparing, summarizing, criticizing, assuming, imagining, making decisions (evaluation of what to do), and applying. (See chapter 6.) List one of these appropriate processes in the left margin by each of the questions you have asked. *Compare your lesson* with the *list of processes* and determine how it can be modified to *include more processes.* Comparing your lesson questions with the critical-thinking science processes, described in chapter 1 on page 9, further assists you in evaluating how sophisticated it is and what it requires students to do cognitively. (Review the Piagetian operations described on pages 33–34 in chapter 2.)
8. Ask divergent open-ended questions to determine how children can use and apply what they discovered.
9. Finish listing the material you will need for the lesson.
10. Include any source content you need to know.

GETTING IDEAS FOR EXPERIMENTS

How to Write Open-Ended Questions

Experimental factors or variables. As pointed out above, in any experimental situation, there are variables or factors being tested. The question, "What effect does water have on the sprouting of seeds?" is asking: What does the factor or variable—water—have to do with the sprouting of seeds?

Look at the problem of sprouting seeds again and think of three open-ended questions that suggest further investigation. You should have little difficulty in doing this. All you have to do is think for a minute what might influence the sprouting of seeds. You may think of factors such as light, temperature, pH (acidity), and seed population (the number of seeds pre-

FIGURE 7-1

METEOROLOGY—WEATHER

WHAT IS A BAROMETER? (K–6)

What Do I Want Children to Discover?
Air Exerts Pressure.
Air Pressure Changes.
Air pressure may indicate the type of weather.
Low air pressure usually indicates rainy or cloudy weather.
High air pressure usually indicates fair weather.

What Will I Need?
Coffee can with plastic snap top
Large balloon
Straw
Glue
Straight pin
Card

What Will We Discuss?
Have each child blow up a balloon and ask:
What is in the balloon?
How do you know there is pressure exerted in the balloon?
How can you discover whether or not air has the same pressure at all times and at all places?
What is a barometer?
What is it used for?
How might location affect the readings of the barometer?

What Must I Know?
The room temperature will affect the barometer the children will make in this activity. It does not, therefore, only measure air pressure differences. It might be desirable to have some students keep their barometers outside class and compare their readings with those in class.

PROCESSES

What Will Children Do?

1. Obtain a coffee can with a plastic snap top, straw, glue, straight pin, and a card.
2. Cover the coffee can with the plastic snap top making certain the can is sealed completely.
3. Place a small amount of glue in the center of the drum and attach a straw as shown in the diagram. Place another drop of glue on the end of the straw and attach the pin.
4. Mark a card with some lines that are the same distance apart. Tack it on the wall as shown in the diagram.

Hypothesizing/ Inferring
What will happen to the plastic snap top if the air pressure on it increases?

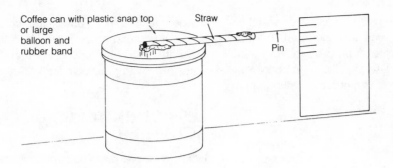

Coffee can with plastic snap top or large balloon and rubber band

Straw

Pin

Hypothesizing/ Inferring	What will happen to the plastic snap top if the air pressure decreases?
What Must I Know?	When air pressure increases, it pushes down on the plastic snap top, causing the straw to give a high reading. When the air pressure is low, the opposite will happen. A falling barometer may indicate that a storm is approaching.
	5. Record the readings of the barometer three times a day for a week.
Comparing	How do the readings of the barometer differ during the day?
Comparing	How do the readings differ from day to day?
Inferring	What causes the readings to vary?
	6. Record the type of weather existing at the time the barometer readings were made.
Inferring	What kind of air pressure exists during fair weather?
Inferring	What kind of air pressure exists during stormy weather?
	7. Compare the readings of barometers in different locations.
Inferring	What reasons can you give for the readings?
Applying	By using the readings of the barometer, predict what the weather will be.
How Will Children Use or Apply What They Discover?	**1.** Does air travel from an area of high pressure to an area of low pressure or from an area of low pressure to an area of high pressure? Why?
	2. What would you do to improve the barometer?
	3. What other materials could you use to make a barometer?
What Must I Know?	If you do not get *any* reading (change of straw moving up or down) after a few days, you may do one of the following.
	1. Seal the snap lid by pouring glue around can top where lid touches can or
	2. Cut stem off large balloon, stretch across can top, and tie securely with string or glue.
	You must seal snap top or balloon so no air enters or leaves can.

sent). Some examples of factors or variables that may be involved in experimental conditions are listed below. You probably will think of many others. Use this list or prepare one yourself to help you as a guide in writing open-ended questions:

☐ Temperature
☐ Light
☐ Sound
☐ Water or humidity
☐ Food or presence of minerals
☐ pH—alkalinity or acidity
☐ Air or other gases or lack of them (space flight conditioning)
☐ Pressure
☐ Type of motion
☐ Fields—gravitational, magnetic, electrical
☐ Friction
☐ Force
☐ Population density

Qualitative questions. Several of the factors or variables listed here may vary in *qualitative* ways. For example, a child may have done an activity to find out whether light is needed for photosynthesis in leaves. The child does not know, however, whether *all* wave lengths of light are necessary. The teacher may then ask the following *qualitative* questions about light in the open-ended questions section of the lesson:

> What colors of light do you think are necessary for photosynthesis to take place?
> How will different colors of light speed up or slow down photosynthesis?

The children may then cover plants with different colored cellophane to find answers to these questions.

Quantitative metrical questions. All of the factors in this list may also involve *quantitative* questions. For example, "How much light is necessary for photosynthesis to take place?" "How do different intensities of light affect photosynthesis?"

Look at the list of factors again and design qualitative and quantitative questions for the various factors that affect the sprouting of seeds. If you can accomplish this task, you will have little difficulty writing open-ended questions to go with your own laboratory exercises.

LESS STRUCTURED DISCOVERY ACTIVITIES

Less structured discovery science activities are to a higher degree *exploratory* lessons where children are encouraged to find out through their own ingenuity as much as possible about some phenomenon. The teacher may provide the problem and materials and then allow a lot of time and freedom for the children to "mess around." For example, she may give the children many different things that roll on inclined planes or ask them to observe as many things as possible. She may also provide metric sticks, hand lenses, flashlights, lemon juice, forceps, and jars to serve as aquaria for the students to use in studying organisms. After allowing the children to investigate for some time, the teacher will collect the animals or equipment and discuss what was discovered. This activity may be followed by more structured assignments, such as writing and reading about their discoveries or doing experiments related to them.

Less structured, hands-on discovery experiences with physical objects are particularly important for preschool and primary children in order for them to develop physical and logical knowledge such as the realization that things can be classified, conserved, and ordered in different ways. However, less structured lessons have relevance for *all* grades. The sophistication of student involvement, is largely dependent on experience, cognitive development, and motivations of the children. Examples of these lessons are shown in figures 7–2 and 7–3.

Providing for Greater Student Autonomy

The purpose of less structured discovery activities is not merely to teach science concepts.

FIGURE 7–2
Less structured discovery activity

WHAT DO FEATHERS DO? (GRADES K–4)

Materials

Bring several different feathers into class. Give them to the students; also provide trays of water.

Opening Questions

What can you find out about these feathers?
What can you do with feathers?

Allow a lot of time for the children to "mess around" with the feathers. Later ask questions such as
What did you find out about your feathers?
What did you do with them?
What do they do?
How do they do it?
How do they vary in shape?
In what other ways are they different?
Which feathers would be the best to have for flying? Why?
Which would be the best to keep a bird warm? Why?
Which would act as a raincoat?
How could we make a wing from feathers?

Some Possible Activities

You might suggest, if the students don't think of it themselves, what would happen if they poured water over wing feathers. Do the same with the down feathers and note what happens.

You might also bring to class a down-filled parka or gloves and let the children place their hands inside to feel how warm they become. Invite the children to drop various types of feathers and note how they float and how lightweight they are. Discuss how birds need strong wings but how they must be lightweight so they don't have to work so hard in flying. Set up a place in your room where children can pin feathers they collect. Talk about how Indians (Native Americans) used feathers. Talk about how the children's grandparents or great-grandparents used feathers.

FIGURE 7-3
Less structured discovery activity

PHYSICAL ACTIVITIES

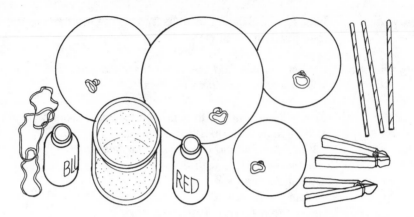

WHAT CAN YOU DISCOVER ABOUT BALLOONS?

Materials

Balloons of different sizes, clothespins, water, food coloring, small funnels, rubber bands, straws

Opening Questions

How could you use these balloons with each other?
How can you keep air in a balloon?
How well will a clothespin keep air in a balloon?
How could you use a straw to let air out of a balloon?
What have you found out about balloons?

Later ask:
How could we have a balloon race?

Some Possible Activities

Fill the balloons with water. Blow up the balloons. Twist them to make different shapes. Have a balloon race by letting the air expand from the tail. See which ones go the farthest. See how well a clothespin will keep air in the balloon by clamping the open end of it closed. See if it keeps the air in more or less time as the air in the balloon is varied. Hold the balloon closed. Put a straw in the end of the opening of the balloon. Wrap a rubber band around the balloon and straw. Let the air escape from the straw to see what will happen to the balloon. Rub a balloon against your leg and see if it will stick to a wall or ceiling.

More importantly, such activities provide experiences where children can work alone or in groups to gain physical, social, and logical mathematical knowledge. They are designed to allow children a great deal of *autonomy* so they may become more self-directive and creative persons. Piaget believes that children construct knowledge only through their own physical and mental actions on objects. The purpose of less structured discovery activities is not necessarily to advance students from one cognitive level to another. However, the activities undoubtedly will contribute to this to some extent. Their main objective, however, is to have children, on their individual cognitive levels, learn to generate questions and solve problems relative to objects without the teacher imposing objectives and directions. If teachers always *tell* children what to do, the children never learn to be responsible for their own learning, nor do they develop well their own creativity and social competence.

Less structured activities often focus the child on performing various types of *actions* on objects: pushing, sliding, rolling, floating, swinging, dropping, attaching-gluing-clipping, listening to sounds, mashing, and stirring. The role of the teacher is to present the materials to the child and ask divergent questions, for example, "What can you do or make with these objects?" and then allow a lot of time for the child to investigate. Teachers should withdraw and only interject with questions when they see the children are losing interest. When they do ask a question, they might have the children focus on some action. For example, "What do you think would happen *if you* were to (state some action here) mash it, place it in water, and so on?"

Look over the lessons illustrated in figures 7–2 and 7–3 once more and create some activities of your own. All you need to do is collect some objects, for example, clothespins, cloth, juice cans, toothpicks, rubber bands, and think of different *actions* the children might perform using these things.

Criteria for Selecting Observational Experiences

Dr. Constance Kamii and Rheta De Vries, specialists in using this approach, especially for

helping young children develop their own physical knowledge, suggested that the following criteria for selecting observational experiences must be met.

1. The child must be able to produce the movement by his or her own action.
2. The child must be able to vary the action.
3. The reaction of the object must be observable.
4. The reaction of the object must be immediate.[3]

Some movements of objects fascinate children and others do not. The reason this difference occurs can be, at least, partially explained in how well they meet Kamii's criteria. Although Kamii applies these criteria only to preschool children, they nonetheless appear to have relevance for other levels as well. For example, witness the acceptance of Pac Man, Astroids, Space Wars, and other video games that can be played on television sets—games that adults also enjoy playing. How well do they meet the above criteria? If physical knowledge activities should relate, not to observation of objects in their static state, but involve *active* transformation, do electronic games allow for this? For a fuller explanation of electronic and/or computer-assisted instruction, see chapter 13.

THE SHORT DISCOVERY LEARNING CYCLE FORMAT

The less structured discovery approach has been used with some modification in several curriculums. It is often incorporated into a generalized format called the *learning cycle* and usually includes the following general components.

1. *Exploration.* Children are involved in hands-on activities where they observe and study some phenomenon.
2. *Invention or concept development.* The teacher may use demonstrations, written materials, or discussion to develop through questioning the discovery of some science concepts or principles related to the material used in the exploratory phase. Terms may be introduced by the teacher, for example, predator, for the concepts the students have developed.
3. *Discovery application, or using what you learn.* The students are involved in applying what they discovered in the concept-development phase.

The learning cycle approach contains many aspects of a structured science lesson such as objectives, but usually they are not spelled out. This format is good for all grades but especially useful for the preschool and primary grades.

The learning cycle method has been supported as being Piagetian in design by Robert Karplus, Anton E. Lawson, John W. Renner, and many other science educators. It is the design that Dr. Karplus followed in producing the SCIS program. Dr. Renner has also used it for an elementary science series.

The learning cycle approach is essentially the same process that Piaget calls the *active method.* It helps students become actively involved and responsible for their own learning. In the exploration phase, they are invited to investigate spontaneously their own interests and to be relatively autonomous in their activity. This is followed by class discussion. Piaget says the active method "presupposes working in common, alternating between individual work and work in groups."[4]

Select some action-oriented activity as suggested above and think how *you* would incorporate it into a learning cycle format. You might like to look at SCIS materials (see chapter 9 and appendix B for information and sources) to see how they have done this in their curriculum.

It should be obvious that less structured lessons are more likely to be investigative than experimental since they may have no control or variables. The justification for giving investigative lessons of this nature is that children must learn about and have multiple hands-on experiences with physical phenomena first, so they can design and carry out experiments later. They must also advance to certain levels of cognitive thought before they are capable of designing investigations in a rational and purposeful manner.

Suggestions for organizing and conducting guided discovery laboratory lessons are presented in chapter 8 on managing the science classroom.

SUMMARY

The discovery approach involves children in learning through laboratory experiences. A large number of resources help teachers use this approach. However, the teachers still need to know how to construct discovery activities of their own. Such personally developed activities may be more appropriate for the class than the ones commercially available.

Laboratory investigations vary in how experimental they are in the structure they provide for the student. Teachers who follow the guided discovery lesson-planning formats included in this chapter learn to write good guided discovery lessons. They also learn the components of a science curriculum. It is important in writing guided discovery lessons that particular attention be given to the critical-thinking, Piagetian operations, and science processes. After writing a lesson, these processes should be identified. If the lesson does not appear to require enough thinking, the list of the processes should be consulted for ideas of other thinking types of questions and activities that might be included.

Prospective and experienced teachers often say they have difficulty originating ideas for experiments. A number of resource books can be used to get ideas for lessons. Teachers can also learn to identify factors or actions that might affect an object or organism. After doing this, an activity may be designed to invite children to test what will happen in an experimental situation if some factor is changed. For example, one factor influencing plants is the amount of light that is present. A guided discovery lesson can be designed to determine the effect of light on plants.

Once an instructor has learned well how to construct guided discovery laboratory lessons, she should feel confident to write less structured ones because she knows the nature of the discovery process. Less guided discovery lessons may be organized around a learning cycle approach where children explore some phenomenon and then develop and later learn to apply science concepts.

SELF-EVALUATION AND FURTHER STUDY

1. Write several guided discovery lessons, being sure to evaluate them on the basis of the thinking process that will be involved in doing them. Have other students and/or teachers read your lessons and suggest improvements, especially in the types of questions you ask.
2. Explain how using the list of thinking processes or factors presented in this chapter helped you become more creative.
3. Teach, and tape on a cassette recorder, one of your lessons to a group of four or five students in your class. Listen to your tape and evaluate your questioning for divergency, wait-time, whether you get student-student-student or student-teacher-student interaction, and so on.
4. Prepare some unguided discovery activities.
5. Prepare a learning cycle lesson.
6. Design an action-centered, less structured activity. Explain how it fulfills the criteria for an activity of this type.
7. The following terms are used almost interchangeably by some teachers. Define each one in your own words and indicate any differences that might exist.

a. Experiment
b. Observational, classificational, and experimental investigations
c. Structured discovery lesson
d. Learning cycle
e. Less structured lessons

8. What is the justification for the statement "We believe you can write better laboratory lessons than you can buy if you follow the procedures presented in this chapter on how to write a discovery laboratory lesson"?

ENDNOTES

1. Harold Pratt et al., "Science Education in the Elementary School," from *What Research Says to the Science Teacher, vol. 3*, Norris C. Harms and Robert E. Yager, editors (Washington, D.C.: National Science Teachers Association, 1981), p. 79.
2. Ibid., p. 76.
3. If you are interested in the preschool to primary level, we suggest you read Dr. Constance Kamii and Rheta De Vries, *Physical Knowledge in Preschool Education—Implications of Piaget's Theory* (Englewood Cliffs, N.J.: Prentice-Hall, 1978).
4. Jean Piaget, *To Understand Is to Invent* (New York: The Viking Press, 1974), p. 108. For more information on the learning cycle, see the SCIS Teacher's Handbooks and Robert Karplus, "Education and Formal Thought—A Modest Proposal" (Paper presented at the Eighth Annual Symposium of the Jean Piaget Society, Philadelphia, Pennsylvania, May 18–20, 1978). Available from the author, Lawrence Hall of Science, University of California, Berkeley, California 94720.

8

How Can You Arrange and Manage an Activity-Based Guided Discovery Science Classroom?

"The biggest stumbling block to the success of laboratory science has been teachers' fear of working in unstructured, disorganized, undisciplined, noisy, chaotic classrooms. Hands-on science may, at times, appear unstructured, noisy, and even chaotic, but it is well-designed chaos. Organization and classroom management are the keys to success. . . . Effective activity-based programs combine stimulating environment with skillful management to make children active learners." (Johanna Strange and Stephen A. Henderson, "Classroom Management," *Science and Children*, 19, no. 3 [November/December 1981], pp. 46–47.)

In this chapter, you will move from a more theoretical understanding of guided discovery science to a more practical one. You will learn how to organize your classroom for optimal student achievement, promote student interaction, and create an environment in which students will be able to do science.

ORGANIZING THE CLASSROOM ENVIRONMENT FOR OPTIMAL LEARNING

Your self-contained elementary classroom must encompass the entire elementary curriculum of math, social studies, reading and language arts, music, art, and other fields. Therefore, the physical arrangement of facilities, equipment, supplies, and other teaching materials must be flexible, and, in most cases, serve more than one purpose or subject area. Guided discovery science teaching necessitates these science areas in your self-contained classroom.

1. activity area
2. temporary or portable science areas
3. material storage areas
4. equipment storage areas
5. student work storage
6. small item storage, e.g., shoe boxes
7. space and suitable containers for living things
8. discovery learning centers
9. research and reading materials center
10. total class teaching area-teacher directed learning
11. audiovisual equipment area

Figure 8–1 shows a self-contained classroom for the primary grades with the science areas listed above. Figure 8–2 shows how classroom space can be organized to fit the needs of older, more mature students in the middle or upper elementary, or middle school. Note the

☐ provision for total class or large group teacher-directed learning
☐ skills reinforcement areas
☐ student choice areas, e.g., art, library, individual activities
☐ subject matter centers—science, social studies, math, etc.
☐ "special" areas, e.g., listening area, manipulative
☐ way the classroom appeals to students' interests

150

☐ areas are flexible and can change as needs change
☐ way each area serves learning needs

The next sections discuss some of the specific areas.

Science Activity Area

Your elementary school classroom probably contains movable furniture. In figure 8–1, the center of the room houses the movable desks, tables, and chairs. The wall space areas provide opportunities for more stationary science equipment and facilities. Science facilities should be grouped as much as possible in one general area of your room. The science equipment, supplies, and other materials you need should be readily available for making, assembling, experimenting, and demonstrating.

For active pupil participation in the discovery science program, you must supply adequate space for all children to work. Even if your classroom is small and crowded, the experiments, demonstrations, construction, and other *active* parts of your science program can still be performed. For instance, space next to and beneath window sills and counter tops can be used for work areas.

If your classroom has flattop desks, you can move them together to make larger work areas. You will find it helpful to get at least one large table in your classroom for doing discovery science activities. Try to get tables that are water- and acid-resistant. Otherwise, use Masonite or laminated plastic such as Formica to cover your desks and tables. If burners will be used, the best tops are stone or composition stone. If you do not have permanent science work areas, you can cover desks and tables with (or use pads of) tempered Masonite. An excellent temporary work area can be made by putting boards or plywood across two wooden

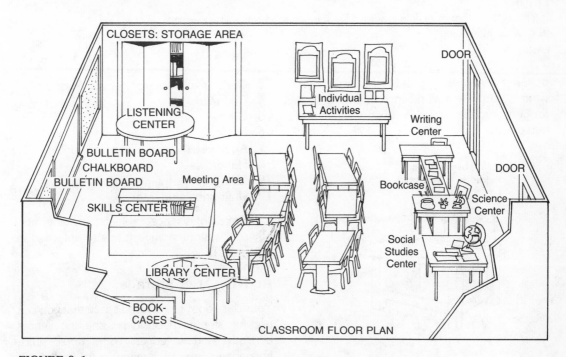

FIGURE 8–1
Primary grades self-contained classroom stressing active involvement of children

The author is indebted to the following for an excellent discussion of how to use the classroom: Johanna Kasin Lemlech, *Classroom Management* (New York: Harper and Row, 1979).

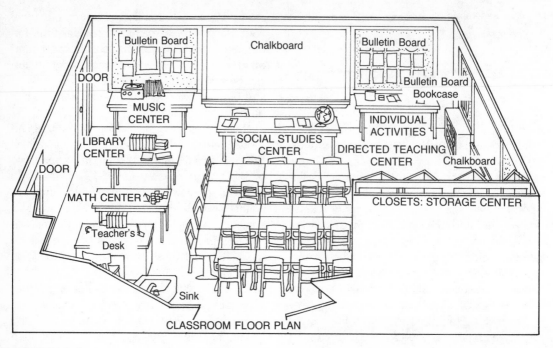

FIGURE 8-2
Intermediate, upper or middle grades classroom stressing active involvement
of children in learning

Lemlech, ibid.

boxes or sawhorses. If possible, you might also want to purchase a workbench and hand tools for your students to use in constructing simple equipment.

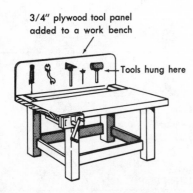

When you plan your work areas, you should also plan for storage of certain equipment and materials.

1. Science supplies
2. Science apparatus and equipment
3. Consumable science items
4. Chemicals
5. Charts
6. Models
7. Audiovisual equipment and supplies
8. Handtools
9. Living things (plants and animals)
10. Unfinished student work

Sources of science cabinets, shelving, and other laboratory storage furniture are listed in appendix D.

Activity Area Storage

Your classroom has unused space that you can use for storage. Consider using the spaces beneath window ledges, countertops, sinks, above and around heating units (radiators), and even under student desks.

You can purchase excellent commercially made cabinets that fit any of these spaces, or your students and/or your custodian and you can construct them. With some creativity, you and your children can arrange these cabinets in a variety of ways.

Small Item Storage: Using Shoe Boxes

With a guided discovery activities science program, you will constantly need to store many small items. Shoe, corrugated cardboard, cigar, and other small boxes provide space for collecting, organizing, and storing small, readily available materials for particular science areas. Figure 8–3 illustrates how to use shoe boxes and cheese boxes for small item storage. Eventually, your shoe box collections can be organized as shown in figure 8–4. You may also use larger cardboard boxes for storage and place them in easily obtained steel shelving especially designed for this purpose.

Storage for Living Things

You should encourage children to bring animals and plants into your classroom. The well-prepared teacher always has the following containers available.

☐ Insect cages
☐ Small animal cages
☐ Aquariums
☐ Terrariums

Insect cages. Use small cake pans, coffee can lids, or covers from ice cream cartons for the cover and base. Roll wire screening into a cylinder to fit the base and lace the screening together with a strand of wire.

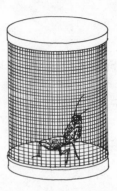

Insect cage with wire screening

You can cut windows in a paper coffee container, oatmeal box, shoe box, or another suitable cardboard container. Cut out the windows and glue plastic wrap, cellophane, silk, a nylon stocking or some other thin cloth over them.

Another home for insects such as ants that live in the soil can be made by filling a wide-mouthed quart or gallon pickle or mayonnaise jar with soil up to two inches from the top.

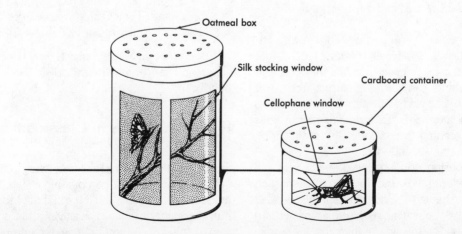

Insect containers with windows

SHOE BOX COLLECTION

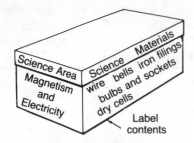

Label contents

CHEESE BOX COLLECTION

Cheese boxes in
2-lb. and 5-lb. sizes or shoe boxes
stacked in groups or
made into drawers. Pot
cover and screw serve
as knobs.

FIGURE 8–3
Using shoe and cheese boxes for small item storage

Cover the jar with a nylon stocking and place it in a pan of water. Put the insects in and cover the jar with black construction paper to simulate the darkness of being underground.

Animal cages. You can use some of the insect containers for small animals, too. Larger animals can be housed in cages that you and your students can easily construct from wire screening. Cut and fold the wire screening as shown in figure 8–5. Tack or staple three sides of the screening to a wooden base and hook the other side for a door.

For housing *nongnawing animals,* you will need a wooden box and sleeping material such as wood shavings. *Gnawing animals* need a wire cage. A bottle with a one-hole stopper and tubing hung on the side of the cage will supply

water. Before proceeding, consult publications such as *Science and Children* and read some of the articles on the care and maintenance of various animals.

Terrariums. The word *terrarium* means "little world." In setting up a terrarium for any animal, you should try to duplicate in miniature the environment in which the animal originally lived. You can make a terrarium with six pieces of glass (four sides, top, and bottom) taped together. One side of the top should be left open as a lid. Place the finished glass terrarium in a large cookie or cake pan. Commercially made terrariums are also available.

Another simple terrarium can be made by each student from a two-liter, plastic soda pop bottle, charcoal, pebbles, topsoil, small plants, and scissors (see figure 8–6).

Suggestions for caring for plants and animals and for setting up different kinds of terrariums can be obtained from

☐ Biological Supply House, Inc., 8200 South Hoyne Avenue, Chicago, Illinois 60620. *Free* by writing on school stationery for Turtox Service Leaflets, especially: No. 10—*The School Terrarium and No. 25— Feeding Aquarium and Terrarium Animals.*

☐ National Science Teachers Association, 1742 Connecticut Avenue, N. W., Washington, D. C. 20009. Send 25¢ for How to Do It Pamphlets, especially: *How to Care for Living Things in the Classroom,* by Grace K. Pratt (Stock No. 471—14288).

Food and other requirements for a variety of water and land animals are presented in appendix I.

Keeping Animals in Classroom for 24 Hours

There are times when children bring animals into your classroom for an overnight stay. Here are some directions to help the children adopt a humane attitude toward the living things they are observing. Although it is recommended

STORAGE OF SHOE BOX COLLECTIONS

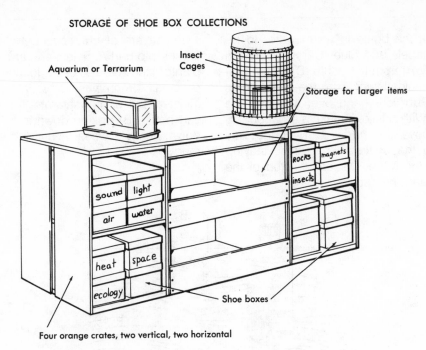

FIGURE 8-4
Construction and storage of shoe box collections

that animals be studied and not removed from their natural habitat, children's curiosity occasionally motivates them to remove them. John J. Dommers of the Humane Society of the United States recommends we adopt the "24 Hour Rule" to serve the best interests of the animals and children:

Small animals, such as insects, turtles, frogs and salamanders, may be kept for a period not exceeding 24 hours, if the habitat in which they were found is simulated as closely as possible in captivity. Children should not handle but observe the animals. They should research information about identification, characteristics, feeding habits, value, etc. The animals should

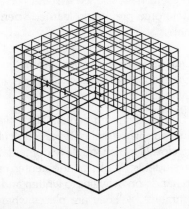

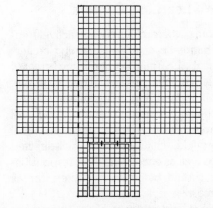

FIGURE 8-5
Constructing a wire cage

Soak the bottle in warm water to remove labels and glue. Carefully pry the bottom (A) from the bottle (B) so the bottom remains intact. Turn the bottle on its side. Rub your hand over it to find the ridge. With scissors, make a slit about 1.5 cm above the ridge. Cut all the way around the bottle at that level, staying above the ridge. Discard the top of the bottle and the cap.

Put layers of charcoal, pebbles, and topsoil into part A. Select and arrange the plants in the soil. You can add moss, bark, or small ornaments to your terrarium. Moisten, but do not saturate, the soil. Invert bottle (B) upside down into A. Push down gently to seal. Your terrarium is ready!

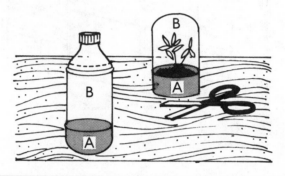

FIGURE 8-6
Constructing a terrarium

Source: Virginia Gilmore, "Helpful Hints—Coca-Cola® Bottle Terrarium." Reproduced with permission by *Science and Children* 16, no. 7 (April 1979):47. Copyright 1979 by the National Science Teachers Association, 1742 Connecticut Avenue, N.W., Washington, D. C. 20009.

then be released, unharmed, in the same area they were found so they can carry on their environmental activities.

Discovery Learning Centers

In classrooms where children are actively engaged in hands-on activities, learning centers are essential. Learning centers are created and directed by the teacher. They motivate, support, guide, and reinforce children's learning. By having learning centers, you will have broader opportunities to meet individual needs, provide children with self-directed learning, as well as encourage their responsibility. There should be learning centers for all content areas.

Set aside at least one area of your classroom as a "discovery science learning center." This center should contain collections, direction or task sheets, activities, and materials that do these things.

1. Present new science materials
2. Reinforce previously learned science materials
3. Develop a scientific skill
4. Drill on specific science information
5. Develop other science interests and creativity.[1]

"Science learning centers allow teachers to design supplemental science curricula which more closely match the developmental levels of their students. Tasks at the center can range from hands-on activities to written and research assignments."[2] They are places where one or more students may work apart from your regular ongoing science activities. Children are free to explore, discover, experiment, or just plain tinker.

Figure 8–7 is a view of a typical upper elementary school classroom using learning centers. The different learning centers are separated by dividers such as movable screens, workbenches, display or bulletin board space, bookcases, planters, and tables or shelves. There should be enough tables, chairs, and appropriate, easily obtainable materials for your children.

Construction of a Learning Center[3]

Building a center is relatively easy. Back panels made of colored tagboard cut to about 45 cm square will stand up and store with excellent stability. Three panel (tri-fold) centers stand up best.

1. To construct a tri-fold, obtain three pieces of sturdy cardboard, three pieces of colored tagboard, duct tape in different colors, rubber cement, plastic laminating film, stick-on letters for titles, plus whatever pictures and instructions you plan to include.
2. Lay the three cardboard pieces next to each other, leaving about 5 millimeters (mm) separation between boards. (See illustration.) Apply the duct tape over the separation or place the duct tape, sticky side up, on the table and lay the cardboard onto the tape. Cover the sticky part of the duct tape with another strip of duct tape. This reinforces the joint. The small gap between boards allows the center to fold easily without crushing the cardboard. Cover the sticky part of the duct tape (in the groove between boards) with masking tape or transparent tape to prevent it from sticking together.
3. Next use rubber cement to glue all needed information on the colored tagboard. Information includes titles, directions, examples, factual information, pictures, and activities to be completed by students. Laminate the tagboard. The lamination makes these parts more durable. You might like to cover and laminate any containers to be used in a matching color.
4. Finally, rubber cement the tagboard to the cardboard. Since the rubber cement may dry out in a year or so, cover the edges of the board with colored duct tape. Laminate all activity cards or game pieces or they will quickly show wear and tear by students. Your center is ready for enthusiastic students to pursue important science learning.

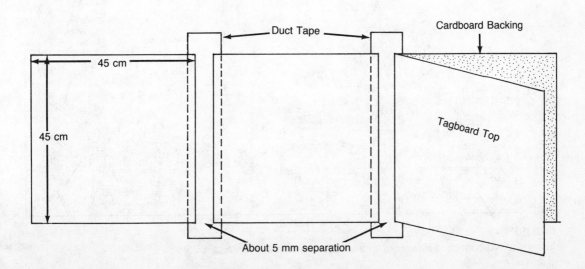

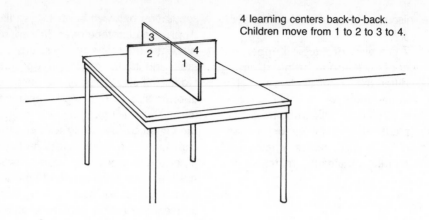

4 learning centers back-to-back.
Children move from 1 to 2 to 3 to 4.

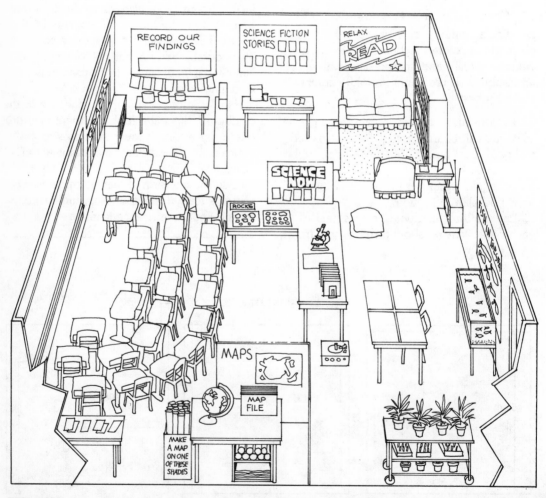

FIGURE 8–7
Integrated self-contained classroom with a variety of learning centers for 25-35 children.

Types of Science Learning Centers

There are many types of science learning centers, including (1) directed discovery science learning, (2) science processes, and (3) open learning centers.[4]

The *directed discovery* learning center is set up to focus on specific science concepts. For this type of center, place materials in shoe boxes with a series of guiding discovery questions, such as, "Using the materials in this box, show that light appears to travel in a straight line." Directed learning centers may be set up with one theme or separate problems.

Another kind of learning center focuses on developing *science processes* such as observing, predicting, and measuring. Using collections of materials and discovery guidance questions, you could ask your children to measure the items in this box in both metric and standard measurements.

The last and most creative type of center is an *open learning* center. You supply many random materials, not according to any one theme or science area. Use minimum direction for your class; for example, "Invent something with the materials in this box."

All three types of learning centers should be based on the following format for planning a learning center. Here is a summary of these important learning center guidelines.

> Learning center objectives should be stated so that they describe what pupils are to learn, how they are to learn, how pupils will know they have learned it—how they will be evaluated.[5]

Format for Planning Your Learning Centers

State purpose. The purpose of a learning center should be clear, both to the teacher and student and stated as a part of the center; e.g., "At this center you will examine some seeds. You will compare sizes, weights, volumes, and shapes of the seeds."

Consider student levels. The center must be appropriate for the students who will be using it. The backgrounds and experiences, the cog-nitive level of operation, the socio-economic level, the maturity level and level of independence, and the psychomotor level must be defined and used as the basis for planning the activities and expected learning outcomes from the center.

Define concepts and skills to be developed. A clear statement of the concepts, sub-concepts, and skills to be developed by the students using the center is necessary if the center is to be a true teaching/learning situation. If these criteria are not met, centers break down into "busy work."

Outline expected learning outcomes. These statements can be in the form of performance, or behavioral, objectives. Here a concise statement of what the student is expected to learn as a result of using the center can also serve as a guideline for evaluating student success.

Select appropriate activities and methods. These must be carefully selected to harmonize with the criteria mentioned above. The activities must serve the purpose of the center and be appropriate to the students using it. They must be so designed that they will assist the student to reach the expected learnings. The directions must be clearly within the ability of the student and presented so that the student can follow them independently. The materials must be readily available.

Do evaluations. Use the objectives for the center as a base to determine whether the student has attained the expected learning, concepts, and skills stated. The center and its materials may need periodic servicing.

Implement change as needed. Student performance will provide insight into how each center can be improved to meet the needs of the students it serves, the curriculum, and the objectives and goals stated for the center.

For other suggestions on how to make your science classroom more compatible with a hands-on, active program, see chapter 10 and the appendices.

A Simple Outline for Planning a Learning Center

Purpose of Center	Characteristics of Students	Concepts and Skills	Activities and Materials	Expected Learning Outcomes	Evaluations	Suggestions for Change
					Students: Center:	

Source: Geraldine R. Sherfey and Phyllis Huff, "Designing the Science Learning Center." Reproduced with permission by *Science and Children* 14, no. 3 (November/December 1976), p. 12. Copyright 1977 by the National Science Teachers Association, 1742 Connecticut Avenue, N.W., Washington, D.C. 20009.

IMPORTANCE OF STUDENT INTERACTION IN GUIDED DISCOVERY SCIENCE

A bright, well-decorated classroom is enhanced by interest centers, attractive and informative bulletin boards, posters, and other visual displays. However, it is just as important for students to have opportunities in their science program to interact, share ideas, draw upon each other's discoveries, and communicate their ideas to each other. Science is a *participa-*

tion activity and if its social aspects are to be fully realized, students must have guided activities involving interaction with each other.

The physical arrangements of the classroom can advance or hinder this interaction. Reexamine figures 8-1, 8-2, and 8-7 to see how furniture is wisely used. Rows are not straight, desks do not face in one direction (usually toward *you*) where children see only the backs of the heads of children in front of them. This enforced "order" impedes the development of active, involved children. The "E" arrangement of children's desks in figure 8-2 has several advantages: it allows the teacher to have the children's attention directed to the chalkboard; children face each other for discussion purposes; and rearranging the desks for other purposes is easy.

Classroom Management in Science Teaching/Learning

However important physical arrangement of your classroom is, the heart and soul of your science teaching is classroom management. Even if you have a well thought out science program, a carefully prepared physical classroom, and adequate supplies, the one thing that can wreck your teaching is faulty *classroom management*, sometimes called *discipline*. Here is a comparison of certain aspects of classroom management and medicine.

Anticipating and Preventing Problems Before They Happen

An ounce of prevention is worth much more than a pound of cure in your science teaching. Thinking and planning can help you spot many, though never all, potential trouble areas. Here are some things to keep in mind as you start planning your science teaching.[6]

Phase 1. Teacher/Children Preparation

☐ Identify *what* you want children to learn and relate it to the cognitive level of your students.

☐ Pick appropriate activities for your children to learn (*how*).

☐ Collect supplies and equipment you and the children will need.

☐ Plan the physical room arrangement and logistics needed for the activity.

☐ Organize the class into working teams.

This aspect of planning needs elaboration, especially for those who are new to teaching, or who have not had groups of children working together in science instead of the total class working together. Divide the class into teams of two to five to provide sufficient involvement and interaction, making sure the groups are balanced in sex, ability, etc. Seat members close to each other. Assigning a group name, or

Category	Medicine	Science Classroom Management
Prevention	check-ups, good nutrition, exercise, sleep, etc.	preassessment/diagnosis; teacher/student preparation; teacher observation; student grouping; pre-activity discussion; material distribution; teacher/student interactions
First-aid treatment	stopping bleeding, bandaging, etc.	separating and quieting problem students; halting disruptive activity
Long-term treatment	vitamin supplements, chemotherapy, limb in cast	individual skills improvement; teacher/student/parent conferences; student removal

letting the children pick their own, encourages group participation in their investigations and later on will help smooth distribution and collection of supplies and equipment. Give specific directions to each group.

☐ Organize science materials *before* starting your activity at stations in your self-contained classroom. Team members share responsibilities for obtaining and returning science materials, eliminating confusion, and expediting movement of materials. Give this considerable planning, as the distribution of materials can make or break your science lesson.

Phase 2. Pre-Activity Discussion

☐ Use verbal directions; pointing, arrows, and questions to help direct and focus children's attention on what will be done when they are working in their groups. *BE VERY SPECIFIC.*

☐ Guide students to identify the problem being investigated, to design the experiment, to determine data-collecting and record-keeping techniques, and to decide what and how equipment and supplies will be used.

☐ Give students time during this stage to discuss, explain what will be done, exchange ideas, etc. This is important for children to internalize what will be done and to form working relationships with other children.

Research has shown that (1) highly anxious students do better if the teacher is less directive; (2) students with low anxiety levels seem to respond better to stronger direction from the teacher; (3) average and low ability students benefit more from greater structure in teacher presentations and materials; and (4) above average students learn better when they have more latitude to imagine, interpret, and rapidly manipulate symbols.[7] Gear your pre-activity discussion to the individual needs of the specific groups with which you are working.

☐ By effectively using open-ended questions, you can guide children toward the goals you have for the activity.

☐ It is very important to establish a reason in children's minds for doing the activity.

☐ List on the board the reasons for conducting the activity, and write down as you discuss how supplies and equipment will be distributed and collected:

Charlie's Group - Give out and collect magnets and iron filings

Alice's Group - Give out and collect dry cells, switches, bulbs and sockets

Remember that science supplies and materials should be assembled at the distribution and collection stations *before* the lesson begins.

Phase 3. Distribution of Science Supplies and Equipment

☐ Assign one group at a time to go to the supply stations and get the needed items. Make certain each group knows exactly what it is to get. Review with the groups what they will do, what they need, and how they will proceed *before* having them go for supplies.

☐ Establish a realistic time limit for supply gathering and collection.

☐ Always check to see that each group has all necessary science supplies.

Phase 4. Doing the Activity

☐ With all the groups in their places with their supplies, review once more what each group will be doing. Sometimes it helps to check by asking the children who have the most difficulty, so that you can be sure all children understand the directions.

☐ For children unaccustomed to group work, try assigning a number to each task. Giving each child a numbered task assures total group participation.

First-Aid Treatment

As the children begin their group work, you take many roles. Here's how to keep the groups working effectively.

☐ Move about the room. Do not plant yourself in the front of the room, but move quietly to each group.

☐ If children are bogged down, ask questions to guide them and move them back on the tasks to be done.

☐ Encourage communication among the students in each group.

☐ Assess the noise level and see if it's appropriate for the specific activity. If it's too noisy, you might
  1. establish beforehand a signal calling for quiet (e.g., putting lights out for a moment, ringing a bell, raising a hand in air). When everyone quiets down, remind the class that it is too loud. Ask the children to quiet down.
  2. move to the offenders and quietly remind them to lower their noise.
  3. conclude the lesson if you are unable to quiet class. Do this only as a last resort.

☐ Praise students who are working well instead of criticizing those who are not work-

ing well. Be specific with your praise so children know exactly the behavior you are praising, such as, "Notice how quietly Ann's group is discussing what effect the length of the pendulum cord has on its swings," or "Class, Jon's so helpful by going around and showing each group how to wire the bell."

☐ Temporarily remove from their groups children who cause problems and ask them to watch groups that are working well together. In a few minutes you might say, "Jason, I know you want to work with your group, so when you're ready, quietly go back to them and see if you can now work quietly and share your materials properly."

☐ Be enthusiastic.

☐ Show respect for children by speaking politely and listening to each child in an unhurried manner.

☐ Do not add to class noise by shouting above children. Calm and quiet children with a firm but soft voice.

Long-Term Treatment

Evaluate your group lessons to see if you need to address any of these problems.

☐ Some children may be too immature for group work. You may have to work with them individually while the rest of the class works in groups.

☐ Additional total class or small group instruction may be necessary for those children who need science concepts/skills improvement before they are able to fully benefit from group work.

☐ Review, sharing of information, and discussions are necessary to follow up students' work.

- ☐ Make sure that all children understand the conclusions and generalizations.
- ☐ Build in time in each lesson for children to clean, disassemble, and return to collection stations all supplies and equipment used. This also establishes responsibility in children and teaches them that teachers are not servants or maintenance people.

- ☐ After each lesson, abstract a minimum set of working rules from the children to be used for future work, such as, *Make certain you know what you must do* or *Find out what materials you will have to use in the lesson.*
- ☐ If there is a chronic offender in your class you might (1) talk with the child; (2) try to

determine her or his interests; (3) ask for the child's perceptions of the problem and schedule a student-parent-teacher conference to see what can cooperatively be done; and if needed, (4) invite the principal to attend with the aid of information from the school psychologist, social worker, or other professional.

Although no classroom management system is foolproof and a substitute for an alert and intelligent teacher, here is a summary of techniques that can help in your guided discovery science teaching.

Simple, Clear Rules and Work Directions

1. Establish with children a minimum set of rules and working directions, which contain primarily fairness and courtesy behaviors. *Wherever possible*, give children a reason for the rule, e.g., "We will ask that only one group come up at a time to the science supply station so we can avoid bumping into each other and spilling things. Understand?" Post the rules on a chart.
2. Determine an appropriate "attention and quieting signal" to which children can automatically respond.
3. Devise a signal telling children to lower their noise level.
4. Set up and review often the system for distributing and collecting science supplies and equipment, as well as your clean-up procedures.

Classroom Management Maintenance and Reinforcement

5. Develop a repertoire of praise and reinforcement for children working cooperatively. These articles give specifics in this area: Donald B. Neumann, "Elementary Science for All Children—An Impossible Dream or a Reachable Goal?" *Science and Children*, 18, no. 6 (March 1981), pp. 4–6, Roger T. Johnson and David W.

Johnson, "Chapter 2—What Research Says About Student-Student Interaction in Science Classroom" and James R. Okey and David P. Butts, "Chapter 3—Linking Teaching Behaviors and Student Behaviors in Science," in *Education in the 80's: Science* (Mary Budd Rowe, Editor), (Washington, D.C.: National Education Association, 1982), pp. 25–52.
6. Present concise directions for each activity that each child can understand. Test often to see if all children know exactly what to do.
7. Provide a short demonstration of what is expected and any new idea or procedure.

Handling Problems

8. Prepare contingency plans for disruptive situations, e.g., spilling of science supplies, "explosive" student behavior (fighting, pushing, etc.), or unexpected science occurrence (hamster gives birth). Remember—if anything can go wrong, it will!
9. Consider beforehand the pro's and con's of first-aid discipline such as removing a student from the situation, physically restraining, etc., so you can effectively use it if necessary.
10. If you feel the lesson is getting away from you, don't hesitate to end it. Evaluate what went wrong and plan the next lesson to eliminate the problem.

For additional help in preparing to teach science through guided discovery, see chapter 10, individualizing a guided discovery program.

SUMMARY

To put a guided science discovery teaching program into effect, you must adequately provide for three aspects of your teaching.

1. classroom environment
2. student interaction
3. classroom management

Most science in the elementary school is taught in self-contained classrooms. This chapter suggested various physical arrangements of the classroom including sample floor plans and storage for materials, small items and living things.

Discovery learning centers in a classroom allow your students to explore, discover, and experiment in less structured situations. This chapter describes how to construct and use learning centers.

Not only the physical arrangement of the room, but also student interaction is critical, since science is a *participation* activity. Teachers must arrange furniture in a flexible and creative way.

Classroom management, or discipline, can make or break your science teaching. Classroom management is compared to medicine; both feature prevention, first-aid, and long-term treatment.

SELF-EVALUATION AND FURTHER STUDY

1. Draw a floor plan on graph paper for your classroom. Arrange the room to include these science areas: activity, equipment and supplies storage, living things storage, discovery learning center, research and library center, conference center, and audiovisual center.
2. Plan innovations of your present classroom that allow you to provide for the areas in item 1 above. Indicate which items would be made in school and which items would have to be purchased. For purchased items, give specific descriptions of item, source, price, and quantity needed.
3. Obtain free materials from a local grocery, fast-food chain, or other source and construct several of the storage areas or shoe box collections.
4. Construct several containers to house insects, small animals, or birds, using the information in this chapter.
5. Set up and maintain an aquarium or terrarium. Once established, add a small animal(s) or fish, as appropriate.
6. Plan and develop a discovery science learning center around a single topic of science.
7. Select a guided discovery science activity and write a plan for classroom management using prevention, first-aid, and long-term treatment. Be specific.
8. Using text readings and others you can find, prepare a list of positive reinforcement statements to encourage and reinforce cooperation among your children.
9. Read about the relationships and specifics of classroom rewards and punishment and learning science, starting with Ann Jensen, ''Classroom Rewards: Do They Work?'' *American Educator*, vol. 7, no. 1, Spring 1983.

ENDNOTES

1. Leon L. Ukens, "Learning Stations and Science Teaching," reproduced with permission from *Science and Children* 14, no. 3 (November/December 1976), p. 13. Copyright 1976 by the National Science Teachers Association, 1742 Connecticut Ave. N.W., Washington, D.C. 20009.

2. Donald C. Orlich et al., "Science Learning Centers—An Aid to Instruction," *Science and Children*, 20, no. 1 (September 1982), pp. 18–19.

3. Ibid., p. 20.

4. For additional information on how to organize learning centers, see Carl J. Wallen and LaDonna L. Wallen, *Effective Classroom Management* (Boston: Allyn and Bacon, 1978).

5. Charles R. Coble and Paul R. Houshell, "Science Learning Centers," reproduced with permission of *Science and Children* 16, no. 1 (September 1978), p. 12. Copyright 1978 by the National Science Teachers Association, 1742 Connecticut Avenue, N.W., Washington, D.C. 20009.

6. The author is indebted to the following for its excellent ideas. You are urged to read this brief but thorough coverage of classroom management: Johanna Strange and Stephen A. Henderson, "Classroom Management," *Science and Children*, 19, no. 3, (November/December 1981), pp. 46–47.

7. See the following for a discussion of structure in learning: John J. Koran, Jr. and Jeffrey R. Lehman, "What Research Says: Teaching Children Science Concepts: The Role of Attention," *Science and Children*, 18, no. 4, (January 1981), pp. 31–32.

9

How Can You Use Ideas from Innovative Science Programs?

"ESS, SCIS, SAPA and similar programs were a lot more effective than most educators, politicians, and parents have given them credit for being. Our quantitative synthesis of the research clearly shows that students in these programs achieved more, liked science more, and improved their skills more than did students in traditional, textbook-based classrooms. The report card for the hands-on curricula is impressive. It seems only fair and in the best interest of students to give these programs another critical look." (James A. Shymansky et al., "How Effective Were The Hands-On Science Programs of Yesterday?" *Science and Children,* 20, no. 3 [November/December 1982], p. 15.)

Knowing our roots in science teaching can help our current teaching. Below is a summary of how elementary school science has evolved.

WHAT FUNDED PROGRAMS HAVE IN COMMON

Many funded, experimental science projects were developed in the late 1950s, 1960s and 1970s to try to reform science education. Some of these projects were SAPA (Science—A Process Approach); SCIS (Science Curriculum Improvement Study); ESS (Elementary Science Study); and ISCS (Intermediate Science Curriculum Study). They had these features in common:

1. *Initiation* of many of these innovations in science teaching was by distinguished pro-

1850s	Memorization of facts for religious explanations
	Descriptions and memorizations in object teaching
	Structured curriculum based upon formal scientific classification and terminology
	Methodology and utilitarianism of science curriculums based upon sequence of major science principles and their applications
1950s	Textbook series and state adoptions
	Textbook series scope and sequence school's science content and methods of teaching
1960s	Curriculums influenced by funded national science projects
	Expanded teacher training in science
1970s	Teaching science as processes and products: discovery and inquiry approach; conceptual schemes
1980s	Individualizing science for all children: handicapped, gifted, normal
	More emphasis on human values, ecology, and the government

fessional scientists rather than professional science educators, state departments of education, or teacher education institutions.

2. For the first time, funds were made available to do curriculum research and development *before* inclusion or exclusion in schools.

3. Each project had a *team* of psychologists and other learning specialists, science educators, scientists, and elementary school teachers. Although each member brought expertise to the project, the give-and-take of working relationships resulted in a blending of the best.

4. Projects were *experimental*. They were tested, rewritten as a result, and retested until the teams were more sure of the procedures and materials. The projects generally wed the knowledge of good teaching and learning practices with the latest in science disciplines.

5. There was a great emphasis upon the *active participation of the learner* in all the new projects. Most of the projects claimed that *all* children could participate, not just select groups. In effect, each of these projects emphasized the open-ended laboratory approach where students use simple equipment in the elementary classroom.

6. Departure from the standard textbook was evident in all projects having a total program. Where printed materials were available for students, they were for purposes of recording what had been observed, planning future activities, and answering questions.

7. There was a definite trend away from teaching *many* science content areas to teaching a relatively *few* content areas.

8. More abstract content was generally introduced earlier in these projects than in former science curricula.

9. Most of the projects *did not* follow the typical science unit, which consciously integrates science with social studies, reading, written expression, and other areas.

10. These projects were much more *quantitative* than descriptive, unlike previous science curricula. *Mathematical* skills and understandings were highly stressed and an integral part of the projects, which used techniques such as measurement, graphing, and recording data.

11. There was a trend toward *open-ended*, relatively unstructured methods of discovery rather than teaching one method of problem solving. Knowledge was viewed as part of a creative process of finding out rather than as something to be accumulated.

12. The movement was away from emphasis upon technology and application of science to more concern with abstractions, theories, and basic ideas of science.

13. *"Packaged programs,"* including hardware and software, were constructed to give a whole program to teachers. These aided the teacher in attempting to adapt new programs to the particular situation. These packages also contained many new curricular innovations that provided the teacher with flexibility to handle a wide range of student abilities and varying teaching conditions.

14. The change in the *teacher's role* in the science program was one of the most dramatic breaks with the past. The teacher was the *guide to*, not the teller of, science. Most projects had extensive provisions for training (and retraining) teachers for this role through implementation programs and dissemination of materials. (*Note:* Specific suggestions for teachers interested in implementing an experimental science project are presented later in this chapter.)

HOW FUNDED SCIENCE PROJECTS DIFFER

Although you saw above that the funded science curriculums have many things in common, they are not identical. Two major differences are

1. A difference in the degree to which they stress *processes* or *content*.

2. The amount of *freedom* or *structure* within the scope and sequence of these processes and content.

Figure 9–1 is a continuum of structure. ESS has the least structure, with individual, nonsequential science modules that are not dependent upon each other for content or processes. SCIS is in the middle, stresses both content and processes, and gives the teacher greater freedom to establish sequence and activities within and between units. SAPA stresses processes and is very sequential.

WHY INVESTIGATE FUNDED SCIENCE PROGRAMS?

According to the research, students in new programs outperformed those in traditional, textbook-based classrooms on *every* criterion measured. In figure 9–2, note that

1. The average student in a ESS, SCIS, or SAPA classroom performed better than 62 percent of the students in traditional classrooms across all performance criteria measured—a 12 percentile-point gain.
2. In the three science curricula, students scored at least 18 percentile points higher than traditional class students on measures of process skills development.
3. SCIS and SAPA scored higher than students in comparable textbook-based classrooms on tests of reading and arithmetic skills. [1]

Regardless of what kind of science program you have, you could benefit from looking at the funded programs to see what could be adapted for your particular classroom and children. Use these criteria to evaluate each program as a possible resource.

How full is the program of science from kindergarten on up?
What parts of the projects are sequential?
Can the teacher pick and choose?
What segments depend upon exposure to a previous one?
How does the project emphasize content over process or vice versa?
To what degree are teachers required to "know science"?
What is the primary technique used for children to learn science in the project?
What ways are there for evaluating results in the project?

ELEMENTARY SCIENCE STUDY (ESS)

Developer: Educational Development Center (EDC), 55 Chapel Street, Newton, Massachusetts 02160
Distributors:

1. Webster Division, McGraw-Hill Book Company at the Distribution Center nearest you:
   Eastern: Princeton Road, Hightstown, New Jersey 08520
   Midcontinent: Manchester Road, Manchester, Missouri 63011
   Western: 8171 Redwood Highway, Navato, California 94947
2. American Science and Engineering, 20 Overland Street, Boston, Massachusetts 02115

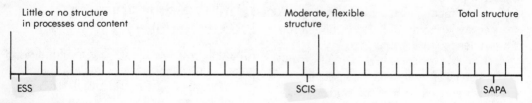

FIGURE 9–1
Funded programs structure continuum

FIGURE 9–2
Performance improvement for students in classrooms using ESS, SCIS, SAPA as compared to students in traditional classrooms[2]

Performance Area	Percentile Points Gained		
	ESS	SCIS	SAPA
Achievement	4	34	7
Attitudes	20	3	15
Process Skills	18	21	36
Related Skills	—*	8	4
Creativity	26	34	7
Piagetian Tasks	2	5	12

* No studies reported.

The ESS project is designed as *nonsequential* science units to be used at any time in the elementary school years, when and how you please. The units can be integrated into an existing school science curriculum or you may use them independently. They are flexible and have *not* been assigned definite grade levels, but most have a range of three or more grades. The broad purposes of the 56 units are to present students with scientifically sound accounts of phenomena, have them discover the "order and beauty the developers see in science," and stimulate them to think objectively and in a discovery manner.

ESS is highly individual and experimental, giving children access to materials for open-ended, rather than teacher- or textbook-directed investigations. All the materials needed for each unit are supplied in kits. These kits use many items familiar to children from around their houses, such as the heating and cooling kit described in figure 9–3.

ESS is very similar to the British Science 5–13 Program. Science 5–13 is Piagetian-based and stands for the ages of children for whom the units are designed (5 to 13 years old). Science 5–13 uses a thematic approach and offers a series of Teacher's Guides such as: Early Experiences, Science from Toys, Time, Change, Ourselves, and Like and Unlike. (See Chapter 10 for additional information on Science 5–13.)

Other ESS materials. In addition to kits, ESS has developed the following materials to accompany and enrich the activities.

1. Films
2. Filmloops
3. Student worksheets and booklets
4. Teacher's Guides

The Teacher's Guides attempt to provide teachers with as much help as possible while keeping the units free for children to discover things on their own. To accomplish this the guides contain

1. A summary of activities children can reasonably be expected to experience
2. Materials needed for teams of two students working together
3. Suggested procedures that are intended to be models rather than directions
4. Copies of student worksheets or problem cards that accompany the unit
5. Ideas for extending the unit further
6. Notes on scheduling

Figure 9–4 shows material from page 16 of the *Teacher's Guide for Heating and Cooling* illustrating Problem Card 2 and a typical reaction of children.

Types of ESS units. Some of the ESS units are designed for *total class use* in a "regular self-contained classroom" and contain student record sheets, film loops, Teacher's Guides, and student materials. Some of these total class units are

Balancing	Kitchen Physics
Balloons	Microgardening
Batteries and Bulbs	Optics
Colored Solutions	Pendulums

Materials for Heating and Cooling

A Note on the Materials:
   Most teachers find it helpful to have each child bring a shoe box in which to store his own equipment. Empty 2-pound coffee cans can be filled with water and used by each child or group to cool hot objects.

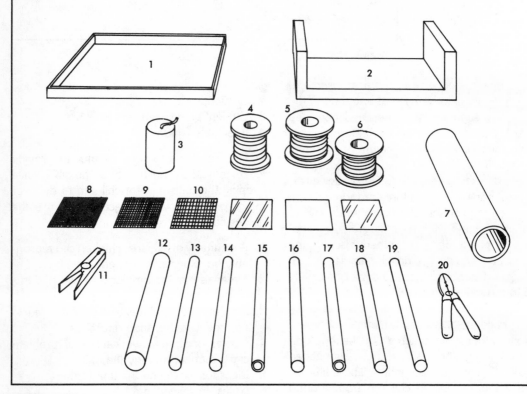

FIGURE 9–3
Looking at innovative science programs for ideas

Source: Adapted from *Teacher's Guide for Heating and Cooling.* Reproduced by permission of the Elementary Science Study of Education Development Center, Inc. Copyright © 1971 by Education Development Center, Inc.

Gases and "Airs"	Rocks and Charts
Growing Seeds	Sink or Float
Heating and Cooling	Slips and Slides
Ice Cubes	Small Things

Other ESS units are less precise and contain only a Teacher's Guide. These less structured, open-ended guides suggest student activities and common materials found locally or from science supply houses. These units may (or may not) involve the whole class and be taught in a series of sequential lessons.

Animal Book	Mealworms
Bones	Mobiles
Brine Shrimp	Mosquitoes
Butterflies	Musical Instrument
Changes	Mystery Powders
Clay Boats	Peas and Particles
Daytime Astronomy	Pond Water
Eggs and Tadpoles	Recipe Book
Life of Beans and Peas	Starting From Seeds
Light and Shadows	Structures
Mapping	Tracks
Match and Measure	Where Is the Moon?

A large variety of materials will add to the interest of the unit. Many teachers keep a "junk box" and encourage the students to bring in new materials for heating and cooling experiments.

Flames, Candles, and Alcohol Lamps:

For the experiments in heating and cooling, a flame is used to heat the various items. In trial classrooms, candles were used as heat sources. The classrooms sometimes became smoky, especially when screening was being heated. For this reason, it is a good idea to open the windows and air out the room from time to time.

Supplied in Kit:

(14) 5 solid aluminum rods, ¼" diameter
(13) 5 solid aluminum rods, ⅛" diameter
(17) 5 hollow brass tubes, ¼" diameter
(16) 5 solid brass rods, ¼" diameter
(18) 5 solid copper rods, ¼" diameter
(19) 5 Pyrex glass rods, ¼" diameter
(23) 50 aluminum sheets, 4" × 4"
(22) 50 lead sheets, 4" × 4"
(21) 30 copper sheets, 4" × 4"
 (9) 20 copper screens, 4" × 4", 20 openings per square inch
(10) 20 copper screens, 4" × 4", 10 openings per square inch
 (8) 5 aluminum screens, 4" × 4", 20 openings per square inch
 (5) 25' copper wire, #18 gauge
 (6) 25' copper wire, #22 gauge

(12) 2 solid aluminum rods, ½" diameter
(15) 5 hollow aluminum tubes, ¼" diameter
 (4) 10' aluminum wire, #18 gauge
(20) 1 pair wire cutters
 (3) 100 household candles
 (1) 5 cardboard trays, 14" × 18"
(11) 10 spring-type wooden clothespins
 (7) 1 box aluminum foil
 (2) 1 expansion frame
     1 package soapless steel wool (for cleaning soot from rods and sheets, not shown in figure)
Note: The cardboard trays are used to protect desk tops from melted wax, spilled water and hot objects. The clothespins make good tongs for holding hot objects.

You Will Need to Provide:

shoe boxes, fire extinguisher, buckets or cans for water, "junk box" items, wooden safety matches (enough small boxes so that each child can have a box to strike on), scissors for cutting sheets and screens.

The rest of the units are for *individual* or *small-group* activity in flexible, informal classrooms where much individual work takes place; open-education classrooms use these unstructured units.

Animal Activity
Attribute Games and
    Problems
Balance Book
Batteries and Bulbs II
Drops, Streams,
    and Containers
Geo Blocks

Mirror Cards
Mobiles
Pattern Blocks
Printing Press
Sand
Spinning Tables
Tangrams

Role of teacher in ESS. Your role in ESS is to prepare the classroom, introduce and guide student activity without setting a given or approved pattern, respond and guide questioning, stimulate talking and theorizing about the scientific experiences being investigated, and generally conduct a *nondirective* approach to science teaching. One thing you should be aware of if you intend to work with ESS: It is *not* like the more traditional ways of teaching science and you would do well to request some type of teacher training from the publisher or local university science education department. You should become familiar with what is expected of you, see the printed materials, go over them with the instructor, have a few hands-on workshops where you actively participate in the units, and have some type of

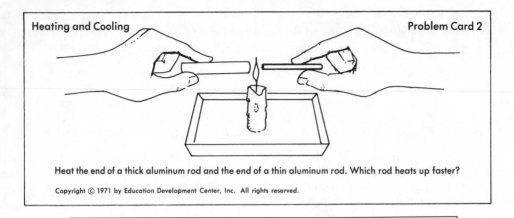

Heating and Cooling   Problem Card 2

Heat the end of a thick aluminum rod and the end of a thin aluminum rod. Which rod heats up faster?

Regarding Problem Card 2, a boy said:
"These rods are the same. They're both aluminum, and they're both solid. They're just different sizes."
What do you think will happen when you heat them?
"I think the thin one will win the race."

Later he said:
"It's incredible, but the thin one never heated up. After 5 minutes, the thick rod was very hot, but after 12 minutes, the thin rod wasn't really hot. It doesn't make sense that it should take that long. I think I'll do it over."

FIGURE 9–4

Source: Adapted from *Teacher's Guide for Heating and Cooling*. Reproduced by permission of the Elementary Science Study of Education Development Center, Inc. Copyright © 1971 by Education Development Center, Inc.

follow-up to assist you as you try out the units with your students. A request from your school administrator to the publisher should bring you teacher-training sessions.

Using ESS for special education. For information about ESS units appropriate for children with learning difficulties, see chapter 10 on Individualizing Science Teaching.

ESS evaluation. The developers of ESS contend that their materials have been tested and that they stimulate children to manipulate the materials provided in the kits, to raise questions, and to think investigatively.

Researchers found that ESS stimulates children's interests in informal talk. There is also evidence of involvement and pleasure on the part of children in working with ESS units, as well as improved student performance in science processes.[3]

Because ESS is not traditional in its approach, it cannot be evaluated in the traditional paper-pencil tests. Two kinds of evaluation are recommended by William Aho and his associates in their book *McGraw-Hill Evaluation Program for ESS*:

1. Honest appraisal approach (teacher considers child's efforts, contributions, and performances and makes judgment about what has been learned)
2. Behavioral-objective approach (using unit and evaluation objectives for the 56 ESS units and simple check sheet found in manual)

SCIENCE CURRICULUM IMPROVEMENT STUDY (SCIS)

Developer: Science Curriculum Improvement Study, University of California, Berkeley, California 94720 (Robert Karplus)

1. *SCIIS*
Delta Education, Box M, Nashua, New Hampshire 03061
Authors: Herbert Thier, Robert Karplus, Chester Lawson, Robert Knott, and Marshall Montgomery (all were on the original SCIS project team)
2. *SCIS II*
American Science and Engineering, Inc. (AS & E), Education Division, 20 Overland Street, Boston, Massachusetts 02215
Authors: Lester Paldy, Leonard Amburgay, Francis Collea, Richard Cooper, Donald Maxwell, and Joseph Riley

The SCIS projects differ from ESS in that they are *total* programs; they are also *structured* and specific *relationships* exist between units. SCIS also differs from SAPA in that it stresses *both* processes and content (SAPA has a heavy emphasis upon process only) and al-lows greater freedom for teacher choice in selecting and conducting activities within and among SCIS units. Also, the sequential arrangement of SCIS units is not necessarily meant to be graded.

Currently, there are *three* versions of SCIS being sold commercially. The original SCIS, as well as the new SCIIS, were developed by the same team (Thier, Karplus, Lawson, Knott, and Montgomery) and published by the same commercial concern, Rand McNally. SCIS II was developed by another team (Paldy, Amburgay, Collea, Cooper, Maxwell, and Riley) and produced commercially by American Science and Engineering, Inc. Here are summaries of each of the projects, giving similarities and differences compared to the original SCIS.

SCIS Learning Strategy

The SCIS projects are based upon a hierarchy of scientific concepts in the physical and life sciences. Figure 9–5 shows the hierarchy of subject areas. Level one introduces children to concepts in the physical science area of "material objects" such as object, property, material, serial ordering, change, and evidence. The Life

STRUCTURE AND SEQUENCE OF UNITS

K	BEGINNINGS

	Physical/Earth Science Sequence	Life/Earth Science Sequence
1	MATERIAL OBJECTS	ORGANISMS
2	INTERACTION AND SYSTEMS	LIFE CYCLES
3	SUBSYSTEMS AND VARIABLES	POPULATIONS
4	RELATIVE POSITION AND MOTION	ENVIRONMENTS
5	ENERGY SOURCES	COMMUNITIES
6	SCIENTIFIC THEORIES	ECOSYSTEMS

FIGURE 9–5

Source:The Rand McNally SCIIS Program, *Interaction and Subsystem: Teacher's Guide* (Chicago: Rand McNally & Co., 1978), p. xiii.

Science area of "organisms" gives children exposure to concepts of organism, birth, death, habitat, food web, and detritus. It is expected that a class usually spends one-half of the year in the appropriate life science unit and the other half in the physical science unit. Although the units are separate entities, they need not be taught exclusively and may be taught as best seen by the teacher. The teacher may arrange activities and provide new ones to meet the specific needs and interests of individual children progressing at varying rates and levels of learning.

The main purpose of the project is to develop *scientific literacy* in children (functional understanding of science concepts) and an inquiring, open mind. To achieve these aims, SCIS has developed a *materials centered approach* in which the elementary classroom actually becomes a laboratory. Children manipulate specially designed equipment and observe, sometimes freely and sometimes under teacher guidance. Next, the teacher introduces scientific concepts that describe or explain what the children have observed. This is called the "invention lesson." Invention lessons are followed by other direct experiences that present further examples of the concept. These are called "discovery lessons," since the child is expected to recognize that the new concept has applications to situations other than the initial one. The SCIS learning strategy includes:

1. *"Student exploration"* of materials the teacher provides
2. *"Teacher invention"* or explanation of the concept
3. *"Student discovery"* or applications of concept to another set of materials and/or circumstances

Characteristics of SCIS Programs

Figure 9–5 shows all seven levels of the three SCIS programs. Booklets are available for each unit, accompanied by laboratory equipment and materials kits. Student activity booklets are also available for recording observations, and teacher's guides present this information.

1. General background and introduction of the study and its philosophy and intent
2. Overview of the science content included in the unit and general objectives for teaching and learning the concepts involved
3. Clues for the teacher on different approaches to teaching any given lesson
4. Further teaching hints through use of the Student Activity Pages
5. Within each lesson:
   a. Materials
   b. Objectives of the learning experiences
   c. Teaching suggestions
   d. Suggested use of student activity pages
   e. Replica of student activity pages (for review lessons or recording)

Figure 9–6 shows a sample from the *Teacher's Guide to Organisms*, a level one Life Sciences unit, about the difficult subject of death. Rather than avoid the subject, SCIS plans for the inevitable happening when students work with living organisms. The teacher is presented with a range of suggested activities to help children deal with the concept of the death of an organism.

Teacher and student roles in SCIS. The teacher's role in SCIS is to prepare materials, guide the children's explorations, and be a close observer of how the children progress. To do this, you do *not* need a special science background; however, in-service training by SCIS consultants is strongly recommended and can be obtained by contacting the publisher or your local university science education center.

Students *actively* participate in classroom activities with simple equipment, as well as through outdoor field investigations. In this way, the students in the SCIS project are helped to grow into self-directed learners.

Evaluation and SCIS. Because SCIS is not a traditional science project, it cannot be evaluated by traditional methods such as written tests. Teachers must continuously evaluate students' progress. By knowing what a child is

6 Death in an Aquarium

TEACHING SUGGESTIONS

An exploration activity—observing changes in a dead organism—leads to invention of the concept *death*. This activity can be done only after an organism dies. If necessary, go on to Part Three and return, at the appropriate time.

Observations. If several organisms die in one aquarium, remove and discard all dead bodies but one. Decomposition of more than one body could change the conditions in the aquarium, making it impossible for the other plants and animals to survive. The decomposition of one guppy or one snail probably will not seriously endanger the other living organisms and will give the children an opportunity to observe what happens after an organism dies. However, you may wish instead to put the animal and some aquarium water in a covered jar for study.

Figure 6-1. As a fish decomposes, the gases produced may lift it to the water surface.

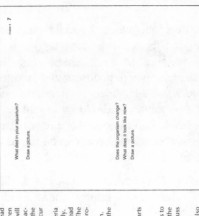

Figure 6-2. Decomposition beginning.

Using student manual page 7. Whether the dead organism is a guppy, snail, or plant, have the children write its name in the manual. The dead animal will eventually disintegrate, but the specific changes accompanying the process cannot be predicted. Ask the children to observe the day-to-day changes that occur and picture them in the manual. Possibilities are:

- The water may turn cloudy and white as bacteria and protozoa feeding on the organism multiply.
- Green algae may appear, first around the dead body and then throughout the aquarium. The decaying organic matter acts as a fertilizer, promoting growth of algae.
- A fuzzy white mold may appear on a dead fish.
- A white scum may appear on the surface of the water.
- A dead fish may float.
- There may be an unpleasant odor.
- As the organism is broken down, the soft parts may disappear into the water.

As changes occur, ask the children what happens to the dead organism. Do the broken-down parts of the body remain in the aquarium? Let the children discuss what might happen to the parts.

Decomposition of plants. The children may also study the decay of aquarium plants. Though the

What died in your aquarium?

Draw a picture.

Does the organism change?
What does it look like now?
Draw a picture.

FIGURE 9-6

Source: Rand McNally SCIIS Program, *Organisms: Teacher's Guide* (Chicago: Rand McNally & Co., 1978), pp. 25–26.

doing, the teacher guides the child into new discoveries. SCIS presents the teacher with feedback activities in each chapter of the teacher manuals, including observation, written student work on lab sheets, convergent and divergent questioning, and other informal evaluation methods. A more formal evaluation program has been developed and can be found in these two SCIS publications.

1. *Evaluation Supplements* (Berkeley, Calif.: Science Curriculum Improvement Study, University of California, 1974).
2. Robert Karplus and Herbert Thier, *SCIS Teacher's Handbook* (Berkeley, Calif.: Science Curriculum Improvement Study, University of California, 1974).

Research and SCIS

Research has shown that students who have completed the SCIS program show a more positive attitude toward science, experimenting, and scientists than students not exposed to SCIS.[4] John Renner found that first graders using SCIS also made greater gains in word matching, listening, and number on the Metropolitan Reading Readiness Test (MRT) than non-SCIS groups.[5]

Jane Bowyer and Marcia Linn found that SCIS subjects scored significantly higher on scientific literacy tests.[6] For a thorough compilation of research studies and articles related to SCIS, read Ashley G. Morgan et al., *A Bibliography of Research and Articles Related to Science Curriculum Study (SCIS)* (Atlanta: Georgia State University Center for Improving Elementary School Science and Mathematics, 1979), 19 pages.

All copyrights on the original SCIS program passed on January 1, 1978, from the copyright holders, the University of California, to the public domain. As a result, SCIIS and SCIS II came into being.

SCIIS program. SCIIS was originally published by Rand McNally, and is a revision of the original SCIS by the original team from the University of California at Berkeley. Rand McNally SCIIS is now published by Delta Education, Inc. in Nashua, New Hampshire. Basically, SCIIS is the same program as SCIS, using suggestions from field testing to produce modifications. In fact, it is so close in concepts, teaching methods, and evaluation that Rand McNally and Delta Education, Inc. offer a conversion kit for changing from SCIS into SCIIS. Here are some of the major changes.

1. Level five of the Physical/Earth Science module was enlarged to include "solar energy."
2. Level five of the Life/Earth Science module now includes the "pyramid of numbers" and "competition."
3. Level six of the Physical/Earth Science module was a major change from the model Electric and Magnetic Interaction to Scientific Theories, which now includes "electricity," "magnetic field," and "light rays."
4. Some activities were changed, incorporating hardier organisms than previously and introducing either some new material not covered before or better ways of handling present materials.
5. "Earth science" was added to each of the two major sequences, renaming them Physical/Earth Science and Life/Earth Science.
6. New material was added, emphasizing the student's physical relationship to the earth and its ecological nature.
7. Teacher's Guides were redesigned to be larger and include more drawings to help make the text material more understandable.
8. To make SCIIS more useful with individualization, *Extending Your Experience* (EYE) cards were added as supplementary materials. These cards are used by students for enrichment, remediation, or extension of the basic concepts. The Teacher's Guide suggests how they can be used, as figure 9–7 shows.
9. Evaluation procedures were added for each chapter and included in the appendix of the Teacher's Guide.

SCIIS EXTENDING YOUR EXPERIENCE CARDS

23. Mix Liquids with Water. The children look for liquids that mix with water and do not separate out again. The discussions that take place as your pupils try to explain and defend their choices will provide many opportunities for them to develop their oral language ability.

24. Float Liquids on Water. As children produce their collections, ask questions that cause them to explain and defend their choices. Informally introduce the meaning of *float* to those who are having trouble. In Chapter 18 they will have further experiences with objects floating and sinking in water.

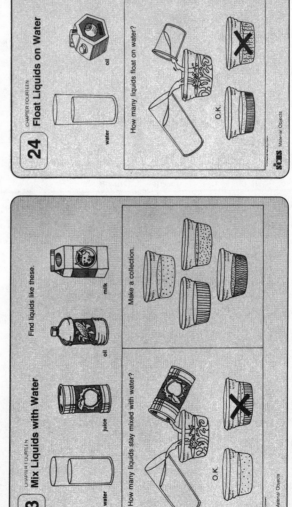

FIGURE 9–7

Source: Herbert D. Thier et al., *Material Objects (Level 1)—Teacher's Guide* (Chicago: Rand McNally-SCIIS, 1978), p. 60.

10. Storage and handling has been made easier by redesigning and packaging.
11. Delivery systems, supply sources, and services for teachers have all been improved.

SCIS II Program

SCIS II is published by American Science and Engineering (AS&E), the group which had been the exclusive designer and producer of all of the materials (except printed matter) used in the original SCIS program. The authors were all involved in training teachers in the original SCIS. SCIS is used as the foundation for the SCIS II program with these major changes.

1. New content was added, such as "earth science" in the fourth and sixth levels.
2. One or more concepts were added in each unit.
3. The title of the fourth level physical science was changed to Measurement, Motion, and Change, and concepts were modified to show the earth science emphasis.
4. The title of the sixth level physical science was changed to Modeling Systems, with more emphasis upon weather (air temperature, barometric pressure, and atmosphere).
5. The Teacher's Guide was changed to stress what teachers need most—classroom management.
6. Activity Cards were added for individualization and enrichment and for correlating science activities with math and language arts.
7. Student Duplicating Masters have replaced student lab manuals, in an effort to simplify classroom management and cut costs of the materials.
8. Original SCIS terms—*exploration, invention, discovery*—were replaced by *exploration, concept, application.*
9. Greater stress is placed upon evaluation devices, such as the Section Check Up included in each activity in the Teacher's Guide. A sample of one is shown in figure 9–8.
10. Packaging is more flexible than in the original SCIS, and the program is available in several different packaging options, including a conversion kit for SCIS users.

AAAS SCIENCE—A PROCESS APPROACH (SAPA)

Developer: The Commission on Science Education of the American Association for the Advancement of Science (AAAS), 1515 Massachusetts Avenue, N.W., Washington, D.C.

1. *SAPA*
   Distributors: Xerox Education Division, 1200 High Ridge Park, Stamford, Connecticut 06904
2. *SAPA II*
   Ginn and Company, A Xerox Educational Company, 191 Spring Street, Lexington, Massachusetts 02173.

SAPA differs from both ESS and SCIS in that it is a *total* program for grades K–6. It is the most structured of the three projects; completely *process-oriented*; activities and sequences must be strictly followed; and the teacher has less freedom for innovation than with the other two projects.

Currently there are *two* versions of SAPA being sold commercially. The original SAPA and SAPA II are produced and marketed through Ginn and Company, a Xerox Education Company subsidiary. Here are sketches of both of the SAPA programs, showing similarities and differences.

Original SAPA program. By the very title of the project—Science, A Process Approach—you can see that the American Association for the Advancement of Science Commission on Science Education placed its emphasis upon the basic *process* skills to further learning in science. The commission chose these eight categories of processes for their science lessons for grades K–3.

☐ Observing
☐ Classifying
☐ Using Space/Time Relations
☐ Using Numbers
☐ Communicating
☐ Measuring

Section Check Up

Two Animals

The *Mealworm and Butterfly* writing sheet (Figure 8) will give you feedback about the children's understanding of Chapter 7.

Three Animals, Three Plants

The *Who Has What?* record sheet (Figure 9) is a checkup for the children's understanding of Section Two. It also challenges them to recall observations of plants and to think about ways in which plants and animals are similar and different.

Have the students place a check mark in a box if the item is correct (*Larva, Fruit Fly*). Have them put an *X* if an item is not correct (*Larva, Pea*).

Who Has What?

	Fruit Fly	Pea	Bean	Mealworm	Butterfly	Corn
Larva						
Pupa						
Adult						
Egg or Seed						
Needs Food						
Moves						
Has Legs						
Shows Growth						
Shows Development						

Copyright · 1978 by American Science and Engineering, Inc

Figure 9

Mealworm and Butterfly

Look at the pair of larvae below.   What is different?

What is similar?   List the properties that are different.

List the properties that are similar.   Do the same for the other pairs.

	Mealworm	Butterfly	Similarities	Differences
Larva				
Pupa				
Adult				

Figure 8

Source: Lester G. Paldy et al., *SCIS II Sampler Guide* (Boston: American Science and Engineering, Inc., Education Division, 1978), p. 25.

FIGURE 9–8
SCIS II

Source: Lester G. Paldy et al., *SCIS II Sampler Guide* (Boston: American Science and Engineering, Inc., Education Division, 1978), p. 25.

☐ Predicting
☐ Inferring

In grades 4–6, these categories of processes are introduced.

☐ Formulating Hypotheses
☐ Controlling Variables
☐ Experimenting
☐ Defining Operationally

☐ Formulating Models
☐ Interpreting Data

Each exercise is arranged so that one specific skill from the above processes is taught in a six-year "hierarchy." Therefore, this program cannot be taught piecemeal, but requires strict adherence to sequential order.

Science content is not omitted, but introduced in each lesson for each grade while the child participates in the preceding processes. The content is not systematically related to particular scientific disciplines but is derived from familiar objects and phenomena in the child's world. The science lessons are arranged in an orderly, sequential progression. Objectives to be completed at the conclusion of each exercise are described very specifically in terms of expected student behaviors. SAPA is the only one of the three projects that stresses behavioral objectives. To determine if these behavioral objectives have been attained, appraisal exercises are provided for each lesson. These are discussed further in chapter 3.

The format followed by the original SAPA exercises is

1. Statement of objectives (behavioral skills expected by completion of exercise)
2. Rationale (teacher's description of why the exercise is included, plus other helpful background data)
3. Vocabulary (words not used in previous exercises)
4. Materials (may be obtained locally or from AAAS)
5. Originating problem (for arousing student interest in topic)
6. Instructional procedure (to be done in sequence since each builds on skills developed in preceding ones)
7. Appraisal (to determine whether objectives have been attained)

Teacher and student roles in SAPA. The teacher's role in SAPA is to prepare classroom materials and lessons in advance, initiate student activities through demonstrations and instructions, and lead discussions about the experiments performed. The teacher is more *directly* involved and assesses and records student performance more than with ESS or SCIS. As a necessary concrete aid to the teacher, and also as a basis for evaluating student performance, SAPA describes skill mastery of a process skill in behavioral-objective terms. SAPA provides a visible record of what each student is to learn, the sequence in which it must be learned, and when the student has or has not learned it. A color-coded Planning Chart, giving a sequential arrangement of all the behavioral objectives for the entire program, is provided for the teacher. Each of 17 columns is a stage containing a group of modules that can be taught in any order. As you can see in a section of the Planning Chart for the lower grades (figure 9–9), behavioral objectives are stated and reference is made to where (module) you can obtain the activities to help children learn them. You would then go to one of the Science Materials Kits, which contain all of the objects needed for a class of 30 students for one year's study. A teacher's guide comes with the kit. Clear labeling and instructions guide you through the compartments in the kit, and you get a lot of printed matter to assist you in teaching. Inservice programs are available through the company or local university science education departments. Instructions for teaching are very explicit, usually with specific directions to teachers such as, "Do this and then ask these questions. . . .", or "Your students do this and then you ask. . . ."

Although SAPA has been criticized for strong adherence to, and possible negative or abusive uses of, sequential behavioral objectives, Howard Hausman of the Council for Basic Education points out

> While SAPA may have contributed to this plague by popularizing the idea of behavioral objectives, it can hardly be blamed for the misuses of the concept. The authors of SAPA have been able to enunciate objective statements about important skills and processes fundamental to the genuine learning of science, although their compilation may not be in total agreement with that of other experts. They

have provided instruments for assessing student attainment. It is significant that the SAPA processes or derivatives of them have been introduced into all new science programs appearing since SAPA's advent. Moreover, as older textbook series issue new editions they invariably stress the process skills which they claim are built into their programs. The contribution of SAPA is impressive if imitation is a measure.[7]

In SAPA, students observe and *actively* investigate materials individually or in groups; they are more teacher-directed than in ESS or SCIS. Late-entering students may need remedial work or flexible placement in a lower-level learning group from the hierarchical Planning Chart shown in figure 9–9. The 105 modules in SAPA are grouped as follows if you want to use them as approximate grade equivalents.

☐ Modules 1 through 12 or 15 constitute kindergarten.

☐ Modules 13 through 24 or 16 through 30 constitute first grade.

☐ Modules 12 through 15 are for every other year.

To arrive at the proper grade level for your class, you need to refer to the SAPA Planning Chart.

Figure 9–10 is a sample of the kind of instructional procedure supplied to the teacher for conducting activities with the upward movement of materials in liquids. Notice how specific the directions are to the teacher in how to set things up, what behavioral objectives are stressed, what procedures to follow, what specific questions to ask, and what your students should know after being exposed to these activities.

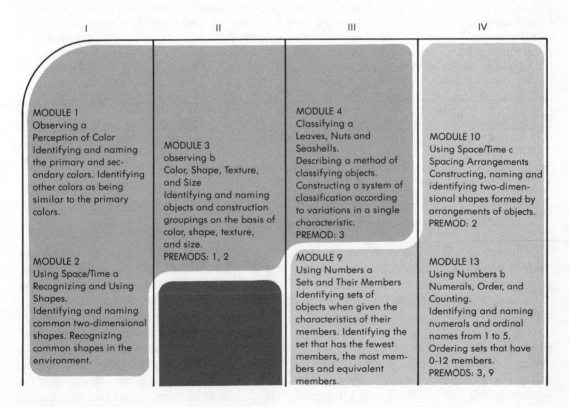

FIGURE 9–9

Source: *Architecture of a Revision, Science . . . A Process Approach II, The Modular Science Curriculum* (Lexington, Mass.: Ginn and Company, A Xerox Education Company, 1977), p. 8.

Instructional Procedure

Just before the science period, make the following preparation which the children should not see. Dip a strip of yellow blotting paper about 40 centimeters long and 5 centimeters wide in a shallow dish of water, and keep it there until the wet part of the strip is substantially longer than the water is deep.

Show the children the partially wet strip and the dish of water. Tell them that you did not spill water on the paper. Ask, How do you think the paper got wet? If someone suggests that the strip was in the water, hold it vertically alongside the dish to show that the wet area goes up much higher than the depth of water in the dish. Someone should say that only a small part of the strip had to be in the water. However, if no one does say this, ask a child to come to the demonstration table. Give him two dry strips of red blotting paper and a wide-mouth container half-filled with water. Suggest that he dip the strips into the water to different depths and observe what happens. Let another child repeat the demonstration, if you wish.

FIGURE 9–10

Source: Adapted from *Science—A Process Approach*, Part E, "Upward Movement of Materials in Liquids." (Washington, D.C.: American Association for the Advancement of Science, 1968), pp. 3–4.

There are also film loops recommended for students needing additional help in catching up with the rest of the class, or for advanced students who could benefit from enrichment activities.

Evaluation and research in SAPA. Evaluation in the SAPA program is very structured and will be thoroughly investigated in the next section dealing with SAPA II, since the two versions are similar. SAPA has the most elaborate system of testing of all three major science projects. Each exercise contains a manipulative testing device based upon behavioral objec-tives. In addition, *group* contemporary tests are given after each exercise. There are also diagnostic science process tests for placement and fifth-grade reading tests.

Douglass Macbeth found that kindergarten children who were involved in SAPA showed more extensive attainment of process skills than a non-SAPA control group.[8] Jerry Ayers and Mary Ayers, in working with Appalachian kindergarten children, found that SAPA influenced the children's readiness for reading by refining their abilities to use logic.[9] Two studies found that SAPA works equally well for children in all socioeconomic groups. H. H. Walbesser and H. L. Carter discovered that all groups appear to perform equally well in the behavioral objectives of SAPA.[10] Phyllis Huff and Marlin Languis, working with kindergarten children from inner-city schools in Columbus, Ohio, found that SAPA produced a positive effect upon the development of language output, vocabulary, general meaning and skills, sentence structure, word definition, and listening behavior.[11]

SAPA II program. As time passed and SAPA had been used extensively, it became necessary to revise the program. Ginn and Company provided money for the AAAS Commission on Science Education to respond to incorporating these factors into the original SAPA.

1. Important changes in science education since the inception of SAPA
2. Increased emphasis upon flexibility in teaching
3. Heightened interest in individualization of learning

Classroom teachers who used SAPA were the major contributors to the revision work. SAPA II emerged in 1975 as a result of data collected from Trial Centers, studies from the Eastern Regional Institute for Education, special conferences and symposia, consultants, rewriting, and trial testing. Although SAPA II is close in concepts, teaching methods, philosophy, and evaluation to SAPA, here are some ways it differs.

1. There is a deeper concern for and understanding of the environment and its problems. Extensive material on the environment has been integrated throughout SAPA II.
2. Students apply each of the processes of science to environmental exercises.
3. Teaching flexibility is built into the SAPA II modular-structure curriculum. At each stage, a teacher may choose among several different modules, and within some modules, alternate exercises allow the teacher to choose among different content options for the same process. This is an attempt to get away from the rigidity of SAPA's original structure.

4. There is a more child-centered and humanistic approach. Science is presented as a powerful human tool to be used to solve problems and satisfy curiosity.
5. Value development is added to intellectual skills, information gathering and processing, and motor control.
6. The generalizing of experiences in each module is a means of asking children to relate what they have learned to new contexts.
7. Physical changes in SAPA II's packaging give a continuum of 105 ungraded modules designed for easy storage and efficient use.
8. Individualization of activities is stressed by items such as "latent image" worksheets. These sheets, reproduced on special spirit duplicating masters, contain not only questions and space for students' answers, but also responses that are invisible until the lesson is done and the sheet is rubbed with a special marker. Images then appear and students get immediate feedback and can check their answers. A sample of a latent image duplicating master for an observation or inferences evaluation is shown in figure 9–11.
9. To help teachers implement SAPA II in a wide range of classroom organizations (traditional or open classrooms, large or small groups, individualization), a sound filmstrip Orientation Package is offered covering the introduction, basic processes, metric system, integrated processes, and teaching strategies.
10. Ordering and packaging combinations are more flexible, allowing teachers to combine modules in three ways for their individual classroom needs:
    a. In grade sets—15 modules combined in a sequence designed to fulfill one part of the overall hierarchy of behavioral objectives.
    b. In clusters—a cluster combines a sequence of content-related modules that

SAPA II "LATENT IMAGE" SPIRIT MASTER EVALUATION
Observation or Inference?

With your pencil, put a ✓ on the line <u>under</u>
the ☐ if you think the person is making an
inference. If you think the person is making
an observation, put a ✓ on the line under the ◯.

When you are finished, get a magic pen
and fill in the <u>shape</u> above your check ✓.
If you are right, a smile ☺ will appear!

Activity 2

Give each child a copy of the sheet *Observation or Inference?* Show the children a large
sealed paper bag that has a ball in it. Tell the children that the statements on the sheet
were made by children who were trying to find out what was in a similar closed paper
bag. Have those children with sufficient reading skills complete the sheet independently. Ask them to share the magic pens (image developers). Have the remaining
children work in a group with you. Read to the children the directions on the sheet. Then
read each statement aloud, pausing after each for the children to mark their sheets.
When the children have completed the sheets discuss their answers. Finally, let the
group use the magic pens.

Materials

Observation or Inference?, 1 spirit master, (*Module 33*)
Paper bag, 1
Ball, 1 (*Module 40*)
Pens, 5, image developers (*Module 33*)

FIGURE 9–11

teach a particular skill or science topic, for example, the Metric System cluster contains 7 modules teaching metric measurement to students.

c. Individually—enrichment or innovative modules, for example, "Listening to Whales" or environmental modules.

The three funded science projects presented above—ESS, SCIS, and SAPA—have had a great impact upon science education, as explained in the following sections.

IMPACT OF FUNDED SCIENCE PROJECTS

Science Textbook Revisions

The National Science Teachers Association, with funding from the National Institute of Education of the Department of Education, reviewed science textbooks and funded programs. NSTA compared "Frequently Used Science Textbooks," NSF Texts (SCIS, ESS, SAPA), and what they called "New Generation Texts," on the characteristics in figure 9–12. NSTA concluded, "There is a marked contrast between the first group of texts and the other two. *The influence of the NSF programs is very evident in the program characteristics of the third group.*"[12]

Textbook authors and publishers have been influenced by funded science projects. They have adapted many of the better points of these projects into their textbooks, resulting in high-quality textbooks for the elementary schools. Among the more visible science textbook improvements are

1. There has been a greater effort to improve the accuracy of scientific information.
2. A *discovery* or laboratory-centered approach is apparent in more recent textbooks because of the greater emphasis on question and answer techniques rather than the dialogue or telling techniques so popular in some previous elementary science textbooks.
3. Authors are beginning to develop styles of writing that convey the fascination and intellectual excitement inherent in scientific disciplines.
4. Emphasis on science processes is appearing more frequently in current textbooks, including manipulative activities.
5. Several of the publishers are including (very often as optional) kits of materials to carry out the experimental activities included in their texts.
6. Limited opportunities are beginning to appear in texts for developing scientific attitudes as well as skills for creative and critical thinking.
7. The format of modern textbooks is much more inviting than that of previous texts; there is more extensive use of pictures and other illustrations and sequential photos of scientific phenomena. Film loops and films are also available to supplement the books.

Congruence of Existing Program Characteristics to Desired States			
Characteristics	Frequently Used Texts	NSF Texts	New Generation Texts
1. Interdisciplinary	Low to None	High to Good	High
2. Alternatives	None	High	High to Low
3. First Hand Experience	Low	High to Good	Good
4. Involved in Data-Gathering	Easily Avoided	High	High
5. Alternative Modes	Single-Mode Text	Single-Mode Text Hands-On	Combination
6. Reflects How Children Learn	Low	High	High

FIGURE 9-12[13]

8. Fewer comprehensive science units are explored in greater depth than the numerous isolated lessons of the past.

WHERE ARE WE GOING IN SCIENCE TEACHING?

What trends will you see in science education projects in the 1980s and 1990s? The revised versions of SCIS and SAPA show some of the observable trends in science education.

1. Science programs employ a more *humanistic approach* in which the child's life is used to emphasize and correlate the science concepts introduced.
2. There is an increase in showing the direct *relationships of people's lives and conditions* to the processes and concepts of scientific investigations.
3. More emphasis is placed on relating the science programs to *environmental and ecological issues.*
4. *Values and social aspects of science and technology* are integrated into the science curriculum.
5. A broader *integration of science with other curricular areas* such as language arts, social studies, and mathematics is taking place.
6. The programs make wider use of *more flexible techniques* and *individualization of instruction* because more students are mainstreamed in the elementary school classroom, such as physically or emotionally handicapped and gifted children.

Trends 2 and 6 can be observed in the increased number of funded programs with these emphases. Examples of funded programs that incorporate these trends follow.

Science and Fate Control

Increasing numbers of funded science programs are employing a more humanistic approach in which children's lives are used to highlight and correlate the science concepts. An exemplary program of this type is the Health Activities Project (HAP) developed by the Lawrence Hall of Science of the University of California at Berkeley, supported by a grant from the Robert Wood Johnson Foundation, and published by Hubbard Publishers of Northbrook, Illinois. HAP is a series of scientifically formulated activities designed to develop concepts of "self" and health care such as

☐ How the body works and changes
☐ That the body can be controlled to increase performance, improve skills, develop strength, make decisions that result in healthier, more efficient living
☐ How technological devices are used to evaluate health
☐ How to look at the preventative aspects of health[14]

Notice that HAP is also concerned with helping children raise their consciousness so they can control their bodies and improve their personal performance. This is what is referred to in chapter 4 as "fate control." HAP currently has four modules: Breathing and Fitness, Sight and Sound, Heart Fitness, and Action. Each module has activity folios for students to use in their activities, activity sheets to fill out, teacher's guides and charts, and labeling supplies. Figure 9–13 shows a sample of the kinds of activities and materials used in the Breathing Fitness Module. Notice the stress on awareness and control of body.

Bringing Science to the Handicapped and Gifted

Public Law 94–142 and supporting legislation mandate that we provide physically handicapped children with the optimal means for becoming fully integrated into mainstream classrooms. One such group of handicapped children is the visually impaired. It is very likely that you will some day have such students in your mainstream classroom. Chapter 10 on individualizing science describes activities for bringing science to the handicapped and gifted.

WHAT ALL OF THIS MEANS FOR YOU

You may be asking, "All of this research, innovation, and experimentation is great, but what does it have to do with *me*? I'm only a classroom teacher, not a science education researcher." It has a *lot* to do with any elementary school teacher who must include science in the curriculum.

More educational ideas and materials are being produced than ever before. What used to take 30 years to accomplish, from a new educational idea to actual classroom teaching, now occurs rapidly. We must all be more involved in professional growth activities, through preservice and in-service training, than ever before in our professional history.

Teacher-education courses must present the new programs in science education to *all* prospective teachers. If this is done *before* teachers enter the profession, it is less expensive and more effective than "retraining" teachers through in-service education. There must be a commitment by those responsible for preservice science education courses to include factual materials about, and hands-on activities for, the most recent science education projects.

Elementary school teachers (*and administrators*) currently in service will have to study these programs *in depth* before committing themselves to any specific project. How can this be done?

1. Request that the colleges teach about formerly funded science projects, especially ESS, SAPA, and SCIS. If you are teaching, take a course in innovative science programs for the elementary schools. If one is not currently offered by your local college, request that one be given. The course you take should have you doing the science activities in the same way children will experience them; merely talking about the projects is not enough.
2. A group of teachers in your school or school district could send for information about science projects from the sources listed in this chapter. Make a list of the things you want to investigate, among which might be concerns such as
   a. How do the units cover the elements of science and learning espoused by your school or school district?
   b. Are there many varied activities for children to obtain information, attitudes, and so on?
   c. How are the concepts appropriate for the interests and abilities of your particular students?
   d. In what ways do the concepts challenge the children?
   e. How does the project provide for systematic development of concepts?
   f. How do the teacher's guides provide you with sufficient science and pedagogical information for you to guide the children to discover the goals of the program?
3. Contact the *distributor* of any project, who will usually arrange for a consultant to speak to you about your interests and concerns about the project without any commitment. It is always best to prepare a list of questions ahead of time.
4. Once your school or school district decides upon a *specific* project to follow, contact the distributor. The distributor will usually set up a series of free in-service workshops for all the teachers using the program. Consultants giving workshops are often former classroom teachers or college professors especially trained in the new science project.
5. Become familiar with the materials, science concepts, and teaching strategies during the workshops. *Try the activities yourself!* When you feel comfortable with the activities your students will do, you can then be a good guide for them.
6. Make certain you have *all* the materials needed for the project. New science projects depend on materials, student record sheets, and evaluation sheets where appropriate.
7. Share your success and failures with your fellow teachers *and the consultant or*

Using the breath control device, student teams measure and record data involving their ability to keep a cylinder suspended inside the tube. They learn that practice improves their control.

Working together alternating between being the subject, recorder and the measurer, students use the lung volume bag to measure their lung capacity, then discover the relationship between lung capacity and height. The result is a new respect for their lungs and the knowledge that various factors affect lung volume.

Breathing Fitness Module

Exploring Breath Rates. After learning how to measure their breathing rates, the students investigate the effects of breathing style, breath holding and exercise on breath rate.

Breath Recovery. The students measure and compare their breath recovery after sprinting and after jogging.

Breath Control. The students measure and practice improving their breath control.

Measuring Lung Volume. The students measure their maximum lung volumes and investigate the relationship between lung volume and height.

Through a series of breathing exercises, students explore when, how, and why breathing rates change. They learn about voluntary and automatic breathing, the diaphragm and rib movement during normal, shallow, and deep breathing.

Students experiment to determine their breathing rates before and after exercises. They analyze the difference between resting, after-breath holding, and their after exercise breathing rates.

FIGURE 9–13

Source: *Kids Love Hap.* Developed by the Lawrence Hall of Science of the University of California at Berkeley. Reproduced here by permission of Hubbard Publishers, P.O. Box 104, Northbrook, Illinois 60062, pages 2 and 4–5.

Students count and record breath recovery rates following a 100 meter sprint, then after a jog, and compare the difference. After the exercises, they discuss what breath recovery is, their comparative findings, and why recovery from vigorous exercise takes longer than recovery from lighter activity. They conclude that faster breath recovery rates indicate better physical fitness.

Order the
BREATHING & FITNESS MODULE

CLASS KIT FOR 27 STUDENTS	ORDER NO.	PRICE
	6001	$215.00

- **ACTIVITY FOLIOS, ACTIVITY SHEETS AND TEACHER'S GUIDE**

  - (1) **Exploring Breath Rates** Folio
  - (1) **Breath Recovery** Folio
  - (1) **Breath Control** Folio
  - (1) **Measuring Lung Volume** Folio
  - (1) **What's HAPpening?** Teacher's Information Folio
  - (4) Reproducible Activity Sheets
  - (1) Plastic Pouch

Four 4-Page Activity Folios with (4) Student Activity Sheets and a What's HAPpening? Folio in a Plastic Pouch.

- **CHARTS AND LABELING SUPPLIES**

  - (1) **Our Breathing Fitness** Chart
  - (1) **Our Lung Volumes Chart**
  - (50) Orange Labeling Dots
  - (100) Green Labeling Dots
  - (50) Red Labeling Dots
  - (1) Erasable Crayon

Large 25" x 38" Durable, Reusable Plastic Charts with Special "Write On-Wipe Off" Surface.

Students record their resting breath rates and their breathing rates after holding their breath, then discuss the difference.

- **APPARATUS & EQUIPMENT**

  - (14) Lung Volume Bags
  - (14) Mouth Piece Holders
  - (28) Mouth Pieces
  - (9) Breath Control Meters
  - (4) Meter Tapes
  - (20) Rubber Bands
  - (1) HAP Clock
  - (1) "C" Cell Battery

  - (1) Disinfectant Kit
    - Bleach
    - Detergent
    - Brush
    - Bucket
  - (1) Equipment Storage Box

Kit Contains All the Equipment and Supplies Necessary to Conduct the Activities Described in the Adjacent Copy.

distributor. Constant self-evaluation and sharing of ideas will help you achieve the goals of the project.

If you become involved in teaching any of the new science projects, you will be part of a new and exciting venture. You have a *new* role in developing the science curriculum. Part of this role is being the *only* member of the educational team (professional scientist, child psychologist, curriculum writer, classroom teacher, and so on) setting up a new science project who knows a great deal about the actual teaching relationships *with children.* In addition, you are on the "firing line" of testing the value of any new science program with children.

Many of the decisions on new science projects will eventually rest with you. Therefore, you must be well informed on the current science projects and texts, so you can help select, carry out, and evaluate innovation in science education in the elementary schools. The unique contribution and potential power of the elementary school teacher are summarized by this statement of Hubert H. Humphrey, former school teacher and vice-president of the United States.

> What you really need is a little teaching power. Who knows better what ought to go in a classroom? Who knows better about the kind of teaching tools that work? Who knows better about young people than those who work with them and live with them? Who knows better what the purposes of education are than a trained teacher?

Your role as *guide,* not teller, may be a difficult transition for you. This shift from "purveyor of all knowledge" to intelligent arranger of the learning environment is, however, easily within your reach. To assist you in moving toward this goal, read chapters 6, 7, 10, and 11. With a little practice, your classroom will become a stimulating, open-ended, laboratory-centered science program. Should you want additional information about ESS, SCIS, SAPA, or any other funded science project, see the chart in appendix B.

SUMMARY

The past 100 years have seen radical changes in elementary school science programs, reflecting the century's unprecedented social, economic, scientific, and technological transformations. Each change in science programs was born out of the needs and interests of its time. Programs of the 1950s, 1960s, and 1970s showed intense interest in science as both processes and products using the discovery approach and conceptual schemes.

Experimentation, innovation, and reform in elementary school science were accelerated by massive grants of money from federal, state, and local governments, as well as private foundations such as the Ford Foundation.

Science projects share common elements such as a trend toward open-ended methods of discovery rather than *one* method of problem solving, and they view knowledge as part of a creative process of finding out, rather than the mere accumulation of information.

Funded science projects (e.g., ESS, SAPA, SCIS) differ in the amount of structure in their teaching/learning approach and whether they stress process or content. This chapter looked at the revised versions of the three most popular funded projects, ESS, SCIS, and SAPA.

Innovative science projects have had a substantial impact on many aspects of science in the elementary schools. Science textbooks reflect the discovery activity orientation of these projects. Teachers in those districts that have adopted new science projects must become familiar with them, and this chapter suggests how to do this. *You* are the key to whether the new science programs succeed or fail.

A key trend in science for the 1980s and 1990s is the wider use of teaching activities for *all* children, especially the mainstreaming of handicapped children.

SELF-EVALUATION AND FURTHER STUDY

1. Select an innovative science project (ESS, SCIS, SAPA, HAP, or SAVI) and contrast it either to a local or state school science curriculum or a major science textbook series approach. How are they different? Similar? Which do you prefer? Why?
2. Which of the science projects fits most easily into schools with a "conventional" science program? Why? With open classroom science? Why?
3. Select a unit from ESS that fits into what you are currently teaching in science and integrate it into your teaching.
4. Pick any innovative science project and give examples of how it attempts or does not attempt to present these trends in science education:
   a. Humanistic approach relating concepts to children's lives
   b. Environmental and ecological orientation
   c. Values and social aspects of science
   d. Integration of other subject areas with science
   e. Individualization of teaching strategies
5. Imagine that you have been asked by your principal or supervisor to pick one of the new elementary school science projects to use in teaching your students. React to these items.
   a. What criteria would you use to pick one?
   b. How would you go about collecting data to make your choice?
   c. Which innovative science project would you pick? Why?
   d. How would you evaluate your teaching?

ENDNOTES

1. James A. Shymansky et al., "How Effective Were The Hands-On Science Programs of Yesterday?" *Science and Children*, 20, no. 3 (November/December, 1982), pp. 14–15.
2. Ibid., p. 15.
3. R. B. Nicodemis, *An Evaluation of Elementary Science Study as Science—A Process Approach* (Washington, D.C.: Department of Health, Education and Welfare, Office of Education, 1968). R. E. Rogers and A. M. Voelker, "Programs for Improving Science Instruction in the Elementary School: ESS," *Science and Children* (January/February, 1970).
4. Lawrence F. Lowery et al., "The Science Curriculum Improvement Study and Student Attitudes," *Journal of Research in Science Teaching*, 17, no. 4 (July 1980), pp. 327–35 and Gerald H. Krockover and Marshall D. Malcolm, "The Effects of the Science Curriculum Improvement Study Upon A Child's Attitude Toward Science," *School Science and Mathematics*, 78, no. 7 (November 1978), pp. 575–84.
5. John W. Renner et al., *Research, Teaching, and Learning with Piaget Model* (Norman, Okla.: University of Oklahoma Press, 1976).
6. Jane B. Bowyer and Marcia C. Linn, "Effectiveness of the Science Curriculum Improvement Study in Teaching Scientific Literacy," *Journal of Research in Science Teaching*, 15, no. 3 (May 1978), pp. 209–19.

7. Howard J. Hausman, *Choosing a Science Program for the Elementary School*, Occasional Papers Number Twenty Four (Washington, D.C.: Council for Basic Education, October 1976), p. 19.

8. Douglass Russell Macbeth, "The Extent to Which Pupils Manipulate Materials and Attainment of Process Skills in Elementary School Science," *Journal of Research in Science Teaching* 11, no. 1 (1974), pp. 45–51.

9. Jerry B. Ayers and Mary N. Ayers, "Influence of SAPA on Kindergarten Children's Use of Logic in Problem Solving," *School Science and Mathematics* 73 (December 1973), pp. 768–771.

10. H. H. Walbesser and H. L. Carter, "Acquisition of Elementary Science Behavior by Children of Disadvantaged Families," *Educational Leadership* 25 (May 1968), pp. 741–48.

11. Phyllis Huff and Marlin Languis, "The Effects of the Use of Activities of SAPA on the Oral Communication Skills of Disadvantaged Kindergarten Children," *Journal of Research in Science Teaching* 10 (1973), pp. 165–73.

12. Harold Pratt et al., "Science Education in the Elementary School," in *What Research Says to the Science Teacher, volume 3*, Norris C. Harms and Robert E. Yager, editors (Washington, D.C.: National Science Teachers Association, 1981), p. 84.

13. Ibid., p. 84.

14. *Kids Love HAP*. By permission of Hubbard Publishers, P.O. Box 104, Northbrook, Illinois 60062, pages 2 and 4–5.

10

How Can You Individualize Science for *All* Your Children?

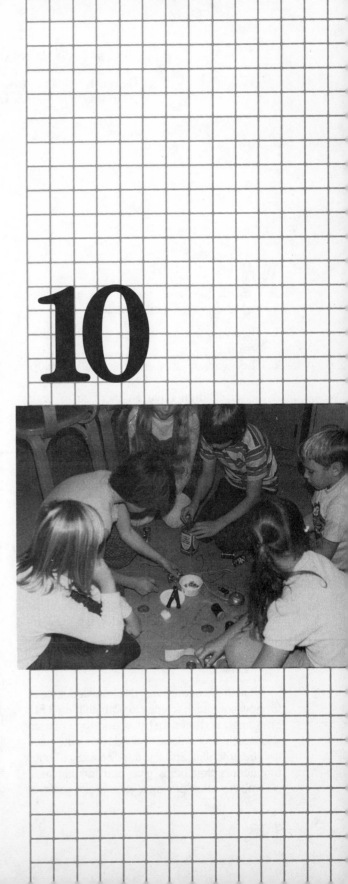

> "... given the blessed variety of students, varying in gifts and destination—there is nothing so unequal as the equal treatment of unequals." (Paul F. Brandwein, "On certain areas of Doubt and Uncertainty in Science Education," *Kappan* [May 1980].)

Much has been said in this text about how children differ. Let's review.

1. They vary in the Piagetian operations they perform.
2. They vary in their neurological development.
3. Some children have an increase in brain mass much sooner than others. Dr. Herman Epstein said this signals a readiness to process information in new, cognitive ways.
4. Children vary a great deal in the degree to which they use their cerebral hemispheres.
   a. Some have a preference for *right* cerebral interaction. They tend to process information in a more holistic manner in music, visual input, body movement, or fantasy. They are often intuitively creative people.
   b. Other children are quite different in the ways their brains process stimuli from the environment. They prefer *left* cerebral interaction and learn better by linear, verbal, mathematical, and analytical processes.

What implications does this knowledge have for how you teach science to your children? For one thing, it shows that you and the children you teach are unique individuals. You have unique potential, and it is the discovery of your uniqueness that helps give you identity as a person. No other person is exactly like you and no other person can become what you have become. This chapter emphasizes the need for individualizing your science teaching, especially for the gifted, hearing-impaired, and visually, physically and mentally handicapped. It also discusses the special need to involve young girls more in elementary science to develop their potentials. *All children are unique in some way.*

The beauty of humanity is the diversity of its talents. The beauty of children is that they have the potential for manifesting these talents. The beauty of teaching is the satisfaction that comes from helping children develop their talents.

WHAT IS INDIVIDUALIZING SCIENCE?

You may have more individualization in your classroom than you realize. To see where you stand, respond to James A. Shymansky's system for monitoring your individualization efforts in figure 10–1. Check the box at the conclusion of this chapter for your individualization score.

The elements in Shymansky's system for monitoring individualization are

1. presenting a variety of instructional materials
2. selecting different media for different students

1. Is your instruction based on one text-book and/or laboratory manual?
   ☐ No—score 1   ☐ Yes—score 0

2. In class today, were different students learning through different media?
   ☐ Yes—score 1   ☐ No—score 0

3. Were students given the option of work-ing on different topics or activities?
   ☐ Yes—score 1   ☐ No—score 0 (skip to No. 5)

4. Who designed the activities that stu-dents worked on?
   ☐ Student—score 1   ☐ Teacher—score 0

5. Did you spend more time interacting with individual students or small groups of less than six than with large groups?
   ☐ Yes—score 1 (go to No. 6) ☐ No—score 0 (stop)

6. Did you spend more time today check-ing on materials, checking and making assignments, and grading work than you did working with students on the science activity, individually, in small groups, and large groups combined?
   ☐ No—score 1   ☐ Yes—score 0

FIGURE 10–1
System for monitoring your individualization efforts

3. giving students the option of working on different topics or activities
4. having students design activities
5. encouraging teacher interaction with indi-viduals or small groups
6. having more teacher time spent on working with individuals and small group activities than checking on materials, assignments, grading, *etc.*

Curriculum Materials for Individualizing Science

Most elementary science programs can be adapted for individualizing. Some curricula, however, have been specifically designed with this purpose in mind. Here is a list of critical reviews of seven valuable programs.

☐ *Evaluating Instructional Systems—PLAN, IGE,—EPIE Educational Product "In Depth" Report #58* (New York: Educa-tional Products Information Exchange In-stitute, 1974).

☐ Samuel N. Henrie, sr. ed., *A Sourcebook of Elementary Curricula Programs and Projects* (San Francisco: Far West Labora-tory for Educational Research and Devel-opment, 1972).

☐ Richard E. Haney, "Teaching Science in IGE Schools," *Science and Children* (Oc-tober 1978), pp. 22–24.

☐ Richard E. Haney and Juanita S. Soren-son, *Individually Guided Science* (Read-ing, Mass.: Addison-Wesley Publishing Co., 1975–77). This is one of nine vol-umes in the IGE Leadership Series.

☐ *Environmental Studies* (Menlo Park, Calif.: Addison-Wesley Publishing Co., 1972).

☐ *Science 5/13* (London, England: Mac-Donald Educational Schools Council, 1973).

☐ *United Sciences and Mathematics for the Elementary School* (Newton, Mass.: Edu-cation Development Center, 1976).

Suggested ESS units to purchase for individ-ualizing. If your school system does not have sufficient funds to purchase the kits, obtain some of the following teacher's guides. In most cases, you can find the materials locally at little expense. These units have been particularly popular with teachers.

Tangrams[2]	Behavior of
Attribute Games	Mealworms
Mirror Cards	Bones
Drops, Streams and	Tracks
Containers	Batteries and Bulbs
Mystery Powders	

Suggested 5–13 units. Another curriculum designed around the unit and based on Piaget is the British-initiated program Science 5–13.

The 5–13 stands for the ages of children for which the different units are designed. This program consists of a number of teacher's guides packed with suggestions. They lend themselves particularly well to the thematic approach or as resources for ideas about small group or individualized instruction. Some available units are

---

Early Experiences—An excellent book for preschool-primary grades.

Time	Ourselves
Science with Toys	Trees
Change (upper elementary only)	Coloured Things

PRACTICAL SUGGESTIONS FOR INDIVIDUALIZING SCIENCE EDUCATION

Regardless of your teaching situation—self-contained, multimedia, or systems approach—you can use these suggestions to extend individualization of instruction for your students. The list is not exhaustive; alert teachers will adapt and vary these ideas for their unique classrooms, as well as discover new ideas. Do not be afraid to try any procedure you believe will provide broader and richer science experiences for your students. Encourage your students to be constantly alert to other things they could be doing in science.

1. Set up an enrichment center for your science-oriented students. This center will offer optional, free-time recreational science activities similar to the kinds of activities students get in intramural sports, band, art or photography club, and dramatics. Ideally, an entire room will be provided for the enrichment center, but it can function in a corner of a classroom, library, multimedia or audiovisual room, or any other room.

Dr. Alan McCormack prepared special materials to be used in enrichment centers. He suggested that in the enrichment center 100 or more challenges should be available on posters or "Challenge Cards." Students should be free to choose any one that interests them and try to solve it. Usually they have two options once a challenge is selected.

a. Solve it completely on their own with simple equipment and science supplies in the center, from home, or from the teacher.

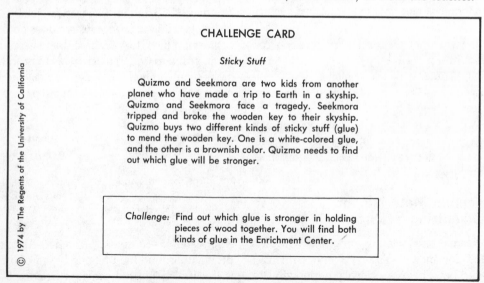

CHALLENGE CARD

Sticky Stuff

Quizmo and Seekmora are two kids from another planet who have made a trip to Earth in a skyship. Quizmo and Seekmora face a tragedy. Seekmora tripped and broke the wooden key to their skyship. Quizmo buys two different kinds of sticky stuff (glue) to mend the wooden key. One is a white-colored glue, and the other is a brownish color. Quizmo needs to find out which glue will be stronger.

Challenge: Find out which glue is stronger in holding pieces of wood together. You will find both kinds of glue in the Enrichment Center.

© 1974 by The Regents of the University of California

FIGURE 10–2

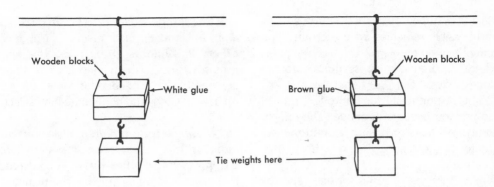

b. Request a "Solution Card" and a corresponding box of materials specifically designed to go with it.

The solution cards have instructions for doing an experiment or using a method to solve the challenge, but, of course, not a *specific* answer. Divergent questions are used on the solution cards to stimulate the student's thinking without giving cookbook answers. By having two options presented to the students, they can choose the amount of structure suitable for them at that particular time. Next time it may be a different selection. Figures 10–2 and 10–3 are samples of challenge and solution cards Dr. McCormack prepared while working at the Lawrence Hall of Science at the University of California.

2. Have students take an active role in changing their own school grounds environment by

a. Participating in a general cleanup of grounds.

b. Making a survey of needed improvements and possible remedies for playground and school ground problems such as worn paths where children cut across grass, eroding slopes, "dust-bowl" play areas, and so on.

c. Taking responsibility for improving one of the problem areas in b above. They might plant small trees or bushes around the perimeter of the school grounds with money they raise.

d. Writing letters to agencies for help, such as ecology groups and county agricultural agents.

e. Reclaiming eroded areas by planting bushes, trees, or ground cover.

3. Encourage students to conduct a survey of people and places in their community as possible resources for science programs. A file can be made of the kinds of science topics studied in school and the places and persons who might contribute in each, like those below.

4. Encourage students to set up a rock garden, birdhouse, bird feeder, birdbath, or other out-of-doors project on the school grounds. Assist them in collecting information about what is needed (and why) for setting up, maintaining, and continuing their selection.

5. Suggest that children visit museums, planetariums, observatories, parks, botanical gardens, or other out-of-school places. Parents should be included in the planning by meetings or by notes sent home to them. They could accompany their children and guide their learning if requested or necessary.

6. Have volunteer children visit the classrooms of younger children to explain science projects, bring in and discuss raising their pets, give slide talks of recent trips, show how their musical instrument works, and so on. Some schools have a cadre of "cadet teachers" of older children to teach younger children.

Biological Sciences	Chemistry	Earth Science	Physics
Biology department (local college)	All kinds of factories	Abandoned quarry	Airport
Farm	Chemistry department (local college)	Field	Astronomical observatory
Fish hatchery	Drugstore	Geology department (local college)	Electronics factory
Food processing plant	Electroplating shop	Museum	Gas station
Greenhouse	Oil refinery	Seashore	Physics department (local college)
Hospital	Plastic industry	Stream	Power dam or electricity generator plant
House excavation	Water purification plant	Weather station	Radio station
Park	Chemical engineer	Astronomer	Television station
Pharmaceutical lab	Chemist	Geologist	Telephone exchange
Vacant lot	Druggist	Mining engineer	Newspaper printing plant
Dentist	Photographer	Pilot or navigator	Architect
Druggist		Weatherman	Builder
Farmer			Automobile mechanic
Florist			Electrician
Laboratory technician			Electronics engineer
Nurse			
Pet shop owner			
Physician			

7. *Accumulate science kits or teacher's guides such as those from Elementary Science Study* (ESS) or Science 5–13 and encourage individuals and small groups of children to "mess around" with them. Students can use these kits during leisure or free time, during "science time," or at home if you think the children are mature enough for this responsibility. Refer to chapter 9 for more information about ESS and Science 5–13.

8. *Secure a copy of television program listings and teacher's guides* if they are available from your local commercial and educational television stations or by writing directly to one of the major national networks.

- ☐ American Broadcasting Company, Inc. (ABC), 1330 Avenue of the Americas, New York, New York 10019.
- ☐ Columbia Broadcasting System, Inc. (CBS), 51 West 52 Street, New York, New York 10019.
- ☐ National Broadcasting Company (NBC), RCA Building, 30 Rockefeller Plaza, New York, New York 10020.

Make a list of pertinent science shows under these headings.

- ☐ Program
- ☐ TV channel
- ☐ Local date, time
- ☐ Science topic covered

Suggest that children view programs of interest to them or assigned to them and report to the class. If you think it is needed or desirable, arrange a worksheet with some specific questions to guide the students' viewing.

9. *Set up science surprise boxes* and encourage students to work with them. The science surprise box is an activity that is popular with students, especially slow learners. Periodically you can display a labeled box. On the front of the box you can print a statement of its content in riddle form such as

> I am hard.
> I can push something without your seeing me push it.
> I can pull something without your seeing me pull it.
> I am iron and nickel.
> What is my name?

One use of the opening of the surprise is to introduce an area of study to the class. In the above box, of course, there would be a magnet. Some teachers put one of the surprise boxes out each day on a table for use by individual students at their leisure. It is also valuable for students to make their own surprise boxes and share them with their classmates. For excellent suggestions on additional boxes, see Eddie L. Whitfield and Eva D. Samples, "Small Box Science: Independent Learning Exercises for Younger Children," *Science and Children*, 18, no. 7 (April 1981), p. 9.

10. *Students can pick a scientific topic, collect display materials from magazines and newspapers, and set up a bulletin board.* By keeping the bulletin board up no longer than one week, you will give all the children an

Solution Card
Sticky Stuff

Materials:
4 wooden blocks (all equal in size)
  string
4 cup hooks
1 weight set
2 different glues

Solution:

1. This won't be tough to do. Take four wooden blocks and make sure they are exactly the same size. Screw a cup hook into the middle of the large face of each block. Place the blocks in pairs, and glue each of the pairs together with one of the glues to be tested. Let the glues dry overnight. Suspend each pair of blocks with strings as shown in the drawing below. Then, add weights to another string tied to the lower side of the blocks. Continue adding weights till one pair of blocks pulls apart.

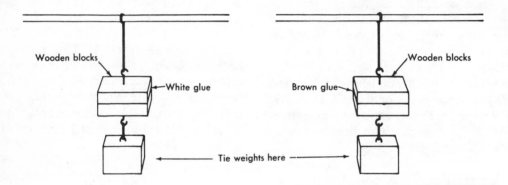

Which variables must be kept the same in both parts of this experiment?
What variable did you change?
What did you find out?

2. Seekmora tried another experiment to test the glue's strength. She glued two wooden blocks together with white glue, and another two with brown glue using equal amounts of glue and blocks exactly the same size. After the glue dried overnight, Seekmora tried to pull the white-glued blocks apart. Quizmo succeeded, but Seekmora did not. Seekmora then decided that white glue was stronger.

What do you think of Seekmora's conclusion?
What variables would you control?
What variables would you change?

New Challenges:

1. Try to think of another (maybe better) way of testing the glues' strength. Find some materials and try your experiment. Compare your results with those of the experiment suggested in #1.
2. Try the "What Does Good Glue Do on a Rainy Day?" Challenge Card.

FIGURE 10–3

Source: Reprinted with permission from the Enrichment Center Trial Editions, by the Lawrence Hall of Science. Copyright 1974 by the Regents of the University of California.

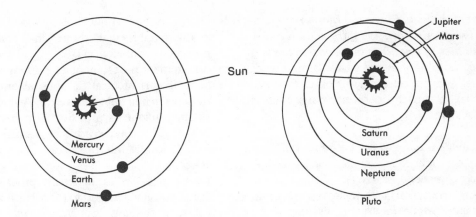

FIGURE 10-4

opportunity to participate in making one. This also increases children's interest in looking at the bulletin boards as they have participated in their construction, and the boards do not get "stale."

11. Have several students work together in a panel discussion of a science topic such as the problems of scientific exploration. These questions might be used, for instance, as the focus for the discussion.

> What provisions would you need to take to the moon? Mars? Antarctica? Mohave Desert?
> What types of research or studies do you think should be carried out when you get there?

If you tape the discussion, ask students later to conduct self-evaluations of their contributions as well as those of their classmates.

12. Assist students in the upper elementary grades to prepare personal progress files. Each student should get a file into which he or she places summaries of all types of science activities that he or she has completed.

13. Contact your local museum to see if they have any special science program that your students individually or as a group might attend.

14. Introduce the science discovery chart to your class. The science discovery chart is a

bulletin board or chart that has pieces of string going from the board to objects near it. Students print what they think the object is on small cards, along with their names. They pin the cards to the end of the string. After several children have had a chance to pin their cards on the board, the teacher then discusses their answers. A typical chart might show some simple machines: inclined plane, pulley, lever, screw, wheel, and axle. The discovery chart can be used to review or introduce an area of science. Figure 10-4 is a chart showing the different heavenly bodies in the solar system.

15. Secure many different science trade-books on a variety of reading levels. Ask students to read a book of their choice and report about the book to their peers in any way they choose—orally, by tape-recording, with a drawing, in writing, and so on. There are many high-interest, low-vocabulary science books, so all students (including very young children or those with reading difficulties) can benefit from books such as

- ☐ *What Is It Series* (Chicago: Benefic Press).
- ☐ *All About Books* (New York: Random House, Inc.).
- ☐ *Webster Classroom Science Series—Let's Read About Series* (St. Louis: Webster Publishing Co.).
- ☐ *About Book Series* (Chicago: Melmont Publishing Co.).

16. Help students to see the human orientation of science by providing them with many biographies of scientists on as wide a reading level as possible. Several students may work together and put on a play or other dramatic presentation showing particular parts of their scientist's life.

17. Provide a table or bookcase for children to display their collections of rocks, leaves, birdnests, insects, or coins. They can explain their collections with signs, reports, or an audiotape cassette for classmates to play by themselves.

18. Make up a series of pictorial riddles on 5″ x 8″ index cards or larger on oaktag. Here's how to make your own riddles.

a. Select some concept or principle to be taught or discussed.

b. Draw a picture, show an illustration, or use a photograph that shows the concept, process, or situation.

c. An alternate procedure is to present something that is atypical or unusual and ask students to find out what is wrong with it. An example might be a picture of a big man being held up on a seesaw by a small man. Ask, "How is this possible?" (See figure 10–5.)

d. Devise a series of divergent process-oriented questions related to the picture which will help students gain insights into what principles are involved.

19. Organize a science club for highly interested and motivated students. The club can meet before or after school, during free time during the day, or Saturdays. Perhaps a parent can serve as guide or leader. Students from this

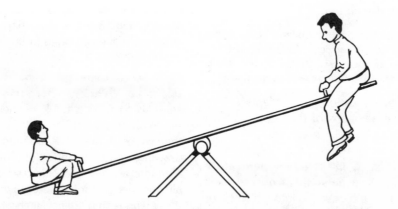

How Does a Lever Work?
(Grades 5–8)

What do you notice about this picture?
What are all the ways this is possible?
(Teacher's Note: There are over 100 possible explanations: The board is nailed in place. The big individual has just pushed up. He is filled with air, pillows, etc. He only appears larger since the board is rotating and he is closer to you. This is in outer space. The board is not made of the same material on each side of the pivot point or fulcrum, etc. How many more can you add?

FIGURE 10–5

club may also function as science cadet teachers or science helpers. Many schools find these students are excellent resources for teachers throughout the school.

20. Extend the science club with a weekly or monthly school science newspaper. Students from kindergarten on up love to contribute art, pictorial riddles, brain-teasers, book or TV reviews, etc. News of which classes have the rock collections, pets, insects, plays, or dioramas can be inserted so all may share the science activities of the entire school.

21. Use computers and microcomputers in your classroom. For practical applications see chapter 13 on mathematics and the computer in elementary science. This twenty-page pamphlet contains information on the use of computers: *Guidelines for Computers in Education.* A Position Statement Prepared by the Association of Mathematics Teachers of New York State, July 1982.

SCIENCE FOR GIFTED AND TALENTED STUDENTS

So far this chapter has focused upon enrichment for *all* children. Some students, however, may have unusual skills, interests, attitudes, and motivations in science. Often, teachers are at a loss to provide for these gifted and talented students. Gifted students stand out from other students because they *usually*, but not always

- [ ] speak well and have large and varied vocabularies
- [ ] display longer attention spans
- [ ] are extremely curious
- [ ] possess excellent academic skills, especially reading
- [ ] comprehend and follow directions very well
- [ ] seek out activities and hobbies in science areas
- [ ] enjoy puzzles and games of an open-ended type, e.g., Rubik's Cube, electronic games and computers, etc.[3]

- [ ] are more interested in broad concepts and issues than other children

These students love to participate in many of the activities previously mentioned in this chapter. In addition, there are many ways of challenging their intellects by providing them with meaningful enrichment activities. If you have children with the attributes mentioned above, these suggestions may prove useful.

Learn with and from your gifted students. Most elementary school teachers have not majored in science and, therefore, may find that some of their gifted students know more about certain areas of science than they do. Not feeling totally competent with science should not stop you from having gifted students do more advanced work than the rest of the class. Children enjoy seeing their teachers get excited about the results of students' work. In addition, this approach tends to break down the traditional view of teacher as giver of knowledge. You can truly become a teacher/facilitator/arranger of the learning environment, an adult questioner, and a constant positive critic. It may help you to keep a perspective when you feel inadequate in science by remembering that for all their knowledge, gifted students are still elementary school children socially, emotionally, and physically. They need your mature adult guidance and professional training in education and psychology.

Encourage gifted students to do simple, unstructured experiments. Gifted students should be challenged to do simple, unstructured experiments to find answers which are not easily available from texts or encyclopedias. These experiments differ from the cookbook kind because they do not have predetermined results or step-by-step procedures worked out in advance.

Keep these things in mind while guiding gifted students through unstructured experimentation.

- [ ] Start by using the combined talents of the class or group. Later, when routines are established, individuals may explore on their own.

☐ Keep the experimentation within the limits of time, talents, and easily available apparatus. Explore these limitations *before* suggesting problems.

☐ Be alert to the open-endedness of this type of experimentation. Frequently, questions will arise such as "Suppose we varied the experiment in this way, what will happen?"

☐ Do not assume that the gifted child will continue to have a sustained interest in the problem. You must continually check on progress.

Gifted students should use mathematics more frequently. Mathematics is the language of science, and gifted students should be encouraged to use it as much as possible. They should be as much involved with "how much" or "what relationships exist between" as they are in answering the "how," "what," and "why." Wherever possible, ask students to quantify their findings.

With the increased availability of microcomputers both at home and in school, gifted children especially are drawn to these challenging electronic machines. See chapter 13 for materials on the use of microcomputers in elementary school science.

Work with parents of gifted students. Encourage parents of gifted students to obtain books, magazines, and science kits and materials and to discuss science with their children. Often, desirable scientific learning situations arise when the family takes a vacation. Stress the importance of the parents' buying or taking from the library supplemental booklets such as the How and Why Wonder Books and the Golden Books. Explain the desirability of motivating and supplying "intellectual fuel" for the gifted child. Assure the parents of gifted children that their children are not freaks and, given continual opportunities, will be leaders as they mature and grow up.

Give leadership roles to gifted students. Ask gifted students to be science assistants to

help with preparing materials, dispensing and collecting equipment and supplies, collecting information about experiments, and assisting less able classmates with some aspect of their science work. Often, peer teaching/learning is more effective than learning from teacher-pupil exchanges. Students gifted in science may also create teaching models related to the science units being studied. These models may be weather instruments, electrical devices, atomic or solar systems, or scale models of local environmental or ecological systems.

ENCOURAGING GIFTED AND TALENTED IN THE MAINSTREAM SCIENCE CLASSROOM

Most highly motivated, bright students need little encouragement. For those that do, these suggestions may be useful.

1. Provide recognition for their efforts.
2. Provide extra credit for novel ideas or products.
3. Stress positive comments in all teacher-pupil exchanges.
4. Offer special privileges for specified performances.
5. Permit high-achieving students to be "teacher."
6. Encourage student-initiated projects and activities for those who have completed assignments.
7. Make special arrangements for high-achieving students to take selected subjects in higher grades.

8. Introduce elementary age students to research methods.
9. Teach debating skills and encourage students to sponsor and participate in debates on topics of their choice.
10. Have high-achieving math students create mathematical puzzles.
11. Encourage students to write scripts for TV and radio programs and "participate in" the programs.
12. Have students present a synopsis of a magazine or newspaper article to the class in a way that is interesting and understandable.
13. Have a "crazy idea" session where only unusual notions can be discussed.
14. Conduct a traditional brain-storming session.
15. Let them express themselves in art forms such as drawings, creative writing, and role playing.
16. Have them dramatize their readings.
17. Have a great books seminar to introduce students to the classics.[4]

Special Provisions for the Gifted Out of the Classroom

It is very difficult, if not impossible, to provide information and activities to your gifted children in all their areas of interests in the classroom. These out-of-classroom ideas may be helpful to you.

1. Make library services available to them. If the school library is inadequate, take them on regular trips, if possible, to a public library. Arrange to secure hard-to-get materials from state or university libraries.
2. Try to guide the children to the resources they need. Refer them to encyclopedias, dictionaries, and other reference sources.
3. Develop a catalog of other resources which students can use, possibly containing addresses of agencies providing free and inexpensive materials or local community resources.
4. Form interest clubs with students as officers.
5. Identify people in the community who are available to work with individual gifted students. Help those who are knowledgeable in their fields but do not know how to manage or teach children.[5]

Teaching Methods That Encourage Gifted Students

In our society, children's thinking is often trained to focus on *the right answer*. This sometimes discourages gifted students from taking risks in academic situations. They may be confused or feel threatened with failure when they are faced with tasks in which there are no clear answers, or in which there may be a variety of correct answers. Try some of these techniques to encourage them.

1. Use a questioning technique rather than giving information.
2. Use hypothetical questions beginning with "What if . . .?"
3. Ask students to develop situations where no one answer is correct.
4. In subjects such as arithmetic, where specific answers are required, encourage students to estimate their answers.
5. Have students check your written work for errors; let them see that all adults are fallible.
6. Instead of information only, emphasize concepts, theories, ideas, relationships, and generalizations.
7. Provide opportunities and assignments which rely on independent reading and research.
8. Have students give reports on their individual research and experimentation; this helps them acquire a sense of sharing their knowledge.
9. Provide foreign language materials—books, periodicals, recordings, newspapers—for young gifted children.[6]

ECONOMICALLY, SOCIALLY, AND/OR CULTURALLY DISADVANTAGED CHILDREN

Gifted students offer a special kind of challenge to the elementary school teacher. Another kind of challenge is meeting the needs and interests of children on the other side of the continuum, those who are *not* school-oriented, often feel hostile to school and society, and lack the academic skills necessary to cope with the average curriculum of our schools. For want of more accurate descriptions, we refer to these children as economically, socially, or culturally disadvantaged.

It is almost impossible to pick up a professional text or journal, watch TV, or read a newspaper or magazine without some reference to economically and/or socially disadvantaged children. Causes, effects, and proposals for this urgent social problem should rank among our nation's highest priorities. These children, although from a variety of racial and cultural backgrounds, seem to exhibit similar characteristics.

1. They have a lack of experiences in childhood, which most of us take for granted, with things such as gardens, elevators, pets, trains, and open countryside.
2. They want action rather than introspection.
3. They respond better to structure and organization than to a more flexible situation.
4. They benefit more from **simple, more** concrete, scientifically **demonstrable explana**tions than from symbolic, circuitous interpretations.
5. They want informal, sympathetic, non-patronizing relationships rather than intensive, formal ones.

When you study the needs, interests, and expectations of disadvantaged children, you are struck with how pertinent a laboratory-centered science program is, with an emphasis upon actual manipulation of concrete materials. You will find these kinds of activities are excellent ways of meeting the needs of *all* children, but they are especially valuable for disadvantaged children. Don't forget that culturally, socially, or economically disadvantaged children can be found in rural and suburban, as well as urban, areas.

The following sources reveal that students of low ability, underachievers, and disruptive students actually *outperformed* counterpart groups in conventional single-mode classroom settings (usually just textbook) when given a multi-mode, optional-activity approach to elementary school science.

T. E. Allen, "A Study of the Behaviors of Two Groups of Disruptive Children When Taught with Contrasting Strategies: Directive vs. Non-directive Teaching." Unpublished doctoral dissertation, The Florida State University, 1976.

J. E. Penick et al., "Studying the Effects of Two Quantitatively Defined Teaching Strategies on Student Behavior in Elementary School Science Using Macroanalytic Techniques." *Journal of Research in Science Teaching*, 13, no. 4 (1976), pp. 289–96.

J. A. Shymansky et al., "A Study of Self-Perceptions Among Elementary School Students Exposed to Contrasting Teaching Strategies in Science." *Science* Education, 58, no. 3 (1974), pp. 331–41.

_____, "How Teaching Strategies Affect Students: Implications for Teaching Science," *What Research Says to the Science Teacher, volume 1,* Mary Budd Rowe, editor (Washington, D. C.: National Science Teachers Association, 1978), pp. 31–39.

Frank Riesman, *The Culturally Deprived Child* (New York: Harper & Row, 1962).

_____, "Education of the Culturally Deprived Child," *The Science Teacher* (November 1965).

Use the student's immediate environment.
All children are concerned with the world around them and disadvantaged children are no exception. However, the environment of disadvantaged children is very restricted and, in many ways, different from that of their teacher. Joan Rosner listed these ten objects that disadvantaged children might see first as they step outside their building in the city and suggested

them as the possible starting points for a city kid's science program.[7]

1. Concrete sidewalk
2. A bird eating food scraps
3. A curb-side tree
4. Ants crawling on the sidewalk and along its edges
5. A dandelion
6. People-people-people-people
7. Automobiles, trucks, taxis
8. Gutters and sewers
9. Trash cans overflowing
10. Bare, hard, compacted soil on a shortcut through a vacant lot, or a curbside grassland

Rosner expands upon each of these city aspects, giving practical applications for science study such as

Concrete Sidewalk

What is concrete? What natural materials are used to make it? Are there cracks? If so, what may have caused them? Is anything green growing in the cracks? If so, what? (Probably moss and weeds.) How did these little plants get into the cracks? Discuss seed and spore dispersal. Introduce the concept of plant succession and relate it to the natural process which produced forests from bare rock. Examine the moss and weeds with a magnifying glass. Compare their structure. Scrape some of the moss out with a knife. Moisten it and place it in a covered dish. Leave it in the classroom in a spot where it can get

sunlight for a half hour a day.

If there are no plants in the crack, scrape out some of the soil. Place it in an egg carton, moisten it slightly, and keep it for several weeks in a warm spot in the classroom. Does anything germinate?

On a hot day, feel the sidewalk. Take the temperature of the concrete and compare it with the surface temperature in an adjacent weed patch. Which is hotter? Which retains heat longer? How might retention of concrete affect the city's temperature during a prolonged hot spell? What is meant by the statement that "cities make their own climates"?[8]

Survey your students to see how many of them have never experienced some of the common things *you* take for granted. Then *do something about it!*

Capitalize on real problems. As you broaden the children's exposure to the world around them, you will raise many questions in their minds. Questions like these are uppermost in the minds of disadvantaged children and could be the focus for science studies.

Why are there more rats and roaches in city buildings than other places?

How do you get rid of them?

How do cities get food for all the people living there if there aren't any farms in the cities?

What happens to the garbage and toilet wastes when they leave our buildings?

Why are some people's skins different colors?

How can curb trees grow in a city right through concrete? Why does the city plant them?

Why are there wire cages around city trees?

Where does the electricity come from when we turn on the light switch?

Why do people take dope? What does it do to you? Where does it come from?

Often these children do not get answers to their questions in their early childhood from parents or others and, therefore, stop asking. Always respond to their questions, even if it is only with, "Let's find out about that tomorrow."

In *Home Sick? Try House Sense*, an innovative comprehensive housing curriculum for New York City neighborhoods, the problem of rats becomes a practical study for urban kids.

Here is a sample of a follow-up worksheet children will use with their families and Bureau of Pest Control to do something about the situation. In this way, science becomes real in their lives.[9]

CHILDREN WITH GENERAL LEARNING DISABILITIES

Other children who can benefit from activity-based science programs are the approximately 4.5 million who are labeled "mentally retarded." About 350,000 of these children are enrolled in some form of schooling.

Definitions vary widely for the severity of mental retardation. The American Association on Mental Deficiency (AAMD) uses this definition of mental retardation.

> Mental retardation refers to subaverage general intellectual functioning which originates during the developmental period and is associated with impairment in adaptive behavior.

Many noted persons in the field, however, propose that the term *mental retardation* be abandoned because it has negative connotations and because it does not relate to education. They generally suggest that the alternative term to use is *general learning disabilities*. While the latter definition helps us develop a more positive and/or restrictive definition of mental retardation, the major professional organizations actively serving the retarded advocate the use of the AAMD definition.

Educators often classify retardation according to these levels of severity: *mildly retarded* (referred to as "educable mentally retarded"), *moderately retarded* ("trainable mentally retarded"), and *severely retarded*. Research at Colorado State College and Florida State University has found that moderately retarded students can learn some basic concepts. Mildly retarded students, in addition, can learn to predict, compare, group or classify, control a variable with help, outline a simple investigation, measure, observe, and communicate, and interpret simple data.[10]

What a Pest!

DIRECTIONS: Look at all of the pictures below. Read each question with the entire class.

ACTIVITY: Circle the correct answer (s). Some questions may have more than one correct answer! Discuss your answers to each question with your classmates.

1. *CIRCLE* the picture of the rat.

A.    B.   C.   D.    E.

2. *CIRCLE* the picture(s) of the things a rat needs.

A. 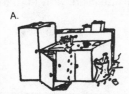   B.   C.    D.

WATER   FOOD   A DAILY BATH   SHELTER

3. *CIRCLE* the picture(s) of the places where a rat would like to live.

A.    B.   C. 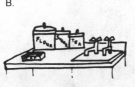   D.

4. *CIRCLE* the picture(s) of what to do to get rid of rats.

A.   B.   C.   D.

"AIR-MAILING" GARBAGE   CLEAN, DRY COUNTERS, SEALED CONTAINERS   CALL THE HEALTH DEPT.   COOPERATION

CONCLUSION: Discuss with your classmates other ways to get rid of rats. Discuss what problems rats cause. Remember rats can bite, destroy property, and cause disease.

Show this worksheet to members of your family. With them, discuss whether any of the conditions shown in the photographs could be found in your building or neighborhood. If your parents or guardians know that rats are living in your neighborhood, tell them they can contact the Bureau of Pest Control for information, advice, and possible assistance in eliminating the rats. Tell them to call: Bureau of Pest Control at 285-9503, the Health Department Central Complaint number.

Answers: 1. D; 2. A,B,D; 3. A,C,D; 4. B,C,D

Mildly retarded students can be effectively educated in the regular self-contained elementary school classroom with individualized instruction and the help of specialists such as a resource teacher. This is called mainstreaming. Moderately retarded students generally need a highly specialized program and are commonly placed in self-contained classes with children with the same learning disabilities.

Most likely, you will at some time have children who are mildly retarded. These children often have difficulty centering on one aspect of an activity at a time. Therefore, it is best to limit your goals for each lesson. If you want to discuss the children's findings at the conclusion of a lesson, collect all the materials from the children *before* starting the discussion, because these children are easily distracted by the materials before them and will not pay attention to the discussion.

Meeting Special Needs of Mildly Retarded Students in Science

Here are some practical suggestions for meeting special needs of these children in your regular classroom science program.

1. It is vital for these children that you emphasize *concrete*, meaningful content. It is important to use examples from the child's environment such as colors of a school bus, grass, or their clothing when talking about colors.
2. Reinforce mastery of new materials through *repetition* and use of multimedia. For instance, after working with children on germinating seeds, reinforce by reading a story, showing a filmstrip, or listening to a tape.
3. Teach sequenced information from the easy to the difficult. If these children are to learn to cut paper strips to measure non-numer-

ically the growth of their plants, start them cutting short straight lines, then move into cutting longer straight lines, and then to two-dimensional cuts.

4. Increase attention initially by highlighting relevant dimensions and by minimizing unnecessary stimuli, e.g., darken room and present materials about magnets on the overhead or opaque projector.

5. Secure commercially prepared materials. The Biological Sciences Curriculum Study (BSCS), Boulder, Colorado, designed and field tested activity-centered science curricula for mildly retarded children. They presently have two available from commercial companies: *Me Now,* for elementary-aged children, and *Me and My Environment,* for older children. Materials include filmstrips, models, film loops, teacher's guides, 35 mm. daylight projection slides, test booklets, student worksheets, charts and picture cards, and scientific equipment. Presently BSCS is planning a similar type of curriculum for the primary level.

6. Use ESS for special education. Thirty-one ESS units have been identified as appropriate for children who have *learning difficulties*. A guide has been designed primarily for use by teachers of mildly retarded children, but other teachers will find it valuable. If interested, you may send for a copy through the distribution center nearest you: Ask for David W. Ball, *ESS Special Education Teacher's Guide* (St. Louis, Missouri: Webster/McGraw-Hill, 1978).

Units selected for special education are divided into three categories: perceptual, psychomotor, and other appropriate units. They follow the same sequence:

a. Description of audience (that is, type of child, grade range, and so on)
b. Overview giving unit description and what it can do for the child
c. Specification of objectives
d. "Ways of getting started" for unit initiation
e. "Keeping it going"
f. "Other classroom tips"
g. Evaluation checklist
h. Time required
i. Ordering information

If you work with exceptional children, you will find this new guide extremely helpful.

Visually Impaired Children

You will probably have visually impaired students in your classroom. These children are ". . . any students who need special aids and/or instruction to read ordinary print, as well as the student who must read braille. This includes both totally blind students and partially sighted students."[11]

Elva R. Gough suggests that it is very important for the visually handicapped to be well oriented with the laboratory and the equipment. When appropriate, students should prepare braille labels and affix them to the scientific equipment; braille grades can be affixed to papers and quizzes.

The Lawrence Hall of Science of the University of California at Berkeley, with the aid of a grant from the Health, Education and Welfare Department, has produced Science Activities for the Visually Impaired (SAVI). It is a discovery-oriented science curriculum, developed by many of the original SCIS team, and reflecting many of the SCIS ideas. SAVI consists of three sets of activity folios, with sections on overview, background, purpose, materials, anticipating (what to do before starting), doing the activity, and follow-up. Figure 10–6 is an example of how the developers of SAVI provided metric measurement activities for visually impaired students.

Examples of other science programs for the handicapped are Adapting Science Materials for the Blind (ASMB) and Science Enrichment for Learners with Physical Handicaps (SELPH). If you are interested in finding out more about science programs for the handicapped and gifted, *see*

1. Appendix B of this book, Curriculum Projects Update
2. Office of Education, Bureau of Education for the Handicapped, Washington, D.C.

3. Elva R. Gough, "Common Sense and Sensitivity in Teaching the Blind," *The Science Teacher* 45, no. 9 (December 1978): 34–35
4. The *whole* issue of *Science and Children* 13, no. 6 (March 1976) entitled "Science for the Handicapped" with these three parts:
   ☐ Part 1—Definition and Discussion
   ☐ Part 2—Science Programs
   ☐ Part 3—Activities
5. The *whole* issue of *Science and Children* 16, no. 6 (March 1979) entitled "Science and Giftedness," containing 17 articles on science and the gifted
6. Helenmarie H. Hofman and Kenneth S. Ricker, *Sourcebook: Science Education and the Physically Handicapped* (Washington, D.C.: National Science Teachers Association, 1979)

Science Enrichment for Learners with Physical Handicaps

The Science Enrichment for Learners with Physical Handicaps (SELPH) Project, Lawrence Hall of Science, University of California, is presently working on adapting SAVI materials for use with disabled students. This project is also designing learning centers to be used in mainstreamed classrooms for the orthopedically disabled. These centers will have materials that are hands-on, multisensory, discovery-oriented science activities.

The Hearing Impaired

It is particularly important when working with hearing impaired students that you use the chalkboard a lot and identify the science concepts you are teaching in written form. You can also use language cards. When these children are involved in activities, place them in circles with other children so they can easily see what is going on. When you demonstrate, use lots of visual aids, pantomime, and body language. A particularly helpful source for teaching the visually and hearing handicapped is Doris E. Hadary and Susan Hadary Cohen, *Laboratory Science and Art for Blind, Deaf, and Emotionally Disturbed Children, A Mainstreaming Approach* (Baltimore: University Park Press, 1978).

SCIENCE EDUCATION IN THE BALANCE

During the past spring and fall, SAVI answered the cry for metric measurement activities for visually impaired students with the SAVI **Measurement Module.** The six hands-on activities contained in this module introduce youngsters to standard units of metric measurement.

In order to develop the concept of *mass*, we needed a measuring tool that would be suitable for use by the visually impaired. We finally decided to use a balance instead of a spring scale or other device and this decision resulted in some unexpected dividends for the project.

We looked at a lot of balances before we made the decision and even built a few of our own. Finally, we chose a simple, vacuum-formed model that is commercially available at a reasonable price. Then, we went to work on it!

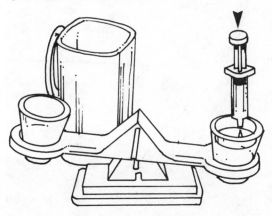

First, we cut the bottoms of the two balance pans so that a paper or plastic cup could be dropped securely into the hole and then removed easily. Then, we added a tactile balance indicator. These slight modifications made it possible for blind students to determine weight to an accuracy of one gram!

The removable cup was the breakthrough we needed to make accurate weighing easy for visually impaired students. Both the weights (20g, 10g, 5g, 1g plastic pieces) and the objects or substances to be weighed automatically center in the cups, thus eliminating discrepancies due to the position of objects in the cups. An object, substance, or liquid can be removed from the balance *cup and all*; a new cup can then be inserted and a new material weighed. There's no more trouble "getting all the powder out," or "transferring the beans"; the objects stay in the cups.

The students use the balances to verify that 50 ml of water (measured with a modified SAVI syringe) weigh 50g, thereby establishing the relationship between volume and mass.

Since its introduction, the SAVI balance has crept into other modules. The forthcoming **Kitchen Interactions** Module will feature an activity that focuses on the concept of *density*. Density is defined operationally using the SAVI balance: equal volumes of two different liquids are compared on the balance and the heavier one is identified as the *denser* liquid.

FIGURE 10–6

Source: *SAVI Update—Science Activities for the Visually Impaired,* January 1979, Lawrence Hall of Science, University of California, Berkeley, California, p. 2. Copyright 1979 by the Regents of the University of California.

Special Needs of Girls in Science

In the United States and Canada, there are fewer women in the scientific professions than in some other nations. Recent research by Dr. Herman Epstein has shown that in early adolescence, girls precede boys in the increase in the mass of their brains. This increase is mainly due to a large number of new nerve cell interconnections being produced. Dr. Epstein believes that when these interconnections are produced, it is critical for girls to have educational experiences requiring the use of their minds in new cognitive, formalistic ways. Women teachers, who have often themselves experienced educational environments where they were not challenged, may continue to perpetuate the situation because of personal feelings of inadequacy they have relative to science. Dr. Mary Budd Rowe, who spent years analyzing elementary children's thinking, emphasized this point when she said

> Girls at all socio-economic levels act with respect to science as though they are handicapped. . . . It is tempting to speculate that one reason so little science is being given to the groups who most need it may be related to the feelings of low confidence that so many women have when it comes to science. Wouldn't it be too bad if our children were kept in a deficit condition because many of their teachers do not know or/ (sic) understand what the treatment could accomplish for them?[12]

For additional information and activities for special children, see the appendices for lists of resources for books, activities, and other teaching ideas.

SUMMARY

Individualized instruction is not new; it was the main system of instruction in the one-room schoolhouse. Research has shown that achievement in individualized schools is as high as, or higher than, in traditional classes. However, there is greater interest, better attendance, more enjoyment by students, and a more positive attitude toward teaching and schools by teachers and parents.

Most elementary science curricula can be adapted for individualized instruction. Those that are particularly helpful are ESS and Science 5–13. Some curricula have been specially designed for this purpose, including individualized Science (IS), Individually Guided Education (IGE), and Program for Learning in Accordance with Needs (PLAN).

Several practical suggestions for individualizing science are

1. Enrichment centers
2. Challenge and solution cards—OBIS
3. Student school ground activities
4. Out-of-doors activities
5. Visitations to museums, parks, etc.
6. Children teaching children
7. Science kits
8. Creative use of television
9. Science surprise boxes
10. Student bulletin boards
11. Student panel discussions
12. Student personal progress files
13. Use of museums
14. Science discovery charts
15. Science tradebook reports
16. Biographies of scientists
17. Student displays

18. Pictorial riddles
19. Science clubs
20. School or classroom newspaper

These suggestions are for *all* children. Some of your students, however, may have unusual talents, interests, and motivations in science. This chapter includes additional suggestions for *gifted* children in activities such as learning with and from your gifted students, encouraging them to perform simple *unstructured* experiments, having them use mathematics more frequently, working with their parents, and giving them leadership roles.

Economically, socially, and/or culturally disadvantaged children present different kinds of challenges. Suggestions for these children are in the discussion about using the student's immediate environment.

Mainstreamed children need special consideration in presenting science. Special science curricula have been designed for the mildly retarded and the visually handicapped. Several resources are also available for the visually and hearing handicapped.

To combat cultural bias and take advantage of earlier brain development, girls need challenging science experiences to ensure that they become better thinkers and have greater professional opportunities.

Scoring information on figure 10–1, System for Monitoring Your Individualizing Efforts on page 199: Add up your scores. If you got six points, your science program is individualized. Now refine other efforts such as questioning skills. If your score is three to five, you are headed in the right direction and are ready to take the next steps. If your score is less than three, yet you think you have an individualized program, you need to take a closer look. That's nothing more than you'd expect your students to do in the event they too achieved less.

SELF-EVALUATION AND FURTHER STUDY

1. Find science activities suitable for a handicapped child in your class or school to perform while your other students are investigating a science topic. Use references in this chapter or others you find more suitable.
2. Blindfold yourself and try to move around a laboratory. Have someone lead you through the laboratory first. Try to enumerate the things the guide should point out to you. Keep this list and use it when you have a visually impaired student in your class.
3. Put ear plugs in your ears and have another student teach you a science lesson. What problems did you encounter? What can you do to overcome some of these problems?
4. Construct some challenge cards of your own. Look at science resource books or texts to get ideas.
5. Make some discovery science charts.
6. Make some science surprise boxes.
7. Make a storyboard using several related pictures or pictorial riddles. Mount these on cardboard and cover them with plastic for protection.
8. Outline how you'd invite and use student-produced display science material.
9. Investigate in depth some of the science curriculum materials mentioned in this chapter.

10. Read the following excellent article to see how hemispheric preference is related to high ability and low ability elementary children: M. Shannon, and Dale R. Rice, "A Comparison of Hemispheric Preference Between High Ability and Low Ability Elementary Children," *Educational Research Quarterly* (Fall 1983), 7 (3), pp. 7–15.

ENDNOTES

1. James A. Shymansky, "Rating Your Individualized Program," *Science and Children*, 17, no. 5 (February 1980), p. 33.
2. An excellent source for constructing hundreds of Tangrams of your own is Joost Elffers, *Tangram, The Ancient Chinese Shapes Game* (New York: Penguin Books, 1976).
3. For additional information on identification and encouragement of, and programs for, gifted students, see Donald F. Sellin and Jack W. Birch, *Psychoeducational Development of Gifted and Talented Learners* (Rockville, Maryland: Aspen Systems Corp., 1981); and Norris G. Haring, editor, *Exceptional Children and Youth, third edition, Behavior of Exceptional Children, second edition* (Columbus, Ohio: Charles E. Merrill Publishing Co., 1982).
4. Thomas M. Stephens and Joan S. Wolf, "The Gifted Child," *Behavior of Exceptional Children, second edition,* Norris G. Haring, editor (Columbus, Ohio: Charles E. Merrill Publishing Co., 1978), p. 404.
5. Ibid., p. 404.
6. Ibid., pp. 404–5.
7. Joan Rosner, "Ecology for Urban Children," *The World Around You Environmental Education Packet* (New York: The Garden Club of America, 1972).
8. Ibid.
9. *Home Sick? Try House Sense:* A Comprehensive Housing Curriculum for New York City Neighborhoods, prepared by New York City Department of Housing Preservation and Development, Office of Program and Management Analysis in cooperation with the New York City Board of Education, Division of Curriculum and Instruction, 1982, p. 219.
10. William Sweeters, "A Study to Determine if Educable Mentally Retarded Children Can Learn Selected Teaching Objectives through Individualized Discovery Oriented Instruction" (Ph.D. diss., Colorado State College, 1968); and N. M. Robinson and H. B. Robinson, *The Mentally Retarded Child: A Psychological Approach, second edition* (New York: McGraw-Hill, 1976).
11. Elva R. Gough, "Common Sense and Sensitivity in Teaching the Blind," *The Science Teacher* 45, no. 9 (December 1978), pp. 34–35.
12. Mary Budd Rowe, "Help Is Denied to Those in Need," *Science and Children*, March 1975, p. 25.

11

How Can You Encourage Creativity and Critical Thinking?

For years, people believed that being creative was sort of like having curly hair; either you were born with it or you weren't. Now a large body of research suggests that creativity does not have to be left to chance but in fact can be nurtured. While early scholars defined creativity primarily in terms of what it produced, recent thinking deals more with creativity as a *process*. (John E. Penick, "What Research Says: Encouraging Creativity", *Science and Children*, 20, no. 5 [February 1983], p. 32.)

One of the goals of education is to foster and encourage creativity and critical thinking. However, too often only children with high IQs or precocious language and reading skills receive attention. Few science teachers consider students' science interests and potential talents. Evaluate yourself with figure 11–1, the check-list for recognizing a child's talent in science. How do you rate? Notice that these attributes (for teachers and students) are clustered around the following aspects of creativity.

☐ Creative teachers and students are *more flexible* and can *cope better* with new situations.

☐ Creative people are *more observant*; they see and value things others do not.

☐ Creative students and teachers are *more adaptable and sensitive* to their surroundings and to other people.

☐ In general, creative children are *more self-sufficient, more secure, more flexible and dependable,* and show a healthier participation in group activities. They are open to experience and actively seek solutions to problems they set for themselves.[1]

UNDERSTANDING THE CREATIVE PROCESS

Previous chapters discussed giving children experiences that prepare them to develop creative ideas, think critically, and solve problems. Providing children with concrete activities prepares them because they raise questions in their minds, do some preliminary exploration, and identify and clarify the problem. Students can play with possible solutions once they identify problems, discuss them with you and their classmates, and then explore them further. One insight leads to another and, through your guidance, students can apply what they learned in one situation to new situations. How

FIGURE 11-1[2]

Checklist: Recognizing a Child's Talent in Science

Student's name: _____

1. Demonstrates intense absorption in self-selected tasks. _____
2. Is consistently productive; does not await direction from adults. _____
3. Generates questions on his or her own; uses peers and adults as resources. _____
4. Wants to discover what makes things work; takes things apart and reassembles the pieces. _____
5. Manifests curiosity about what he or she sees, feels, and hears. _____
6. Shows interest in a variety of subjects: weather, animals, humans, etc. _____
7. Enjoys collecting items relating to his or her science interests. _____
8. Wants to label items in collections. _____
9. Expresses a particular science interest by devising unique games. _____
10. Invents new ways to work with common materials. _____
11. Possesses a "let's try" approach in play. _____
12. Examines pictures in books and magazines to learn about the world (even when he or she cannot read). _____
13. Is a thorough observer, paying unusual attention to detail. _____
14. Easily and quickly spots details other children miss. _____
15. Uses words in unique ways to express feelings, observations, and knowledge. _____
16. Uses metaphors or analogies, indicating a linkage of perceptions. _____
17. Talks in a conversational manner; listens and responds appropriately. _____
18. Organizes materials in a way that is meaningful; orders and groups, for example. _____
19. Shows interest in and some understanding of numbers, counting, quantity, and measurement. _____
20. Is an avid explorer; enjoys nature. _____
21. Enjoys exploring materials, both old and new. _____
22. Is easily motivated by field trips, books, and new materials. _____
23. Responds positively to adult suggestions that broaden the task being pursued. _____
24. Accepts a challenge; expresses little fear of the unknown or of the difficulty. _____
25. Is persistent in science tasks. _____
26. Contributes ideas when a problem arises. _____
27. Is imaginative in associating ideas with materials. _____
28. Is independent in thought and work habits. _____
29. Enjoys the spatial challenge of new and difficult puzzles. _____
30. Is self-confident; frequently assumes a leadership role. _____

NOTE: You may wish to designate your own scale for recording behaviors, such as frequently, occasionally, and rarely, or a hierarchy of 1 to 5; or simply yes or no. Variation depends on data.

can you encourage children to play with problems and enjoy seeking answers?

CLASSROOM ENVIRONMENT TO ENHANCE CREATIVITY

Teachers who exhibit creative behavior themselves provide classroom environments which enhance creativity. These teachers avoid these cultural and emotional blocks in their classrooms.

- ☐ the effects of conformity
- ☐ excessive faith in logic
- ☐ fear of mistakes or failure
- ☐ self-satisfaction
- ☐ lack of independence
- ☐ reliance on authority
- ☐ negativism
- ☐ perfectionism[3]

One way to avoid cultural and emotional blocks in your classroom is to hold off on your evaluation during the brainstorming and "messing about" stages of creative thinking. Evaluation at this stage has been found to inhibit curiosity, stifle inquiry, and encourage undue dependence on you. Even praise can be a stifling thing if seen as another form of evaluation. Your students cannot separate praise from evaluation. Therefore, praise can *reduce*, rather than increase, students' intrinsic motivation.

Instead of praising (evaluating) students, encourage them. Try

1. giving children attention when they need it
2. watching children in their work to know what they are doing
3. listening attentively to what each child has to say (see chapter 6 on developing questioning techniques and sensitive listening skills)
4. questioning children about their work to show your interest and to be able to guide

and encourage in directions you feel are important for the child

5. developing nonverbal gestures to encourage, such as a wink, an arm on the shoulder, a nod, etc. (Individuals vary in their need for and reaction to verbal and nonverbal praise and encouragement. Some will do anything to avoid public praise in front of their peers, while others will do anything for it. Tailor your use of praise and encouragement to the individual.)

6. fostering choice of studies wherever possible, so that students can experience inner satisfaction from the activity rather than receive an external reward from you

7. keeping children's work and sharing it with them often, so that they can see the growth in their skills over a period of time. This is excellent encouragement for many children.

OPPORTUNITIES FOR SELF-SELECTED SCIENCE STUDIES

Another way to encourage creativity and critical thinking is to let students select for themselves aspects of science to study. Figure 11–2 shows a continuum from "other-directed" (usually teacher) learning to "self-directed." Few schools are totally one or the other in all subject areas; most contain elements of each in the various curricular areas. Where are you in this learning continuum? Previous chapters gave many suggestions for moving your classroom and teaching toward more self-direction, especially chapter 10.

Some teachers have found that they are able to expand self-direction in their science programs by starting with more mature and highly motivated students. Grouping three to five of these students together and encouraging them to study what interests them can stimulate much creativity and critical thinking. Here are some practical approaches to initiate self-directed science activities.

Science Task and Activity Cards

Science task cards and activity cards can be used at science centers or other areas in your classroom.

Self-Directed Learning	Other-Directed Learning
Schools	**Schools**
structure, not stricture	norm-based evaluation
build on student interest	lock-step grade levels
freedom of expression; variety of materials	rigid schedule
interdependence of people	adult-determined curriculum
continuous evaluation	subject matter emphasis
open climate	ditto sheets
child-centered curriculum; no bells	quiet classrooms
displays of students' work	rigid scope and sequence
flexible seating arrangements	homogeneous grouping
time for planning; few rules	many rules
Teachers	**Teachers**
adjust to change; trust students	insecure
encourage problem solving	all children doing the same thing
flexible; listen well	seats in rows
plan with students; care for individuals	few smiles
excited about learning	very directive
engage in professional activities	look for specific answers
wholistic attitude	single, fixed focus
provide descriptive feedback to students	provide judgmental feedback
negotiable pace for students	determine students' pace
ask divergent questions	ask convergent questions
Students	**Students**
responsible; mature	conforming
trusting; self-reliant	conditioned
flexible	passive
adventurous; happy	do only what is asked
self-disciplined; resourceful; inquisitive	wait to be asked
playful; curious; eager	restrained
enthusiastic	copy teachers' behavior
learn from mistakes	dependent on teachers
accept criticism; evaluate selves	underachieving

FIGURE 11–2

Words and phrases associated with learning

Source: Edwin P. White, "Why Self-Directed Learning?" *Science and Children*, 19, no. 5 (February 1982), p. 39.

Usually, the differences between activity and task cards are

☐ *activity cards* are open-ended, *not* self-contained (i.e., they do not include all data students will need, so they must go to other sources)

☐ *task cards* are self-contained (contain all data and materials to complete task), and have a readily identifiable skill focus

Follow these simple directions to make your own task or activity cards.

1. Pick science topics of interest to your children.
2. You can color-code the tasks and activities, e.g., "fun" activities (puzzles, riddles, etc.) on red cards; observing and inferring skills on green cards; library skills (research) on yellow cards.

3. Describe the task or activity in simple language and with a simple drawing, if possible.
4. For the task card, supply all the information and materials that will be needed to complete the task.
5. For the activity card, suggest other sources that students can use to complete the activity, e.g., "Go to the library and prepare a three-page report on water pollution in our community."
6. See examples of task and activity cards in figures 11–3 and 11–4.

7. You can use one card to perform *both* a task and an activity, as indicated in the examples.

When students become familiar with task and activity cards, ask them to prepare them for classmates. This will give them creative activities as well as increase your supply of cards. It often helps to have students work in pairs, especially if one of the pair has difficulty reading the directions or carrying out the tasks. It is also valuable to have students make small box collections of science materials to use with task and activity cards.

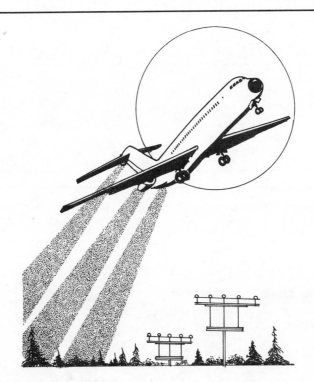

For an Activity Card
    Write a short story about what you see happening in this picture. Then share your story with the rest of the class.

For a Task Card
    Write a short story about what you see happening in this picture. After you're finished, go back and underline what you *observed* with a *red* pen. Then underline what you *inferred* with a *black* pen. Then share your story with the rest of the class.

FIGURE 11–3
Activity and task card for upper elementary grades

Are There Hotter Spots in Our Classroom?

Get: 3 thermometers from HEAT shoebox and some masking tape

Do: ☐   Put three thermometers on a table and see if they all are at the same temperature. If not, replace any that are different until you have three with the same reading.

☐   Use masking tape and attach thermometers to the wall like this:
a) one near the floor b) one about the top of your head c) one as close to the ceiling as you can (see picture)

☐   After 30 minutes check the temperature readings of each thermometer. Do the same after 60 minutes.

☐   What differences did you observe? Which was the highest temperature? Which was the lowest temperature?

☐   If you found differences, why do you think that happened?

FIGURE 11-4
Task card for primary or middle elementary grades

Small Box Creative Science Activities

Another way to provide creative science activities is to build up a collection of small box science activities. As shown in chapter 8 on Classroom Arrangement and Management, an area of the classroom can be set aside as a science center for storage and use of these collections. Task cards giving directions on conducting the activity can be attached to the outside of the box (or recorded on cassette tapes for nonreaders). Here is how to set up a touch box for young children.

1. Cut out a small hole in the cover of the box just large enough for a young child to insert a hand. Cover the hole with cloth so children cannot see into the box, but can still reach in.

2. Place in the box: rock, feather, cotton, bottle top, sandpaper, etc.
3. On task card, list these directions:
   a. Reach into the box through the cloth-covered hole, but do *not* look into the box.
   b. Feel the objects and try to identify them by touch only.
   c. Which ones were *hard*? Which ones were *soft*?
   d. Which ones were *rough*? Which ones were *smooth*?
   e. What other ways did they feel?

To get concise directions for constructing small box science collections, read Eddie L. Whitfield and Eva D. Samples, "Small Box Science— Independent Learning Exercises for Younger Children," *Science and Children*, 18, no. 7 (April 1981), p. 9.

Hilda Taba's Work

Hilda Taba and her colleagues produced these major approaches to stimulating creativity and critical thinking.

- ☐ Developing concepts
- ☐ Attaining concepts
- ☐ Developing generalizations
- ☐ Exploring feelings
- ☐ Resolving interpersonal problems
- ☐ Analyzing values
- ☐ Applying generalizations[4]

The basis of these strategies is to involve children through questioning; in answering questions, they perform mental operations enhancing their creativity and mental development. Review chapter 6 on questioning before you read the following discussion.

Developing concepts. Have students identify and label certain concepts related to a topic or problem. One approach is to ask a class what they know about a topic, for example, trees, birds, spiders, snakes, the ocean, space flight, or the moon, and then proceed, following the steps in the strategy. Another technique is to involve students in something, for example, hearing or reading a story about some scientific discovery, watching a film, taking a field trip, or watching a demonstration. Then ask, "What did you find out about . . . ?" List the answers on the chalkboard, group them according to similarities, and label.

Strategy: Developing Concepts

1. What do you know about butterflies? (Identifying)

2. How would you group these items? (Grouping)
3. What would you name these groups? (Labeling)
4. What members of each could be placed in another group? (Relating)
5. What could you write or tell the class in one sentence about all the groups? (Summarizing)

Attaining concepts.   Here you give the class the *name of a concept* and control to a higher degree the progress of the lesson. After naming the concept, give several examples of it. Next, list a number of related nonexamples. Then write on the chalkboard a mixture of examples and nonexamples. Ask the students to separate these examples into their respective groups. This strategy is usually used when the meaning of some concept requires clarification before involvement in other lessons. For example, concepts such as animal, ecology, mammal, machine, pulley, or insect may be introduced in this manner and then related to other parts of a group.

Strategy: Attaining Concepts
1. These are examples of insects. (Observing, listening)
2. These are or are not examples of insects: flies, butterflies, wasps, spiders. (Observing, listening)
3. Present a mixture including several examples and some nonexamples. Ask: Which of these things are examples? (Comparing, selecting)
4. What do you think an insect is? (Stating)
5. How would you define an insect? (Defining)

Developing generalizations.   This strategy involves the students in higher levels of thinking in relating several concepts. The product of this approach is a sentence stating some specific principle, for example, "Disease may be caused by microorganisms," rather than a word concept, ecology.

Strategy: Developing Generalizations
1. What did you notice or find out about microorganisms? (Selecting, evaluating)

2. What happened to the bread kept in a wet plastic bag compared to the dry bread? Why did it happen? (Inferring)
3. What does this indicate about the conditions mold requires to grow? Why do you think so? (Generalizing)
4. What is the significance of the data? Or what can you say about microorganisms? (Generalizing)

Exploring feelings.   Students are involved in exploring their own and others' feelings. They learn better how others perceive a situation, understand their own emotions, and generalize when appropriate about people's affectivity. The strategy is designed so students do not feel threatened as might be the case if asked directly what their values are about a topic, for example, mercy killing of deer or infected horses. Rather, a situation is provided, and the students are encouraged to explore and react to it. This method is effective in environmental science topics.

Strategy: Exploring Feelings
1. Present some situation and ask, "What happened in this situation?" For example, Roger and a small pony in Texas. One day he noticed it appeared sick. His father called the veterinarian, who came to look at the pony. The vet said the pony had an infectious disease that might spread to other animals. The government, furthermore, requires that sick animals be put to death to stop the spread of the disease. (Summarizing)
2. How do you think the people involved felt? How did Roger feel? How did his parents and brothers and sisters feel? How did the veterinarian feel? How did the local government agricultural agent feel when he heard of the disease? (Inferring)
3. What experiences have you had that are similar? (Describing)
4. How did you feel? (Describing, emoting)
5. Why did you feel that way? (Explaining)

Interpersonal problem solving.   This strategy involves confronting students with conflicts between individuals or groups. Ask the students to relate similar experiences, propose and defend solutions, and consider and evaluate alternatives to the problem. Taba and her associates warn that students, because of their own egocentricity, may not proceed to the higher levels of exploring criteria and alternatives in making judgments. You can circumvent this by moving the group along the other steps in the strategy.

Strategy: Interpersonal Problem Solving

1. Present a situation involving interpersonal conflict, for example, a man representing an electrical power company proposes to a state planning commission that a dam be placed on the river just below a beautiful natural lake. A Sierra Club representative argues against this proposal, stating that the dam would prevent the free movement of salmon up the river. A heated argument then occurs between the power company engineer and the Sierra Club conservationist. (Listening)
2. What happened? (Describing)
3. What did each of the people (groups) do? (Summarizing)
4. What should each do? Why? (Evaluating)
5. When has something like this happened to you? What did you do? (Summarizing)
6. As you look back on what happened to you, how would you respond now? (Evaluating)
7. Why? (Evaluating)
8. What things might you have done differently? (Explaining)

Analyzing values.

This strategy requires that students assess the values of individuals or groups to help students perceive that people may have different values. It is not necessarily trying to have students develop higher values themselves. The approach involves presenting a class with a situation involving individuals or groups and asking students to make inferences about the values the individuals or groups have that may have dictated their responses, ways of living, and so on. Students are also asked to analyze their own values relative to the topic presented.

Strategy: Analyzing Values

1. Present a situation depicting some value orientation. For example, a group of Boy Scouts planted several trees in the park area and along the banks of a river. (Listening)
2. What did they do to improve their community? (Inferring)
3. Why do you think individuals (groups) do that? (Inferring)
4. What does this indicate about their values or what they think is important? (Inferring)
5. If you were confronted with a similar situation, what would you do and why? (Hypothesizing)
6. What does this indicate about what you value? (Inferring)
7. How do these people differ in their values compared to you? What differences do you see in what you and other people value? (Inferring)

Applying generalizations.

This approach invites students to use generalizations obtained from previous learning and apply them to similar new situations.

Strategy: Applying Generalizations

1. Ask, "Given these conditions . . . what do you think would happen if children planted grass seed and trees on a hill that had a lot of gullies?" (Applying)
2. Why do you think that would happen? (Inferring)
3. What is needed for your statement to happen? (Supporting hypotheses)
4. What other explanations can be given for what might happen? (Inferring)
5. If as you said, there was less erosion, what would happen after that to the amount of erosion? (Hypothesizing)

Of course, you can use various parts of this model in class discussion and then break for individual or small group investigation so students gain more information before continuing to use various parts of the method.

USING THE YES/NO METHOD IN CREATIVITY AND CRITICAL THINKING

J. Richard Suchman devised an inquiry approach to help students construct and build theories. In this research, a set of 25 color films were made into 8 mm cartridges, each presenting puzzling events that students attempt to explain. The films are silent and do not contain any captions; for this reason, the films can be used by any grade although they have been suggested mainly for the upper elementary grades. The problem films are the endless-loop cartridge type and the titles are

1. The Stalled Car
2. The Cannon
3. The Baseball Catcher
4. The Man and the Dumbbell
5. The Five Pendulums
6. The Ice Cubes
7. The Balloon in the Jar
8. The Restaurant
9. The Train and the Track
10. The Spring Carts
11. Walking
12. The Sailboat and the Fan
13. The Wrenches
14. The Diving Bottle
15. The Knife
16. Drinking Boiling Coffee
17. The Spring
18. The Amusement Park
19. The Pendulum and the Peg
20. The Man and the Wheel
21. The Eight Pendulums
22. Boiling by Cooling
23. Puck on a String
24. The Long Pendulum
25. The Shrinking Balloon

Some of the film loops may be too difficult for elementary school children. Elementary teachers have found 1, 6, 7, 8 14, 15, 18, and 23 useful with children in middle grades. Many of the other film loops are appropriate for the talented and gifted child. If you cannot afford to purchase the entire set, purchase 3 or 4 selected loops. One of the problem film loops is shown to children. This is a description of the *inquiry session* (Suchman's name for the thinking session that follows the film) ground rules. After seeing the problem event, the students attempt to construct a reasonable theory to account for it. They usually do this by making a guess at a theory and then gathering data to test it. The bulk of the inquiry session is normally devoted to data-gathering questions raised by the students and answered by the teacher.

Inquiry sessions are conducted under these simple rules.

1. The questions should be phrased in such a way that they can be answered *yes* or *no*.
2. Once called upon, a student may ask as many questions as he or she wishes before yielding the floor.
3. The teacher does not answer *yes* or *no* to statements of theories, or to questions that attempt to obtain the teacher's approval of a theory.
4. Any student can test any theory at any time.
5. Any time the students feel a need to confer with one another without the teacher's presence, they should be free to call a conference.
6. Inquirers should be able to work with Experimental Kits, Idea Books, or Resource Books at any time they feel the need.[5]

Note that the method has components similar to other discovery-inquiry techniques outlined in this text. It differs, however, in how students initially are required to phrase their questions: the teacher answers only yes or no, at least in the first phase of this approach. After students have investigated the problem and collected information, the teacher brings the class together and acts as a discussion leader in a manner similar to other inquiry discussion methods. Generally, the class procedures go through four phases.

1. Presentation of a discrepant event.
2. Discussion in which students phrase questions to the teacher that may be answered only by yes or no.
3. Students may investigate to gather further information relative to their theory.
4. Class reconvenes and teacher leads a discussion, helping students to develop a theory. Teacher may clarify, focus students' attention on certain aspects of the problem, and summarize their ideas.

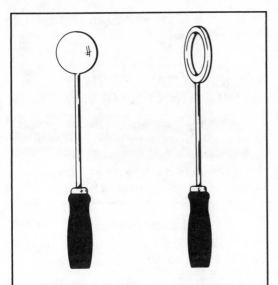

Ball and Ring Inquiry Session

PUPIL:	Were the ball and ring at room temperature to begin with?
TEACHER:	Yes.
PUPIL:	Would the ball go through the ring at first?
TEACHER:	Yes.
PUPIL:	After the ball was held over the fire, it did not go through the ring?
TEACHER:	No.
PUPIL:	If the ring had been heated instead of the ball, would the results have been the same?
TEACHER:	No.
PUPIL:	If both had been heated, would the ball have gone through then?
TEACHER:	That all depends.
PUPIL:	If they both had been heated to the same temperature, would the ball have gone through?
TEACHER:	Yes.
PUPIL:	Would the ball be the same size after it was heated as it was before?
TEACHER:	No.
PUPIL:	Could the same experiment have been done if the ball and ring were made out of some other metal?
TEACHER:	Yes.

FIGURE 11–5
Ball and ring apparatus

Source: Richard J. Suchman, ''Inquiry Training in the Elementary School,'' *The Science Teacher* 27 (November 1960), p. 42.

Figure 11–5 shows a portion of an inquiry session reported by Suchman in his early research. The session dealt with the film ''Ball and Ring Demonstration,'' in which a brass ball just fitting through a brass ring is heated. An unsuccessful attempt is then made to pass the ball through the ring. Figure 11–5 shows the ball and ring apparatus used in this inquiry session. A portion of a class interaction, after the class has seen some discrepant event and discussed it for some time is outlined. Note how the teacher aids the students in understanding and constructing a theory.

Using the yes or no answer with pictorial riddles. The yes or no answer approach can be adapted easily to other teaching activities, in addition to using it with demonstrations. Figure 11–6 is an example.

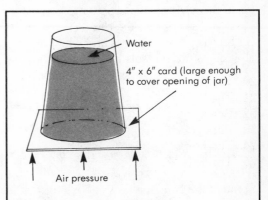

1. Present a pictorial riddle.
2. The class is told they may ask any questions that can be answered by yes or no.

Teacher's Note: The air pressure that is pushing below this 3'' by 5'' card is keeping the water in the jar. When air leaks in under the card, the water will pour out of the jar.

3. The teacher, knowing the above explanation, answers questions about it as appropriate.

FIGURE 11–6

ORGANIZING TIME FOR CREATIVE INVESTIGATIONS

When teachers study discussion methods like Suchman's approach, they generally think of using them only with large groups. This limits their effectiveness in developing students' critical thinking. All discussion methods can be modified for more student-centered involvement, particularly in the upper elementary grades. For example, a teacher might divide a class period as follows.

Teacher's Role

1. Teacher or students originate a problem, for example, "Write down all the ways you can think of to help decrease pollution in our town."
2. After students have had time to individually write their ideas, the teacher divides the class into groups of four or five students and tells them:

"Look over all of your ideas. Pick one or two of the ones you think are best and develop them. Appoint a reporter to present the ideas you selected to the class."

3. Teacher observes class and when he or she senses the students have more or less completed the task, asks them to reconvene for large class discussion.
4. Teacher asks the class which of the ideas they would most like to implement.

5. Teacher asks how they should get organized.

The general format for this class activity is

1. Teacher or students originate a problem.
2. Students work individually on it.
3. Students confer in groups and share information on the problem.
4. A member from each group reports information to total class.
5. Class discussion occurs. The activity may end here or continue to the next phase.

6. Students do something with what has been done in class.

OTHER ACTIVITIES THAT STIMULATE CREATIVITY

The source of activities to stimulate your and your students' creativity is the environment of your classroom with all its curricular areas. Here are some suggestions for you to brainstorm for use with your class.[6]

Students' Involvement

Students individually write down their creative ideas. They spend time as needed. Time: Estimated, 5 minutes.

Students discuss their ideas and what they need to do to implement them. Time: 10–15 minutes.

Students reconvene for large group discussion. A member for each group presents his or her group's ideas to the class. Time: 10 minutes.

Students discuss the ideas as a class and center on those they would like to implement. Time: 10–15 minutes.

Students organize into groups and define their role and assign individual tasks. The implementation of tasks may continue in class or as outside work. Time: 10 minutes.

A New Perspective

Encourage students to look at their environments *from a new perspective*.

Looking at the world through someone else's eyes. Have your children role-play different objects or people in their environment. Primary grade children could role-play a seed germinating, wriggling under the ground, peek-

ing its head up through the soil and swaying back and forth in the sun and wind. Older children could role-play an astronaut in space coping with the physical adjustments to eating, walking, working, and playing in weightlessness.

Changing your eye view. Ask your children to imagine they are only *10 cm* tall. To fully comprehend what that might be like, have them lie on the floor of the classroom or on the grass of the play area outside the school. What does the world look like from that perspective? Now ask them to imagine that they are 5 *meters* tall. How have their perceptions changed? How do they feel now? How do things look now?

Changing the colors you can see. Distribute colored toothpicks over a small area outside the classroom before class. Have children make "glasses" from a paper bag and colored cellophane as in the diagram below. Pick colors for the cellophane that match the colors of the toothpicks. Now take the class outside and ask them to put on their colored glasses and find as many toothpicks as they can. Is it easier to find some toothpicks with certain colored glasses? Which ones? How does this relate to some insects and animals?

Body twisting. Another way for your children to change their perspectives is "body twisting," or getting themselves into unusual positions to see the world in unusual ways.

A. Cut a paper bag to form a window or slot as shown below:

B. Tape colored cellophane (red, green, or blue to match colors of your toothpicks) on window or slot. Another variation of this activity is called *Secret Messages.* Have children write notes with several colors of crayons. Then have them use filters made of different colored cellophane to filter the crayons and "read" the colored crayon messages.

Have children stand on their heads, lie only on their backs limiting the movement of their heads from side to side, *etc.*

Fantasy

Encourage children to *fantasize* often. After studying about snow, you might ask children to imagine they are snowflakes. Have them act out what it would be like to melt, *freeze*, evaporate, stick to another snowflake, *etc.*

Brainstorming

Give your children opportunities to *brainstorm.* Select any common object, such as a pencil. Ask the children to observe the pencil's characteristics or properties and how these relate to its function. A child might see that the soft, black lead leaves a mark on paper and that's why it was chosen for its function. After you have exhausted looking at characteristics and properties related to function, you could extend this activity for some of your more creative students by asking, "How would you improve on the design or selection of materials (or both) of this pencil?" Other questions might be "Name as many ways as you can to use this pencil," "How could the pencil be changed to serve other functions?"

Fun Machines

Make a *fun machine*. Invite each student, one at a time, to the front of the room to demonstrate some moving part of a machine. By the time the activity is completed, the entire class is involved and moving like parts of some large machine. Afterwards discuss what machines do and encourage creative expression in art, poetry, and writing. Students may also make some type of machine from rubber bands, cardboard, spools, pipe cleaners, etc.

Fun Movements

The following are a few examples of movement activities that may be used to get students relaxed or to wake them up if they appear sluggish. They can also be used as a basis for creative writing or to teach various concepts of science. In each case, ask the students to "stand up, close your eyes, and imagine you are any of the following."

☐ A candle burning very slowly
☐ A sweater on a hanger slowly slipping toward the floor
☐ A tree being blown by a gentle and then strong wind
☐ Wallpaper becoming unglued and slowly peeling from the wall

SUMMARY

One of the goals in science teaching is to encourage creativity and critical thinking. To help identify creative behavior and skills in students and ourselves. A checklist for recognizing a child's talent in science was presented. After understanding the creative process, ideas were given for enhancing the classroom environment for creativity, including the role of encouragement. Specific activities that encourage creativity and critical thinking with step-by-step directions include science task and activity cards; small box creative science activities; Hilda Taba's strategies for stimulating creativity and critical thinking; Richard Suchman's Yes/No Inquiry Approach; using a Yes/No approach with pictorial riddles; helping students brainstorm by encouraging them to view their environments from different perspectives; using their bodies to act out happenings; fantasizing; looking for unique uses for common objects; and making fun machines.

SELF-EVALUATION AND FURTHER STUDY

1. Select several children and use the *checklist: Recognizing a Child's Talent in Science* to identify their strengths.
2. Make a list of encouragement techniques you could use instead of praising or evaluating children's creative efforts. Include nonverbal actions.
3. Pick several science topics that you are studying with your class and make task and activity cards for them.
4. For either the task or activity cards in number 3 above, construct small box creative science activity collections, including all necessary directions and materials.
5. Prepare several Hilda Taba lessons that you can use with your science class.
6. Try a Suchman-type creative science lesson in a class with children using only the Yes/No technique described in this chapter.
7. Plan and carry out science lessons using the activities that ask children to look at their environments from a new perspective.
8. Have a brainstorming session with a group of children.

ENDNOTES

1. John E. Penick, op. cit., p. 32. The author is indebted to this article for many excellent ideas about creativity in this chapter.
2. Margaret McIntyre, "Early Childhood—Identifying Children with Potential," *Science and Children*, 19, no. 7 (April 1982), pp. 44–45.
3. Much information (including this list) in this chapter is from John E. Penick, "Developing Creativity As a Result of Science Instruction," *What Research Says To The Science Teacher, Volume 4*, Robert E. Yager, editor (Washington, D.C.: National Science Teachers Association, 1982), pp. 42–52.
4. For a more detailed explanation of the inductive approach, see Hilda Taba et al., *A Teacher's Handbook to Elementary Social Studies—An Inductive Approach*, 2d ed. (Reading, Mass.: Addison-Wesley Publishing Co., 1971).
5. J. Richard Suchman, *Putting Inquiry into Science: Learning-Inquiry Development Program* (Chicago: Science Research Associates, Inc., 1966), p. 4.
6. For additional ideas for stimulating creativity in your students see Michael J. Moravcsik, "Creativity in Science Education," *Science Education*, 65, no. 2 (April 1981), pp. 221–227; Lawrence S. Bass, "Problem-Solving Science," *Instructor*, 90, no. 9 (April 1981), pp. 93, 96, 98; Claude D. Crowley, "Having a Field Day in the Schoolyard," *Teacher*, 98, no. 2 (September 1980), pp. 96, 99–100; Rodger Bybee, "Creativity—Nurture and Stimulation," *Science and Children*, 17, no. 4 (January 1980), pp. 7–9.

How Can You Integrate Guided Discovery Science With Other Subjects?

> **"If teachers add process teaching to the curriculum, something else has to be subtracted. . . . . or teachers need to find ways in which to combine a number of different 'learnings' into one activity."**
> **(Daniel Paul, "A Special Day—On that day, everything you do, all day long, should be related to a particular process," *Science and Children*, 19, no. 7 [April 1982], p. 24.)**

As an elementary school teacher, there are too many pressures on you to do too many things with your children, with too little time to do it all. We are at a time in history when we are being held more accountable for our teaching. It is also a time when there is a diminished emphasis upon science and science teaching in elementary schools by both the public and the funding agencies.

You must be efficient and judicious with your precious class time in order to "fit science in" and still help your children develop skills in all the other self-contained classroom subjects. One excellent way to do this is to integrate science with other subjects. This chapter deals mostly with integrating science with reading/language arts, while chapter 13 looks at mathematics and computers in science.

INTEGRATING SCIENCE WITH OTHER SUBJECTS

Research shows that when science is integrated with other curricular areas, both science and the other subjects are learned more effectively by children. Therefore, as you approach a science area of study, try to plan how other subjects could be woven into the study. Figure 12–1 shows how one fourth-grade teacher integrated teaching the scientific process of classification into other curricular areas. Use this model in your own subjects.

HOW DISCOVERY SCIENCE AND READING ARE SIMILAR

Reading and discovery science emphasize the same intellectual skills and both are concerned with thinking processes:

> Other skills appear to be "built in" for use in the discovery process being stressed by most new science materials. The scientific experiences are designed so that the student will be asked to define problems, locate information, organize information into graphic form, evaluate findings, and draw conclusions. . . . It becomes obvious that this type of science curriculum demands a myriad of skills concomitant with those of a well developed reading program.[1]

In the context of Stephen Lucas and Andrew Burlando's points, you are currently engaged in teaching reading in your science program, whether or not you realize it. When you help your students develop *scientific* processes, you are also helping them develop *reading* processes. Figure 12–2 gives examples of problem-solving skills in science and the corresponding reading skills. Notice the correspondences. For instance, when you are working on "observing" in *science*, children are also learning to discriminate shapes, sounds, syllables, and accents for *reading*. The skills of predicting, classifying, interpreting, and so on are essential to logical thinking as well as to forming the basic skills for learning to read and decode.

242

Integrating Science with Other Subjects
Results of a Brainstorming Session

4th Grade	Subject Areas				
Science Skill (Topic)	Language Arts Reading Writing Spelling	Science Physics Chemistry Biology Geology	Mathematics Measuring Graphing Time Geometry	Social Studies Economics Geography History Sociology	Art, Music, Physical Education
Classification	Write five sentences on the board. Underline nouns; circle verbs, etc. Have children find the common elements in each. Have children write all the space words they can think of on the board. Have them classify them into five groupings. Ask other students to figure out the system. Cut a simple outline apart. Have students reorganize each line into major ideas and sub-ideas. Visit the library, review with students how books are classified.	Draw sixteen two and three dimensional geometric shapes on a colored ditto. Copy and have students develop an identification key. Distribute pictures of foods provided by American Dairy Council or have children cut ads from paper. Classify pictures into food groups, or classify by part of the food eaten, such as fruit, leaf, root, etc. Teach the hardness scale, give each child a mineral to test.	Have children cut out ten different pictures from a magazine. Using a metric chart with headings of liters, meters, and grams, place each picture in the appropriate column. Then make rows for centi, deci, kilo, etc.	Play twenty questions. Say, I'm going to buy _____." To determine what you are going to buy, the children must ask good classification questions, such as, "Is it natural or manufactured?" Teach them to try to divide things into two categories.	Display the primary colors, blue, yellow, and red on an overhead projector. Experiment by combining them in different ways; record the findings.

FIGURE 12-1

Daniel Paul, ibid., p. 25.

Both science and reading are concerned with processes *and* content. *Content* can be thought of as subject matter. "More specifically, it is the accumulation of details, concepts, and generalization of a particular curriculum.

Process consists of the reading and scientific skills necessary to acquire and apply content.[2]

Your students started to talk before they could read. They first had to be able to recognize relationships between sounds and graphic symbols. They used processes to distinguish between vowels and consonants, learning the sounds of letters, letter blends, and syllables. Then your students began to build up a reserve of frequently used "sight words," words not easily sounded out (for example, *mustache*). Other reading skills, such as structural or contextual clues, are used to help attack new words. Once children master basic vocabulary, they are exposed to many comprehension skills: reading for the main idea, following directions, solving problems. Again, you can see the parallel between reading and science skills.

Does Science Teaching Teach Reading?

There is evidence that early experience with science helps children with language and logic development, regardless of their socio-economic status.[3] Several studies found that young children's experiences with natural phenomena in active science programs improved their reading readiness and reading skills. See chapters 9 and 10 for research on increase in reading skills for SCIS, SAPA, and ESS students, as well as disadvantaged blind, deaf, and other handicapped students. Also see Appendix B for additional research.

THE MARRIAGE OF SCIENCE AND READING

A recent journal article posed this provocative dilemma:

> Despite all the work in beginning reading instruction and in science, little has been recommended in the way of marrying what would seem to be a most natural, productive, and effective union; reading and science.[4]

What are the things you can do right now in your science program that will enhance your students' reading abilities, and what things in your reading program will enrich your science teaching? What can you do to be the "matchmaker," to wed your science program and your reading program? What are you currently doing with reading in your science program that should be enlarged and expanded?

Using Printed Science Materials with Nonreaders

One of the best techniques for working with nonreaders is to read to them. Investigations of the effects of reading aloud to children *regularly* showed significant increases in quantity of vocabulary growth, knowledge of word meanings, visual decoding, motor decoding, and reading comprehension achievement. Two important elements in improving reading performance are the regularity of reading to children and the length of time the reading aloud is done. It was found that the most effective frequency was daily reading aloud and the most effective length of time was a minimum of ten minutes per session. Younger children may benefit more from being read to than older children. Reading aloud to young children also affects their reading interests. After being read to, young children are more eager to read for themselves the books that had been read aloud to them. This tendency was shown by Sarah Graham, a librarian in Rochester, New York, when she kept records of what books children signed out from her school library for a year. She found science was the second most popular category of books. The first was fiction, and some of these books were in science fields or science fiction.[5]

Reading aloud to your students need not be limited to younger children. Reading aloud to children who are in the lowest range of reading achievement in *any* grade produces reading growth. L. Fearn discovered that when fourth graders heard taped readings of stories, those at the lower extremes of reading achievement showed the greatest growth in comprehension and total reading scores.

David Cornelius sums up the values of reading to children in your science program this way:

> I think that the best solution to the problem of teaching youngsters to comprehend written scientific materials is the technique that is frequently used to teach reading in the first place—namely, we must read aloud to our students. . . . reading aloud to students—no more than 3 to 5 minutes once a day—might be done while introducing a new topic, highlighting

EXAMPLES OF PROBLEM-SOLVING SKILLS IN SCIENCE	CORRESPONDING READING SKILLS
Observing	Discriminating shapes Discriminating sounds Discriminating syllables and accents
Identifying	Recognizing letters Recognizing words Recognizing common prefixes Recognizing common suffixes Recognizing common base words Naming objects, events, and people
Describing	Isolating important characteristics Enumerating characteristics Using appropriate terminology Using synonyms
Classifying	Comparing characteristics Contrasting characteristics Ordering, sequencing Arranging ideas Considering multiple factors
Designing investigations	Asking questions Looking for potential relationships Following organized procedures Reviewing prior studies Developing outlines
Collecting data	Taking notes Surveying reference materials Using several parts of a book Recording data in an orderly fashion Developing precision and accuracy
Interpreting data	Recognizing cause and effect relationships Organizing facts Summarizing new information Varying rate of reading Inductive and deductive thinking
Communicating results	Using graphic aids Logically arranging information Sequencing ideas Knowledge of technical vocabulary Illuminating significant factors Describing with clarity
Formulating conclusions	Generalizing Analyzing critically Evaluating information Recognizing main ideas and concepts Establishing relationships Applying information to other situations

FIGURE 12–2
Skills important both to science and reading

Source: Glenda S. Carter and Ronald D. Simpson, "Science and Reading: A Basic Duo," *The Science Teacher* 45, no. 3 (March 1978), p. 20.

a set of lab directions, summarizing a particular unit, or interjecting an appropriate bit of current events.[6]

We all can find times in our discovery science programs when it would be useful and appropriate to read aloud to our students. Which times are best for you in your discovery science program? How can you interject more reading aloud in your science activities?

Give your students many opportunities to *listen* to how science *sounds*. Besides providing children with experience using another sense (hearing), giving children the chance to listen also helps them see that words in books are merely spoken words put down in written form. This in turn helps children begin to see a relationship between oral and spoken language.

"Inventing" new words for children. Words are the verbal labels you must choose to focus clearly and explicitly your students' attention on the conceptual ideas they have been investigating. In your discovery science program, you have supplied many sensory, hands-on activities for your students. After they have experienced exploratory manipulative ac-

tivities, you might "invent" words and terms for what they have been doing.

1. Group your students near you so all can see anything you demonstrate, can hear your questions, and are able to communicate with each other.
2. Carefully plan and interestingly introduce an activity the children have done themselves before this lesson.
3. During the activity, introduce the label (word) for the concept you want to develop. For instance, if you show a large magnet lifting a toy truck you could say: "When the magnet lifts the truck, we can say it is *evidence of interaction* (new "invented" word) between the magnet and the truck." *Write "Interaction" on the chalkboard at this point* (gives visual as well as oral introduction of new word to children). This repeats an activity your students have already done, but adds a new word for the concept. (See figure 12–3)
4. Now perform a *new* activity using interaction. For instance, pour vinegar over baking soda, and ask: "What do we call what is happening to the vinegar and baking

FIGURE 12–3
"Inventing" term interaction

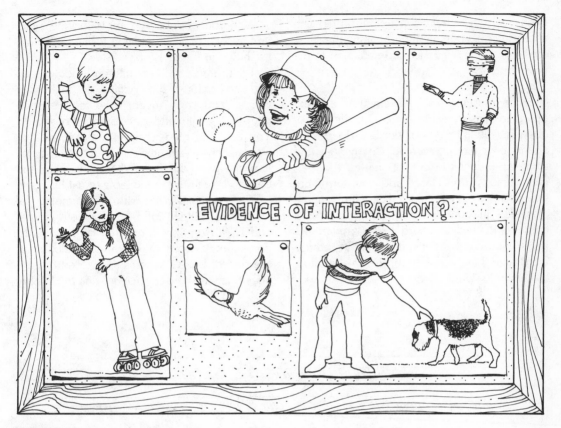

FIGURE 12–4
Evidences of interaction bulletin board

soda? (the bubbles are *evidence of interaction*)

5. Ask your students about the similarities and differences in the two demonstrations. You are trying to stress that something happens between the objects—magnet and truck, vinegar and soda.

6. Ask your students to focus upon the changes in both demonstrations and show them how we interpret this *evidence of interaction* between objects.

7. To reinforce and to see which children understand the concept of evidence of interaction, ask, "Give us an example where *you* have seen evidence of interaction between objects."

8. Focus the children's attention on examples given to clarify objects and evidences of interaction.

9. As a follow-up, have children cut pictures out of magazines at home of evidences of interaction.

10. Next day, make a bulletin board of evidences of interaction from magazine pictures using the words *evidence of interaction* often as reinforcement, as seen in figure 12–4.

Science educators also use the term *operational definition* to describe the inventing of science words growing out of your students' activities. Operational definitions use *actions* to describe what is happening, such as *evidences* of interaction. Note, however, as Piaget suggested, that the invention of terms must come after the children have actually handled various materials. Otherwise you will be teaching by rote. Numerous follow-up activities are then needed to reinforce the concept presented with a variety of new situations containing the same concept, that is, evidence of interaction in the environment.[8]

Science dictionaries. As children are exposed to sensory experiences and the subsequent inventing by you of words and terms for science concepts, you can help them make and keep up-to-date science dictionaries. As a science topic is investigated and new terms are introduced, a "class science dictionary" can be displayed in your Science Center or on a corner of the bulletin board. Using large primer paper, you can keep a running list of science words and their meanings for the area studied, as shown in figure 12–5.

With younger children, try to include a picture instead of or in addition to the definition, as shown in figure 12–6.

Try to interest older children in looking up and researching the *origins* of interesting words. You can "invent" the term *etymology*—the origin and development of words. You can also read to them about interesting words such as *sandwich* and, in this case, tell how the word was named for a gambler too busy to leave his gaming table to eat his roast.

To become familiar with the etymology of words see Wilfred John Funk's *Word Origins and Their Romantic Stories* for general words. For scientific word origins and development, see one of Isaac Asimov's specialized dictionaries, such as *Words of Science and the History*

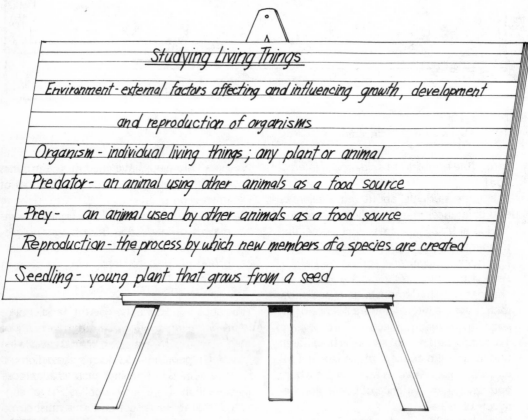

FIGURE 12–5
Science dictionary

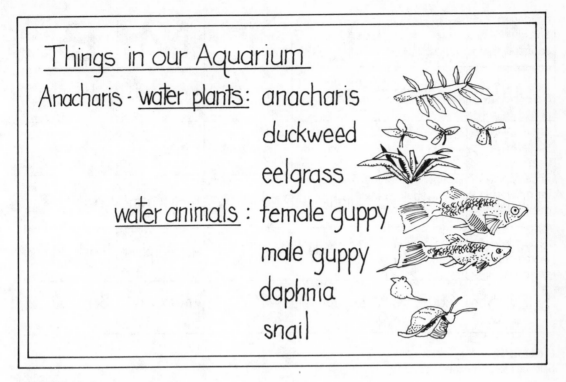

FIGURE 12-6
Science dictionary with pictures

Behind Them. Have your students keep a "science words etymology dictionary" and have them share it with each other and other classes.

Science word categories game. Another way to stimulate science vocabulary development after direct experiences with science concepts is the Science Word Categories Game. First, each player draws a grid with five spaces across the top and down as shown in figure 12-7. The students take turns suggesting one of the five different science categories of items such as plants, animals, electricity, ecology, and scientists and list these categories on the left-hand side of the grid. Then the children pick any five-letter word in which none of the letters is repeated, such as the word *climb.*

The object of the game is to think of words in each category that begin with the same letter at the top of the grid. Set a time limit. The winner is the child who has filled in the most words at the end of the established time. Children may use the class science dictionary, their own dictionaries, or standard class dictionaries. Encourage more creative children to make up their own science word dictionaries for the rest of the class to work on.

Expanding Science Vocabulary Through Record Keeping

Keeping records is as important to science as breathing is to people. It is through records that we compare and analyze scientific experimentation. Children need to do this, too. Through their own record keeping, your students will expand their scientific vocabulary.

Collecting, recording, and reading their science record books, science logs, and science lab reports (or any other name given by you)

C	L	I	M	B
PLANTS cabbage	lilac	iris	milkweed	bean
ANIMALS cat	lion	iguana	mouse	bat
ELECTRICITY current	light	induction	magnetism	bellwire
ECOLOGY community	life cycle	insecticide	metamorphosis	bacteria
SCIENTISTS Currie	Leyden	IGY	Marconi	Bernouli

FIGURE 12-7
Science word categories game

gives them much practice in learning and constantly using new science words. The first records your students keep may contain a minimum of words but lots of pictures. One record may be an "experience chart" made by the total class or a small group, in which you record on primer chart paper things your students observed and shared with the class after a field trip walk around the park near your school. The chart may look like the one shown in figure 12–8.

Record keeping for *older* children can include brief descriptions of what they did, in addition to specific evidences of the number of objects observed and counted. At first, you may want to use a *group* activity such as the experience chart. As your students learn how to give brief descriptions of what they did in groups, they are ready to start their own individual record keeping. You can duplicate a page such as the one shown in figure 12–9, where your students record their "sink and float experimentation." Another record-keeping experience for your students is the science log (see the discussion of "Teacher- or Student-Made Science Mini-books or Logs").

USING TEXTBOOKS IN DISCOVERY SCIENCE

Even though your science program is discovery- or process-oriented, do not overlook the potential value of science textbooks, especially if you use them judiciously. Your students can be helped to see reading as a process to enrich their firsthand experimentation. Textbooks are a resource of science's products of reliable and tested facts, concepts, and principles. Instead of "reinventing the wheel" for every step of our investigations about the wonders of the universe, we can use reading as one of science's processes to find and share other people's information and to check our own findings for validity.

Our Trip to the Park

Things We Saw	Things We Heard	Things We Smelled
Sally: Branches moving in wind	Birds singing	
Greg: Little bugs crawling		Fresh air
Tom: A birds nest	An airplane	Flowers
Amy: Yellow flowers in grass	Dog barking	
Jon: Squirrel running	Twigs snapping	Dirt (soil)
Jill: Water drops on grass	Our class laughing	Wet grass

FIGURE 12–8
Experience chart of observations

Here are some ways you can use your science textbooks to enrich and expand your students' scientific explorations.[8]

1. *Selecting appropriate reading levels.* Using the cloze and Piagetian measures for cognitive levels or other methods, select textbooks that your students can read. Try to get a variety of levels of texts, so you may individualize assignments. When investigating a science topic, list pages in each of the levels where your students can find information about that topic. Allow your students to select the level of their choice or suggest particular pages to specific children. Most science textbook series have a wide range of reading levels for each science topic between grades.

2. *Organizing your class for science reading.* Group your students in any way that facilitates using books to find information, to check the validity of experimentation, or for any other purpose you intend. Sometimes it is practical to group students homogeneously if you are working on skills and only a small group of your students need help. Other times, you may find that you can use heterogeneous groupings.
   a. Form a "buddy system" by pairing children having trouble reading with better readers who are more cognitively advanced.
   b. Form groups of four to six children who have varying levels of reading abilities. Let them read and discuss your assignments cooperatively.

3. *Individualizing textbook assignments.* So each of your students will get the maximum benefit from using science textbooks, incorporate some of these individualization techniques into your classroom.
   a. If you have poor readers, or immature or "deprived" children, reading to them may be useful. By listening to you as they follow their textbook, they hear words at the same time they are learning to decode and thus learn to read independently. To be most effective, try reading to and with your students under these conditions:
   1. Have students put other work away.
   2. Pick a special "listening place" such as on a rug or the lawn under a tree in warm weather, so your students can sit or lie down.
   3. Read with expression and enthusiasm, so the children can see the relationships between written and spoken language.

You have been working with things that sink or float. What did you do to find out which objects sink or float? Draw a picture.

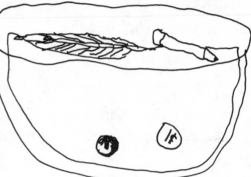

We put objects in the bowl of water. If the object floated, we put it in box with label Float. If it sank, we put it in box Sink. Then we tried all the objects in the Float box to check if they all floated. We did the same with the objects in the Sink box.

What did you find about which objects sink or float? Record your observations on the chart below.

OBJECT	MADE OF	SINK	FLOAT
PENNY	METAL	X	
PENCIL	MOSTLY WOOD		X

FIGURE 12-9
Experience chart for group science activity

4. Stop occasionally and ask questions. Invite questions, too. Be careful, though, that the kind of questions and their frequency do not detract from the reading, but whet your students' interest.

5. Stop occasionally and ask the children to read the next portion to themselves to find a particular answer to your question or to prepare to read to the class if they want to.

6. Ask for a volunteer to read to the class only after the students have had an opportunity to read and prepare first. Avoid asking poor readers to read to a group anything they are seeing for the first time and have not prepared. Sometimes it is valuable to put sections of your textbook on audiocassettes for poor readers to use either with or in place of the text. Commercially prepared cassette and picture science programs for the elementary level, such as those by Coronet Films, are also available. They provide oral reinforcement and assistance and help with word recognition and concept development. Your better readers will get practice with oral reading by making the cassettes for you. Supplement reading assignments for poor readers with other learning activities such as films, filmstrips, tradebooks, and field trips.

b. You can enrich the textbook assignments for your better readers by
1. Improving assignments to your better readers. All your reading assignments should include these three elements:
   a. *Content*—specifically indicate what you expect your students to get from reading the text: finding facts, interpreting, drawing conclusions, etc.
   b. *Motivation*—relate the assignment to ongoing work and to previous materials, demonstrate its relevence.
   c. *Skills*—indicate how an assignment should be read, such as what type of recall is expected.
2. Guiding your students to learn to locate and organize information from their textbooks. Teach them reading skills and enhance comprehension and retention of science concepts in written materials. Become familiar with techniques for teaching your students reading/study skills in science, such as those listed in figure 12–10.

USING NONTEXTBOOK READING MATERIALS

There are many opportunities for you to use other nontextbook reading materials in your discovery science program to enhance both your science and reading processes and content. For example

1. Children's literature
   a. Tradebooks
   b. Minibooks or science logs
   c. Fiction/science fiction
   d. Comics
2. Children-made reading materials
   a. Creative writing
   b. Data collections (surveys, and so on)
   c. Other written communications

Children's Literature

Literature of all kinds supplies a variety of enrichment science learning experiences. Chil-

I. *Locating information*
   In text:
   1. Tables of contents
   2. Indexes
   3. Appendices
   4. Glossaries
   5. Footnotes
   6. Bibliographies
   7. Chapter headings
   8. Unit titles
   9. Keys
   10. Cross-references
   Reference books:
   1. Encyclopedia
   2. Dictionaries
   3. Atlases
   4. Almanacs
   5. Periodical indexes
   6. Library card catalogs
II. *Selecting information*
   Recognizing main ideas
   Differentiating between relevant and irrelevant ideas
   Differentiating between supporting and nonsupporting ideas
   Noting important details
III. *Organizing information:*
   Note-taking
   Outlining
   Summarizing information
IV. *Using graphic aids:*
   Maps   Tables
   Graphs   Cartoons
   Charts   Illustrations
V. *Following Directions*
IV. *Developing reading flexibility*
   Scanning for specific information
   Skimming for general ideas
   Slow, careful reading and rereading for detailed mastery

FIGURE 12–10
Reading/study skills in science

Source: Jill D. Wright and Paul B. Houshell, "Enhance Reading Through Science," *The Science Teacher* 45, no. 7 (October 1978), p. 35.

dren's literature and science complement each other. You will find excellent resources for using children's literature in your discovery science program in the following science reading materials.

Science minibooks. Would you like to increase the number of printed science materials available to your students by 25 or even 100? Would you like to make the printed science materials you currently have more attractive to your students? Would you like to use science textbooks ready to be destroyed by your school district or school to enhance your discovery science program? If the answer to any or all of these questions is positive, you should become familiar with the construction and use of "minibooks."

Minibooks are small books that are either commercially made, teacher-made, or student-made. Commercial minibooks are made by assembling as many and as wide a variety of reading-level science books as you can get. The books you pick for making minibooks should be those that can be separated into parts and can be cut up. Using a single-edged razor blade, slit the paper glued near the binding within the front and back covers. Separate each chapter (or part of a chapter) into specific

science topics. You or your students can make cardboard or oaktag front and back covers. Staple them together and have the children illustrate the covers with drawings, magazine pictures, or other illustrative materials. If your original science textbook had 8 units of approximately 50 pages each, you will now have 50 separate books of 8 pages each! A 50-page unit on "Plants and Food for the World" can be further divided into separate minibooks on topics such as kinds of leaves, plants that "eat" animals, how leaves make sugar, and how leaves change color.

Teacher- or student-made minibooks or logs. In addition to securing commercially prepared books for reassembly into minibooks, you and your students can make your own minibooks or logs. Select a size that appeals to you and the children. It may be dictated by the materials you have available to you, for example, the size paper (8-1/2" x 11") used in most schools. Have the children put in their minibook things they have studied and found for a particular science topic, a field trip, and so on.

FIGURE 12–11

1. Experiments of other activities
2. Observational records
3. Drawings
4. Magazine pictures
5. Handwritten or typed science content

Have your students add front and back covers, illustrate them, and bind them together. They can share their minibooks with each other, and some schools have even set up a special "Our Own Minibook" section in their libraries. This is an excellent opportunity to integrate science with reading, writing, art, mathematics, and other subjects.

Using fiction in discovery science programs.
Sometimes in our zeal to help children grow and develop, we forget how *they* use *their* senses to investigate *their* worlds. Students constantly weave from "reality" to "fantasy" as they acquire and test huge amounts of information about their environments. Although well intentioned, we often push the development of reading, math, spelling, and science and avoid or discourage fantasizing. However,

as noted in chapter 11, research on the functions of the right and left brain hemispheres show two distinct ways of learning. The left hemisphere deals with logic, rational thinking, and the use of language and numbers, and the right hemisphere uses the senses, creativity, intuition, metaphorical thinking, fantasy, spatial relationships, music and color. Some of our students will do better in science if we allow them to use the creative and intuitive right hemisphere.

Here is a right-hemisphere technique suggested by Virginia Johnson. This reinforces what you have read in chapter 2 and relates it to science and reading. Note that the "Fantasy on Metamorphosis" lesson presented in figure 12–13 will give your students experience with a science concept and also a chance to use their right hemispheres to fantasize. This allows them to wed the rational with feeling and intuition. You will find the "fantasy exercise" will also help motivate some of your nonparticipating students, since they may be "right-brained." Try them. (The *writing* of fiction by children is explored later in this chapter.)

FIGURE 12–12

Fantasy—Caterpillar to Butterly

Concept—Metamorphosis, the life cycle of an insect.

Get in a comfortable position. Sit relaxed in your seat. When you are ready close your eyes.

Imagine you are curled up tight inside a ball/something tells you it is time to break out of the ball/you begin to squirm and wiggle/the ball begins to break/it tears open/you crawl out and are very hungry/you crawl onto a juicy green leaf/you take a bite and it tastes so good/you eat and eat/now you begin to grow larger/and larger/you eat until you are a large, green, fuzzy caterpillar/you are no longer hungry/it's time for a rest/you begin to look for a place to take a nap/you choose a stem and begin to spin a soft cocoon around your body/it's warm and dark inside the cocoon/the cocoon sways gently in the breeze/you sleep/while you sleep your body begins to change/you wiggle, and jerk, and squirm in your sleep/you start to wake up and want to get out/your legs are just below your head/you crawl and bite and struggle/a hole appears in the top of the cocoon/you pull and squeeze/you crawl out into the bright sunlight/your shoulders itch/you are tired, but you have to wiggle the bumps on your shoulders/the bumps are moving/you are stretching and unfolding them/you are pumping a liquid into the bumps/before long they open into large, soft, beautiful green wings/slowly you fan your wings in the breeze/you are so proud of your new wings that you wiggle the feathery antennae on your head.

Now you just want to fly/and mate/and lay eggs/you fly in the sunlight for a few minutes./

Fly back to the tree. You are back in the classroom. Open your eyes.

This activity may introduce or follow up a lesson on insects. Cocoons or chrysalides can be kept in the classroom in appropriate containers. If you are lucky, you may observe a moth or butterfly emerge. The caterpillars of the mourning cloak butterly are recommended. The small dark caterpillars may be found on elm trees and will eat only fresh elm leaves until they form chrysalides. These may be found in late summer or early fall. It will take about two weeks for the butterfly to develop. This is a good September activity.

The following questions will help students discuss their fantasy experience, and give them the opportunity to express feelings they had during the fantasy.

Questions
1. How did it feel to eat and still be hungry?
2. When were you happiest—eating, sleeping, or flying?
3. Why weren't you hungry when you were a butterfly?

Metaphors
1. The caterpillar was hungry as a _____
_____

2. What machine is like a caterpillar? A butterfly?

Body movements can also be used after this exedrcise. The children can act out the different stages of the butterfly's development. Music may develop the flight of the butterfly. Art and creative writing assignments are an excellent follow-up to this fantasy experience.

Make *sure* the information presented in the fantasies is accurate. Children remember what they experience during a fantasy exercise.

The following books are excellent sources of activities, ideas, and techniques for similar science activities:

- James Adams, *Conceptual Blockbusting* (San Francisco: W. H. Freeman and Co., 1974).
- Gloria Castillo, *Left-Handed Teaching* (New York: Praeger Publishers, 1974).
- Richard DeMille, *Put Your Mother on the Ceiling* (New York: The Viking Press, 1973).
- Gay Hendricks and Russel Wills, *Centering Books* (Englewood Cliffs, N.J.: Prentice-Hall, 1975).
- Robert McKim, *Experiences in Visual Thinking* (Monterey, Calif.: Brooks/Cole Publishing Co., 1972).
- Robert Ornstein, *Psychology of Consciousness* (San Francisco: W. H. Freeman and Co., 1972).
- Max Rennels, "Cerebral Symmetry: An Urgent Concern for Education." *Phi Delta Kappan,* March 1976.
- Robert Samples, "Are You Teaching One Side of the Brain?" *Learning* 3 (February 1975): 25–28.

FIGURE 12–13
Fantasy on metamorphosis

Source: Virginia Johnson, "Fun, Fantasy, and Feeling," Reproduced with permission by *Science and Children* 15, no. 4 (January 1978), pp. 21–22. Copyright 1978 by the National Science Teachers Association, 1742 Connecticut Avenue, N.W., Washington, D.C. 20009. This article discusses right-hemisphere learning in science.

The use of comics in discovery science programs. Regardless of your opinions of comic books, it is hard to overlook their use in our society. Comics are read by the whole range of our population, not only by people with limited vocabularies or reading interests. In fact, comics are enjoying a boom among high school and college students. Many of the comic books have science fiction themes. The popularity of science fiction in movies and television probably has a lot to do with this. You would be hard pressed to find a student who has not seen and fallen in love with *Star Wars, Superman, E.T., 2001: A Space Odyssey, Planet of the Apes*, or *Star Trek*. A whole earlier generation was also hooked on science fiction serial movies such as Flash Gordon and Buck Rogers.

One of the best ways to use comics is a way of introducing a new science topic to your students. You could flash a cover of a comic book popular with the children on a screen using an opaque projector, or make a transparency and show it on an overhead projector, or simply pass the cover around as you point out some particular aspect. One teacher used Plastic Man doing his contortions to introduce how scientists have helped us develop plastics and other man-made materials. Some comic book characters you can use to introduce new science topics are listed below.

Comic book characters and their situations can also be used in pictorial riddles, tests, and evaluative devices. See chapter 3 for suggestions of how they may be effectively used in your discovery science program evaluation.

Other Science-Language Activities

There are many opportunities in your discovery science program to enrich and enlarge your students' science and communication skills through written and oral activities such as creative writing, science fiction writing, data-collection activities, and teacher/pupil communication.

Creative writing and science. Combining science and creative writing can be beneficial to your science program and can encourage children's imaginations to soar. One of our goals in science education is to get children to think not only *vertically* (logically, analytically, precisely) but also laterally and more holistically. *Lateral thinking*, according to Edward deBono of Cambridge University in England, moves sideways from established or ingrained ways of looking at problems with novel and unusual approaches. Lateral thinking is *not* looking for the best answer, only for a variety of alternatives. From this perspective, you can see that what deBono calls "lateral thinking" is what we are most familiar with as *creativity*. Chapter 4 explores holistic thinking and right and left hemispheres in depth. Here are some ways to stimulate lateral thinking or creative, holistic

Comic Character	*Science Topic*
Molecule Man or Mole Man	Problem solving
Iron Man, Quicksilver, Silver Surfer, Cobalt Man, the Metal Men, and Golden Arrow	Metals or minerals, geology
E-Man, Doctor Solar, Atom Smasher, The Atom, Captain Atom	Nuclear and other forms of energy
Sea Devils, Aqualad, Aquaman	Water, chemistry
Sandman, Rusty	Chemical reactions
Metamorpho	Elements and compounds
Coal Man, Carbon Copy Man, Sugarfoot	Organic chemistry, metals, minerals, rocks
Superman, Doc Savage	Metals, alloys, rocks, minerals

thinking using science language both orally and in writing:

Encourage creative writing by stimulating your students to write their own fiction, implementing the science concepts learned in your discovery science program. Combining scientific knowledge with their creative writing allows the children to reinforce concepts and also to develop their creative and critical-thinking skills. They also

☐ are motivated to check scientific facts
☐ look for additional data if needed
☐ develop research skills
☐ practice science vocabulary in meaningful new situations
☐ increase their oral- and written language skills

H. Kay Reid and Glenn McGlathery suggest these science creative-writing theme ideas, which are adjustable to any grade level in an elementary or middle school.[9]

1. *"Just-So"* (Rudyard Kipling's stories)— Explain how the monkey got a long tail or the leopard its spots; or any other animal characteristic basic to protection, motion, or eating can be used.
2. *Trash Machine*—Collect pieces of litter and design your machine. How does it work and how does it help us?
3. *Cloudy "Daze"*—Study the clouds and use your imagination. What do you see? Identify the object and explain why it is there.
4. *Earth History*—You are a visitor from outer space. Find evidence of the inhabitants of this planet. List what you find and speculate about its uses. (This could be a litter pick-up activity, but need not be limited to that.)
5. *"Picnic Pets"*—Were the insects present at your picnic friends or foes? How did they move?
6. *Germs*—Imagine an unusual germ that moves about in strange ways (wheels or skis for feet). How does it attack the body and how does the body fight back?
7. *Erosion*—Imagine you're a stream bed or a field. What causes you to erode? Can anything be done to save you?
8. *Planting Time*—Imagine you're a dandelion or tree seed. The wind removes you from your "family." How do you find a new home? What are your first years like?
9. *Frosty Freeze*—(a magic snowman) What type of weather does a snowman like best, and why?
10. *Machines*—Invent your own machine. How does it work? What simple machines are used in it? What can it be used to do?
11. *Daydreaming*—Imagine what type of daydream might an elephant, or a monkey, or a deer have.
12. *Use Your Senses*—Taste cotton candy. Feel a new baby. Smell a bakery. Hear the ocean roar. How does a raindrop taste or feel?
13. *Forest Living*—You live in a forest. Who are your friends? How do you survive?

What sounds do you hear? Variations: You live in the desert. You live by a lake.

14. *Anthropologist*—You were looking for dinosaur bones. You fell in a hole and you went back millions of years. What was it like?

15. *Submarine Ride*—You travel underwater to study life. What is it like on the ocean floor? What do you meet in murky depths?

16. *Birthday Surprise*—You are given a jungle pet for a present. How does it get along in its new environment? What are its needs? Is it happy?

17. *Sleuthing*—Write a description of an animal, plant, etc. Have other children guess its identity from your descriptive phrases.

18. *Caught in a Snowstorm*—Use your senses to describe your predicament. Paint a word picture of the situation.

19. *Girabbit*—Imagine an animal that is half giraffe and half rabbit. How would it move? What does it eat? What are its habits? What problems does it have? What other two animal combinations can you imagine?

20. *Save the Animals*—Imagine that you are an endangered animal. Write a letter to the world about your need to be protected and why we should help. Where do you live? How important are you to nature's balance?

21. *All the Facts*—Imagine you're a newscaster. Report your finds of a study made outdoors using who, what, where, when, and how. Report on an invasion from outer space. Variation: You are a weather forecaster. Write a weather report for today and tomorrow. What weather conditions are present? What do you predict as a long-range forecast?

22. *Before It's Too Late*—Earth is a spaceship. How can we keep the ship safe? Write a letter to "Dear Everyone" explaining your ideas. How do you feel? How do we preserve Earth?

23. *Inventor*—You have just developed a new vegetable. Describe its looks, use, and health value. How is it an improvement over other vegetables?

24. *Detective*—You are looking for a missing queen ant. You must invade an ant colony to find her. How will she be protected? How will you recognize her?

25. *If I Went Through a Washing Machine Wringer and Came Out Flat*—How would being flat change your life? Would there be any advantages? How would you relate to your environment?

26. *If I Were Very Small*—How would you have to adjust your life to survive? Variations: If I Had Wings, If I Had a Shell.

27. *Inventor*—Invent something to help you do some despised job or prevent an unwanted situation.

28. *Visit to Another Planet*—Describe your space flight and landing. Is there life on the new planet as we know it? What is the soil like? How could you adjust to living there?

29. *Interview*—Interview an animal. Does it have problems? Where does it like to play?

30. *Story Titles*—"The Day the Animals Talked," "Spaceship in our Yard," "The

Laughing Frog." Give each child a different title and have him write a story about it.

31. *Book Covers*—Borrow book jackets on animals and nature from the library. Have each child choose one and write a story to go with the cover.

32. *Survivor*—You survived a flood, tornado, or hurricane. You are alone. Describe the situation and what you do.

33. *Haiku*—Write a poem about nature. The haiku form has three lines. Five syllables are in the first and third lines. Seven syllables are in the second, for example

> Fall brings new colors
> Bright orange, yellow, and brown
> Marking summer's end
> —Laurie McGlathery

Don't forget to stimulate your students' creative-thinking abilities by asking divergent (as suggested in chapter 6) thought-provoking questions like these:

1. Why do you think a particular character behaved in a certain way?
2. What are some other ways the character could have handled the problem?
3. What might happen if . . . ?
4. Suppose you substitute a different animal (or any thing with different attributes). How would this alter the situation?

SCIENCE AND SOCIAL STUDIES

There are many natural opportunities for the alert teacher to integrate a science and a social studies program. Obviously, you do not want to diminish either the science or social studies, and, indeed, there are times when it is wiser to teach each separately. Humanistic values of science in a social context were discussed in chapter 4. For an excellent discussion of how humanistic values could be used in your science program, read this short article: Cynthia Sunal, "Science and Social Studies—Taking the Global View", *Science and Children*, 17, no. 4 (January 1980), pp. 22–23.

Here are some ways that science and social studies can be conducted together to enhance children's learning of both.

☐ In studying heat and heat transmittal, children could investigate how their school is heated, insulated, and cooled by having the custodian show them the heating/cooling systems and trace the movement of heat in the building.

☐ Children's bicycles, roller skates, and other toys could be examined when you are studying about machines, gears, and mechanical advantage.

☐ Radio, television, and electronic games could be used to study light and sound in communication.

☐ As students study plants or animals, they could be introduced to population concepts and the problems associated with overpopulation.

☐ In a science unit on weather and climate, you have an opportunity to help children see the interrelationship between geographical areas, and how pollution in one area could cause acid rain or other pollu-

tants to fall on people thousands of miles away.

☐ Insect studies lend themselves to exploring ways of avoiding or ridding urban areas of rodents, roaches, and other disease-carrying animals.

You must decide when, how much, and for how long to integrate science with social studies.

ART AND SCIENCE

Many suggestions for using art in science are scattered throughout this book in such things as bulletin boards, use of visual aids and projected objects, posters, drawings, etc. Here are some ways of getting children involved with aesthetic or artistic appreciation and skills through integration with science.

1. While studying light, cover the ends of flashlights with different colored cellophane, using several layers to produce strong colors. Darken the room and have children experiment with various colors.
2. In discussions about the properties of matter, give each child several different kinds of textured papers, such as sandpaper, watercolor paper, or oatmeal paper. Have children draw or scribble on papers with crayons to discover the different textures.
3. Mobiles are excellent ways to graphically show such things as the solar system or weather elements.
4. Puppets of all kinds (paperbag, hand, tennis ball, etc.) allow children to engage in artistic and fantasy extensions of science.

5. Making objects with clay or other maleable substances permits children to produce three-dimensional representations of mental images.
6. Working with wood and tools (saws, hammers, drills, screwdrivers, etc.) lets children see how people use knowledge of machines to make work easier.

Besides being very enjoyable, art provides children with opportunities for both right and left brain development, as do physical activities.

PHYSICAL ACTIVITIES AND SCIENCE

Often, it is difficult to approach theoretical concepts with elementary school children, especially those in the primary grades. We have difficulty helping these children see the *how* and *why* of physical occurances; activities like games, dances, and role-playing can help us explain physical occurances. Story-dances about familiar physical phenomena, in which children role-play invisible entities, have these advantages for science learning:

1. Dances that tell a story have an ancient and universal appeal that helps to motivate students.
2. Students involved in physical activity are not as easily bored as those listening passively.
3. Sufficient roles are required so that the whole class can have a part. Nobody has to sit and watch. (Even students in wheelchairs can play.)

4. Each dance is short, usually less than five minutes. Time is available for two or three repetitions with a chance for trading roles.
5. No stage equipment is required—only a roll of masking tape or some chalk to outline objects on the floor.[10]

Dances that help children "see" invisible particles are possible in such areas as matter, energy, particles, and motion in melting ice, boiling water, electricity, atoms and subatomic particles, and electrons. By acting as the microscopic particles, they can act out such concepts as molecules slowing down or speeding up or the movement of electrons. They can visualize what happens in expansion and contraction of metals due to heat or cold by moving further together or apart as metal molecules, as shown below.

Help children to conceptualize invisible particle theories by using more physical move-ment. However, in relating physical activities to science, consider the appropriateness of the cognitive level. For example, the concept of particles and their relationships seems to be too abstract for pre-operational or early concrete operational children.

SUMMARY

When science is properly integrated, in an un-forced and natural way, with other subjects, children's learning in *both* science *and* the other subject is enhanced.

Discovery science programs enhance and enrich the language development of children. Reading and discovery science require the same intellectual skills. Students, through ac-tive involvement with physical objects, learn the cognitive processes (such as class inclusion, conservation, and ordering) required to read

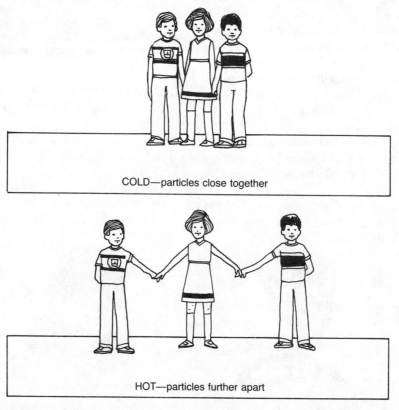

COLD—particles close together

HOT—particles further apart

FIGURE 12-14

better in science better than they learn them through reading alone. One of the best techniques is to read frequently to nonreaders to encourage the development of reading skills.

Selecting appropriate cognitive reading levels of textbooks for your students can present problems. Techniques have been presented in this chapter for using the cloze test and Piagetian assessment for the independent, instructional, and frustration levels of reading. Other factors for textbook use in your discovery science program have also been explored.

Specific techniques for developing vocabulary for science reading have been presented, such as inventing new science words, using science dictionaries, playing science word categories games, using science word associations and science word-attack skill games, keeping records, and effectively using science textbooks.

Activities have been explored for effectively using other nontextbook reading in your science program such as children's literature (tradebooks, minibooks, science fiction, comics,) and creative writing, written data collection, and person-to-person written communications.

Specific activities were also presented for integrating science with social studies, art, and physical activities.

This chapter cautioned that science is a legitimate subject and should not be diluted or diminished when combined with any subject matter. If the full impact of your science program cannot be realized by integration, then don't integrate it.

SELF-EVALUATION AND FURTHER STUDY

1. Help your students make a science pictorial dictionary using drawings or magazine photos on large primer chart paper.
2. Construct a science word category game for a group of children.
3. Following a field trip, help your class write an experience chart of the experience on large primer chart paper. Illustrate it with your or your students' drawings. Use the children's words whenever possible.
4. Gather old or discarded science textbooks and tradebooks and help your students make minibooks.
5. Working with a group of children, help them make science logs following a science study.
6. Plan and conduct a fantasy exercise with a group of children.
7. Pick a science theme and plan science creative-writing activities for your students.
8. Find cartoons or other forms of humor and prepare several lateral-thinking exercises.
9. Prepare a form for a large index card to be used as a written teacher/pupil, one-to-one communication. Duplicate the form and use it with your students.
10. Textbook and tradebook selection for your science program must be given much thought. Use the following as beginning articles to help you pick for your class:
    ☐ *Science and Children*, "Resource Reviews;" "Outstanding Science Trade Books for Children" (an annotated bibliography prepared annually).

☐ Seymour Simon, "Behold the World: Using Science Trade Books in the Classroom," *Science and Children*, 19, no. 6 (March 1982), pp. 5–6.

☐ Richard J. McLeod, "Selecting a Textbook for Good Science Teaching," *Science and Children*, 17, no. 2 (October 1979), pp. 14–16.

11. Develop activities in expository and descriptive writing for your elementary science program using these references:

☐ Jeffrey Lehman and Jane Harper Yarbrough, "25 (Scientific) Writing Activities," *The Science Teacher*, 50, no. 2 (February 1983), pp. 27–30.

☐ Shirley Koeller, "Expository Writing: A Vital Skill in Science", *Science and Children*, 20, no. 1 (September 1982), pp. 12–16.

☐ Marylu Shore Simon and Judith Moss Zimmerman, "Science and Writing," *Science and Children*, 18, no. 3 (November/December 1980), pp. 7–10.

12. Select several science study areas and, using the "Integrating Science With Other Subjects" chart, plan integration activities with social studies and other subjects for your elementary school class.

13. Devise art activities that naturally lend themselves to science topics.

14. Plan a dance-play to help children visualize invisible particles in science theory you are studying.

ENDNOTES

1. Stephen B. Lucas and Andrew B. Burlando, "The New Science Methods and Reading," *Language Arts* 52 (September 1975), pp. 769–70.

2. Judith Thelen, *Improving Reading in Science* (Newark, Del.: International Reading Association, 1976), pp. 1–2.

3. For an excellent review of research in science teaching and reading, see Ruth T. Wellman, "Science: A Basic for Language and Reading Development," in *What Science Says to the Science Teacher,* vol. 1, ed. Mary Budd Rowe (Washington, D.C.: National Science Teachers Association, 1978), pp. 1–12.

4. Philip White and Lynne List, "And Never the Twain Shall Meet? A Forgotten Process Approach," *The Journal* 4, no. 3 (October 1974), p. 42.

5. Sarah B. Graham, "Do Children Read Science Books," *Science and Children* 15, no. 5 (February 1978), p. 29.

6. David W. Cornelius, "A 'Once Upon A Time' Approach to Reading," *The Science Teacher* 46, no. 2 (February 1979), p. 38.

7. For a thorough presentation of inventing of new terms, see Herbert D. Thier, *Teaching Elementary School Science—A Laboratory Approach* (Lexington, Mass.: D. C. Heath, 1970), no. 139–42.

8. The following sources were used, and you are urged to refer to them for elaboration upon the brief introduction offered here: Roach Van Allen, *Language Experiences in Communication.* Copright © 1976 by

Houghton Mifflin Company. Used by permission. James Moffett and Betty Jane Wagner, *Student-Centered Language Arts and Reading, K–13,* second edition. Copyright © 1976 by Houghton Mifflin Company. Used by permission. Jill D. Wright and Paul B. Hounshell, "Enhance Reading Through Science," *The Science Teacher* 45, no. 7 (October 1978), pp. 34–36.

9. H. Kay Reid and Glenn McGlathery, "Science and Creative Writing." Reproduced with permission by *Science and Children* 14, no. 4 (January 1977), pp. 19–20. Copyright 1977 by the National Science Teachers Association, 1742 Connecticut Avenue, N.W., Washington, D.C. 20009.

10. For an expanded discussion of the use of physical activity in elementary school, *see* Lloyd D. Remington, "Let's Get Physical in Science," *Science and Children*, 19, no. 7 (April 1982), pp. 13–15.

13

How Can You Use Mathematics and Computers in Your Science Teaching?

"Computers have been major scientific research tools since the 1950s; but despite promising starts in the 1960s and 1970s, their effectiveness in teaching science has not yet been felt. The time has arrived for science teachers to explore the possibilities for computer-based learning." (Jerry J. Doyle and Vincent N. Lunetta, "Class, Open Your Microcomputers (Hardware, software, bytes and discs—a primer)," *The Science Teacher,* 49, no. 8 [November 1982], p. 25.)

The preceding chapter covered the interrelationships between science and other areas of elementary school teaching. In this chapter, you will discover the close relationships between science, mathematics, and computers. These disciplines develop the cognitive abilities of children. Mathematics, to a large degree, is the *language* of science; by using it in activities, children gain better insights into scientific concepts and principles. Involvement in scientific activity enhances mathematical logical reasoning. Computers, especially new generations of software, can significantly improve mathematics and science learning. "Microcomputers offer an opportunity to revolutionize the way science and mathematics are taught and learned."[1]

Mathematics has always been integrally involved with the advancement of science. This involvement continues with the development of computers. Throughout the history of science, there have been periods of rapid growth and of inactivity. This uneven development often depended on the lack of sophisticated mathematical tools to analyze natural phenomena. Breakthroughs in mathematics, such as non-Euclidean geometry, which eventually enabled us to better understand outer space, have heralded technological advancements-in this case, space exploration. The development of computers advanced the exploration of

space even further by combining sophisticated mathematics with mind-numbing speed and accuracy. In a similar way, the calculus of Leibniz and Newton gave us insights into rates of change, necessary for studying moving objects, which, in turn have helped us understand the movement of planets and satellites. Because of the growing importance of computers to science and mathematics, science teachers must become as familiar with them as we did years ago when other "revolutionary" teaching tools, the movie and slide projectors, were introduced.

INTERRELATIONSHIP OF SCIENCE AND MATHEMATICS IN SCHOOLS

Because science and mathematics are so integrally involved, much elementary school science activity has mathematical implications and many mathematical problems have scientific ramifications. In its publication, *Theory into Action in Science Curriculum Development,* NSTA emphasized the importance of the role of mathematics in teaching science:

One cannot speak realistically of a sound science curriculum without considering the important role played by mathematics. . . . Mathematics is the language by which one describes the order in nature and which in turn leads to a clearer understanding of that order.[2]

Developing Cognitive Abilities Through Science and Mathematics

Piagetian operations are required for children to achieve well in the basics, and this is especially so in science and mathematics. Some of the operations basic to these disciplines are

1. Conservation of substance
2. Conservation of length
3. Conservation of number
4. One-to-one correspondence
5. Ordering
6. Seriating
7. Classification

Students who do not do these operations well, and this includes many children aged seven to eight, have trouble reading and solving mathematical and scientific problems. They are still *prelogical* (unable to do logic) and *prenumerical* (unable to do things with numbers) in their development. Science and mathematical curricula that involve children in the above

operational tasks help students overcome such inadequacies. Thus, many science and mathematical curriculums include Piagetian activities.

Science and mathematical curricula, particularly in the primary grades, have some necessary duplication because students on the preoperational level need many similar operational experiences, such as conservation, to develop their cognitive abilities. Curricula, therefore, include Piagetian activities in developing operational competencies. These competencies are not only fundamental to science and mathematics but to all subjects that require thinking. For example, Donald Strafford and John Renner found that the Science Curriculum Improvement Study (SCIS) caused significant gains in conservation of length, number, and other abilities in the first grade.[3] Donald Kellogg found that the "Materials Objects" unit was the main contributor to this increase in operational ability. This unit contains many experiences that are also found in some primary mathematical programs.[4]

In another study, Jerry Ayers and George Mason found that using Science—A Process

Approach (SAPA) curriculum materials, kindergarten children did significantly better on the Metropolitan Readiness Test on Number as well as on other abilities.[5] Mary and Jerry Ayers, in a similar study done with kindergarten children in Appalachia, concluded that SAPA significantly helped children develop their thinking-operational abilities.[6]

Because of this research and other studies as well, Dr. Mary Rowe concluded that science is especially important because it helps children develop not only mental operations but also a greater willingness to solve problems. This willingness to solve problems is critical for children learning both science and mathematics. Rowe, furthermore, believes this is especially important for disadvantaged children.

> Without science experiences, disadvantaged children tend to be frightened and frustrated by simple problems. Their problem-coping skills simply do not develop satisfactorily. With it, they usually learn strategies for attacking problems.[7]

Research indicates that science experiences are crucial for facilitating operational abilities not only in the primary grades but in the upper elementary and middle school grades as well. F. Elizabeth Froit found that certain inquiry-oriented science curriculums such as Introductory Physical Science (IPS), Earth Science Curriculum Study (ESCS), and Time, Space, and Matter (TSM) caused significant gains in the number of students capable of doing formalistic reasoning.[8] Formal reasoning is necessary for students to perform adequately in algebra and higher mathematics.

How Scientists Use Mathematics

Scientists use mathematics to collect data. The data they collect can be of two types: dichotomous or metrical. The word *dichotomy* comes from the Greek word *dichotomia*, which means to divide into two parts. The word *metre* comes from the Greek word *metron*, which means to measure.

Here is an example of a dichotomous experiment, an "all (one group) or none (the other group)" situation. If scientists want to

determine whether light is necessary for seeds to sprout, they establish two groups. One group of seeds receives light; the other group, the control, receives no light. From the experiment, they will be able to determine whether light is necessary for the seeds to sprout. However, they will not know *how much* light is necessary.

In setting up an experiment to determine how much light is necessary, scientists would have to design it so they could obtain metrical measurable data. They would have to establish an experimental situation to determine how intense the light would have to be over varied periods to get seeds to sprout. Obviously, this metrical experiment is far more sophisticated than the simple dichotomous experiment, and mathematics is required to determine the intensity of light and the periods of time. However, the scientists' knowledge of the relationship of sprouting seeds to light would be far more sophisticated.

Because mathematics aids in understanding natural phenomena, encourage the metrical aspects as much as possible in elementary science activities. Dichotomous experiments may be done in the primary grades or as an introductory experiment but should be followed by open-ended questions leading to metrical experiments.

How Mathematics Reveals Relationships

Mathematics, in addition to its measurement uses in scientific investigation, is also used to reveal relationships. It helps the scientist organize data and understand it. Look at Newton's formula for the law of gravity.

$$F = \frac{GM_1M_2}{d^2}$$

where F = force
M_1 = mass of one object
M_2 = mass of another object
d^2 = distance between the two masses (objects), squared
G = a constant, its value is 6.67×10^{-11}

What relationships can you see between the force, the mass of the objects, and the distance between objects? What will happen if the distance (d) is increased between the two objects? Substitute some simple number for d in the formula and you will see. What will happen if the mass of one of the objects is increased? Substitute simple numbers for the masses in the formula. The formula enables you to see and retain in your mind the relationships of gravitational force to the masses of any two objects and the distance between them. Newton's formula for the law of gravity is a remarkable intellectual tool that enables you to determine the gravitational relationships of any object to any other object in the entire universe.

THE USE OF MATHEMATICS IN SCIENCE CURRICULUMS

Elementary Science Study (ESS)

Although, as the name indicates, the Elementary Science Study has been mainly concerned with science, many of the units produced actually deal to a great extent with the development of mathematical concepts as well. Some of the many units that deal with this are Mirror Cards (Grades 1–7); Light and Shadows (Grades K–3); Attributive Games and Problems (Grades K–8); Peas and Particles (Grades 4–6); Primary Balancing (no grade listed); Changes (Grades 1–4); Optics (Grades 6–8); Pattern Blocks (Grades K–5); Balloons and Gases (Grades 6–8); Tangram (Grades K–8); Mapping (Grades 6–7); Musical Sound (Grade 6); Matrix Blocks (Grades K–8); Measuring (Grades K–3); Checkerboard (Grade 4); Thermometry (Grades 4–6); Time and Clocks (Grades 3–5); and Counting the Slide Rule (Grades 7–8). For more information on ESS, refer to chapter 9.

Science Curriculum Improvement Study (SCIS)

SCIS uses to a high degree Piagetian operations in its curriculum. Its Teacher's Handbook outlines and explains how these operations are developed in the lessons. Since the operations are basically logical and mathematical, they contribute to the learning of mathematical concepts. Examples of selected activities from the various levels of the curriculum are outlined below (see also chapter 9).

Grade Kindergarten
1. Drawing, sorting, and assembling objects. This physical action leads to the internalization of mental action later and is fundamental to learning numbers.
2. Multiple classification, classifying objects by more than one characteristic. This involves combining or grouping similar objects. It is also basic to using numbers.
3. Class inclusion. Developing the idea that what is said for the major class is also true for subclasses or sets.
4. Conservation of number. The child realizes that rearranging items doesn't affect the number of a set.
5. Conservation of distance. The child realizes that placing something between two objects doesn't affect the distance between them.

Grades K–3—Material Objects
1. Sorting objects according to some property.
2. Reversibility, mentally reversing actions.
3. Serial ordering.

Grades 3–6—Populations
1. Representing data by means of histograms.
2. Sorting liquids according to some property.
3. Graphing.

Grades 4—Relative Position and Motion
1. Describing object location from various viewpoints.
2. Forming correspondences between properties and variables.
3. Describing locations of objects mathematically by coordinating two distances.

Grades 4—Environments
1. Averaging data.

Grades 5—Energy Sources
1. Graphing.
2. Measuring and conserving liquids.
3. Isolating variables, keeping one constant.

Grades 5—Communities
1. Averaging data.
2. Using proportional reasoning.

Grades 6—Ecosystems
1. Using data relative to the cyclic movement of materials.

Science—A Process Approach (SAPA)

SAPA extensively integrates mathematics with science, particularly in three areas: *measuring, using number,* and *using space-time relationships.* Examples of some of the types of activities included under these sections from the primary level are listed below. The following examples are not quoted directly from SAPA but are modified slightly to relate them to Piaget's work (see also chapter 9).

Primary Level
I. Using Space-Time Relationships
  1. Recognizing and using shapes
     a. Making triangles, circles, ellipses
     b. Making people out of triangles, circles, rectangles (the materials used can be pieces of paper or blocks of wood)
     c. Identifying, when given several squares, the largest and smallest square
     d. Playing games with shapes
        (A child holds up one shape and the other children identify it; the child identifying it holds a different shape and the class responds.)
     e. Turning a triangle many ways and having children describe how it looks
     f. Tracing shapes on a chalkboard and naming them
  2. Using correspondence and establishing coordinate orientation
     a. Teacher making a triangle on floor and one on the chalkboard (A child stands in one end of a triangle and points to the corresponding spot on the board. Each child draws on a piece of paper his or her triangle and where he or she stood.)
  3. Using number (one-to-one correspondence)
     a. Matching a row of either real, plastic, or paper drawings of saucers and cups
     b. Pairing children
     c. Asking children if they can think of things that can be paired, for example, a chair for each child.
     d. Placing several blocks and toy cars on a table and asking the children how they would find out whether there are more cars than blocks
  4. Ordering
     a. Placing three shoe boxes filled with lollipops on a table and asking the children how they can tell which has the most and least in it
     b. Introducing several sets, for example, two balls, three blocks, four cars, and asking the children to compare and order the sets from the least to the most

British Nuffield Mathematics 5–13 Project

In the 1960s, a group of British mathematicians, funded by the Nuffield Foundation, decided to revise mathematical instruction so it more appropriately integrated what was known about how children develop and learn. They produced the Nuffield Mathematics 5–13 Project. The 5–13 refers to the ages for which the program has been designed. Basically, this program follows a Piagetian approach since children are involved in concrete experiences before abstract concepts are developed. The general design of instruction follows the "learning cycle" discovery format described in chapter 7. In the primary and lower elementary grades, there is a great deal of overlap between this program and Science 5–13 since they both are attempting to develop similar Piagetian operations.[9]

SCIENCE AND THE METRIC SYSTEM (SI)

Although the movement to adopt the metric system in our country seems to have lost some of its steam, the country is becoming more

ALL YOU WILL NEED TO KNOW ABOUT METRIC
(FOR YOUR EVERYDAY LIFE)

10

Metric is based on Decimal system

The metric system is simple to learn. For use in your every-day life you will need to know only ten units. You will also need to get used to a few new temperatures. Of course, there are other units which most persons will not need to learn. There are even some metric units with which you are al-ready familiar: those for time and electricity are the same as you use now.

Basic Units

METER: a little longer than a yard (about 1.1 yards)
LITER: a little larger than a quart (about 1.06 quarts)
GRAM: about the weight of a paper clip

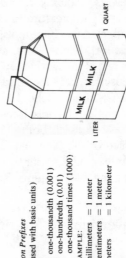

1 METER

(comparative sizes are shown)

1 YARD

1 LITER   1 QUART

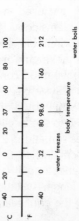

Common Prefixes
(to be used with basic units)

MILLI: one-thousandth (0.001)
CENT: one-hundredth (0.01)
KILO: one-thousand times (1000)

FOR EXAMPLE:
1000 millimeters = 1 meter
100 centimeters   = 1 meter
1000 meters   = 1 kilometer

Other Commonly Used Units

MILLIMETER: 0.001 meter   diameter of paper clip wire
CENTIMETER: 0.01 meter   width of a paper clip (about 0.4 inch)
KILOMETER: 1000 meters   somewhat further than ½ mile (about 0.6 mile)
KILOGRAM: 1000 grams   a little more than 2 pounds (about 2.2 pounds)
MILLILITER: 0.001 liter   five of them make a teaspoon

Other Useful Units

HECTARE: about 2½ acres
TONNE: about one ton

1 KILOGRAM   1 POUND

Temperature

degrees Celsius are used

25 DEGREES FAHRENHEIT

25 DEGREES CELSIUS

°C -40   -20   0   20 37   60   80   100
F   -40   0   32   80 98.6   160   212
         water freezes   body temperature   water boils

FIGURE 13-1

273

metric. The metric system, now termed SI, which stands for the International System of Measurement, is used by all other English-speaking countries. The pressure to change to SI has already affected machine tools, packaging (especially liquor), temperature, etc. Competition with the rest of the world may continue to accelerate business, science, and governmental use of SI. Children in school will have to know *both* systems during this transition period. You will have to teach both. The Metric Information Office of the National Bureau of Standards has published a paper to help individuals compare the two systems (see figure 13–1).

Making Conversions to Metric Measures

The metric system is convenient because conversion factors within the system are powers of ten. For example, in measuring and adding the length of objects together, the metric system is often easier to use than our English system. It is easier to add 4.5 cm and 2.4 cm than add 1 ¾ and 1 ⅛ inches. Also, because the metric system has smaller units (millimetres), it is easier to measure exactly.

Because of the national concern about changing to the SI system, many states are insisting that greater attention be given to using metric measures. Many science curriculum projects and texts use only metric units.

Teachers often think the SI system is difficult; they are used to the English system and have problems converting from it to the metric form. Children, however, do not have difficulty learning the metric measures. Since they do not yet have good concepts of the English system, the SI system seems as easy as the English system. You should not stress converting from the metric to the English system. When a child measures something 2.54 cm long, accept that as a description of its length. Do not ask how many inches long it is. Children's concepts of a unit of length will be just as good without knowing the equivalent in the English system.

Using Metrics in Science Texts and Curricula

Science curricula and text series use the metric system almost exclusively. For example, Charles E. Merrill's *New Elementary Science Program* uses only metrics in its measurements. The Modular Activities Program (MAPS) of Houghton Mifflin uses many activitites from SCIS, ESS, and SAPA in integrating the metric system into its activities. Figure 13–2 shows uses for the Omnimeter. Figure 13–3 presents simple activities to introduce the SI system.

How Teachers Stimulate the Use of Mathematics in Science

Mathematics and science cannot be divorced. The new curriculum projects in mathematics and science include many activities which unite these two disciplines. When using more traditional instructional material, relate mathematics with science activities: use metric measurement, control variables, and organize and report data mathematically, especially with graphs. Let children interpret graphs and set up experiments that measure variables.

COMPUTER-ASSISTED INSTRUCTION

In 1983, almost one of four elementary schools used computers in instruction, and the number increases rapidly every year. You will shortly use some form of computer-assisted instruction (CAI). There are five major ways that computers will help your science teaching (see figure 13–4).

1. "lab" data analysis/processing
2. dialog and tutorial
3. simulating and modeling
4. drill and practice
5. teacher utility (word processing, record keeping, etc.)

"Lab" data analysis and processing. In the pyramid, "lab" data analysis and processing, is

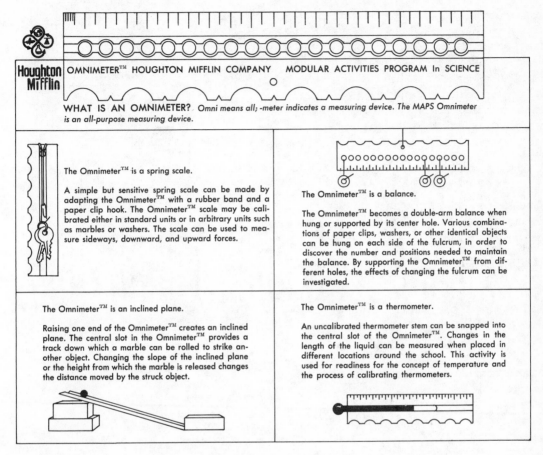

FIGURE 13-2
Omnimeter.

Source: Modular Activities Program (Boston: Houghton Mifflin Co., 1973). Used by permission of the publisher.

based on the four bases: drill and practice, teacher utility, simulating and modeling, and dialog and tutorial. "Lab" data analysis and processing is discussed first because

1. It is easy for elementary school teachers to emphasize drill and practice applications because this is what we know and do ourselves.
2. "Lab" data analysis and processing attempts to use the computer as a tool to aid discovery, not merely as mechanical flash cards.
3. Computers are new to most elementary school science programs. Teachers should emphasize the most creative and innovative uses of computers, rather than the least imaginative, mechanical uses.

Dale Rice has used "lab" data analysis and processing in an interesting way with elementary school children, featuring a two-probe temperature sensor and a computer program with the Apple II microcomputer. Designed specifically for elementary school children, the program shows the temperatures of two loca-

EXAMPLES OF SIMPLE ACTIVITIES TO INTRODUCE CHILDREN TO THE SI SYSTEM

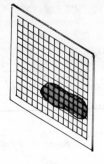

1. Make a paper airplane.
   Measure the size of the wings.
   Fly it.
   Use your metre stick.
   How far did it go?
   Make the wings bigger.
   Fly it again.
   How far did it go?

2. Take a little step.
   Use your metre stick.
   How big was the step?
   Take a big step.
   Use your metre stick.
   How big was your step?

3. How far can you jump?
   Jump.
   Use your metre stick.
   How big was your jump?
   How long was it compared to your step?

4. Measure things in your class.
   Find the smallest thing you can measure.
   Find the largest thing you can measure.

5. How well can you estimate?
   Estimate the length of each of the following:
   Write your estimates.

	Estimate	Measure
Foot		
Head		
Arm		
Long finger		
Little finger		
Thumb		

   Measure each of the above.
   Write your measurements.
   What was your best estimate?

6. Make a metre tape.
   Get some string.
   Hold the string in one hand.
   Make the string six arm spans long.
   Place a knot in one end.
   Put knot at the end of the metre stick.
   Mark off metres on the string.
   Measure the length of the room.
   Measure around something.
   What things did you find
   were more than a metre?
   How many metres high are you?
   How high are you when you stretch?

7. Estimate how far it will go.
   Get a toy car.
   Estimate how far it will go.
   Push it.
   Measure how far it went.

8. How big around is your footprint?
   Get some paper with 1 cubic cm. squares.
   Put your foot on it.
   Trace around your foot.
   Count the number of squares it covered.
   Remember two half squares equal only one
   square.
   How big was your footprint? _____
   cubic cm.

9. A sugar cube has about 1 cubic cm. of volume.
   Put some cubes like this.
   How would you find its cubic cm. volume?
   Put some cubes like this.
   How much is its cubic cm. volume?
   Put some cubes like this.
   How would you find its cubic cm. volume?
   Make your own cube thing.
   How would you find its cubic cm. volume?

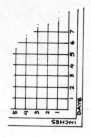

10. Measure a plant growing in centimetres
    for two weeks.
    Record your measurements.
    Make a graph.
    Each line on the graph should be 1 cm. high.
    Place your measurements on the graph.

FIGURE 13-3

FIGURE 13–4

Uses of computer-assisted instruction (CAI) *in science teaching*

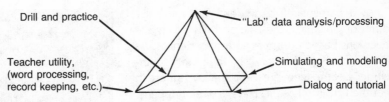

tions simultaneously, e.g., the mouth and the surface of the skin. Both temperatures are displayed at the same time on the television monitor or receiver (called the cathode ray tube or CRT), showing any differences that exist. See the list of microcomputer resources at the end of this chapter for other programs that use "lab" data analysis and processing.

Dialog and tutorial. Another kind of CAI used by science teachers is interactive *dialog or tutorial.* Students could learn how blood circulates, the names of the organs in the circulatory system of a fish, and then be tested to reinforce the concepts learned. Generally, tutorial CAI involves students in *active* dialog, which requires them to answer correctly before going to the next step.

Simulating and modeling. Although difficult to program because of complex computer graphics, *stimulating and modeling* has great potential as a CAI teaching tool. The computer can simulate experiments that are difficult to do in elementary school classrooms, such as wave properties or population growth. Students enjoy the action and direct involvement in the graphic displays; witness the popularity of video games.

Drill and practice. The most common type of computer-assisted instruction is *drill and practice,* which is relatively simple to write. CAI drill and practice is good for teaching things like scientific terminology, classification, and computation.

Teacher utility. The computer has obvious and far-reaching applications in the areas of record keeping, data processing, and other administrative and clerical tasks.

Simulating Real Life[11]

One area of tremendous potential in science education, especially for elementary schools, is the use of the microcomputer as a simulator of real-life events. Students are placed in a situation where they control an environment by interacting with the microcomputer. In this situation, they collect data, correlate results, and learn skills, attitudes, and concepts, as a result of this *active* experience. You must help your children understand the relationship of the computer simulation and reality. Plan activities to help them develop the logical skills needed to make these connections.

An example of such a simulator software program is *Odell Lake,* produced by the Minnesota Educational Computing Consortium (M.E.C.C.). *Odell Lake* is entertaining, educational, and highly interactive. It provides a discovery-based learning experience about the food chain in a Cascade Mountain lake. In this program, the student chooses to be one of six different fish: whitefish, blueback salmon, mackinaw trout, chub, rainbow trout, or dolly varden. After selecting a fish, the student sees this frame that shows what the fish will look like.

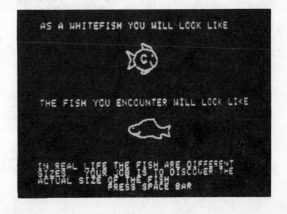

As a particular fish, students will meet the other organisms in the lake and have to make decisions based upon previous experiences. As a fish meeting another fish, their options include: escape deeper; escape shallow; ignore it; eat the fish; or chase it. Here is what happens.

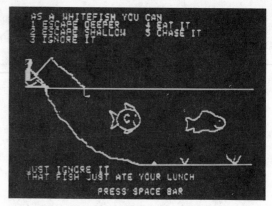

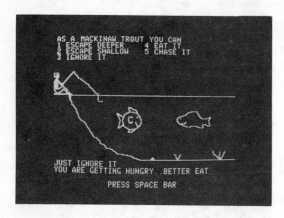

A student who makes the right decision is rewarded—he or she survives and/or eats the other fish. A student making the wrong decision learns a valuable experimental lesson and is eaten or loses a meal. Here's an encounter with another fish.

Children begin to see underlying relationships in the lake as they progress through the program. They eventually meet otters, water insects, and more. Interest runs high and students carry their excitement back into classroom discussions and further study.

This type of simulator microcomputer program provides an exciting, *active* learning experience that allows the student to enjoy a discovery lesson, while absorbing valuable ecological concepts. You must provide closure and analysis and encourage expressions of the concepts learned through such activities as drawing posters of the food web, and role playing various participants in the interactions.

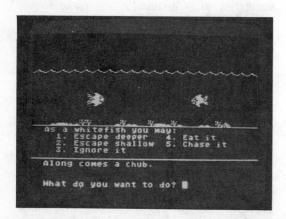

Here's what happened in this situation when the student chose wrong.

MICROCOMPUTERS IN SCIENCE TEACHING

Here are some suggestions on using microcomputers to teach science from two educators who are working directly with computer-assisted instruction.

1. Become familiar with the inexpensive computers that are available or are about to become available.

2. Find out what each system looks like and how the parts work.
3. Gain a mastery of basic computer vocabulary such as: *input device*—typewriter, joy stick, touch panel, graphics tablet, etc. *output device*—printer, loudspeaker, television screen, etc. *memory*—means for storing information electronically *central processing unit*—the heart or brain of the computer which carries out logical operations according to a program or a set of very precise instructions. Vocabulary is essential. One teacher has remarked, "I want to ask a question, but I don't even know the words for the things I want to ask about."
4. Learn the procedure for starting up a computer lesson on some common microcomputers.
5. Find out what kinds of lessons are available in your field.
6. Gain hands-on experience with a variety of lessons, simulations, and computer games.
7. Acquire an understanding (an ability to describe and explain) of the capabilities and languages of various computer systems (e.g., Radio Shack TRS-80, Apple, Commodore Pet, and others).

8. Build up a file of articles, books, information sources, and bibliographic resources.[12]

Arranging and Managing Classrooms for Computer Use

Most likely, you will have only one microcomputer in your self-contained classroom. Here are some guidelines to set up a microcomputer for 30–35 students.[13]

☐ Obtain a 25-inch TV of good enough quality that everyone in your class can read the words and numbers printed by the microcomputer.

☐ Place the TV high enough on an audiovisual cart so everyone can see it. Connect it to the microcomputer in an area visible to whole class.

☐ To begin a computer literacy program with elementary school children, it is probably best to obtain one of the many simple microcomputer textbook/software programs.

☐ Go through each session of the textbook with the whole class.

☐ For the hands-on sessions, call one student at a time to the keyboard of the microcom-

puter. While the student does the activity on the microcomputer, the rest of the class follows in their textbooks and watches what is actually happening on the TV screen. Your job during this phase is to point out what the student at the microcomputer is doing.

☐ After five minutes, call on another student to go to the microcomputer to give as many students as possible hands-on experience. You may have to have pairs or groups of threes doing the hands-on part of the activity.

☐ Normal overhead room lighting should be used but avoid glare off the TV screen from windows. Also avoid setting up the TV screen so that it is silhouetted against a bright window.

☐ Arrange to lock the microcomputer up when not used since it is a great temptation. Many schools engrave the name of the school on each component and bolt them to tables.

☐ Arrange your classroom schedule so that children who are responsible can use the microcomputer on a sign-up basis when they have completed their other classroom responsibilities. You will find computer experience is very popular and can act as positive motivation to complete assignments. Encourage this.

☐ Encourage your students to share any software that is compatible with your microcomputer with their classmates.

☐ Periodically review the microcomputer content and skills with simple tests and introduce them to new software as it becomes available.

Evaluating Microcomputer Software

Software (programs and data used to control the microcomputers) varies greatly in suitability for use with your elementary school children. Much software will be purchased in the coming years and you may be called upon to suggest which ones your school should buy. It will take time to develop the skills to do this. Here are some guidelines for selecting and evaluating software for your elementary school science program.

Is the program easy to use? Programs should provide instructions in two places: on the computer screen and in the operations manual. A program should never assume that the user has experience with computers. Equipment should allow users to control the speed of the program by prompting them to proceed by signaling "press any key" or "press return." The program should be able to accept keys being pushed at wrong times, keys being pushed twice, or incorrect responses.

Is the program design flexible? If the user responds correctly, the program should branch into new material. If the user answers incorrectly, good design should allow the student to go back and review program content.

Is the "menu" complete? Programs should be "menu" oriented. A menu is a listing of a program's or lesson's parts, similar to a topic outline. Programs should start with a master menu that allows users to select parts so as to structure their learning. The program should contain sub-menus throughout that allow users to return to the master menu at any point.

Is the program content accurate and well-designed? Programs should be free of content errors or misspellings. Lessons should be interesting to use and contain activities appropriate to the age range of users. To accomplish this, lessons must go beyond simple text presentation or games. Well-designed programs take advantage of graphics, sound, color, and the computer's branching abilities. In science education, for example, a program that simulates a space flight offers users an exciting instructional possibility. Another program might use the computer to solve or monitor laboratory investigations, using students' data to predict results or to produce a graph.

Does the program offer a complete learning package? A good educational software package will use most of the computer's capabilities in order to present students with a well-balanced learning experience. Clearly written, detailed documentation is a must. This includes teacher directions, descriptions of program content and learning objectives, the age level for which the program was written, follow-up activities, and references.

Is the reading level what we need? Printed text should be presented at a reading level appropriate to the user's ability. Programs should avoid large amounts of text. Lessons should be short, requiring no more than 20 minutes each to complete.

Are the graphics employed direct and appropriate? The use of graphics, sound, or a competitive point system where the user plays against the computer or scores points for correct answers can add interest and excitement to a program. But these effects should not distract from the program. All graphics should relate to the subject. Points and/or graphics may be used to reward correct answers, but they should not be used for incorrect answers. Wrong answers should be followed by a simple "incorrect." Correct answers should be followed by a short statement that reinforces the answer and discourages guessing.

Is there a program purchase warranty? Unfortunately, most educational software publishers do not allow you to preview their software. This policy, intended to prevent unauthorized copying, is unnecessary. Most software is recorded on tape or diskette, which is difficult to copy using normal means. However, copyright laws allow purchasers to print one backup copy of the tape or diskette. This is important because tapes and diskettes are easily damaged. The publisher should offer one backup copy at a low cost. Look for tapes or diskettes that are covered by at least a 90-day warranty.

Has the software been reviewed or recommended? Reviews of educational software can be found in several monthly magazines: *Classroom Computer News, The Computer Teacher, Journal of Courseware Review, Electronic Learning, Creative Computing, Kilobaud Microcomputing,* and others.

Microsift, a non-profit clearinghouse for software evaluation, is forming in Portland, Oregon. It is developing a national reviewing process for educational software.[14]

MICROCOMPUTER RESOURCES

This list will help you start to collect information on microcomputers and their uses in your classroom.

Computer Journals or Magazines

- [ ] *Byte* P.O. Box 590, Martinsville, NJ 08836
- [ ] *Classroom Computer News* P.O. Box 266, Cambridge, MA 02138
- [ ] *Computing Teacher* Department of Computer and Information Science, University of Oregon, Eugene, OR 97403
- [ ] *Compute* P.O. Box 789–M, Morristown, NJ 07960
- [ ] *Creative Computing* 39 East Hanover Avenue, Englewood Cliffs, NJ 07950
- [ ] *Microgram* P.O. Box 620, Stony Brook, NY 11790
- [ ] *Electric Learning* 902 Sylvan Avenue, Englewood Cliffs, NY 07632
- [ ] *Personal Computing* 4 Disk Drive, Box 13916, Philadelphia, PA 19101
- [ ] *Popular Computing* P.O. Box 307, Martinsville, NJ 08836

Science Education and Popular Journals

- [ ] "How Computers Are Changing the Classroom," *Better Homes and Gardens,* (April 1983).

☐ Dorothy Cox and Carl F. Berger, "Micro-computers are Motivating," *Science and Children*, 19, no. 1, (September 1981).

☐ Jerry J. Doyle and Vincent N. Lunetta, "Class, Open Your Microcomputers—Hardware, software, bytes & discs—a primer," *The Science Teacher*, 49, no. 8, (November 1982). *Guidelines for Computers in Education, A Position Statement Prepared by the Association of Mathematics Teachers of New York State* (July 1982).

☐ G. Kearsley, B. Hunter and R. J. Seidel, "Two Decades of Computer-Based Instruction Projects: What Have We Learned?" *Technological Horizons Education Journal*, 10, *no. 3, (January 1983).*, 10, no. 4, (February 1983).

☐ William S. LaShier, Jr., "A Scan of Microcomputer Journals," *The Science Teacher*, 48, no.8, (November 1981).

☐ Henry F. Olds, Jr., "On Understanding Computers—References for a Broader Vision," *Learning*, 11, no. 8, (March 1983).

☐ David Grady, "What Every Teacher Should Know About Computer Simulations," *Learning*, 11, no. 8, (March 1983).

☐ Sally Reed, "Plugging Teachers into Computer Era," Education Spring Survey of the *New York Times* (April 24, 1983).

Computer Books for Teachers

☐ Pierre Barrette, Editor, *Microcomputers in K–12 Education- Second Annual Proceedings* (Rockville, MD: Computer Science Press, Inc. 1983).

☐ Karen Billings and David Moursand, *Are You Computer Literate?* (Beaverton, OR: Dilithium Press, 1979).

☐ Joseph Deken, *The Electronic Cottage* (New York: William Morrow & Co., 1981).

☐ Christine Doerr, *Microcomputers and the 3 R's—A Guide for Teachers* (Rochelle Park, NJ: Hayden Book Co., 1980).

☐ David Moursand, *Teacher's Guide to Computers in the Elementary School* (LaGrande, OR: Computing Center, Eastern Oregon State University, 1980).

☐ Seymour Papert, *Mindstorms: Children, Computers and Powerful Ideas* (New York: Basic Books, 1980).

☐ Kay Richard, *One Computer, Thirty Kids* (Indianapolis, IN: Meka Publishing Co., 1980).

☐ Robert Taylor, *The Computer in the School: Tutor, Tool, Tutee* (New York: Academic Press, 1977).

Computers are a revolution in teaching, and you can be part of it. Consider computers another tool in your teaching arsenal. Be curious, but critical. Attend computer workshops, conferences and exhibitions. Most importantly, find out why children are so enthusiastic about computers and learn to share their enthusiasm.

SUMMARY

Mathematics and science have been integrally involved and have contributed to each other's advancement through the ages. Because mathematics and science are wedded in the investigation of natural phenomena, many of the educational objectives of these two disciplines overlap. When scientists collect data, they often do so in a quantitative manner. Mathematics aids the scientist in collecting objective data, revealing relationships, suggesting problem-solving techniques, and replicating experiments. As a scientist works, mathematics and science are often both involved in the inquiry process, requiring many mental inductive or deductive operations.

Educators more recently have increased their effort to integrate science and mathematics in curriculum design. Although as yet there is no completely integrated mathematics and science curriculum for all grades, many modern curriculum projects have made special efforts to develop units or courses for some of the grade levels. Science curriculum projects and the more recently published elementary science texts have also included more investigations using quantitative approaches. All of these curriculums emphasize the use of the metric (SI) system, because scientists use the metric system in their work and because our country probably will change over to this system in the near future.

The computer is becoming more available to elementary classrooms and can be used in science teaching as drill and practice, dialog or tutorial, and especially as simulation or modeling. An example of a simulation software program was presented. Suggestions were given about how to work directly with computer-assisted instruction. Guidelines were suggested for evaluating software for your elementary science computer, along with computer data collection resources, such as computer journals, magazines, and books.

SELF-EVALUATION AND FURTHER STUDY

1. Prepare some metric activities for the grade you will teach. Use examples from this chapter to get ideas.
2. How are Piagetian operations integrated in science and mathematics?
3. Take one of the Piagetian operations outlined in this chapter and design a lesson using it.
4. What are the arguments for and against integrating science and mathematics in a curriculum?
5. Prepare a dichotomous lesson and a metrical experimental lesson using the same activity.
6. Why would it be unwise to teach children addition before they can conserve number?
7. Enroll in a microcomputer course at a local college or through the many teacher professional organizations.
8. Pick a computer journal or magazine from this chapter's list and see what references are available for using microcomputers in your elementary science program.
9. Study software simulation programs available for elementary science, and see how they can be interrelated with your classroom science activities.
10. Visit a microcomputer store and ask for a microcomputer demonstration using a tutorial or other type of program.
11. Research the following articles and plan to set up a microcomputer for use in a self-contained classroom.
    - ☐ Robert F. Tinker, "New Dimensions in Math and Science Software," *Classroom Computer News*, 3, no. 4, (March 1983), pp. 36–39.
    - ☐ Tim Riordan, "How to Select Software You Can Trust," *Classroom Computer News*, 3, no. 4, (March 1983), pp. 56–60.
    - ☐ Peter Coburn et al, "How to Set Up a Computer Environment," *Classroom Computer News*, 2, no. 3 (January/February 1982), pp. 29–33.

ENDNOTES

1. Robert F. Tinker, "New Dimensions in Science and Mathematics Software," *Classroom Computer News*, vol. 3, no. 4 (March 1983), p. 39.
2. Curriculum Committee, National Science Teachers Association, *Theory into Action in Science Curriculum Development* (Washington, D.C.: National Science Teachers Association, 1964), appendix, p. 3.
3. Donald G. Strafford and John W. Renner, "Development of Conservation Reasoning Through Experience," in John W. Renner et al., *Research, Teaching, and Learning with the Piaget Model.* (Norman: University of Oklahoma Press, 1976), pp. 34–55.
4. Donald H. Kellogg, "An Investigation of the Effects of the Science Curriculum Improvement Studies, First-year Unit, Material Objects, on Gains in Reading Readiness" (Ph.D. diss., University of Oklahoma, 1971).
5. Jerry B. Ayers, and George E. Mason, "Differential Effects of Science—A Process Approach Upon Change in Metropolitan Readiness Test Scores Among Kindergarten Children, *Reading Teacher* (February 1969), pp. 435–39.
6. Jerry B. Ayers and Mary N. Ayers, "Influence of SAPA on Kindergarten Children's Use of Logic in Problem Solving," *School Science and Mathematics* (December 1973), pp. 768–71.
7. Mary Budd Rowe, "Help is Denied to Those in Need," *Science and Children* (March 1975), p. 25.
8. F. Elizabeth Froit, "Curriculum Experiences and Movement from Concrete to Operational Thought," in John W. Renner et al., *Research, Teaching, and Learning with the Piaget Model* (Norman: University of Oklahoma Press, 1976), pp. 79–89.
9. The Nuffield Mathematics 5–13 materials may be obtained from John Wiley & Sons, Inc., 605 Third Avenue, New York, New York 10016. The 5–13 Project follows to a high degree the Piagetian orientation of the mathematics curriculum.
10. The author is indebted to the following for information on these topics: Jerry J. Doyle and Vincent N. Lunetta, "Class, Open Your Microcomputers (Hardware, software, bytes and discs—a primer)", *The Science Teacher*, 49, no. 8, November 1982, p. 24–30.
11. The author thanks the Minnesota Educational Computer Consortium (MECC) for supplying the content and photographs for this section.
12. Joseph I. Lipson and Laurette F. Lipson, "The Computer and the Teacher," in *Education in the 80s: Science*, Mary Budd Rowe, editor, (Washington, D.C.: National Education Association, 1982), pp. 145–146.
13. Acknowledgement is made to the following for assistance in the content of this section: Arthur Luehrman and Herbert Peckham, *Computer Literacy: A Hands-on Approach* (New York: McGraw-Hill, 1983), pp. 7–17; chapter "Getting Started—Classroom Management."
14. Dave Garner, "Educational Microcomputer Software: Nine Questions to Ask," *Science and Children*, 19, no. 6 (March 1982), pp. 24–25.

APPENDIX A

Historical Summary of Science Education in the Elementary School

BEFORE 1850

Children recited and memorized factual knowledge.

THEOLOGY

Purpose: Support for theology.
Criticism: Dull, boring memorization and theological base.

1850s

Two distinct influences on American Science Education:

OBJECT TEACHING

1. *British*—Instructional literature for private tutors or parents.
   Purpose: Children's observations and study of nature.
   Criticism: Obtainable only for upper economic classes.

2. *German*—Pestalozzian "object teaching." In America, the Oswego, N.Y., "Method."
   Purpose: Observation, description, and memorization of animate and inanimate objects for preparation for studying science in upper grades.
   Criticism:
   a. Emphasis upon description; interpretation and understanding of events and phenomena neglected.
   b. Extremely fragmented—lacked order.
   c. Capricious due to chance selection of "objects."

1870s

Great influence of Herbert Spencer and rise of popular interest in science and technology in America; science pushed as a field of study in elementary schools.

FIRST ORGANIZED SCIENCE PROGRAM IN ELEMENTARY SCHOOL

Purpose: Introduction of formalized science curriculum, William T. Harris, St. Louis, Mo., Public Schools—first organized curriculum in elementary school, based upon mastering scientific classification and terminology.
Criticism: Old patterns of teaching/learning not suited to changing times and data beginning to appear on how children learn.

1890s

Influenced by National Education Association, William F. Harris, G. Stanley Hall, Colonel Francis W. Parker, Henry H. Strait, Wilbur S. Jackman, Liberty Hyde Bailey.

NATURE STUDY MOVEMENT

Purpose:
a. Emphasis upon laboratory and other direct experiences.
b. Need for special training for science teachers.
c. Nature study movement—helping children learn about and appreciate their environment.

285

Criticism:
a. Emphasis almost exclusively on biological sciences.
b. Fragmented—overemphasis upon identification and isolated bits of data.
c. Overemphasis on sentimental, emotional, and esthetic explanations.
d. Did not challenge thinking of younger children.

1920s	Influence of Charles Saunders Peirce, William James, John Dewey, Gerald S. Craig.

METHODOLOGY AND UTILITARIAN ASPECT OF SCIENCE

Purpose:
a. Emphasis upon pragmatism—meaning of concepts to be found in the working out process of experience.
b. Methods of science equal to, or greater than, actual information gathered.
c. Cognitive aspects also stressed attitudes, appreciations, interests.
d. Utilitarian aspect of science education as related to health, safety, economy.
Criticism:
a. Tendency to overemphasize attitudes, appreciations, interests.
b. Overemphasis upon methodology of science detracted from science content.
c. Overemphasis upon utilitarian view of science and technology.

1930s & 1940s

Influence of National Society for the Study of Education (31st Yearbook in 1932 and 46th Yearbook in 1947)

CURRICULUMS BASED ON SEQUENTIAL MAJOR SCIENCE PRINCIPLES AND THEIR APPLICATIONS

Purpose
a. Sequence and articulations of science programs K–12.
b. Emphasis upon major generalizations or principles of science.
c. Selection of science content based upon personal and social criteria.
d. Emphasis upon understandings and applications of science.
Criticism:
a. Overemphasis upon practical application of principles.
b. Overemphasis upon personal and social aspects.

1950s–60s

Influence of National Society for the Study of Education (59th Yearbook in 1960), National Science Teachers Association, and many individual curriculum experiments, such as PSSC, wholly or partially supported by the American Association for the Advancement of Science, the National Science Foundation, and other public and private sources.

TEACHING SCIENCE AS PROCESS AND PRODUCTS— DISCOVERY APPROACH AND CONCEPTUAL SCHEMES CURRICULUMS

Purpose:
a. Stress helping children learn science information, skills, attitudes to function as intelligent world citizens.
b. Stress characteristics of science process and products.
c. Use structure and content of scientific disciplines for shaping curriculum.
d. Greater use of data on how children learn for selection of activities for teaching science.
e. Stress teaching science through discovery approach.
f. Scientists, learning specialists, and classroom teachers must work together on preparation of science curriculums and instructional materials.
Criticism:
a. Process may be overemphasized to the exclusion of science content.
b. Structure of conceptual schemes may be too inflexible and rigid.

c. Work aimed at average and above-average students, not slow learner and socio-economically disadvantaged children.

d. Teachers need in-service work to improve skills.

1970s–80s	Influence of National Science Teachers Association and "second-generation" science curriculum projects such as SCIIS, SCIS II, and SAPA II.

Purpose:

a. Stress teaching science with a holistic approach.

b. Integrating science with other subjects.

c. Greater awareness of the importance of teacher's and student's feelings and attitudes in teaching science.

d. Stress humanistic teaching of science.

e. Greater integration of values clarification in science teaching.

f. Use of societal issues and controversies for themes in science teaching.

g. Teaching science on three levels: facts, concepts, and values levels.

h. Stress ecological and environmental focus in science teaching.

i. Stress science teaching for all children—handicapped, gifted, and so on.

Criticism:

a. Need for science curricular materials integrating science and other subjects, including values level.

b. Teachers need in-service work to develop skills in more humanistic, values-laden science teaching.

APPENDIX B

National Elementary Science Curriculum Projects Update

PROJECT TITLE, CONTACT, AND ADDRESS	OVERVIEW
Adapting Science Materials for the blind (ASMB) Dennis Schatz, Field Coordinator Lawrence Hall of Science University of California Berkeley, California 94720	Science Curriculum Improvement Study (SCIS) adapted for visually impaired students. Allows visually impaired and sighted students to work together with minimal additional assistance. (1–6)
Conceptually Oriented Program in Elementary Science (COPES) Janice A. Culter, Associate Director New York University 4 Washington Place New York, New York 10003	A spirally constructed program involving a series of learning experiences leading to an understanding of five major conceptual schemes. COPES features a hands-on curriculum involving active exploration in the learning of concepts, a non-reading program (no materials other than worksheets have been written for children), and low-priced, readily available materials. The curriculum is presented in the form of Teacher's Guides; each contains materials for assessing a child's understanding of the concepts. (K–6)
Elementary Science Study (ESS) Adeline Naiman Education Development Center 55 Chapel Street Newton, Massachusetts 02160	A hands-on, "discovery" based approach. Children are able to explore the physical world directly. Fifty-six units. (K–9)
Individualized Science (IS) A. B. Champagne or L. E. Klopfer Learning Research and Development Center 3939 O'Hara Street Pittsburgh, Pennsylvania 15260	For schools seriously interested in individualization, IS includes a full curriculum integrated with an individualized learning management system. Each of the five levels offers three or more biological and physical science units. Entry above the first level is possible. (K–6)

Source: Reproduced with permission by *Science and Children*, March 1977, pp. 16–17. Copyright 1977 by the National Science Teachers Association, 1742 Connecticut Avenue, N.W., Washington, D.C. 20009.

PRESENT EFFORTS	MATERIALS AVAILABLE	COMMERCIAL AFFILIATION
The project is in final form and is being distributed through the Lawrence Hall of Science.	3, 11, A	None
Awareness conferences have been held in 30 states to inform school administrators and key teachers of the availability and usefulness of COPES.	3, 8, 11	None
Project is completed.	1, 3, 4, 5, 6 A, B, E, G	McGraw-Hill Book Company 1221 Ave. of the Americas New York City 10020
Development of materials for grades 7 and 8 being completed.	1*, 2*, 4*, 5*, 6*, 7, 8*, 9, 11*, A, B, C, F	Imperial International Learning Box 548 Kankakee, Illinois 60901

Note: This chart, compiled by the Curriculum Review Center, updates a similar one published in the March 1969 issue of *Science and Children*. The chart includes elementary science projects which are national in scope and currently being used.

PROJECT TITLE, CONTACT, AND ADDRESS	OVERVIEW
Minnesota School Mathematics and Science Center (MINNEMAST) Alan Humphreys, Director MINNEMAST Center 720 Washington Avenue, S E. Minneapolis, Minnesota 55414	Math and science coordinated for kindergarten and primary grades. Many lessons have been used by intermediate grade teachers. Lessons rely on isomorphisms between math and science. Concepts are presented in an activity, data-gathering format. Students use property blocks, Minnebars, and number lined sliderules and graphic displays. (K–3)
Science—A Process Approach (SAPA) Arthur H. Livermore American Association for the Advancement of Science 1776 Massachusetts Avenue, N.W. Washington, D.C. 20036	SAPA II, a revision of the original **Science—A Process Approach,** is an activity-oriented curriculum. Its 105 modules are structured around the various processes of science. There are (1) instructional booklets for teachers (objectives, possible teaching sequences and activities, evaluation measures), (2) kit materials, and (3) storage units. (K–6)
Science Curriculum Improvement Study (SCIS) Jack Fishleder Lawrence Hall of Science University of California Berkeley, California 94720	Upgraded, sequential physical and life science programs. Developed and evaluated by staff, originated by scientists, and adapted to elementary school children's needs. Challenging investigations using a laboratory approach. (K–6)
Unified Sciences and Mathematics for Elementary Schools (Mathematics and Natural, Social, and Communications Science in Real Problem Solving) (USMES) Earl L. Lomon, Project Director USMES, Education Development Center 55 Chapel Street Newton, Massachusetts 02160	Interdisciplinary program that challenges students to solve real problems from their school and community environment. There are no "right" solutions. Students are required to use their own ideas. The problems are "big" enough to require many class activities for effective solutions. (K–8)
University of Illinois Astronomy Program (UIAP) Stanley P.Wyatt University of Illinois Department of Astronomy Urbana, Illinois 61801	Sequential development of the basic understanding of astronomy through a series of modules. Generally applicable science skills (processes) are practiced in unusual and interesting classroom astronomy activities (5–8)

PRESENT EFFORTS	MATERIALS AVAILABLE	COMMERCIAL AFFILIATION
No new materials are being developed. The project, an agency of the University of Minnesota, functions as a nonprofit distribution center. In-service assistance available on request.	1, 5, 6, A, D, J	None
The program is completed and commerically available. The AAAS is currently completing a Leadership Specialist Program with teams of teacher-leaders from school systems throughout the United States with large populations of racial minorities.	2, 3, 4, 5, 8, 9, 11, A, B, D, H, J	Ginn and Company 191 Spring St. Lexington, Massachusetts 02163
Communications with users. Monitoring quality control of equipment and publications.	1, 3, 4, 9 10, 11, A, B, D, G, K	SCIIS Rand McNally & Company Box 7600 Chicago, Illinois 60680 SCIS II AS & E 20 Overland St. Boston, Massachusetts 02215
The project is completing 26 units, revising the How-To-Cards for intermediate grade students and developing cartoon-style How-To booklets for primary grade students. Research is being conducted on various models for utilization, the effects of USMES on schools, and the effects of USMES on students.	5, 9, 10, 11, C, I, K	None
Project is completed 1	Contact regional sales offices of Harper & Row School Department.	Harper & Row, Publishers 10 East 53rd St. New York City 10022

APPENDIX C

Supplies, Equipment, and Materials Obtainable from Community Sources

This is only a partial list of places in the community that are possible sources of items for a science program in the elementary school. Other sources that should not be overlooked are local factories, the janitor of the school, the school cafeteria, radio and television repair shops, florists' shops, the other teachers in the school, the junior and senior high school science teachers, and so on. The materials are there; it just takes a little looking.

There are times, though, when in spite of the most careful searching, certain pieces of equipment or supplies are not obtainable from local sources; there are also many things that schools should buy from scientific supply houses. A partial list of some of the selected, reliable, scientific supply houses serving elementary schools is given in appendix D.

Dime Store or Department Store

balloons
balls
candles
compasses (magnetic)
cotton (absorbent)
flashlights
food coloring
glues and paste
inks
magnifying glasses
marbles
mechanical toys
mirrors
mousetraps
paperbook matches
scissors
sponges
thermometers

Drugstore

adhesive tape
alcohol (rubbing)
bottles

cigar boxes
cold cream
corks
cotton
dilute acids, preferably 1–5%
dilute H_2O_2 (1½%)
forceps
heat-resistant nursing
   bottles
limewater
medicine droppers
pipe cleaners
rubber stoppers
soda bicarbonate
spatulas
straws
sulfur
tincture of iodine, diluted
   to straw color

Electrical Appliance Shop

bell wire
burned-out fuses and
   light bulbs
dry cells

electric fans
electric hot plates
flashlights
flashlight bulbs
friction tape
magnets (from old
   appliances)
soldering iron

Fabric Shop

cardboard tubes
cheesecloth
flannel
knitting needles
leather
needles
netting
silk thread
spools
scraps of different kinds of
   materials

Farm or Dairy

birds' nests
bottles
clay

292

containers
gravel
hay or straw
humus
insects
leaves
lodestone
loam
rocks
sand
seeds

Fire Department

samples of material used
to extinguish various
types of fire
water pumping
equipment

Garden Supply Store

bulbs (tulips, etc.)
fertilizers
flower pots
garden hose
garden twine
growing plants
labels
lime
seed catalogs
seeds
sprinkling cans
spray guns
trowels and other garden
tools

Gas Station

ball bearings
cans
copper tubing
gears
gear transmissions
grease
inner tubes
jacks
maps
pulleys
tools

valves from tires
wheels

Grocery Store

ammonia
baking soda
borax
candles
cellophane
clothespins
cornstarch
corrugated cardboard
boxes
fruits
paper bags
paraffin
plastic wrapping
salt
sponges
sugar
tinfoil
vegetables
vinegar
wax
waxed paper

Hardware Store

brace and bits
cement
chisels
clocks
dry-cell batteries
electric push buttons,
lamps, and sockets
extension cords
files
flashlights
fruit jars
glass cutters
glass funnels
glass friction rods
glass tubing
hammers
hard rubber rods
insulated copper wire
lamp chimneys
metal and metal scraps
nails

nuts and bolts
paints and varnishes
plaster of paris
pulleys
sandpaper
saws
scales
scrap lumber
screening
screwdrivers
screws
steel wool
thermometers (indoor and
outdoor)
3–6 volt toy electric motors
tin snips
turpentine
wheelbarrow
window glass (broken
pieces will do)
wire
yardsticks

Machine Shop

ball bearings
iron filings
iron rods
magnets
nuts and bolts
screws
scrap metals
wire

Medical and Dental Offices and Hospitals

corks
flasks
funnels
glass tubing
hard lenses
litmus paper
microscopes
models, such as teeth
rubber sheeting
rubber tubing
rubber stoppers
test tubes
test tube holders

thermometers
tongue depressors

Music Shop

broken string and drum
  heads
musical instruments
pitch pipes
tuning forks

Pet Shop

air pumps
animal cages
aquariums
ant houses
cages
fish
insects
nets (butterfly, fish, etc.)
plastic tubing
strainers
terrariums

Restaurant, Diner, or Fast Food Outlet

bones (chicken, etc.)
bottles
cans (coffee, 5 gallons)
drums (ice cream)
five gallon cans (oil)
food coloring
gallon jars
  (wide-mouthed,
  pickles, mayonnaise,
  etc.)
gallon jugs (vinegar)
pie tins

For additional sources of common, easily obtained supplies and apparatus suitable for your elementary school science program, see Alfred DeVito and Gerald H. Krockover, "Gear to Gather For the Well-Appointed Science Classroom," in NSTA *Directory of Science Education Suppliers* (Washington, D.C.: National Science Teachers Association, 1983), pp. 11–12.

APPENDIX D

Selected Sources of Scientific Equipment, Supplies, Models, Living Things, Kits, and Collections

American Nuclear Products, Inc.
1232 E. Commercial
Springfield, MO 65803
(417) 869-4432

American Optical Instrument Div.
P.O. Box 123
Buffalo, NY 14240
(716) 891-3000

Analytical Products, Inc.
P.O. Box 845
Belmont CA 94002
(415) 592-1400

Apple Computer, Inc.
20525 Mariani Ave.
Cupertino, CA 95014
(408) 996-1010

Bausch & Lomb
42 East Ave.
Rochester, NY 14603
(716) 338-6000

Bel-Art Products
6 Industrial Rd.
Pequannock, NJ 07440
(201) 694-0500

Carolina Biological Supply Co.
2700 York Road
Burlington, NC 27215
(919) 584-0381

Central Scientific Co.
11222 Melrose Ave.
Franklin Park, IL 60131
(312) 451-0150

Connecticut Valley Biological
 Supply Co., Inc.
82 Valley Rd.
Southampton, MA 01073
(413) 527-4030,
800-628-7748

Delta Education, Inc.
P.O. Box M
Nashua, NH 03061-6012
1-800-258-1302

Education Development Center
55 Chapel St.
Newton, MA 02160
(617) 969-7100

Educational Activities, Inc.
P.O. Box 392
Freeport, NY 11520
(800) 645-3739

Fisher Scientific Co., Educ. Div.
4901 W. Le Moyne Street
Chicago, IL 60651
(312) 378-7770;
(800) 621-4769

Frey Scientific Co.
905 Hickory Lane
Mansfield, OH 44905
(419) 589-9905

Hubbard Scientific
1946 Raymond Dr.
Northbrook, IL 60062
(800) 323-8368
(312) 272-7810

Ideal School Supply Co.
11000 S. Lavergne Avenue
Oak Lawn, IL 60453
(312) 415-0800

Lab-Aids, Inc.
P.O. Box 158
130 Wilbur Pl.
Bohemia, NY 11716
(516) 567-6120

LaPine Scientific Co.
6001 South Knox Avenue
Chicago, IL 60629-5496
(312) 735-4700

McKilligan Supply Corporation
435 Main Street
Johnson City, NY 13790
(607) 729-6511

NASCO
901 Janesville Avenue
Fort Atkinson, WI 53538
(414) 563-2446

Nasco West Inc.
P.O. Box 3837
Modesto, CA 95352
(209) 529-6957

Nova Scientific Corporation
P.O. Box 500
Burlington, NC 27215
(919) 229-0395;
(800) 334-1100

Sargent-Welch Scientific Co.
7300 N. Linder Avenue
Skokie, IL 60077
(312) 677-0600

Science Kit, Inc.
777 E. Park Drive
Tonawanda, NY 14150
(716) 874-6020

Turtox
5000 W. 128th Pl.
Chicago, IL 60658
(312) 371-5500

Ward's Natural Science
    Establishment, Inc.
P.O. Box 1712,
Rochester, NY 14603
(716) 467-8400

Wilkens-Anderson Co.
4525 W. Division St.
Chicago, IL 60651
(312) 384-4433

APPENDIX E

Planning a Learning Center

State Purpose

The purpose of a learning center should be clear, both to the teacher and student and stated as a part of the center, e.g., "At this center you will examine some seeds. You will compare sizes, weights, volumes, and shapes of the seeds."

Consider Student Levels

The center must be appropriate for the students who will be using it. The backgrounds and experiences, the cognitive level of operation, the socio-economic level, the maturity level and level of independence, and the psychomotor level must be defined and used as the basis for planning the activities and expected learning outcomes from the center.

Define Concepts and Skills To Be Developed

A clear statement of the concepts, subconcepts, and skills to be developed by the students using the center is necessary if the center is to be a true teaching/learning situation. Fulfilling this criteria is the point where many centers break down into busy work.

Outline Expected Learning Outcomes

These statements can be in the form of performance—or behavioral—objectives. Here, a concise statement of what the student is expected to learn as a result of using the center can also serve as a guideline for evaluating student success.

Select Appropriate Activities and Methods

These must be carefully selected to harmonize with the criteria mentioned above. The activities must serve the purpose of the center and be appropriate to the students using it. They must be designed to assist the student to reach the expected learnings. The directions must be clearly within the ability of the student and presented so that the student can follow them independently. The materials must be readily available.

Do Evaluations

Use the objectives for the center as a base to determine whether the student has attained the expected learnings, concepts, and skills stated. The center and its materials may need periodic servicing.

Implement Change As Needed

Student performance will provide insight into how each center can be improved or changed to meet the needs of the students it serves, the curriculum, and the objectives and goals stated for the center.

A Simple Outline for Planning a Learning Center.

PURPOSE OF CENTER	CHARACTER- ISTICS OF STUDENTS	CONCEPTS AND SKILLS	ACTIVITIES AND MATERIALS	EXPECTED LEARNING OUTCOMES	EVALUATIONS	SUGGESTIONS FOR CHANGE
					Students:	
					Center:	

Source: Geraldine R. Sherfey and Phyllis Huff, "Designing the Science Learning Center." Reproduced with permission by *Science and Children* 14, no. 3 (November/December 1976): 12. Copyright 1977 by the National Science Teachers Association, 1742 Connecticut Avenue, N.W., Washington, D.C. 20009.

APPENDIX F

Selected References for the Teacher or School Professional Library

PROFESSIONAL BOOKS IN ELEMENTARY SCHOOL SCIENCE

Abruscato, Joe, and Hassard, Jack. *Loving and Beyond: Science Teaching for the Humanistic Classroom*. Pacific Palisades, Calif.: Goodyear Publishing Co., 1976.

Baez, Albert V. *Innovations in Science Education—World-wide*. New York: UNESCO, 1976.

Blough, Glenn O., and Schwartz, Julius. *Elementary School Science and How to Teach It*. 6th ed. New York: Holt, Rinehart & Winston, 1979.

Butts, David P., and Hall, Gene E. *Children and Science: The Process of Teaching and Learning*. Englewood Cliffs, N.J.: Prentice-Hall, 1975.

DeVito, Alfred, and Krockover, Gerald H. *Creative Sciencing: A Practical Approach* (vol. 1) and *Ideas and Activities* (vol. 2) Boston: Little, Brown and Co., 1980.

Friedl, Alfred E. *Teaching Science to Children: The Inquiry Approach Applied*. New York: Random House, 1972.

Gega, Peter C. *Science in Elementary Education*. 4th ed. New York: John Wiley & Sons, 1982.

George, Kenneth D.; Dietz, Maureen A.; and Abraham, Eugene C. *Science Investigations for Elementary School Teachers*. Lexington, Mass.: D. C. Heath & Co., 1974; *and* Nelson, Miles A. *Elementary School Science—Why and How*. Lexington, Mass.: D. C. Heath & Co., 1974.

Goldberg, Lazer. *Children and Science*. New York: Charles Scribner's Sons, 1970.

Good, Ronald G. *How Children Learn Science*. New York: Macmillan, 1977.

Haney, Richard E., and Sorenson, Juanita S. *Individually Guided Science*. Reading, Mass.: Addison-Wesley Publishing Co., 1977.

Hill, Katherine E. *Exploring the Natural World with Young Children* (New York: Harcourt Brace Jovanovich, 1976.

Holt, Bess-Gene. *Science with Young Children*. Washington, D.C.: National Association for the Education of Young Children, 1977.

Hone, Elizabeth, et al. *A Sourcebook for Elementary Science*. New York: Harcourt Brace Jovanovich, 1971.

Hounshell, Paul B., and Trollinges, Ira R. *Games for the Science Classroom*. Washington, D.C.: National Science Teachers Association, 1977.

Hubler, Clark. *Science for Children*. New York: Random House, 1974.

Hurd, Paul DeHart, and Gallagher, James J. *New Directions in Elementary Science Teaching*. Belmont, Calif.: Wadsworth Publishing Co., 1968.

Ivany, J. W. George. *Science Teaching for the Elementary School: A Professional Approach*. Palo Alto, Calif.: Science Research Associates, 1975.

Jacobson, Willard J. and Abby Barry Begman *Science for Children*. Englewood Cliffs, N.J.: Prentice-Hall, 1980.

Karplus, Robert, and Thier, Herbert D. *A New Look at Elementary School Science*. Chicago: Rand McNally & Co., 1967.

Kauchak, Donald and Paul Eggen. *Exploring Science in Elementary Schools*. Chicago: Rand McNally, 1980.

Kuslan, Louis I., and Stone, A. Harris, *Teaching Children Science: An Inquiry Approach*. Belmont, Calif.: Wadsworth Publishing Co., 1972.

Lansdown, Brenda; Blackwood, Paul E.; and Brandwein, Paul F. *Teaching Elementary Science—Through Investigation and Colloquium.* New York: Harcourt Brace Jovanovich, 1971.

Lewis, June E., and Potter, Irene C. *The Teaching of Science in the Elementary School.* Englewood Cliffs, N.J.: Prentice-Hall, 1970.

Navarra, John G., and Zafforoni, Joseph. *Science in the Elementary School: Content and Methods.* Columbus, Ohio: Charles E. Merrill Publishing Co., 1975.

New UNESCO Source Book for Science Teaching. New York: UNESCO, 1975.

Piltz, Albert, and Sund, Robert. *Creative Teaching of Science in the Elementary School.* Boston: Allyn and Bacon, 1974.

Renner, John W., and Regan, William B. *Teaching Science in the Elementary School.* New York: Harper & Row, Publishers, 1973.

——— and Don G. Stafford. *Teaching Science in the Elementary School,* 3rd ed. New York: Harper and Row, 1979.

Rowe, Mary Budd. *Teaching Science as Continuous Inquiry,* 2nd ed. New York: McGraw-Hill Book Co., 1978.

Tale, Larry L., and Lee, Ernest W. *Environmental Education in the Elementary School.* New York: Holt, Rinehart & Winston, 1972.

Trojcak, Doris, *Science With Children.* New York: McGraw-Hill, 1979.

Victor, Edward. *Science for the Elementary School.* 4th ed. New York: The Macmillan Co., 1980; *and* Lerner, Marjorie E. *Readings in Science Education for the Elementary School.* New York: The Macmillan Co., 1975.

SCIENCE EDUCATION PERIODICALS FOR TEACHERS AND CHILDREN

Children and teachers can keep abreast with the rapid development in research in science and science education by referring to the following periodicals. They provide the most information and are an invaluable supplement to science textbooks.

(T)—teacher oriented
(C)—child oriented

American Biology Teacher. The National Association of Biology Teachers, 19 S. Jackson St., Danville, Ill. 61832 (Monthly) (T)

American Forests. The American Forestry Association, 919 17th St., N.W., Washington, D.C. (Monthly) (T)

The American Journal of Physics. American Association of Physics Teachers, 57 E. 55th St., New York, N.Y. 10022 (Monthly) (T)

The Aquarium. Innes Publishing Co., Philadelphia, Pa. 19107 (Monthly) (C&T)

Audubon Magazine. The National Audubon Society, 1130 Fifth Ave., New York, N.Y. 10028 (Bimonthly) (C&T)

Biology & General Science Digest. W.M. Welch Co., 1515 Sedgwick St., Chicago, Ill. (Free) (T)

Chemistry. Science Service, 1719 16 St. N.W., Washington, D.C. 20009 (Monthly) (T)

Cornell Rural School Leaflets. New York State College of Agriculture, Ithaca, N.Y. 14850 (Quarterly) (T)

Current Science and Aviation. American Education Publications, Education Center, Columbus, Ohio 43216 (Weekly during the school year) (C&T)

Geotimes. American Geological Institute, 1515 Massachusetts Ave., N.W., Washington, D.C. (Monthly) (T)

Grade Teacher. Educational Publishing Co. Darien, Conn. 06820 (Monthly Sept.–June) (T)

Journal of Chemical Education. Business and Publication Office, 20th & Northampton Sts., Easton, Pa. 18042 (Monthly) (T)

Journal of Research in Science Teaching. John Wiley & Sons, 605 Third Ave., New York, N.Y. 10016 (T)

Junior Astronomer. Benjamin Adelman, 4211 Colie Dr., Silver Springs, Md. 20906 (C&T)

Junior Natural History. American Museum of Natural History, New York, N.Y. 10024 (Monthly) (C&T)

Monthly Evening Sky Map. Box 213, Clayton, Mo. 63105 (Monthly) (C&T)

My Weekly Reader. American Education Publications, Education Center, Columbus, Ohio 43216 (Weekly during the school year)

National Geographic. National Geographic Society, 1146 Sixteenth St., N.W., Washington, D.C. (Monthly) (C&T)

Natural History. American Museum of Natural History, 79th St. and Central Park West, New York, N.Y. 10024 (Monthly) (C&T)

Nature Magazine. American Nature Association, 1214 15th St., N.W., Washington, D.C. (Monthly Oct. to May and bimonthly June to Sept.) (C&T)

Our Dumb Animals. Massachusetts Society for the Prevention of Cruelty to Animals, Boston, Mass. 02115 (Monthly) (C&T)

Outdoors Illustrated. National Audubon Society, 1000 Fifth Ave., New York, N.Y. (Monthly) (C&T)

Physics and Chemistry Digest. W. M. Welch Co., 1515 Sedgwich St., Chicago, Ill. (Free) (T)

Physics Today. American Institute of Physics, 335 E. 45th St., New York, N.Y. 10017 (Monthly) (T)

Popular Science Monthly. Popular Science Publishing Co., 335 Lexington Ave., New York, N.Y. 10016 (Monthly) (C&T)

Readers Guide to Oceanography. Woods Hole Oceanographic Institute, Woods Hole, Mass. 02543 (Monthly) (T)

School Science and Mathematics. Central Association Science and Mathematics Teachers, P.O. Box 48, Oak Park, Ill. 60305 (Monthly 9 times a year) (T)

Science. American Association for the Advancement of Science, 1515 Massachusetts Ave., N.W., Washington, D.C. 20025 (T)

Science Digest. 959 8th Ave., New York, N.Y. 10019 (Monthly) (T)

Science Education. Science Education Inc., C. M. Pruitt, University of Tampa, Tampa, Fla. 33606 (5 times yearly) (T)

Science Newsletter. Science Service, Inc., 1719 N. Street, N.W., Washington, D.C. 20036 (Weekly) (T)

Science and Children. National Science Teachers Association, Washington, D.C. 20036 (Monthly 8 times a year) (C&T)

Scientific American. 415 Madison Ave., New York, N.Y. 10017 (Monthly) (T)

Scientific Monthly. The American Association for the Advancement of Science, 1515 Massachusetts Ave., Washington, D.C. 20005 (Monthly) (T)

Space Science. Benjamin Adelman, 4211 Colie Dr., Silver Springs, Md. 20906 (Monthly—during school year) (Formerly *Junior Astronomer*) (C&T)

Science Teacher. National Science Teachers Association, National Education Association, 1742 Connecticut Ave., N.W., Washington, D.C. 20036 (Monthly—Sept.–May) (T)

Science World. Scholastic Magazines, Inc., 50 W. 44 St., New York, N.Y. 10036 (T&C)

Sky and Telescope. Sky Publishing Corp., Harvard College Observatory. Cambridge, Mass. 02138 (Monthly) (C&T)

Tomorrow's Scientists. National Science Teachers Association, Washington, D.C. 20036 (8 issues per year) (T)

UNESCO Courier. The UNESCO Publications Center, 801 3rd Ave., New York, N.Y. 10022 (Monthly) (T)

Weatherwise. American Meteorological Society, 3 Joy St., Boston, Mass. 02108 (Monthly) (T)

APPENDIX G

Professional Societies for Science Teachers and Supervisors

American Association for the Advancement of
   Science
1515 Massachusetts Ave., N.W.
Washington, D.C. 20005

American Association of Physics Teachers
335 E. 45th St.
New York, N.Y. 10017

American Chemical Society
Chemical Education Division
1155 Sixteenth St., N.W.
Washington, D.C. 20036

American Nature Study Society
(No permanent headquarters.
Current officers listed in *Nature Teaching Tips.*)

Association for Supervision and Curriculum
   Development
1201 Sixteenth St., N.W.
Washington, D.C. 20036

Central Association of Science and Mathematics
   Teachers
(No permanent headquarters.
Current officers listed in *School Science and
   Mathematics.*)

Council for Elementary Science International
1742 Connecticut Ave., N.W.
Washington, D.C. 20036

National Association of Biology Teachers
1420 N. Street, N.W.
Washington, D.C. 20005

National Association for Research in Science
   Teaching
(No permanent headquarters.)

National Association of Geology Teachers
(No permanent headquarters.
Current officers listed in *Journal of Geological
   Education.*)

National Science Teachers Association
1742 Connecticut Ave., N.W.
Washington, D.C., 20036

APPENDIX H

Noncommercial Sources and Containers for Organisms

ORGANISMS	NONCOMMERCIAL SOURCE	CULTURE CONTAINERS
POND SNAILS	Fresh water ponds, creeks	Aquaria, large battery jars, gallon glass jars
LAND SNAILS	Mature hardwood forests: on rocks, fallen logs, damp foliage	Terraria, large battery jars
DAPHNIA	Freshwater ponds: at water's edge, and associated with algae	Gallon glass or plastic jars
ISOPODS AND CRICKETS	Under rocks, bricks, and boards that have lain on ground for some time; between grass and base of brick buildings	Glass or plastic terraria, plastic sweater boxes (Provide vents in cover.)
MEALWORM BEETLES	Corn cribs, around granaries	Gallon glass jars with cheese cloth
FRUIT FLIES	Trap with bananas or apple slices. (Place fruit in a jar with a funnel for a top.)	Tall baby food jars, plastic vials (Punch hole in jar lids, cover with masking tape and then prick tiny holes in tape with a pin.)
WINGLESS PEA APHIDS*	Search on garden vegetables, e.g., English peas	On pea plants potted in plastic pots, milk cartons (Keep aphids in a large terrarium so they cannot wander to other plants in the school.)

*These species are difficult to obtain from their natural habitats. Unless you have a convenient source, it is better to buy them commercially. Try a local aquarium or pet shop.

Source: Carolyn H. Hampton and Carol D. Hampton, "The Establishment of a Life Science Center." Reproduced with permission by *Science and Children* 15, no. 7 (April 1978): 9. Copyright 1978 by The National Science Teachers Association, 1742 Connecticut Avenue, N.W., Washington, D.C., 20009.

ORGANISMS	NONCOMMERCIAL SOURCE	CULTURE CONTAINERS
GUPPIES	Obtain free from persons who raise guppies as a hobby. (They are usually glad to reduce population when they clean tanks.)	Aquaria, large battery jars
CHAMELEONS*	Dense foliage along river banks or railroad tracks (Catch with net or large tea strainer.)	Prepare cage from broken acquaria. (Broken glass can be replaced by taping cloth screening along sides.)
FROGS*	Along edges of ponds, ditches, creeks (Catch with large scoop net.)	Large plastic ice chest (Set near a sink so a constant water supply can be provided.)
CHLAMYDOMONAS AND EUGLENA	Freshwater pond	Gallon glass jars, aquaria, battery jars
ELODEA (ANARCHARIS)*	Ponds, creeks: usually along edge or in shallows	Aquaria, large battery jars
EELGRASS*	Wading zone of brackish water	Aquaria, large battery jars
DUCKWEED	Edge of ponds or fresh water swamps	Aquaria, large battery jars
COLEUS AND GERANIUM	Persons who raise them (Start by rooting cuttings in 1 part sand, 1 part vermiculite, in plastic bags; keep moist.)	Clay pots, milk cartons, tin cans

APPENDIX I

Food Requirements for Various Animals

FOOD AND WATER	RABBITS	GUINEA PIGS	HAMSTERS	MICE	RATS
Daily					
pellets	rabbit pellets: keep dish half full		large dog pellets: one or two		
or					
grain		corn, wheat, or oats			canary seeds or oats
green or leafy vegetables, lettuce, cabbage and celery tops	keep dish half full 4–5 leaves	2 leaves	1½ tablespoon 1 leaf	2 teaspoons ⅛–¼ leaf	3–4 teaspoons ¼ leaf
or					
grass, plantain, lambs' quarters, clover, alfalfa	2 handfuls	1 handful	½ handful	—	—
or					
hay, if water is also given carrots	2 medium	1 medium			
Twice a week					
apple (medium)	½ apple	¼ apple	⅛ apple	½ core and seeds	1 core
iodized salt (if not contained in pellets)	or salt block	sprinkle over lettuce or greens			
corn, canned or fresh, once or twice a week	½ ear	¼ ear	1 tablespoon ⅓ ear	¼ tablespoon or end of ear	½ tablespoon or end of ear
water	should always be available	necessary only if lettuce or greens are not provided			

Source: Grace K. Pratt, *How to . . . Care for Living Things in the Classroom* (Washington, D.C.: National Science Teachers Association, 1965), p. 9.

FOOD AND WATER PLANTS (FOR FISH)	WATER TURTLES	LAND TURTLES	SMALL TURTLES
Daily			
worms or night crawlers or	1 or 2	1 or 2	¼ inch of tiny earthworm
tubifex or blood worms			enough to cover ½ area of a dime
and/or			
raw chopped beef or meat and fish-flavored dog or cat food	½ teaspoon	½ teaspoon	
fresh fruit and vegetables		¼ leaf lettuce or 6–10 berries or 1–2 slices peach, apple, tomato, melon or 1 tablespoon corn, peas, beans	
dry ant eggs, insects, or other commercial turtle food			1 small pinch
water	¾ of container	always available at room temperature; should be ample for swimming and submersion large enough for shell	half to ¾ of container

FOOD AND WATER PLANTS

FOOD AND WATER PLANTS	GOLDFISH	GUPPIES
Daily		
dry commercial food	1 small pinch	1 very small pinch; medium size food for adults; fine size food for babies
Twice a week		
shrimp—dry—or another kind of dry fish food	4 shrimp pellets, or 1 small pinch	dry shrimp food or other dry food; 1 very small pinch
Two or three times a week		
tubifex worms	enough to cover ½ area of a dime	enough to cover ⅛ area of a dime
Add enough "conditioned" water to keep tank at required level	allow one gallon per inch of fish add water of same temperature as that in tank —at least 65°F	allow ¼–½ gallon per adult fish add water of same temperature as that in tank—70°–80°F
Plants: cabomba, anarcharis, etc.		
water	should always be available	should always be available

	NEWTS	FROGS
Daily		
small earthworms or mealworms or	1–2 worms	2–3 worms
tubifex worms or	enough to cover ½ area of a dime	enough to cover ¾ area of a dime
raw chopped beef	enough to cover a dime	enough to cover a dime
water	should always be available at same temperature as that in tank or room temperature	

APPENDIX J

Free and Inexpensive Materials For Use in the Elementary Science Classroom

1. **"Ad-vailables"** *Science and Children* magazine. The National Science Teachers Association, 1742 Connecticut Ave., NW, Washington, DC 20009. $20/8 issues.
   Regular column describes free or low cost supplementary materials, publications, and events of interest to elementary, middle, and junior high school science teachers.

2. **Educators Guide to Free Audio and Visual Materials.** James L. Berger and Walter A. Wittich, eds. Educators Progress Service, 214 Center St., Randolph, WI 53956. 1980. $13.50.
   Subject, title, and distributor are included in this annotated listing of videotapes, audiotapes, scripts, and audiodiscs. (Revised yearly.)

3. **Free Stuff for Kids.** Meadowbrook Press, 18318 Minnetonka Blvd., Deephaven, MN 55391.
   Materials on many topics, including science. Single copy free. (Revised yearly.)

4. **Consumer Information Catalog.** Consumer Information Center, Pueblo, CO 81009.
   Describes selected federal publications. Most are free or under $3. (Published quarterly.)

5. **Free for the Taking.** Joseph R. Cooke. Fleming H. Revell Co., 184 Central Ave., Old Tappan, NJ 07675. $7.95.

Lists free materials on many science subjects.

6. **Educators Guide to Free Films.** John C. Diffor and Mary F. Horkheimer, eds. Educators Progress Service, 214 Center St., Randolph, WI 53956. $17.75.
   Describes films for educational and recreational use. Listed by subject, title, and distributor. (Revised yearly.)

7. **Educators Guide to Free Filmstrips.** John C. Diffor and Mary F. Horkheimer, eds. Educators Progress Service, 214 Center St., Randolph, WI 53956. $13.
   Comprehensive listing of filmstrips, slides, and transparencies. Listed by subject, title, and distributor. (Revised yearly.)

8. **Educational Media Yearbook.** Libraries Unlimited, Inc., P.O. Box 263, Littleton, CO 80160. $20.
   Contains a multimedia information section with an annotated listing of free materials. (Published alternate years.)

9. **FAA Film Catalog.** Federal Aviation Administration, 800 Independence Ave., SW, Washington, DC 20003. 1976.
   Lists over 75 films, filmstrips, and slides. Description, length, and date of film are included.

10. **Forest Service Films Available on Loan.** Contact your local U.S. Forest Service office. 1973.
    Provides a variety of color/sound films on many topics prepared by the U.S. Forest Service.

Source: Paula J. Zsiray and Stephen W. Zsiray, Jr., "Utilizing Free and Inexpensive Materials In The Science Classroom," *Science and Children*, 19. no. 5 (February 1981), pp. 20–21.

11. **Free and Inexpensive Learning Experiences.** 1220 Maple Ave., Los Angeles, CA 90015. $24 per year.
List materials on a variety of topics including the environment and science.

12. **Free and Inexpensive Learning Materials.** Incentive Publications, P.O. Box 12522, Nashville, TN 37212. 1979. $4.95 plus $1 postage.
Excellent coverage of free and inexpensive materials including science.

13. **Free! The Newsletter of Free Materials and Services.** Ken Haycock, ed. Dyad Services, London, Ontario, Canada. $10 per year.
Annotated list of materials evaluated and recommended by teachers and librarians. (Bi-monthly.)

14. **Freebies: The Magazine with Something for Nothing.** P.O. Box 5797, Santa Barbara, CA 93108. $6/9 issues.
Contains information on how to utilize free and inexpensive materials and where to get them.

15. **Free Magazines for Teachers and Libraries.** Ken Haycock. Ontario Library Association, 2397 Bloor W, Toronto, Ontario, Canada. 1977.
International sources of free magazines indexed by subject and title.

16. **Index to Free Educational Materials/ Multimedia.** National Information Center for Educational Media, University of Southern California, Los Angeles, CA 90007. 1977. $26.50.
More than 20,000 titles indexed by subject and producer/distributor.

17. **Educators Index of Free Materials.** Linda Keenen and Wayne J. Krepel, eds. Educators Progress Service, 214 Center St., Randolph, WI 53956. 1980. $39.50.
Annotated listing of free materials including science topics. (Revised yearly.)

18. **Bibliography of Materials for Environmental Education.** Wisconsin Vocational Studies Center, University of Wisconsin, 1025 West Johnson St., Madison, WI 53706.
Bibliography of environmental education materials. Free loan materials included.

19. **"Materials/Information Center."** *Instructor* magazine, 757 Third Ave., New York, NY 10017. $16
Lists catalogs and other resources offered by advertisers in the current issue.

20. **NWF Conservation Education Catalog.** National Wildlife Federation, 1412 Sixteenth St., NW, Washington, DC 20036. 1981. Free.
Lists materials available on conservation of natural resources.

21. **Free and Inexpensive Materials in Environmental Science and Related Disciplines.** Ann Hope Ruzow. Vance Bibliographies, P.O. Box 229, Monticello, IL 61856. 1978. $2.50. Tabulates sources of materials in environmental sciences.

22. **Educators Guide to Free Science Materials.** Mary H. Saterstrom and John W. Renner, eds. Educators Progress Service, 214 Center St., Randolph, WI 53956. 1980. $15.50. Annotated listing of audiovisual and science curriculum enrichment aids. (Revised yearly.)

23. **Science and Technology Programs.** Available from local Bell Telephone Company. 1980.
Lists free science films available from Bell Telephone Co.

24. **Selected U.S. Government Publications.** Superintendent of Documents, U.S. Government Printing Office, Washington, DC 20402.
Lists selected government publications, many of which apply to science. (Monthly.)

25. **Free Magazines for Libraries.** Adeline Mercer Smith. McFarland and Co., Inc., P.O. Box 611, Jefferson, NC 28640. 1980. $16.95.
Sources of free magazines, many of which deal with science subjects.

26. **Guide to Government Loan Films.** Daniel Sprecher, ed. Serina Press, 70 Kennedy St., Alexandria, VA 22305. 1978. $12.95.

Describes more than 3,000 16mm films available on loan in the U.S.

27. **Guide to Government Loan Films, Vol. 2.** Daniel Sprecher, ed. Serina Press, 70 Kennedy St., Alexandria, VA 22305. 1976. $9.95.

Lists films, filmstrips, and slides available on free loan from federal agencies.

28. **The Book of Free Books.** W. M. Tevarrow. Contemporary Books, Inc., 180 North Michigan Ave., Chicago, IL 60601. 1979.

Annotated selection of books on a variety of subjects including science. Book is out of print, but can be found in many university libraries.

APPENDIX K

Summary of Studies Showing the Relationship between Science Experiences and Language/Reading Development

AUTHORS	GRADES/ LEVELS	LANGUAGE/ READING VARIABLES	TYPES OF CHILDREN	TYPES OF TESTS WHEN RELEVANT
Ayers & Ayers *Sch. Sci. & Math* Dec. '73	K	Word meaning, listening, matching, alphabet, copying	Semiurban Appalachian	Metropolitan Readiness Test (MRT)
Ayers & Mason *Reading Teacher* Feb. '69	K	Word meaning, listening, matching, alphabet, copying	Urban	Metropolitan Readiness Test
Bybee & Hendricks *Sci. Ed.*	K	Language development	Deaf childen	
Campbell Dissertation	4-5-6	Comprehension		
Huff & Languis *J. Res. Sci. Teach.* 1973	K	Vocabulary, word meaning, listening, sentence structure	Inner-city	
Linn & Thier *J. Res. Sci. Teach.* 1975	5th	Logical thinking	Urban, suburban, & rural	

Source: Modified from chart in Ruth T. Wellman, "'Science' A Basic Language and Reading Development," in *What Science Says to the Science Teacher*, vol. 1 ed. Mary Budd Rowe (Washington, D.C.: National Science Teachers Association, 1978), p. 8.

311

AUTHORS	GRADES/ LEVELS	LANGUAGE/ READING VARIABLES	TYPES OF CHILDREN	TYPES OF TESTS WHEN RELEVANT
McGlathery *ERIC ED. 0262671*	K-1	Language development/vocabulary	Contrasting socio-economic	
Maxwell Dissertation	K	Word meaning, listening, verbal expressions	Suburban lower to upper class	Metropolitan Readiness Test Illinois Test of Psycholinguistic Abilities, The Marianne Frostig Developmental Test of Visual Perception
Neuman *USEO Report* March '70	K-1	Vocabulary, listening, alphabet, reading achievement	Central-city Milwaukee	Metropolitan Readiness Test and Achievement Test
Olson Paper presented	6th	Context clues	Middle-class urban	
Quinn Paper presented	6th	Hypothesis formation		
Quinn & Kessler Paper presented	6th	Language development	Upper class suburban	Batel
Renner et al. *Sch. Sci. & Math '73*	K	Word meaning, listening, alphabet	Public city schools	Metropolitan Readiness Test
Renner et al. Research paper	1	Word meaning, listening, alphabet		SRA, Metropolitan Readiness Test

APPENDIX L

Answers to Evaluate Devices Forced-Choice Test (page 70)

1. *d* Observation is best, although the existence of a product or a right answer might also indicate that instructions were followed.
2. *a* The product will reveal the presence or absence of the desired quality.
3. *d* Observation will reveal the method the child used.
4. *b* A paper and pencil test is most economical, although the product is another indicator. If you wanted to know how a student solved the problem, an observation would be best.
5. *d* Observation of the child reading aloud is the best way to monitor inflection.
6. *b* A paper and pencil test is best, but you could ask the learner to give a self-report about the author's tone and mood.
7. *d* Observation and self-report, perhaps using a questionnaire or inventory, are both good indicators.
8. *d* Observation of the child's participation will reveal attainment of this goal.
9. *d* Observation to note whether the child takes his or her turn is the most appropriate measure.
10. *c* A self-report is best, but a parent might use observation.

Index

315